EZ

Occupational Outlook Handbook™

The Editors @ JIST

Based on information from the U.S. Department of Labor

JIST Works
America's Career Publisher™

EZ Occupational Outlook Handbook

© 2007 by JIST Publishing, Inc.

Published by JIST Works, an imprint of JIST Publishing, Inc.
8902 Otis Avenue
Indianapolis, IN 46216-1033
Phone: 1-800-648-JIST   Fax: 1-800-JIST-FAX
E-mail: info@jist.com   Web site: www.jist.com

> **To Educators, Counselors, and Other Professionals:** The *EZ Occupational Outlook Handbook* can be used with JIST's videos, workbooks, and career assessments for workshops, for courses, and in other settings. Call 1-800-648-JIST or visit www.jist.com for more information.
>
> Quantity discounts are available for JIST products. Have future editions of JIST books delivered to you through our convenient standing order program. Please call 1-800-648-JIST or visit www.jist.com for a free catalog and more information.

Acquisitions Editor: Susan Pines
Writer and Development Editor: Dave Anderson
Copy Editor: Jill Mazurczyk
Database Work: Laurence Shatkin
Cover Photo: Dave and Les Jacobs/Blend Images/Getty Images
Interior Designer: Marie Kristine Parial-Leonardo
Interior Layout: Toi Davis
Proofreaders: Paula Lowell, Jeanne Clark

Printed in the United States of America.

12 11 10 09 08 07   9 8 7 6 5 4 3 2 1

Library of Congress Cataloging-in-Publication Data

EZ occupational outlook handbook : based on information from the U.S. Department of Labor / by the Editors at JIST.

p. cm.

Easy occupational outlook handbook

Includes index.

ISBN 978-1-59357-432-1 (alk. paper)

1. Occupations--United States. 2. Job descriptions--United States. 3. Vocational guidance--United States. I. JIST Works, Inc. II. United States. Dept. of Labor. III. Title: Easy occupational outlook handbook.

HF5382.5.U5E97 2007

331.700973--dc22

2007005243

ISBN 978-1-59357-432-1

One of These Pages Contains the Career of Your Dreams

This book is designed to help you explore careers. It includes descriptions for 269 major jobs, which together employ 90 percent of the U.S. workforce.

The job descriptions answer questions such as these:

* What do people in this job do all day?
* Where do they work and during what hours and days?
* What training or education will I need to do the job?
* How much does the job pay?
* Will the job be in demand in the future?
* What jobs are related to this one?
* And did Thomas Edison *really* invent the lightbulb?

Though it contains an immense amount of information, this book is actually very easy to use (it says so in the title, after all). Simply thumb through the Table of Contents to find one or more job titles that interest you and turn to that page. Alternatively you can use the appendices to find jobs listed by personality type or by the education and training required.

The introduction provides additional information that can help you use this book in your career exploration. We hope it helps you to discover jobs and careers that match your interests, goals, needs, and dreams.

And if you really must know about the lightbulb, just turn to page 229.

Acknowledgments and Limitations on Use of the Data

This book features data obtained from the U.S. Department of Labor as used in various works it publishes, including the *Occupational Outlook Handbook* and the O*NET. The data collection process is an enormous one. We are thankful for the department's tireless efforts and immense contributions to the career development field. In using the information, however, we want to warn you of its limitations by adapting the language used by the department in the original works:

The occupational information contained in this book reflects jobs as they have been found to occur, but they may not coincide in every respect with the content of jobs as performed in particular establishments or at certain localities. Users of this information demanding specific job requirements should supplement this data with local information detailing jobs in their community.

In using this book, note that the U.S. Employment Service, the U.S. Department of Labor, and JIST Publishing, Inc., have no responsibility for establishing wage levels for workers in the United States or settling jurisdictional matters in relation to different occupations. In preparing vocational definitions, no data was collected concerning these and related matters. Therefore, the occupational information in this book cannot be regarded as determining standards for any aspect of the employer-employee relationship. Data contained in this publication should not be considered a judicial or legislative standard for wages, hours, or other contractual or bargaining elements.

The use of any information, no matter how carefully collected, researched, screened, or presented, has its limitations. The information provided in the *OOH* and O*NET database—and this book—has been carefully collected and thoughtfully presented. Even so, errors and inaccuracies can be introduced and, for this reason, we can accept no responsibility for any errors in fact nor in any decisions made or actions taken as a result of the information provided. As in all things, we humbly suggest that you accept your own judgment regarding important decisions.

Table of Contents

Professional and Related Occupations 37

Service Occupations 137

Sales and Related Occupations 165

Office and Administrative Support Occupations 179

Installation, Maintenance, and Repair Occupations............................241

Production Occupations..261

Transportation and Material Moving Occupations 283

Job Opportunities in the Armed Forces 293

Appendix A: Job Titles by Personality Type...295

Appendix B: Job Titles by Education and Training Requirements.................303

Introduction

What This Book Can Do for You

Once upon a time, the U.S. Department of Labor created a book with descriptions of the vast majority of jobs in the market. The book was called the *Occupational Outlook Handbook (OOH)*, and it became the most widely used source of career information around. It has helped millions of people explore their career options and make educated decisions. The book is still the most popular source of career information, and it is updated every two years.

It is also more than 700 pages long and weighs as much as a watermelon. Undoubtedly the *OOH* is so popular because of the wealth of information it offers, but it can also be intimidating for some readers. Those people who are in the early stages of career exploration may not even know where to get started with such a thick book.

If it were only possible to squeeze the most pertinent information out of the *OOH* and put it in a format that was simpler to use, easier to read, and more accessible for the everyday job seeker. A book that contained all of the relevant content, but none of the excess, trimmed down for people like you and me.

A book like this one.

Like the book it was based on, this EZ version of the *OOH* presents information on nearly 270 major jobs, and you are very likely to work in one or more of them during your life. Also like the *OOH*, the *EZ OOH* groups similar jobs together, making it simple to explore related jobs you might not know about. Unlike the *OOH*, the job descriptions in this book are only one page long. Yet they still contain all the necessary information about earnings, working conditions, and job opportunities, as well as information the *OOH* doesn't include, such as personality types best suited to the career and interesting facts related to each job.

This introduction will give you information to help you understand and use the book. In looking over these job descriptions, we suggest that you consider every one that interests you. Remember that you are exploring job *possibilities*. The information presented will help you discover what jobs match your personality and what additional training or education you will need to do that job. If a job requires more training or education than you currently have, consider it anyway. After all, there are many ways to finance an education.

Once upon a time there was a golden-haired girl who stumbled upon a house in the woods. She apparently didn't have very good manners because she started eating, sitting on, and sleeping in everything in sight. She was also a little picky. She couldn't have her porridge too hot or her bed too small. She wanted something that was a good fit for her. Nothing too big or overwhelming, but certainly something rich enough to meet her needs. In short, she was looking for something just right.

We think she would have liked this book.

We hope you do, too.

Getting the Most from an *EZ OOH* Job Description

The table of contents lists all the jobs in this book, arranged into groups of similar jobs. Look through the list and choose one or more of the job groups that sound most interesting to you. Make a list of the jobs that interest you, and then read the descriptions for those jobs.

Each job description in this book uses the same format. They all include six sections:

At a Glance: This section provides a short description of the job, including the most common work activities and responsibilities. Essentially, it gives you a sense of what people in this job *do* for a living.

Career in Focus: Most of the occupations from the *OOH* cover a wide range of jobs within a particular field. This section focus on a more specific job within that career category, a highly related job, or an opportunity for advancement. The description can give you a better idea of what people with specific job titles do.

Where and When: This section describes the working conditions of the job, including the work environment, the number of hours, possible job hazards, and other information that can help you decide whether the job is a good fit.

Did You Know? Because career exploration should be exciting and interesting, this section offers facts, anecdotes, or other unique information designed to give you a better perspective on the job.

For More Information: This section offers associations, agencies, and other organizations you can contact for more information. Internet addresses have been listed whenever possible. For even more information, see Appendix C, "Additional Sources of Career Information."

Data Bank: The Data Bank contains the facts and figures you need to make an informed decision, from earnings to job openings. The following section describes how to get the most of this information.

Using the Data Bank

Each job description is accompanied by a data bank that includes the most pertinent information every job seeker is looking for. This can help you compare one job with another to find the one with the right earnings, the most potential, and that best matches your interests. Unless otherwise stated, all of the data found in this section is based on information from the *Occupational Outlook Handbook* and the Department of Labor.

Education & Training: This section tells you the education and training levels most employers expect for someone just starting out in the job. Almost all jobs now require a high school diploma, so we do not include "high school graduate" as an option. Instead, we list the *additional* training or education the average high school graduate needs to get the job.

Here are brief explanations of the categories we've used for the levels of training and education:

- ✳ **Work experience:** Work experience in a related job.
- ✳ **Short-term on-the-job training:** On-the-job training that can be as short as a week or last up to six months.
- ✳ **Moderate-term on-the-job training:** On-the-job training that can last from six months to a year.
- ✳ **Long-term on-the-job training:** On-the-job training that lasts up to two or more years. This training can take the form of apprenticeships, especially in the construction trades and production, installation, maintenance, and repair occupations.
- ✳ **Vocational/technical training:** Formal vocational or technical training received in a school, apprenticeship, or cooperative education program or in the military. This training can last from a few months to two or more years and may combine classroom training with on-the-job experience.
- ✳ **Associate degree:** A two-year college degree, usually from a trade school, technical school, or community college.
- ✳ **Bachelor's degree:** A four-year college degree.
- ✳ **Master's degree:** A bachelor's degree plus one or two years of additional education.
- ✳ **Doctoral degree:** A master's degree plus two or more years of additional education.
- ✳ **Professional degree:** Typically, a bachelor's degree plus two or more years of specialized education (for example, education to be an attorney, physician, or veterinarian).
- ✳ **Plus Related Work Experience:** Some jobs require work experience in a related job *as well as* formal education.

Some descriptions in this section present a range of possible requirements (for example, **vocational/technical training to bachelor's degree**). This means that certain positions within that career or certain industries within that field may require more training than others. Keep in mind that this represents the *minimum* requirements to get the job, and that many employers would prefer individuals with even more education and training. In addition, some occupations may require certification or licensing for entry, advancement, or private practice. Certification and licensing usually require completing coursework or passing examinations.

To research jobs by the education and training level, start your exploration with Appendix B, "Job Titles by Education and Training Requirements."

Starting Salaries: These are projected earnings for people just starting out in the job. They are based on a weighted average of what the lowest 10 percent of earners make in that occupation.

Average Earnings: These figures are based on the earnings of the middle 50 percent of workers in that field. In all cases, earnings are presented as annual income, even if the job usually pays by the hour. This allows you to easily compare one job's potential earnings with another's. In cases where there is a wide salary range based on industry or job title, more than one figure may be given. Cases where the average earnings only apply to particular jobs are noted as well.

Keep in mind, the range of earnings given here excludes both the bottom and top 25 percent of earners. That is, people in these jobs may still make substantially *less* and substantially *more* than the figures listed here. We can all think of actors and top executives who make more than $100,000 dollars a year. Likewise, some waiters and waitresses earn more than $50,000 a year, although the average earnings for these jobs are much lower.

It is generally true, however, that those jobs requiring higher levels of training and education pay more. Earnings also vary widely for similar jobs with different employers or in different parts of the country. Finally, young workers usually earn less than the average because they have less work experience than older workers in the same job.

Total Jobs Held: This provides an estimate of the total number of people currently employed in this job. This is useful when considering potential job openings. The more people in a given career, generally the more openings that will be available from turnover and retirement.

Job Outlook: This tells you whether the job is likely to employ more or fewer people in the future. The possible categories are as follows:

* **Declining:** Employment is expected to decrease.
* **Little change:** Employment is expected to remain about the same or increase as much as 8%.
* **Average increase:** Employment is expected to increase from 8% to 18%.
* **Above-average increase:** Employment is expected to increase from 18% to 27%.
* **Rapid increase:** Employment is expected to increase by 27% or more.

Annual Job Openings: This figure represents both the number of new jobs that will be created as well as the number of already established positions that will become available each year. It's important to note that even jobs expecting a decline in job growth may still have thousands of openings each year due to turnover and retirement.

Related Jobs: This section lists similar jobs you can consider, all referenced elsewhere in this book.

Personality Type: This section describes the personality type whose interests best match the work and environment required of each job. Personality types are derived from the work of vocational psychologist John Holland. The information here is based on O*NET jobs that are linked to each *OOH* job title. The O*NET, or Occupational Information Network, is a database of job information developed and continuously updated by the U.S. Department of Labor. Jobs may fit more than one personality type.

We recommend you look over the following types and find the two or three that you think best describe your personality and interests. As you research the job descriptions, pay attention to the personality types listed in the Data Bank. While a personality type that differs from your own shouldn't keep you from considering a job, one that matches your personality and interests might be an even more appealing career choice. In short, if you are an artistic person and the job says it is a good fit for artistic people, you may be on to something.

Descriptions of the Six Personality Types

Realistic: These occupations frequently involve practical, hands-on problems and solutions. Workers often deal with plants, animals, and real-world materials like wood, tools, and machinery. Many of the occupations require working outside and do not involve a lot of paperwork or working closely with other people.

Investigative: These occupations frequently involve working with ideas and require lots of critical thinking and analysis. These occupations can involve searching for facts and solving complex problems.

Artistic: These occupations frequently involve working with forms, designs, and patterns. They often require self-expression, and the work can be done without following a clear set of rules.

Social: These occupations frequently involve working with, communicating with, and teaching people. They almost always involve helping or providing service to others.

Enterprising: These occupations frequently involve starting up and carrying out projects. They often require leading people, taking risks, and making important decisions. They often deal with business.

Conventional: These occupations frequently involve following set procedures and routines. They often entail working with data and details more than with ideas. Usually there is a clear line of authority to follow.

To research jobs by personality type, start your exploration with Appendix A, "Job Titles by Personality Type" found in the back of the book.

Dare to Compare

Make photocopies of the worksheet on the following page and use it to compare the jobs that interest you most. Simply fill in the information about each job, giving each characteristic (earnings, working conditions, education requirements, and so on) a rating from 1 (undesirable) to 5 (most desirable). Adding the ratings and comparing the totals for each can give you some idea of which jobs you'd like to pursue further.

Career Comparison Worksheet

Job Characteristic Ratings Scale

←— 1 —— 2 —— 3 —— 4 —— 5 —→

Undesirable   **Desirable**   **Most Desirable**

	Job 1	Job 2	Job 3
Job Title			
Job Description Does the "At a Glance" description appeal to you?			
Working Conditions Does the "Where and When" of the job appeal to you?			
Education Required Jobs that match your current or future educational level are more desirable.			
Average Earnings Generally, the higher the earnings, the more desirable the job.			
Job Outlook Generally, the better the outlook, the more desirable the job.			
Personality Type Jobs that match your perceived personality type may offer more satisfaction.			
Totals			

Management and Business and Financial Operations Occupations

Administrative Services Managers

At a Glance

Administrative services managers work for large and small businesses and government agencies. They manage the services that keep businesses running smoothly: mailroom, food, travel, data processing, security, parking, printing, purchasing, and payroll. They can work as office managers, contract administrators, or unclaimed property officers. In large companies, they may manage other workers. In small companies, they may be responsible for any or all of these services themselves.

Data Bank

Education and Training: Bachelor's degree plus related work experience

Starting Salaries: $31,000

Average Earnings: $45,000–$87,000

Total Jobs Held: 268,000

Job Outlook: Average increase

Annual Job Openings: 25,000

Related Jobs: Office and administrative support worker supervisors and managers; cost estimators; property, real estate, and community association managers; purchasing managers, buyers, and purchasing agents; top executives

Personality Type: Enterprising

Did You Know?

Facility managers looking for advice can find it in *American School and Hospital Facility,* a magazine designed for managers of institutional buildings. It includes articles on everything from the best floor cleaner to the latest grounds security surveillance systems. In fact, whatever your ideal career is, there is probably a magazine for it.

Career in Focus: *Facility Manager*

Facility managers plan, design, and manage workplace facilities. They are responsible for budgeting, buying and selling real estate, and making renovations. They may assist with the architectural design of the buildings. Often they are responsible for keeping the facility safe and well-maintained. Such jobs require a combination of engineering skill and business experience.

Where and When

Administrative service managers generally work in comfortable office settings. Most work a standard 40-hour week, though some overtime may be expected to meet deadlines. Depending on the type of job, frequent travel could be required.

For More Information

* International Facility Management Association, 1 East Greenway Plaza, Suite 1100, Houston, TX 77046-0194. Internet: www.ifma.org.

* Association of Higher Education Facilities Officers, 1643 Prince St., Alexandria, VA 22314-2818. Internet: www.appa.org.

* Institute of Certified Professional Managers, James Madison University, MSC 5504, Harrisonburg, VA 22807.

Advertising, Marketing, Promotions, Public Relations, and Sales Managers

At a Glance

Advertising, marketing, promotions, public relations, and sales managers can be found in almost every industry and are responsible for helping businesses sell their products and services. They coordinate market research, marketing strategy, sales, advertising, promotion, pricing, product development, and public relations activities. Advertising managers dictate what kind of advertising campaign will best sell the product, including the kinds of media used (radio, television, magazines, and so on). Marketing managers estimate how much of a product will sell and to which markets. Promotions managers direct programs that combine advertising with discounts, rebates, and contests to increase sales. Public relations managers help companies create a positive image in the community through interviews, press releases, and special events. Sales managers assign sales territories, set goals, and help train and motivate the sales force. Most of these managers are responsible for coordinating a team of workers to meet goals under strict deadlines.

Career in Focus: *Creative Director*

The creative director is an advertising manager who is specifically responsible for the written and visual parts of an ad campaign. This career combines business sense and experience with an imaginative and artistic personality.

Where and When

Advertising, marketing, promotions, public relations, and sales managers work in comfortable office settings. Long hours, including evenings and weekends, are common. In fact, about two-thirds of these managers usually work more than 40 hours per week. Substantial travel may be involved. The high stress of meeting deadlines can make this a challenging but rewarding career.

For More Information

* American Association of Advertising Agencies, 405 Lexington Ave., New York, NY 10174-1801. Internet: www.aaaa.org

* Public Relations Society of America, 33 Maiden Lane, New York, NY 10038-5150. Internet: www.prsa.org

Data Bank

Education and Training: Bachelor's degree plus related work experience

Starting Salaries: $41,000

Average Earnings: $60,000–$125,000

Total Jobs Held: 647,000

Job Outlook: Above-average increase

Annual Job Openings: 77,000

Related Jobs: Actors, producers, and directors; advertising sales agents; artists and related workers; demonstrators, product promoters, and models; market and survey researchers; public relations specialists; sales representatives, wholesale and manufacturing; writers and editors

Personality Type: Artistic; Enterprising

Did You Know?

As the top-selling soft drink in the world, Coca-Cola spends a hefty sum to keep its brand on the minds of consumers. Their annual advertising and marketing budget hovers around $2.5 billion. With that kind of investment, the new slogan better be catchy.

Computer and Information Systems Managers

At a Glance

Computer and information systems managers plan and direct the installation and use of computer systems. They hire computer programmers and support specialists and plan what new technology is needed to keep their company successful. They also decide what workers and equipment are needed to do certain jobs. Often they are involved in the upkeep, maintenance, and security of computer networks as well. Such responsibilities require them to constantly stay aware of the latest advances in technology.

Data Bank

Education and Training: Bachelor's degree plus related work experience

Starting Salaries: $53,000

Average Earnings: $75,000–$123,000

Total Jobs Held: 280,000

Job Outlook: Above-average increase

Annual Job Openings: 25,000

Related Jobs: Computer programmers; computer software engineers; computer systems analysts; computer scientists and database administrators; computer support specialists and systems administrators

Personality Type: Enterprising

Did You Know?

According to IBM, there are more than 100,000 known viruses threatening our computers. Whether they are protecting against a worm or weeding out the spam, computer and information systems managers have their work cut out for them in protecting their business's networks and data.

Career in Focus: *Network Manager*

Otherwise known as LAN/WAN (local area network/wide area network) managers, these individuals are responsible for designing and maintaining the network that connects all workers within an organization. When an employee on the second floor can't log in or a computer virus suddenly spreads throughout the network, you can be sure this manager is on the case.

Where and When

Computer and information systems managers work in comfortable office settings. They sometimes need to work evenings and weekends to solve unexpected problems, because companies often need their computer systems in order to keep their businesses running. Extensive computer use can lead to eyestrain and back, hand, and wrist problems.

For More Information

* National Workforce Center for Emerging Technologies, 3000 Landerholm Circle SE, Bellevue, WA 98007. Internet: www.nwcet.org

Construction Managers

At a Glance

Construction managers plan and direct construction projects, including roads, bridges, plants, schools, hospitals, and other buildings. On small projects they are responsible for all the people, materials, and equipment at a job site. They direct the building process from the concept stage through the final construction. They hire and schedule workers, make sure materials are delivered on time, and oversee the safety of the work site. They are also responsible for staying within budget. Anyone interested in being a construction manager needs a background in building science, business, and management, as well as experience in the construction industry.

Career in Focus: *Specialty Trade Contractor*

Most construction managers are concerned with all aspects of construction. But some aspects of a building are important enough to require a construction manager who specializes in that line of work, often known as a specialty trade contractor. Examples of specialties include plumbing, heating and air-conditioning, and electrical work. After all, you don't want just anyone overseeing the plumbing work in your new house.

Where and When

Construction managers often work out of a central office where they coordinate activity. However, they spend a great deal of time on site as well, which could mean extensive travel. In addition, they are usually on call 24 hours a day to deal with delays, bad weather, and emergencies. Though safety precautions are always taken, work around a construction site can still be hazardous.

For More Information

* American Institute of Constructors, 717 Princess St., Alexandria, VA 22314. Internet: www.aicnet.org
* Construction Management Association of America, 7918 Jones Branch Dr., Suite 540, McLean, VA 22102-3307. Internet: www.cmaanet.org
* American Council for Construction Education, 1717 North Loop 1604 E, Ste 320, San Antonio, TX 78232. Internet: www.acce-hq.org
* National Center for Construction Education and Research, P.O. Box 141104, Gainesville, FL 32614. Internet: www.nccer.org

Data Bank

Education and Training: Bachelor's degree

Starting Salaries: $42,000

Average Earnings: $55,000–$96,000

Total Jobs Held: 431,000

Job Outlook: Average increase

Annual Job Openings: 28,000

Related Jobs: Architects, except landscape and naval; civil engineers; cost estimators; landscape architects; engineering and natural sciences managers

Personality Type: Enterprising

Did You Know?

There is an increased demand for certification of construction managers. Volunteer certification programs such as those offered by the American Institute of Constructors (AIC) and the Construction Management Association of America (CMAA) provide proof to potential employers and clients of a manager's knowledge and experience.

Education Administrators

At a Glance

Education administrators manage the day-to-day activities in schools, preschools, daycare centers, and colleges and universities. They also direct the educational programs of businesses, correctional institutions, museums, and community service organizations. Education administrators set standards and goals and establish the policies and procedures to carry them out. They develop academic programs, monitor students' progress, and train and motivate teachers. They also may prepare budgets and handle relations with parents, students, employers, and the community. They might be school principals, college presidents or deans, or school-district superintendents. Many education administrators begin their careers as teachers.

Data Bank

Education and Training: Bachelor's degree plus related work experience

Starting Salaries: $42,000

Average Earnings: $54,000–$87,000

Total Jobs Held: 441,000

Job Outlook: Average increase

Annual Job Openings: 58,000

Related Jobs: Administrative services managers; office and administrative support worker supervisors and managers; human resources, training, and labor relations managers and specialists; counselors; librarians; instructional coordinators; teachers—preschool, kindergarten, elementary, middle, and secondary; teachers—postsecondary

Personality Type: Enterprising; Social

Did You Know?

Do you have what it takes to be Principal of the Year? Every year Metlife and the National Association of Secondary School Principals choose one among 50 state principals to win this prestigious honor. It comes with a $5,000 grant and an honorary banquet in Washington, DC. It may not be as glamorous as Miss America, but the competition is still intense (though there is no swimsuit competition as far as we know).

Career in Focus: *College Registrar*

College registrars keep track of college students' records. They register students, record grades, prepare student transcripts, plan commencement, and oversee the preparation of college course offerings. Most students (and many parents) know them primarily for one other responsibility: collecting tuition and fees. Contrary to what many students would say, they really are nice people.

Where and When

Unlike most teachers, the majority of educational administrators work 11 or 12 months out of the year, often more than 40 hours per week. While the job is mostly indoors in comfortable settings, the stress level can be high. These administrators must deal with the concerns of students, parents, teachers, and government agencies all at once.

For More Information

* The National Association of Elementary School Principals, 1615 Duke St., Alexandria, VA 22314-3483. Internet: www.naesp.org

* The National Association of Secondary School Principals, 1904 Association Drive, Reston, VA 20191-1537. Internet: www.nassp.org

* The Educational Leadership Constituent Council, 1904 Association Drive, Reston, VA 20191. Internet: www.npbea.org/ELCC/index.html

* American Association of Collegiate Registrars and Admissions Officers, One Dupont Circle NW, Suite 520, Washington, DC 20036-1171. Internet: www.aacrao.org

Engineering and Natural Sciences Managers

At a Glance

Engineering and natural science managers plan and direct research, development, and production in large and small companies and labs. They hire and supervise engineers, chemists, and biologists. They manage and review the work in a business or lab and help determine salaries. They also decide what workers and equipment are needed to do certain jobs. Many coordinate the design, installation, and operation of equipment in industrial plants. These positions require a good mix of administrative and managerial skills with a scientific or engineering education and background. In fact, most of these managers begin their careers as engineers or scientists.

Career in Focus: *Science Manager*

Most science managers specialize in a particular branch of science, such as biology, chemistry, or geology. They coordinate the research of others and oversee testing, quality control, and production. Most have their Ph.D. in their chosen scientific field and conduct their own research as well.

Where and When

Engineering and natural science managers work in offices or laboratories and are sometimes exposed to potentially harmful substances. Most of these managers work at least 40 hours per week. They are often under pressure to meet deadlines and stay within budget.

For More Information

* American Society for Engineering Management, 614 Pine St., Suite 206B, PO Box 820, Rolla, MO 65402-0820. Internet: www.asem.org

Data Bank

Education and Training: Bachelor's degree plus related work experience

Starting Salaries: $61,000

Average Earnings: $78,000–$124,000

Total Jobs Held: 232,000

Job Outlook: Average increase

Annual Job Openings: 20,000

Related Jobs: Engineers, mathematicians, agricultural and food scientists, atmospheric scientists, biological scientists, conservation scientists and foresters, chemists and materials scientists, environmental scientists and hydrologists, geoscientists, medical scientists, physicists and astronomers, top executives

Personality Type: Enterprising; Investigative

Did You Know?

For a long time the vast majority of management jobs in engineering (or any jobs in engineering for that matter) were held by men. But in the last two decades, more and more women have moved up the ranks to become engineering managers. In fact, today's engineering companies are actively recruiting women at all levels. Nearly 25 percent of all engineering and science managers today are women, though that's still well below the average of 45 percent for all occupations.

Farmers, Ranchers, and Agricultural Managers

At a Glance

American farmers, ranchers, and agricultural managers direct the activities of one of the world's largest agricultural producers. Farmers and ranchers own and operate family-owned or leased farms. They are responsible for preparing, planting, fertilizing, cultivating, and harvesting crops. After the harvest, they make sure that the crops are properly packaged, stored, or marketed. Livestock, dairy, and poultry farmers must feed and care for their animals. Horticultural specialty farmers oversee the production of ornamental plants; flowers, bulbs, and shrubbery; and fruits and vegetables grown in greenhouses. Agricultural managers manage the day-to-day activities of one or more farms, ranches, and nurseries. They all focus on the business aspects of running a farm.

Data Bank

Education and Training: Long-term on-the-job-training to bachelor's degree plus related work experience

Starting Salaries: $30,000

Average Earnings: $39,000–$65,000

Total Jobs Held: 1,285,000

Job Outlook: Declining

Annual Job Openings: 116,000

Related Jobs: Agricultural engineers; agricultural and food scientists; agricultural workers; purchasing managers, buyers, and purchasing agents

Personality Type: Realistic; Enterprising

Did You Know?

Like most other businesses, farming has become more complex due to changes in technology. The result is that many farmers and agricultural managers now use computers and scanners to keep track of inventory and manage their businesses. Being a successful farmer means keeping track of economic trends as well and having good business sense, making it an even more demanding job than before.

Career in Focus: *Aquaculture Farmer*

Aquaculture farmers raise fish and shellfish for food or recreational fishing. They must stock, feed, and protect the aquatic life raised in ponds or floating net pens. It's easier to trust the Gorton's fisherman when you know he raises his own fish in a floating pen.

Where and When

The work of farmers, ranchers, and agricultural managers is demanding. The hours are long and the work can be quite physical. Work usually increases or decreases with the season. In addition, this line of work can be dangerous. Farm machinery can cause serious injury, and exposure to chemicals is a concern.

For More Information

* Center for Rural Affairs, P.O. Box 406, Walthill, NE 68067. Internet: www.cfra.org

* National FFA Organization, The National FFA Center, Attention Career Information Requests, P.O. Box 68690, Indianapolis, IN 46268-0960. Internet: www.ffa.org

* American Society of Farm Managers and Rural Appraisers, 950 Cherry St., Suite 508, Denver, CO 80222. Internet: www.asfmra.org

* Alternative Farming System Information Center (AFSIC), National Agricultural Library USDA, 10301 Baltimore Ave., Room 132, Beltsville, MD 20705-2351. Internet: www.nal.usda.gov/afsic

Financial Managers

At a Glance

Financial managers work for all kinds of businesses and agencies. They analyze data in order to offer advice on how to maximize profits. They prepare financial reports and make sure the business pays its taxes and has enough money to operate. They watch over the cash flow, manage the company's stocks, and communicate with investors. They also decide whether the business needs to borrow money, lend money, or invest in stocks and bonds. Controllers direct the preparation of reports that summarize the organization's financial position. Treasurers and finance officers direct the organization's financial goals, objectives, and budgets. Other managers oversee the firm's credit and collections and monitor the flow of cash.

Career in Focus: *Risk and Insurance Manager*

Risk and insurance managers oversee programs to minimize risks and losses that might arise from financial transactions and business operations. They also manage the organization's insurance budget. They are watchdogs, making sure a company doesn't stretch its financial resources too far.

Where and When

While they do get to work in comfortable office settings and often have access to the latest technology, financial managers are also prone to working long hours. They often work more than 50 hours per week. The job can be stressful and may require some travel as well.

For More Information

* Financial Management Association International, College of Business Administration, University of South Florida, Tampa, FL 33620-5500. Internet: www.fma.org

* Association for Financial Professionals, 7315 Wisconsin Ave., Suite 600 West, Bethesda, MD 20814. Internet: www.afponline.org

* CFA Institute, P.O. Box 3668, 560 Ray Hunt Dr., Charlottesville, VA 22903-0668. Internet: www.cfainstitute.org

* Global Association of Risk Professionals, 100 Pavonia Ave., Suite 405, Jersey City, NJ 07310.

* Institute of Management Accountants, 10 Paragon Dr., Montvale, NJ, 07645-1718. Internet: www.imanet.org

Data Bank

Education and Training: Bachelor's degree plus related work experience

Starting Salaries: $44,000

Average Earnings: $63,000–$118,000

Total Jobs Held: 528,000

Job Outlook: Average increase

Annual Job Openings: 63,000

Related Jobs: Accountants and auditors; budget analysts; financial analysts and personal financial advisors; insurance sales agents; insurance underwriters; loan officers; securities, commodities, and financial services sales agents; real estate brokers and sales agents

Personality Type: Enterprising

Did You Know?

While a bachelor's degree is a minimum requirement for landing a job as a financial manager, many companies are seeking individuals with even more education: preferably a master's degree in business administration, economics, finance, or risk management. The number of students graduating with M.B.A.s continues to rise, suggesting keen competition for careers like these.

Food Service Managers

At a Glance

Food service managers are responsible for the daily operations of restaurants and other establishments that serve food and drinks. They coordinate the activities of the kitchen, dining room, and banquet operations, and ensure that customers are satisfied with their dining experience. Food service managers select and price the food on a restaurant's menu. They hire and train workers and manage staffing, payroll, and bookkeeping. They also oversee food preparation, order supplies and ingredients, and make sure the restaurant is clean and well-maintained. Managers must be able to communicate with a diverse clientele and staff and motivate employees to work as a team.

Data Bank

Education and Training: Work experience

Starting Salaries: $24,000

Average Earnings: $33,000–$53,000

Total Jobs Held: 371,000

Job Outlook: Average increase

Annual Job Openings: 61,000

Related Jobs: Lodging managers, sales worker supervisors, food and beverage serving and related workers

Personality Type: Enterprising

Did You Know?

Have you ever heard of Hamburger University? Students come from around the world to attend McDonald's manager training school in Oak Brook, Illinois. There they learn about maintaining product quality, hiring and supervising workers, advertising and publicity, equipment repair, and other aspects of restaurant management. The training lasts two weeks, and graduates are qualified to manage a McDonald's restaurant. They do not, as far as we know, get fries with that.

Career in Focus: *Special Food Services Manager*

Though the name might suggest that they serve exotic fare like poached ostrich eggs or alligator steaks, special food services managers are actually contractors who supply food services at institutional, governmental, commercial, or industrial locations. In other words, they may supply the food for a school cafeteria, a hotel buffet, or the entire menu at a nursing home.

Where and When

These managers are among the first to arrive and the last to leave. They often work 12 to 15 hours per day and 50 or more hours per week. Those who work in schools, factories, and hospitals may have more regular hours. Managers must be calm under pressure as they are the ones called upon to resolve problems. Dealing with angry customers or uncooperative employees can be stressful. Managers may also experience muscle aches, cuts, or burns.

For More Information

* National Restaurant Association Educational Foundation, 175 West Jackson Blvd., Suite 1500, Chicago, IL 60604-2702. Internet: www.nraef.org

* The International Council on Hotel, Restaurant, and Institutional Education, 2613 North Parham Rd., 2nd Floor, Richmond, VA 23294. Internet: www.chrie.org

Funeral Directors

At a Glance

Although Americans express a wide range of beliefs, funeral practices usually share some common elements: preparing the remains, performing a ceremony that honors the deceased and addresses the spiritual needs of the family, and carrying out the final burial or cremation of the body. Funeral directors, also called morticians or undertakers, arrange and direct these tasks for grieving families. They also help the family plan the funeral, prepare the obituary notice, and handle the paperwork. Funeral directors often run the business as well: They prepare bills, keep financial records, and hire and manage a staff.

Career in Focus: *Embalmer*

Most funeral directors are also licensed embalmers. Embalming is a sanitary, cosmetic, and preservative process that prepares the body for burial or cremation. Embalmers wash the body and replace the blood with embalming fluid to preserve the tissues. They may also reshape and reconstruct disfigured or maimed bodies using materials such as clay, cotton, plaster of paris, and wax. This job may not be for everybody.

Where and When

Funeral directors can work long, irregular hours, in part because they are often on call. There are very few worries about health concerns in working with human remains so long as strict regulations are followed.

For More Information

* The National Funeral Directors Association, 13625 Bishop's Dr., Brookfield, WI 53005. Internet: www.nfda.org
* The American Board of Funeral Service Education, 38 Florida Ave., Portland, ME 04103. Internet: www.abfse.org/index.html

Data Bank

Education and Training: Associate degree

Starting Salaries: $26,000

Average Earnings: $37,000–$63,000

Total Jobs Held: 30,000

Job Outlook: Little change

Annual Job Openings: 3,000

Related Jobs: Social workers, psychologists, physicians and surgeons

Personality Type: Enterprising

Did You Know?

It might be possible to bury the dead in your backyard provided it's big enough. State laws vary widely on whether bodies must be buried in cemeteries or can be laid to rest on a private residence. Regulations are established for how far the burial must be from a dwelling (or water source) to how far down in the ground the remains should be. We do not recommend opening up a cemetery in your backyard, however, no matter how big it is.

Human Resources, Training, and Labor Relations Managers and Specialists

At a Glance

Human resources, training, and labor relations managers and specialists find the best employees they can and match them with jobs in their company. They interview job candidates and train new workers. They may hold job fairs to find applicants. They are often responsible for handling employee benefits and creating and maintaining a fair pay system. They help to resolve conflicts among workers or between workers and management. They also provide some employee training and are concerned with maintaining worker satisfaction. They often provide for mental and physical health services, on the job safety programs, and child care. Increasingly, they take part in the company's strategic planning, discussing how personnel resources can best be used.

Data Bank

Education and Training: Bachelor's degree to bachelor's degree plus related work experience

Starting Salaries: $27,000

Average Earnings: $39,000–$67,000

Total Jobs Held: 819,000

Job Outlook: Above-average increase

Annual Job Openings: 114,000

Related Jobs: Counselors, education administrators, public relations specialists, lawyers, psychologists, social and human service assistants, social workers

Personality Type: Enterprising; Investigative; Social

Did You Know?

Human resource managers are responsible for taking care of the economy's most important natural resource. No—not oil. People. By 2014, the number of people in the U.S. labor force is expected to reach 162 million. And that population is expected to grow even more diverse, meaning that human resource managers and specialists must be especially sensitive to cultural differences in order to be successful.

Career in Focus: *Recruiter*

Recruiters maintain contacts within the community and may travel considerably, often to college campuses, to search for promising job applicants. Recruiters screen, interview, and occasionally test applicants. They also may check references and extend job offers. These workers must keep informed about equal employment opportunity (EEO) and affirmative action guidelines and laws.

Where and When

Most human resources managers work a standard 35- to 40-hour week in comfortable office settings. Although many work in the office, some travel extensively.

For More Information

* Society for Human Resource Management, 1800 Duke St., Alexandria, VA 22314. Internet: www.shrm.org

* American Society for Training & Development, 1640 King St., Box 1443, Alexandria, VA 22313-2043. Internet: www.astd.org

* International Foundation of Employee Benefit Plans, 18700 W. Bluemound Rd., P.O. Box 69, Brookfield, WI 53008-0069. Internet: www.ifebp.org

* Labor and Employment Relations Association, University of Illinois at Urbana-Champaign, 121 Labor and Industrial Relations Bldg., 504 E. Armory Ave., Champaign, IL 61820. Internet: www.lera.uiuc.edu

* American Society for Healthcare Human Resources Administration, One North Franklin, 31st Floor, Chicago, IL 60606. Internet: www.ashhra.org

Industrial Production Managers

At a Glance

Industrial production managers plan the activities needed to produce millions of goods every year in the United States. They direct scheduling, staffing, equipment, quality control, and inventory in factories. Their main job is to get goods produced the right way, on time, and within budget. They decide what equipment and workers to use and in what order. They also monitor the production run to make sure it stays on schedule and to fix any problems that arise. They are often responsible for thinking up ways to improve the production process as well. For that reason they must keep up with changes in technology and new innovations by competitors.

Career in Focus: *Quality Control Manager*

Quality control managers are primarily responsible for ensuring that a product meets certain standards. They sample products before they are shipped and make recommendations for how they might be improved. They are also responsible for troubleshooting problems in the production process. One can only assume that Hanes Inspector #12 has already made it up to management level.

Where and When

Most industrial production managers spend equal time in the production area and their offices. While in the production area, they must follow the established health and safety practices and wear protective clothing and equipment. Most work more than 40 hours per week to meet production deadlines. Some facilities work around the clock, requiring the need for late shift managers or managers on call.

For More Information

For more information, contact local manufacturers or schools with programs in industrial management.

Data Bank

Education and Training: Work experience

Starting Salaries: $44,000

Average Earnings: $58,000–$98,000

Total Jobs Held: 160,000

Job Outlook: Little change

Annual Job Openings: 13,000

Related Jobs: Engineers, management analysts, operations research analysts

Personality Type: Enterprising

Did You Know?

In 1913 Henry Ford introduced moving assembly belts into his auto plants, starting a small industrial revolution. By 1918 half of all cars on the road were Ford Model-T's. Ford is famous for the changes he made to automobiles, production methods, and economic theory. He is also famous for having written about the Model T, "Any customer can have a car painted any color that he wants so long as it is black."

Lodging Managers

At a Glance

Vacationers and business travelers expect good food, a friendly staff, and a comfortable room. Lodging managers are responsible for providing these things. These managers hire, train, and supervise the people who work in hotels, motels, and inns. They set room rates, handle billing, order food and supplies, and oversee the day-to-day operations. Managers who work for hotel chains may staff a new hotel, refurbish an older one, or reorganize one that is not operating well. Some of these managers specialize in one aspect of the lodging business, whether it's helping to coordinate special events, managing housekeeping, or overseeing the food operations. All lodging managers are primarily responsible for keeping their guests happy and comfortable.

Data Bank

Education and Training: Work experience

Starting Salaries: $23,000

Average Earnings: $30,000–$56,000

Total Jobs Held: 58,000

Job Outlook: Average increase

Annual Job Openings: 10,000

Related Jobs: Food service managers; sales worker supervisors; property, real estate, and community association managers

Personality Type: Enterprising

Did You Know?

Did you know you can actually pay $10,000 a night for a hotel room? In fact, many of the most luxurious suites in the world's five-star hotels go for that rate or more. The Bridge Suite at the Atlantis resort in the Bahamas runs $25,000 a night. Of course, such prices often get you a 5,000-square-foot room complete with private cinema, and maybe even a chauffeured Rolls-Royce for personal use. But at that rate, you might just be better off buying a house everywhere you go.

Career in Focus: *Front Office Manager*

Front office managers coordinate reservations and room assignments. They also train and direct the hotel's front desk staff. They ensure that guests are treated courteously, complaints and problems are resolved, and requests for special services are carried out. They are also the ones who address all those questions you have about mysterious telephone and cable charges on your bill.

Where and When

Most hotels are open around the clock, meaning lodging managers commonly work nights and weekends and spend much of their time on call. Coordinating a wide range of activities and managing a staff can be stressful. Conventions and large groups of tourists can require managers to work extra hours. Dealing with angry guests can be difficult at times, especially since kicking them out is seldom an option.

For More Information

✳ American Hotel and Lodging Association, 1201 New York Ave. NW, Suite 600, Washington, DC 20005-3931.

✳ Educational Institute of the American Hotel and Lodging Association, 800 N. Magnolia Ave., Suite 1800, Orlando, FL 32853-1126. Internet: www.ei-ahla.org

✳ International Council on Hotel, Restaurant, and Institutional Education, 2613 North Parham Rd., 2nd Floor, Richmond, VA 23294-4442. Internet: www.chrie.org

Medical and Health Services Managers

At a Glance

Medical and health services managers—also called health care administrators or health care executives—organize and supervise the delivery of health care. They determine staffing and equipment needs. They also direct the public relations, marketing, and finances of hospitals, nursing homes, clinics, and doctor's offices. They may be in charge of an entire organization or only one department within it. Medical and health services managers must be constantly aware of changes in technology and medicine. Because of the rising cost of healthcare, these managers are also often responsible for improving efficiency to reduce cost without sacrificing quality.

Career in Focus: *Health Information Manager*

Health information managers are responsible for maintaining and protecting patient records. Federal regulations require that all health care providers maintain electronic patient records and that these records be secure. Health information managers ensure that databases are complete, accurate, and available only to authorized personnel.

Where and When

While the pay is often good, most medical and health services managers work long hours. Most health care facilities operate around the clock, and administrators and managers may be called at all hours to deal with problems. Some travel can also be required to conferences or other facilities. These managers often work out of comfortable private offices or share space with other managers and staff.

For More Information

* Association of University Programs in Health Administration, 2000 North 14th St., Suite 780, Arlington, VA 22201. Internet: www.aupha.org

* American College of Healthcare Executives, One N. Franklin St., Suite 1700, Chicago, IL 60606-4425. Internet: www.healthmanagementcareers.org

* American College of Health Care Administrators, 300 N. Lee St., Suite 301, Alexandria, VA 22314. Internet: www.achca.org

* Medical Group Management Association, 104 Inverness Terrace East, Englewood, CO 80112-5306. Internet: www.mgma.org

Data Bank

Education and Training: Bachelor's degree plus related work experience

Starting Salaries: $41,000

Average Earnings: $55,000–$90,000

Total Jobs Held: 248,000

Job Outlook: Above-average increase

Annual Job Openings: 33,000

Related Jobs: Insurance underwriters, social and community service managers

Personality Type: Enterprising

Did You Know?

The number of patients using some form of home health care has been rising. More than a million patients rely on qualified professionals to help treat them in their homes. Medical and health service managers are responsible for coordinating their care as well. With the cost of hospital stays rising, home health care can be a good option financially and is sometimes better for the comfort of the patient.

Property, Real Estate, and Community Association Managers

At a Glance

Property and real estate managers maintain and increase the value of real estate. They oversee apartment buildings, rental houses, businesses, and shopping malls. They sell empty space to renters, prepare leases, collect rent, and handle the book-keeping. They also make sure the property is maintained and handle complaints from renters. Managers may purchase supplies and equipment for the property. They make arrangements for repairs that cannot be handled by regular maintenance staff. They make sure that their properties comply with all government regulations and building codes. Some property and real estate managers act as a property owner's economic adviser as well.

Data Bank

Education and Training: Bachelor's degree

Starting Salaries: $19,000

Average Earnings: $28,000–$61,000

Total Jobs Held: 361,000

Job Outlook: Average increase

Annual Job Openings: 58,000

Related Jobs: Administrative services managers, education administrators, food service managers, lodging managers, medical and health services managers, real estate brokers and sales agents, urban and regional planners

Personality Type: Enterprising

Did You Know?

Property managers don't just manage apartments and houses. Did you ever wonder who is in charge of all that open space at the shopping mall? Mall property managers provide security, replace light bulbs, hire cleaning crews, and make sure the lawns are mowed and the flowers are watered. They collect rent from the stores and restaurants (the mall's tenants), and make sure the mall is clean, comfortable, and open for business.

Career in Focus: *Community Association Manager*

Community association managers work for condominium or neighborhood owners' associations. They collect dues, prepare budgets, negotiate with contractors, and help resolve complaints. They interact with homeowners and other residents on a daily basis. They are hired by the volunteer board of directors of the association. They oversee the maintenance of property and facilities that the homeowners own and use jointly, such as playgrounds and swimming pools.

Where and When

Although they work out of offices, these managers spend most of their time away from their desks, investigating problems, showing apartments, or managing staff. Some of these managers are required to live in the apartments or neighborhoods where they work. Night and weekend work is common, though many receive time off during the week to make up for having to work weekends.

For More Information

* Institute of Real Estate Management, 430 N. Michigan Ave., Chicago, IL 60611. Internet: www.irem.org

* Building Owners and Managers Institute, 1521 Ritchie Hwy., Arnold, MD 21012. Internet: www.bomi-edu.org

* Community Associations Institute, 225 Reinekers Ln., Suite 300, Alexandria, VA 22314. Internet: www.caionline.org

* National Board of Certification for Community Association Managers, 225 Reinekers Lane, Suite 310, Alexandria, VA 22314. Internet: www.nbccam.org

Purchasing Managers, Buyers, and Purchasing Agents

At a Glance

These workers look for the highest quality merchandise at the lowest possible price for their employers or for resale. They find the best products, negotiate the price, and make sure the right amount is received at the right time. They study sales records and inventory levels, identify suppliers, and study changes in the marketplace. Wholesale and retail buyers purchase goods for resale, such as clothing or electronics. Purchasing agents buy goods and services for use by their own company or organization, such as raw materials for manufacturing or office supplies. Many managers assist in planning sales promotions.

Career in Focus: *Merchandise Manager*

Merchandise managers buy finished goods for resale. They are employed by wholesale and retail establishments, where they commonly are known as *buyers*. Wholesale buyers purchase goods directly from manufacturers or from other wholesale firms for resale to retail firms, commercial establishments, and other organizations.

Where and When

Most purchasing managers, buyers, and purchasing agents work in comfortable offices, though they commonly work long hours, evenings, or weekends—especially before holiday and back-to-school seasons. Many of them travel several days out of the month, sometimes internationally.

For More Information

* American Purchasing Society, North Island Center, Suite 203, 8 East Galena Blvd., Aurora, IL 60506. Internet: www.american-purchasing.com
* Institute for Supply Management, P.O. Box 22160, Tempe, AZ 85285-2160. Internet: www.ism.ws
* National Institute of Governmental Purchasing, Inc., 151 Spring St., Suite 300, Herndon, VA 20170-5223. Internet: www.nigp.org

Data Bank

Education and Training: Work experience to bachelor's degree plus related work experience

Starting Salaries: $30,000

Average Earnings: $39,000–$68,000

Total Jobs Held: 520,000

Job Outlook: Little change

Annual Job Openings: 49,000

Related Jobs: Advertising, marketing, promotions, public relations, and sales managers; food service managers; insurance sales agents; lodging managers; sales engineers; sales representatives, wholesale and manufacturing

Personality Type: Enterprising

Did You Know?

Purchasing specialists often work closely with other employees in their own organization, an arrangement sometimes called "team buying." For example, before submitting an order, they may discuss the design of products with company engineers, talk about the quality of purchased goods with production supervisors, or mention shipment problems to managers in the receiving department. This may also keep them from having to take all the blame when something doesn't go as well as they hoped.

Top Executives

At a Glance

Although they carry a wide range of titles—CEO, COO, board chair, president, superintendent, or commissioner—all top executives are responsible for guiding their business or corporation, government organization, or nonprofit institution to reach its goals. Top executives make policies and direct operations. They meet with other executives, boards of directors, government heads, and consultants to discuss policy and direction. They are responsible for the organization's ultimate success or failure, so they are always under pressure. They provide the company's vision and share it with its employees and the public.

Data Bank

Education and Training: Bachelor's degree plus related work experience

Starting Salaries: $41,000

Average Earnings: $61,000–$104,000

Total Jobs Held: 2,251,000

Job Outlook: Average increase

Annual Job Openings: 246,000

Related Jobs: Administrative services managers; education administrators; financial managers; food service managers; advertising, marketing, promotions, public relations, and sales managers

Personality Type: Enterprising

Did You Know?

In addition to being responsible for the success of a company, top executives are increasingly held accountable for the ethics of their business practices. After the Enron bankruptcy and scandal, the American public has been even more skeptical of top executives and their dealings. Still, for every CEO who finds himself before a grand jury, there are plenty more who share their success with others, such as Bill Gates, whose charitable foundation gives billions of dollars to people and programs in need.

Career in Focus: *Chief Financial Officer*

Chief financial officers (CFOs) direct the organization's financial goals, objectives, and budgets. They oversee investments and cash flow, raise capital, deal with mergers and acquisitions, and manage a business's expansion. In short, they control the company's purse strings.

Where and When

Top executives usually get the biggest offices with the cushiest chairs, but it comes at the price of long hours, including evenings and weekends. Many executives spend a good deal of time traveling, often outside of the country. In addition, top executives are always under pressure to succeed and to look after the welfare of their employees.

For More Information

* American Management Association, 1601 Broadway, 6th Floor, New York, NY 10019. Internet: www.amanet.org

* International Public Management Association for Human Resources, 1617 Duke St., Alexandria, VA 22314. Internet: www.ipma-hr.org

* National Management Association, 2210 Arbor Blvd., Dayton, OH 45439. Internet: www.nma1.org

* Financial Executives International, 200 Campus Dr., P.O. Box 674, Florham Park, NJ 07932-0674. Internet: www.fei.org

* Financial Management Association International, College of Business Administration, University of South Florida, 4202 East Fowler Ave., BSN 3331, Tampa, FL 33620-5500. Internet: www.fma.org

Accountants and Auditors

At a Glance

Accountants and auditors prepare and check financial reports and taxes. Public accountants perform a broad range of accounting, auditing, tax, and consulting activities for corporations, governments, nonprofit organizations, or individuals. Management accountants record and analyze the financial information of the companies they work for. They are responsible for budgeting, performance evaluation, and cost and asset management. Internal auditors verify the accuracy of their organization's internal records and check for mismanagement, waste, or fraud. Government accountants maintain and examine the records of government agencies. They also audit the records of private businesses. Increasingly, accountants act as personal financial advisors, helping clients develop personal budgets, manage investments, and plan for retirement.

Career in Focus: *Forensic Accountant*

Forensic accountants investigate white-collar crimes such as securities fraud and embezzlement, bankruptcies and contract disputes, and money laundering. They combine their knowledge of accounting and finance with law and investigative techniques in order to determine whether an activity is illegal. Forensic accountants often appear as expert witnesses during trials. Think of it as *CSI* with a lot more math.

Where and When

Most accountants and auditors work in office settings. Some are self-employed and can work from home. Those whose primary responsibility involves auditing other companies' finances have to travel extensively. While most work the standard 40-hour week, overtime is common during tax season.

For More Information

* American Institute of Certified Public Accountants, 1211 Avenue of the Americas, New York, NY 10036. Internet: www.aicpa.org

* National Association of State Boards of Accountancy, 150 Fourth Ave. North, Suite 700, Nashville, TN 37219-2417. Internet: www.nasba.org

* Institute of Management Accountants, 10 Paragon Dr., Montvale, NJ 07645-1718. Internet: www.imanet.org

* The Institute of Internal Auditors, 247 Maitland Ave., Altamonte Springs, FL 32701-4201. Internet: www.theiia.org

Data Bank

Education and Training: Bachelor's degree

Starting Salaries: $32,000

Average Earnings: $41,000–$68,000

Total Jobs Held: 1,176,000

Job Outlook: Above-average increase

Annual Job Openings: 157,000

Related Jobs: Budget analysts; cost estimators; loan officers; financial analysts and personal financial advisors; tax examiners, collectors, and revenue agents; bill and account collectors; bookkeeping, accounting, and auditing clerks; computer programmers; computer software engineers; computer support specialists and systems administrators

Personality Type: Conventional

Did You Know?

In the 1920s, Al Capone boasted that he owned the city of Chicago. Raking in millions of dollars in gambling, prostitution, and alcohol (during the age of prohibition), the police seemed helpless to stop him. That is, until government accountants stepped in and looked at his financial records. Capone was finally convicted and imprisoned, not for the murders he ordered, but for the taxes he didn't pay.

Appraisers and Assessors of Real Estate

At a Glance

Real estate appraisers and assessors estimate the value of all kinds of property, from farmland to shopping centers. Their evaluations are used to help decide property taxes, mortgages, sale prices, or whether property is a good investment for a client. Assessors determine the value of all properties in an area for tax purposes, and they primarily work for the government. Appraisers evaluate properties one at a time for a variety of purposes. After visiting the property, the appraiser or assessor will determine the fair value by considering things such as lease records, location, previous appraisals, and income potential. They then put all of their research and observations together in a detailed report.

Data Bank

Education and Training: Vocational/technical training

Starting Salaries: $22,000

Average Earnings: $31,000–$62,000

Total Jobs Held: 102,000

Job Outlook: Above-average increase

Annual Job Openings: 9,000

Related Jobs: Construction and building inspectors; real estate brokers and sales agents; urban and regional planners; claims adjusters, appraisers, examiners and investigators; cost estimators

Personality Type: Conventional; Enterprising

Did You Know?

Property taxes are the primary source of income for local governments, and much of our everyday life—such as our public school systems—depends on them. Assessors are responsible for researching and helping set the property tax for each city and county. Based on government figures, the states with the highest local property taxes per capita are New Jersey, Connecticut, New York, and Rhode Island.

Career in Focus: *Residential Appraiser*

Residential appraisers focus on appraising homes or other residences. Sellers use appraisers to know what their home is worth. Buyers use appraisals to decide if the price is right and if the property will keep or increase its value. In addition, banks and other lending institutions use appraisers when deciding whether to give home loans.

Where and When

While they spend much of their time researching and writing reports, appraisers and assessors are able to spend more and more time onsite due to advances in mobile technology. Four out of ten appraisers are self-employed and can often work out of their home.

For More Information

* The Appraisal Foundation, 1029 Vermont Ave. NW, Suite 900, Washington, DC 20005-3517. Internet: www.appraisalfoundation.org

* Appraisal Institute, 550 W. Van Buren St., Suite 1000, Chicago, IL 60607. Internet: www.appraisalinstitute.org

* National Association of Real Estate Appraisers, 1224 North Nokomis NE, Alexandria, MN 56308. Internet: www.iami.org/narea/home.cfm

* American Society of Appraisers, 555 Herndon Pkwy., Suite 125, Herndon, VA 20170. Internet: www.appraisers.org

* International Association of Assessing Officers, 314 W 10th St., Kansas City, MO 64105. Internet: www.iaao.org

Budget Analysts

At a Glance

Budget analysts help businesses decide how much money they need in order to run and how best to spend it. They check reports and accounts during the year to make sure the business is staying within its budget and spending its money wisely. Budget analysts work in private industry, nonprofit organizations, and the public sector. They are always on the lookout for new ways to improve efficiency and make the most of the company's resources. Budget analysts create a plan for the coming year and beyond, and then help the chief operating officer, agency head, or other top managers analyze the proposal. Computer software has greatly increased the amount of information that budget analysts are able to analyze.

Career in Focus: *Cost Accountant*

A cross between a budget analyst and an accountant, cost accountants record, research, and analyze the costs (in terms of time and resources) associated with running the company. Like budget analysts, they are interested in finding ways to use their company's resources more efficiently.

Where and When

Most budget analysts work at least 40 hours per week in comfortable office settings. They often work independently, though they usually work under deadlines, especially during mid-year and end-of-year reviews.

For More Information

* Association of Government Accountants, 2208 Mount Vernon Ave., Alexandria, VA 22301. Internet: www.agacgfm.org
* National Association of State Budget Officers, Hall of the States Building, Suite 642, 444 North Capitol St. NW, Washington, DC 20001-1511. Internet: www.nasbo.org

Data Bank

Education and Training: Bachelor's degree

Starting Salaries: $37,000

Average Earnings: $48,000–$74,000

Total Jobs Held: 58,000

Job Outlook: Average increase

Annual Job Openings: 6,000

Related Jobs: Accountants and auditors, cost estimators, economists, financial analysts and personal financial advisors, financial managers, loan officers, management analysts

Personality Type: Conventional

Did You Know?

Balancing the budget is not an easy task, especially if you are the federal government. With a yearly budget of about 2.5 trillion dollars (not to mention the 8 trillion dollars of debt and the money that's owed to social security), one can only imagine the headaches of budget analysts trying to find ways to stretch the U.S. tax dollar and make it pay for everything lawmakers want it to.

Claims Adjusters, Appraisers, Examiners, and Investigators

At a Glance

Individuals and businesses purchase insurance policies to protect against loss. In the event of a loss (such as a house fire), policyholders submit claims, seeking compensation. Insurance claims adjusters and claims investigators check to make sure that the claims filed are covered by their company's policies. Then they decide how much should be paid (called the settlement) and authorize the payment. If the claim is not covered, they deny payment. They are often asked to testify in legal disputes. Appraisers travel to see damaged property and assess how much the damage is worth.

Career in Focus: *Insurance Investigator*

Insurance investigators handle claims in which the company suspects criminal activity, such as arson, staged accidents, or unnecessary medical treatments. Investigators can access certain personal information, such as Social Security numbers, aliases, driver's license numbers, addresses, phone numbers, criminal records, and past claims histories to establish whether a person has ever attempted insurance fraud. Investigators often consult with legal counsel and can be expert witnesses in court cases.

Where and When

Most claims adjusters, appraisers, examiners, and investigators work a standard 40-hour week in comfortable office environments. Many claims adjusters must also work outside of the office inspecting damaged automobiles and buildings. Sometimes they need to adjust their schedules to meet with clients on evenings and weekends. They may have some extended travel with long investigations, for instance, visiting the scene of a natural disaster to assess the total damage.

For More Information

* American Institute for Chartered Property Casualty Underwriters and the Insurance Institute of America, 720 Providence Rd., P.O. Box 3016, Malvern, PA 19355–0716. Internet: www.aicpcu.org

* International Claim Association, 1255 23rd St. NW, Washington, DC 20037. Internet: www.claim.org

* Independent Automotive Damage Appraisers Association, P.O. Box 12291 Columbus, GA 31917–2291. Internet: www.iada.org

---

Data Bank

Education and Training: Long-term on-the-job-training

Starting Salaries: $27,000

Average Earnings: $36,000–$60,000

Total Jobs Held: 263,000

Job Outlook: Average increase

Annual Job Openings: 30,000

Related Jobs: Cost estimators; bill and account collectors; medical records and health information technicians; billing and posting clerks and machine operators; credit authorizers, checkers, and clerks; bookkeeping, accounting, and auditing clerks; construction and building inspectors; accountants and auditors; private detectives and investigators; automotive body and related repairers; automotive service technicians and mechanics

Personality Type: Conventional; Enterprising

Did You Know?

Insurance companies insure the rest of us, but who insures insurance companies? Believe it or not such companies exist. They are called reinsurance companies, and they are responsible for helping other insurance companies cover the cost of claims when catastrophes and natural disasters strike, such as Hurricane Katrina, which caused an estimated $150 billion of damage.

Cost Estimators

At a Glance

When a company is thinking about developing a new product, the owner needs to know how much it will cost to produce. Cost estimators research and evaluate all of the resources that will be necessary including materials, new machinery, additional labor, taxes, and insurance. A cost estimator then finds the least-expensive way to make the best product. They decide what supplies to use, estimate labor costs, and report back to the owner. Computers play an integral role in this line of work, because estimating often involves complex mathematical calculations.

Career in Focus: *Construction Cost Estimator*

More than half of all cost estimators work in construction. These estimators gather information on the proposed building site and the availability of electricity, water, and other services. They then research, analyze, and compile a cost summary for the entire project, including the costs of labor, equipment, materials, and subcontracts. Construction cost estimators also may be hired to track actual costs as the project develops.

Where and When

Cost estimators split their time between doing research in the comfort of their offices and visiting the site or factory floor. Although they normally work 40-hour weeks, overtime is common. In some industries, frequent travel is also required.

For More Information

* American Society of Professional Estimators, 2525 Perimeter Place Drive, Suite 103, Nashville, TN 37214. Internet: www.aspenational.org
* Association for the Advancement of Cost Engineering (AACE International), 209 Prairie Ave., Suite 100, Morgantown, WV 26501. Internet: www.aacei.org
* Society of Cost Estimating and Analysis, 101 S. Whiting St., Suite 201, Alexandria, VA 22304. Internet: www.sceaonline.net

Data Bank

Education and Training: Work experience to bachelor's degree

Starting Salaries: $30,000

Average Earnings: $40,000–$68,000

Total Jobs Held: 198,000

Job Outlook: Above-average increase

Annual Job Openings: 15,000

Related Jobs: Accountants and auditors; budget analysts; claims adjusters, appraisers, examiners, and investigators; economists; financial analysts and personal financial advisors; insurance underwriters; loan officers; market and survey researchers; operations research analysts

Personality Type: Conventional

Did You Know?

A company called a cost estimator to estimate the value of a load of scrap copper in the Mojave Desert. The manager warned the estimator that he might have trouble with the job. When the estimator arrived on site, he understood why. The company had been having such problems with thieves, it had dug a huge pit and put the copper inside. Then, for added security, it had thrown *rattlesnakes* on top of the copper. The estimator just peered into the pit and made his best guess.

Financial Analysts and Personal Financial Advisors

At a Glance

Financial analysts and personal financial advisors help businesses and individuals with their investment decisions. They gather and analyze financial information in order to make recommendations to their clients. Financial analysts research the economic performance of other companies and industries for institutions with money to invest. Personal financial advisors help individuals by giving them a range of investment options that meet the amount of risk they will accept. Some advisors buy and sell financial products, such as mutual funds or insurance, and a number of them take on the responsibility of managing their clients' investments for them. All of these workers must be able to use spreadsheet and statistical software to analyze financial data, spot trends, and develop forecasts.

Data Bank

Education and Training: Bachelor's degree

Starting Salaries: $35,000

Average Earnings: $46,000–$94,000

Total Jobs Held: 355,000

Job Outlook: Above-average increase

Annual Job Openings: 45,000

Related Jobs: Accountants and auditors; financial managers; insurance sales agents; real estate brokers and sales agents; securities, commodities, and financial services sales representatives

Personality Type: Investigative; Social; Enterprising

Did You Know?

What's the difference between a bull and a bear? When you are being chased by one, probably not much (except bulls can't climb trees). In the stock market, however, a bull market indicates a prolonged period of time where prices *rise* faster than they have in the past (generally indicating economic growth). A bear market on the other hand indicates a period of time where prices *fall* faster. Investors obviously prefer the bull over the bear.

Career in Focus: *Ratings Analyst*

Ratings analysts evaluate the ability of companies or governments to repay their debts on bonds. On the basis of their evaluation, a management team can assign a rating to a company's or government's bonds. Based on these ratings, investors can make more sound decisions about where to invest their money.

Where and When

Though they have the benefit of working in comfortable office settings, most financial analysts and personal financial advisors work long hours. Meetings with individual clients sometimes have to be scheduled for evenings or weekends. Financial analysts may have to travel to visit companies and talk to potential investors. Four out of ten of these workers are self-employed.

For More Information

* The Financial Planning Association, 4100 E. Mississippi Ave., Suite 400, Denver, CO 80246-3053. Internet: www.fpanet.org

* Certified Financial Planner Board of Standards, Inc., 1670 Broadway, Suite 600, Denver, CO 80202-4809. Internet: www.cfp.net/become

* American Academy of Financial Management, 2 Canal St., Suite 2317, New Orleans, LA 70130. Internet: www.financialanalyst.org

* CFA Institute, P.O. Box 3668, 560 Ray C. Hunt Dr., Charlottesville, VA 22903. Internet: www.cfainstitute.org

Insurance Underwriters

At a Glance

How much should an insurance company charge for insurance? That depends on how likely a customer is to have an accident. Using national statistics, underwriters first decide whether a person applying for insurance is a good risk. They then help write the policies and decide how much to charge. If they set the rates too low, the company will lose money. If they set the rates too high, the company will lose business to competitors. Most underwriters specialize in one of three major categories of insurance: life, health, and property and casualty. Life and health insurance underwriters may further specialize in group or individual policies.

Career in Focus: *Property and Casualty Underwriter*

Property and casualty underwriters usually specialize in either commercial or personal insurance for a particular type of risk, such as fire, homeowners', automobile, or liability insurance. In cases where casualty companies provide package insurance, the underwriter must be familiar with *all* the different lines of insurance.

Where and When

These jobs tend to be desk jobs in comfortable office settings. Most underwriters typically work a standard 40-hour week, and travel is usually kept to a minimum.

For More Information

* Insurance Information Institute, 110 William St., New York, NY 10038. Internet: www.iii.org
* LIMRA International, P.O. Box 203, Hartford, CT 06141.
* American Institute for Chartered Property and Casualty Underwriters and Insurance Institute of America, 720 Providence Rd., P.O. Box 3016, Malvern, PA 19355-0716. Internet: www.aicpcu.org
* American College, 270 South Bryn Mawr Ave., Bryn Mawr, PA 19010-2196. Internet: www.theamericancollege.edu

Data Bank

Education and Training: Bachelor's degree

Starting Salaries: $30,000

Average Earnings: $39,000–$69,000

Total Jobs Held: 101,000

Job Outlook: Little change

Annual Job Openings: 13,000

Related Jobs: Accountants and auditors; actuaries; budget analysts; cost estimators; financial analysts and personal financial advisors; financial managers; loan officers; insurance sales agents; claims adjusters, appraisers, examiners, and investigators

Personality Type: Conventional

Did You Know?

Underwriters often calculate risk based on national averages. Underwriters look at accident statistics from all over the country to decide which drivers are most likely to be involved in an accident. They use this information to create a profile of a high-risk driver. For example, anyone under the age of 21 or over the age of 70 tends to be considered "high-risk" for automobile insurance. Driving a red Ferrari isn't going to help keep your rates down either. Though if you can afford a Ferrari, you probably don't care.

Loan Officers

At a Glance

Individuals often need loans to afford a house, a car, or a college education. Businesses need loans to start companies, buy inventory, or invest in equipment. Loan officers help these individuals and businesses apply for those loans. They help potential clients fill out the applications, answering any questions. Then they collect and analyze information on a potential client's work, assets and debts, and credit rating. Loan officers usually specialize in commercial, consumer, or mortgage loans. Commercial loans help companies start up or expand; consumer loans help individuals buy cars, make renovations, or pay for other personal expenses; and mortgage loans are made to purchase real estate. Loan officers often act as sales people as well, trying to give potential clients the best deal and rate with as little risk to the bank as possible.

Data Bank

Education and Training: Bachelor's degree

Starting Salaries: $28,000

Average Earnings: $36,000–$70,000

Total Jobs Held: 291,000

Job Outlook: Little change

Annual Job Openings: 38,000

Related Jobs: Securities, commodities, and financial services sales agents; financial analysts and personal financial advisors; real estate brokers and sales agents; insurance sales agents

Personality Type: Enterprising

Did You Know?

More and more students are planning to go to college, yet tuition continues to rise. That means more school loans taken by both parents and students alike. The average student earning a four-year degree graduates with almost $20,000 in debt. This is good news for loan officers who see college graduates as a sound investment—after all, they are bound to get a job and start paying it back eventually. Aren't they?

Career in Focus: *Loan Collection Officer*

Loan collection officers contact borrowers with overdue loan accounts to help them find a method of repayment and keep them from defaulting on the loan. If they cannot agree on a repayment plan, the loan collection officer begins the "collateral liquidation" process: the lender seizes the collateral used to secure the loan—a home or car, for example—and sells it to repay the loan.

Where and When

Most loan officers work a standard 40-hour week in comfortable office settings. Travel can be frequent, especially for commercial loan officers. Many loan officers intentionally carry heavy caseloads, which can cause them to work extra hours. Business picks up when interest rates drop, making loans more attractive to consumers, but increasing the stress on loan officers.

For More Information

* Mortgage Bankers Association, 1919 Pennsylvania Ave. NW, Washington, DC 20006-3404. Internet: www.mortgagebankers.org

Management Analysts

At a Glance

Companies hire management analysts to solve problems. They analyze a company's policy and performance and suggest ways to improve that organization's structure, efficiency, or profits. The work varies from project to project. Some analysts and consultants specialize in a specific industry, such as health care or telecommunications. Others specialize by type of business function, such as human resources, marketing, or information systems. Once they have analyzed the problem and decided on a course of action, consultants report their findings and recommendations to the client. For some projects, management analysts help implement the suggestions they have made.

Career in Focus: *Technology and Electronic Commerce Consultant*

Recently, advances in information technology and electronic commerce have provided new opportunities for management analysts. Companies often hire consultants to help them enter and/or remain competitive in the new electronic marketplace. These analysts must mix their knowledge of computers and technology with their business sense to find the right solutions for their clients.

Where and When

Most management analysts split their time between their home office and the site of the client they are helping, so frequent travel is common. Overtime is also common, and the stress of meeting client's demands on tight schedules can make this a challenging job. Many management analysts are self-employed, however, and can set their own schedule and workload.

For More Information

❋ Association of Management Consulting Firms, 380 Lexington Ave., Suite 1700, New York, NY 10168. Internet: www.amcf.org

❋ Institute of Management Consultants USA, Inc., 2025 M St. NW, Suite 800, Washington, DC 20036. Internet: www.imcusa.org

Data Bank

Education and Training: Bachelor's degree plus related work experience

Starting Salaries: $38,000

Average Earnings: $50,000–$90,000

Total Jobs Held: 605,000

Job Outlook: Above-average increase

Annual Job Openings: 82,000

Related Jobs: Accountants and auditors; budget analysts; cost estimators; financial analysts and personal financial advisors; operations research analysts; economists; market and survey researchers; administrative services managers; financial managers; human resources, training, and labor relations managers and specialists; top executives

Personality Type: Enterprising

Did You Know?

Most everybody can use a little outside support from time to time, including the federal government. In order to prepare for a possible avian flu epidemic, in the spring of 2006 the U.S. Department of Health and Human Services (HHS) awarded Tunnell Consulting a multi-million dollar contract to assist them in preparing for a potential pandemic. Government departments with problems like these are just one possible client for management analysts.

Meeting and Convention Planners

At a Glance

Meeting and convention planners make sure that such gatherings come off without a hitch. They arrange speakers and locations, acquire the necessary provisions and equipment, and deal with any problems that may arise. They work for nonprofit organizations, professional associations, hotels, corporations, and the government. Planners often must negotiate contracts with facilities and suppliers. They are also responsible for measuring how well the meeting's purpose was achieved by collecting and analyzing survey data. An important part of being a planner is establishing and maintaining relationships. Meeting and convention planners interact with a variety of people and must be good communicators.

Data Bank

Education and Training: Bachelor's degree

Starting Salaries: $25,000

Average Earnings: $32,000–$54,000

Total Jobs Held: 43,000

Job Outlook: Above-average increase

Annual Job Openings: 4,000

Related Jobs: Food service managers; actors, producers, and directors; travel agents

Personality Type: Enterprising

Did You Know?

There are conventions for just about everything from tattoos to biotechnology to frozen foods, and planning some of these can be a monumental task. For example, more than one million people attend the annual Chicago Auto Show, where new cars are showcased for the coming year. Such conventions are not only important for the attendees, but also for the area hotels and restaurants, who are more than happy to provide those people with a place to sleep and eat.

Career in Focus: *Convention Service Manager*

Convention service managers work in hotels, convention centers, and similar establishments and act as the contact person between the meeting facility and event planners. They present food service options to outside planners, coordinate special requests, suggest hotel services based on the planners' budgets, and offer any other assistance.

Where and When

This job is fast-paced and requires a great deal of energy and sharp organization skills. Planners travel regularly, and working hours can be long and irregular, especially right before and during the meeting or convention. Some physical activity in the form of moderate lifting may be required. The job offers a high level of independence.

For More Information

* Convention Industry Council, 8201 Greensboro Dr., Suite 300, McLean, VA 22102. Internet: www.conventionindustry.org

* Professional Convention Management Association, 2301 S. Lake Shore Dr., Suite 1001, Chicago, IL 60616-1419. Internet: www.pcma.org

* Meeting Professionals International, 3030 LBJ Fwy., Suite 1700, Dallas, TX 75244-5903. Internet: www.mpiweb.org

Tax Examiners, Collectors, and Revenue Agents

At a Glance

Taxes are one of few certainties in life (see the entry on Funeral Directors for another). As long as governments collect taxes, there will be jobs for tax examiners, collectors, and revenue agents. These individuals work for the federal, state, and local governments and review tax returns to make sure people and businesses are paying the right amount. They send notices to those who have made mistakes, conduct audits, and track down those who are trying to avoid taxes altogether. Tax examiners often handle the simpler tax returns—those of individuals or small businesses. Revenue agents work on the more complex returns of large corporations. All must be trustworthy and have an eye for details.

Career in Focus: *Tax Collector*

Tax collectors, also called revenue officers in the IRS, deal with overdue accounts. When a collector takes a case, he or she first sends the taxpayer a notice. The collector then works with the taxpayer on how to settle the debt. A big part of a collector's job at the federal level is setting and following up on payment deadlines. Collectors must maintain accurate records.

Where and When

Most of these individuals work a standard 40-hour week, though overtime may be necessary during tax season. They work in comfortable office settings, and much of their job involves using computers and managing paperwork. Tax collectors have the stressful and sometimes unpleasant job of dealing with overdue taxpayers.

For More Information

* Internal Revenue Service, 1111 Constitution Ave. NW, Washington, DC 20224. Internet: www.jobs.irs.gov/index.html

Data Bank

Education and Training: Bachelor's degree

Starting Salaries: $25,000

Average Earnings: $34,000–$63,000

Total Jobs Held: 76,000

Job Outlook: Little change

Annual Job Openings: 4,000

Related Jobs: Accountants and auditors, budget analysts, cost estimators, financial analysts and personal financial advisors, financial managers, loan officers

Personality Type: Conventional

Did You Know?

As far back as ancient Egypt, governments have been collecting taxes. Most ancient books, including the Torah, the Bible, and Hindu Sutras, mention paying taxes. Some kings collected animals, crops, or slaves from taxpayers; later governments demanded gold or jewels. Today, the IRS accepts money orders, personal checks, and charge cards. Contrary to popular belief, they do not take first-born children.

Professional and Related Occupations

Actuaries

At a Glance

Actuaries analyze risk. Most of them design insurance plans that will help their company make a profit. Actuaries estimate the probability and likely cost of events such as death, sickness, injury, disability, or loss of property. Actuaries also answer financial questions, including questions about pensions and investments. Most actuaries are employed in the insurance industry, specializing in life and health insurance or property and casualty insurance. They study statistics and social trends to decide how much money an insurance company should charge for insurance. Actuaries in other financial services industries manage credit or price investment offerings. Some actuaries are self-employed and work as consultants.

Data Bank

Education and Training: Bachelor's degree plus related work experience

Starting Salaries: $43,000

Average Earnings: $58,000–$112,000

Total Jobs Held: 18,000

Job Outlook: Above-average increase

Annual Job Openings: 3,000

Related Jobs: Accountants and auditors, budget analysts, economists, market and survey researchers, financial analysts and personal financial advisors, insurance underwriters, mathematicians, statisticians

Personality Type: Conventional

Did You Know?

Because of their knowledge of insurance, actuaries are often called as expert witnesses in lawsuits. For example, they might testify about the expected lifetime earnings of a person who was disabled or killed in an accident. This testimony is used to determine how much money an insurance company must pay the individual's family.

Career in Focus: *Pension Actuary*

Pension actuaries work under the provisions of the Employee Retirement Income Security Act (ERISA) of 1974. They are primarily responsible for evaluating pension plans covered by that Act and reporting on the plans' financial soundness to participants, sponsors, and federal regulators.

Where and When

Actuaries have desk jobs in comfortable office environments. Most of them work a standard 40-hour week. Travel is minimal, but still a possibility. They spend a majority of their time using a computer, so they may experience physical stress on the back, wrists, and eyes.

For More Information

* American Society of Pension Actuaries, 4245 N. Fairfax Dr., Suite 750, Arlington, VA 22203. Internet: www.aspa.org

* Society of Actuaries (SOA), 475 N. Martingale Rd., Suite 600, Schaumburg, IL 60173-2226. Internet: www.soa.org

* Casualty Actuarial Society (CAS), 1100 N. Glebe Rd., Suite 600, Arlington, VA 22201-0425. Internet: www.casact.org

* American Academy of Actuaries, 1100 17th St. NW, 7th Floor, Washington, DC 20036. Internet: www.actuary.org

Computer Programmers

At a Glance

Computer programmers write, update, test, and maintain the programs that make computers work. They provide detailed, step-by-step instructions for the computer, telling it which information to access, how to process it, and what equipment to use. If the software does not produce the desired result, the programmer must correct the errors. Programmers work in what are known as programming languages (COBOL, Java, C++), and they generally know more than one of them. Many programmers also update, repair, modify, and expand existing programs. Programmers in software development companies may work directly with experts from various fields to create software ranging from games and educational software to programs for desktop publishing and financial planning.

Career in Focus: *Systems Programmer*

Systems programmers write the programs that maintain and control computer systems, such as operating systems, networked systems, and database systems. These workers make changes in the instructions that determine how the network, workstations, and central processing unit of the system handle the jobs they have been given. Because of their knowledge of the entire system, these workers are often asked to solve complex computer programming problems.

Where and When

Programmers generally work in comfortable office settings. They may be required to work long hours or weekends to meet deadlines or fix critical problems. Like other workers who spend long periods of time in front of a computer, programmers are susceptible to hand and wrist problems, back discomfort, and eyestrain.

For More Information

* Association for Computing Machinery, 1515 Broadway, New York, NY 10036. Internet: www.acm.org

* Institute of Electrical and Electronics Engineers Computer Society, Headquarters Office, 1730 Massachusetts Ave. NW, Washington, DC 20036-1992. Internet: www.computer.org

* National Workforce Center for Emerging Technologies, 3000 Landerholm Circle SE, Bellevue, WA 98007. Internet: www.nwcet.org

---

Data Bank

Education and Training: Bachelor's degree

Starting Salaries: $36,000

Average Earnings: $48,000–$83,000

Total Jobs Held: 455,000

Job Outlook: Little change

Annual Job Openings: 28,000

Related Jobs: Computer software engineers, computer scientists and database administrators, computer systems analysts, mathematicians, engineers, statisticians, operations research analysts

Personality Type: Investigative

Did You Know?

Two-thirds of computer programmers hold a college degree or higher, and about one out of every five has a graduate degree. Employers are most interested in people familiar with the latest programming languages, which means computer programmers must constantly learn about the latest innovations in their field.

Computer Scientists and Database Administrators

At a Glance

Computer scientists work as theorists, researchers, and inventors. Some work for universities. Others work for research companies on projects ranging from creating programming languages to designing robots. Database administrators find ways to help businesses organize and store data. They also work with companies, creating and maintaining the integrity of their computer networks. Database administrators often plan and coordinate security measures as well. Network systems and data communications analysts design, test, and evaluate systems such as local area networks (LANs), wide area networks (WANs), and other data communications systems.

Data Bank

Education and Training: Associate degree to doctoral degree

Starting Salaries: $30,000

Average Earnings: $47,000–$85,000

Total Jobs Held: 275,000

Job Outlook: Above-average increase

Annual Job Openings: 26,000

Related Jobs: Computer programmers, computer software engineers, computer and information systems managers, engineers, mathematicians, statisticians

Personality Type: Investigative

Did You Know?

The Internet that is so vital to today's personal, education, and business worlds started as a military research project by computer scientists back in the 1960s. Recognizing the network's potential beyond simply linking military radar systems, the Internet underwent several versions before its widespread public acknowledgement in the 1990s. Today it is estimated that more than one billion people use the Internet. Every revolution has to start somewhere.

Career in Focus: *Webmasters and Web Designers*

The vast expansion of the Internet has prompted the need for occupations related to the design, development, and maintenance of Web sites. For example, webmasters are responsible for all technical aspects of a Web site, including the speed of accessing approved content. Web developers, also called Web designers, are responsible for day-to-day site creation and design.

Where and When

Computer scientists and database administrators normally work in offices or laboratories. They typically work 40 hours per week. Telecommuting is a popular option as well, as more and more work can be done from home. Like most other jobs involving heavy computer use, eyestrain, back discomfort, and hand and wrist problems can occur.

For More Information

* Association for Computing Machinery (ACM), 1515 Broadway, New York, NY 10036. Internet: www.acm.org

* Institute of Electrical and Electronics Engineers Computer Society, Headquarters Office, 1730 Massachusetts Ave. NW, Washington, DC 20036-1992. Internet: www.computer.org

* National Workforce Center for Emerging Technologies, 3000 Landerholm Circle SE, Bellevue, WA 98007. Internet: www.nwcet.org

Computer Software Engineers

At a Glance

Computer software engineers research and design computers and programs. Software engineers analyze users' needs and design, construct, test, and maintain computer applications software to meet those needs. They may also identify problems in business, science, and engineering and then design specialized computer software to solve those problems. Software engineers must possess strong programming skills, but they are more concerned with analyzing and solving programming problems than with actually writing code (which is more the job of a computer programmer).

Career in Focus: *Computer Systems Software Engineer*

Computer systems software engineers coordinate the construction and maintenance of a company's computer systems and plan that company's future growth. They coordinate each department's computer needs—ordering, inventory, billing, and payroll, for example—and make suggestions about the software required. They might set up the company's networks as well.

Where and When

Computer software engineers generally work in comfortable offices or laboratories. Those who work as consultants can expect to travel frequently. Like other workers who spend most of their time typing in front of a computer, software engineers are prone to back discomfort, eyestrain, and hand and wrist problems.

For More Information

* Association for Computing Machinery (ACM), 1515 Broadway, New York, NY 10036. Internet: www.acm.org
* Institute of Electronics and Electrical Engineers Computer Society, Headquarters Office, 1730 Massachusetts Ave. NW, Washington, DC 20036-1992. Internet: www.computer.org
* National Workforce Center for Emerging Technologies, 3000 Landerholm Circle SE, Bellevue, WA 98007. Internet: www.nwcet.org

Data Bank

Education and Training: Bachelor's degree

Starting Salaries: $48,000

Average Earnings: $62,000–$98,000

Total Jobs Held: 800,000

Job Outlook: Rapid increase

Annual Job Openings: 91,000

Related Jobs: Computer systems analysts, computer scientists and database administrators, computer programmers, computer support specialists and systems administrators, statisticians, mathematicians, engineers, actuaries

Personality Type: Investigative

Did You Know?

Computer software engineers are projected to be one of the fastest-growing occupations in the next ten years. Those with at least a bachelor's degree in computer engineering or computer science should have very good job opportunities as businesses continue to adapt to advances in technology. In addition, the continued growth of the Internet will provide more and more job possibilities for creative engineers.

Computer Support Specialists and Systems Administrators

At a Glance

What happens when a company's computers crash? They call in the computer support specialists, the troubleshooters of the computer world. These workers find and fix problems for big businesses and individual computer owners. They provide advice to users as well as the day-to-day maintenance and support of computer networks for companies. Many work at "help desks" where they answer telephone calls and e-mail messages from customers who need guidance. Systems administrators help companies decide what kind of system they need. Then they design, install, and support the organization's computer network. They also monitor and adjust the performance of existing networks.

Data Bank

Education and Training: Associate degree to bachelor's degree

Starting Salaries: $32,000

Average Earnings: $39,000–$65,000

Total Jobs Held: 1,027,000

Job Outlook: Rapid increase

Annual Job Openings: 164,000

Related Jobs: Computer programmers, computer software engineers, computer systems analysts, computer scientists and database administrators

Personality Type: Investigative

Did You Know?

There is no denying the positive impact that e-mail and the Internet have had on modern business. The ability to instantly send and receive prices and reports and to ask and answer questions is invaluable. But it comes at a cost. As more and more workers are linked online, more and more time is wasted trading jokes, recipes, and gossip. It has been estimated that companies lose $54 billion per year due to the lack of worker productivity related to e-mail and Internet use.

Career in Focus: *Computer Security Specialist*

Computer security specialists plan and coordinate an organization's information security—protecting the data stored on computer systems from viruses, theft, loss, and other threats. They educate users about computer security, install security software, monitor the network for security breaches, respond to cyber attacks, and, in some cases, gather data and evidence to be used in prosecuting cyber crime. The number and variety of cyber attacks have increased in recent years, resulting in an increased demand for these specialists.

Where and When

These individuals generally work in comfortable office settings for a standard 40-hour workweek, though they may be on call to fix unexpected technical problems. Many of these support specialists interact directly with customers and fellow employees and need good people skills. Like other workers who spend long periods of time in front of a computer, programmers are susceptible to hand and wrist problems, back discomfort, and eyestrain.

For More Information

* Association of Computer Support Specialists, 333 Mamaroneck Ave., #129, White Plains, NY 10605. Internet: www.acss.org

* System Administrators Guild, 2560 9th St., Suite 215, Berkeley, CA 94710. Internet: www.sage.org

* National Workforce Center for Emerging Technologies, 3000 Landerholm Circle SE, Bellevue, WA 98007. Internet: www.nwcet.org

Computer Systems Analysts

At a Glance

Computer systems analysts help businesses and organizations decide which computer systems will best help them grow. Systems analysts may plan and develop new computer systems or devise ways to apply existing systems' resources to new operations. They often set up and test the new technology as well. Many systems analysts are involved in networking, which involves connecting computers together within a company or to the Internet.

Career in Focus: *Software Quality Assurance Analyst*

While all computer systems analysts are sometimes involved in testing the programs and systems they put in place, software quality assurance analysts do more in-depth testing of products. In addition to running tests, these individuals diagnose problems, recommend solutions, and determine whether program requirements have been met.

Where and When

Computer systems analysts generally work in comfortable offices or laboratories. Though they typically work a 40-hour week, evenings or weekends may be necessary to meet deadlines. As the technology continues to change, more and more computer professionals are able to telecommute as well. Like other workers who spend long periods of time in front of a computer, programmers are susceptible to hand and wrist problems, back discomfort, and eyestrain.

For More Information

* Association for Computing Machinery, 1515 Broadway, New York, NY 10036. Internet: www.acm.org

* Institute of Electrical and Electronics Engineers Computer Society, Headquarters Office, 1730 Massachusetts Ave. NW, Washington, DC 20036-1992. Internet: www.computer.org

* National Workforce Center for Emerging Technologies, 3000 Landerholm Circle SE, Bellevue, WA 98007. Internet: www.nwcet.org

Data Bank

Education and Training: Bachelor's degree

Starting Salaries: $42,000

Average Earnings: $54,000–$85,000

Total Jobs Held: 487,000

Job Outlook: Rapid increase

Annual Job Openings: 56,000

Related Jobs: Computer programmers, computer software engineers, computer and information systems managers, computer scientists and database administrators, engineers, mathematicians, statisticians, operations research analysts

Personality Type: Investigative

Did You Know?

The average lifespan for a personal computer is two years. Technology changes so rapidly that newer and faster machines are necessary to meet the demands of new software for business and personal use. Computer systems analysts have to be constantly aware of these changes in technology so they can keep businesses competitive.

Mathematicians

At a Glance

Mathematicians use mathematical theory, computation, and computers to solve economic, engineering, scientific, and business problems. Mathematicians work in two areas: theory and applications. Theoretical mathematicians look for relationships between new math principles and old ones. Most work as part of a university faculty where they teach and conduct research. Applied mathematicians use math to solve practical problems in business, government, and everyday life. Much of this work is done by individuals who aren't formally called mathematicians, such as economists, statisticians, and computer scientists.

Data Bank

Education and Training: Master's degree

Starting Salaries: $43,000

Average Earnings: $58,000–$102,000

Total Jobs Held: 3,000

Job Outlook: Declining

Annual Job Openings: Less than 500

Related Jobs: Actuaries; statisticians; computer programmers; computer systems analysts; computer scientists and database administrators; computer software engineers; operations research analysts; teachers–postsecondary; teachers–preschool, kindergarten, middle, elementary, and secondary; engineers; economists; market and survey researchers; financial analysts and personal financial advisors; physicists and astronomers

Personality Type: Investigative

Did You Know?

While the number of jobs that hold the formal title "mathematician" are declining, some of the hottest and best-paying fields require math as one of the most important, if not *the* most important skill. Increasingly, individuals graduating with a degree in mathematics are going into careers in computer science and software development, engineering, and financial analysis. Those interested in sticking with a career in pure math will likely have to earn their doctorate and compete for university jobs.

Career in Focus: *Cryptanalysts*

Some mathematicians, called cryptanalysts, analyze and decipher encryption systems designed to transmit military, political, financial, or law enforcement-related information in code. Sometimes these mathematicians are asked to crack an enemy code during times of war or keep a computer hacker from getting access to customer's credit card numbers, making this job both brainy and cool at the same time.

Where and When

Mathematicians generally work in comfortable office settings. They may need to travel to conferences or seminars as part of the job. Those who work at the university level are required to balance teaching, research, and publishing responsibilities.

For More Information

* American Mathematical Society, 201 Charles St., Providence, RI 02904-2294. Internet: www.ams.org

* Society for Industrial and Applied Mathematics, 3600 University City Science Center, Philadelphia, PA 19104-2688. Internet: www.siam.org

Operations Research Analysts

At a Glance

Operations research analysts help businesses operate efficiently by applying mathematical principles to real world problems. Large companies search for the most effective use of their resources, and operations research analysts help these companies coordinate their money, materials, equipment, and people. First, analysts define and study the problem. Next, they gather information by talking with people and choosing which mathematical model they will use. Finally, they present their findings and recommendations to the company's management. They often specialize in one industry and are sometimes involved in top-level planning and management.

Career in Focus: *Government Operations Analyst*

Probably no other institution in America has as many resources to coordinate as the federal government. In fact, the fields of "operation research" and "management science" have been used extensively by the U.S. military. Because of its size and scope, inefficiencies in government operations are common, and analysts are often required to find and fix them. For their efforts, operations research analysts working for the federal government earn an average annual salary of nearly $90,000.

Where and When

Operations research analysts work regular hours in comfortable office settings. They may be required to work long hours to meet deadlines, and they spend much of their time using a computer to research and compile data.

For More Information

* Institute for Operations Research and the Management Sciences, 7240 Parkway Dr., Suite 310, Hanover, MD 21076. Internet: www.informs.org
* Military Operations Research Society, 1703 N. Beauregard St., Suite 450, Alexandria, VA 22311. Internet: www.mors.org

Data Bank

Education and Training: Master's degree

Starting Salaries: $36,000

Average Earnings: $47,000–$81,000

Total Jobs Held: 58,000

Job Outlook: Little change

Annual Job Openings: 7,000

Related Jobs: Computer systems analysts, computer scientists and database administrators, computer programmers, engineers, mathematicians, statisticians, economists, market and survey researchers, computer and information systems managers, management analysts

Personality Type: Investigative

Did You Know?

One of the primary tools of operations research analysts is "game theory." It is a branch of applied mathematics that studies decision making in situations where each party seeks the best course of action. It has been used to analyze everything from animal behavior to nuclear strategy. It has found its most consistent and practical use in economics. American mathematician John Nash won the Nobel Prize in economics for his work in game theory, and was later biographied in the film *A Beautiful Mind*.

Statisticians

At a Glance

Statistics is the application of mathematics to the collection, analysis, and presentation of data. Statisticians collect information from surveys and experiments. They decide where and how to gather the information, who to survey, and what questions to ask. They primarily use the information they collect to make predictions about the economy or to assess various social problems in order to help business and government leaders make decisions. Other fields that use statisticians include biology, engineering, medicine, public health, psychology, education, and sports.

Data Bank

Education and Training: Master's degree

Starting Salaries: $33,000

Average Earnings: $45,000–$84,000

Total Jobs Held: 19,000

Job Outlook: Little change

Annual Job Openings: 2,000

Related Jobs: Mathematicians, operations research analysts, computer systems analysts, computer scientists and database administrators, computer programmers, computer software engineers, engineers, economists, market and survey researchers, computer and information systems managers, management analysts

Personality Type: Investigative

Did You Know?

You might know who holds the Major League record for homeruns in a season (Barry Bonds, 73), but do you know who holds the record for most strike-outs in a career (Reggie Jackson, 2597) or the most sacrifice flies (Eddie Murray, 128)? And did you know that St. Louis pitcher John Grimes hit a total of six batters with pitches during a game in July of 1897? Sports statisticians keep track of even the most obscure player and team statistics, though some devoted fans can recite the lifetime numbers of their favorite players as well.

Career in Focus: *Government Statistician*

Four out of every ten statisticians work for the federal, state, or local governments. Government statisticians measure everything from population growth to consumer confidence to unemployment. Other government statisticians work for scientific, environmental, and agricultural agencies. Statisticians are also involved in our national defense, determining the likely effectiveness of military strategies.

Where and When

Statisticians work regular hours in comfortable office environments. They are sometimes required to travel to gather data or give presentations. Those who work at colleges and universities usually have to balance teaching and research responsibilities.

For More Information

* American Statistical Association, 1429 Duke St., Alexandria, VA 22314-3415. Internet: www.amstat.org
* American Mathematical Society, 201 Charles St., Providence, RI 02904-2213. Internet: www.ams.org

Architects, Except Landscape and Naval

At a Glance

Architects design buildings and other structures, everything from churches, houses, and hospitals to college campuses and industrial parks. They are not just concerned with the overall appearance of the buildings they design, they also make sure the buildings are functional, safe, and economical. They draw plans of every part of a building, including the plumbing, heating, air-conditioning, communication, and electrical systems. They also help choose a building site and decide what materials to use. They may be involved in all phases of development, from the initial discussion with the client through the entire construction process. Architects spend a great deal of time explaining their ideas, so they must have good communication skills. Most architects today use computers in their work, and many are self-employed.

Career in Focus: *Museum Architect*

Some architects end up specializing in one type of building, such as houses, office buildings, or hospitals. One field that has produced a wide range of styles is museum architecture. Like the paintings and artifacts inside them, the actual museum building acts as a kind of display, and museum architects are careful to balance the need to make the buildings functional with the desire to make them works of art.

Where and When

Architects spend most of their time in offices either developing their drawings and models or discussing them with clients. They sometimes visit the construction sites to review the building's progress. Most work a standard 40-hour week, though deadlines can cause them to work overtime.

For More Information

* The American Institute of Architects, 1735 New York Ave. NW, Washington, DC 20006. Internet: www.aia.org

* Intern Development Program, National Council of Architectural Registration Boards, Suite 1100K, 1801 K St. NW, Washington, DC 20006-1310. Internet: www.ncarb.org

Data Bank

Education and Training: Bachelor's degree

Starting Salaries: $38,000

Average Earnings: $49,000–$82,000

Total Jobs Held: 129,000

Job Outlook: Average increase

Annual Job Openings: 7,000

Related Jobs: Construction managers, landscape architects, engineers, urban and regional planners, interior designers, commercial and industrial designers, graphic designers

Personality Type: Artistic

Did You Know?

Sometimes flaws in architectural design can become famous. Take the cathedral bell tower in the Italian city of Pisa for example. Begun in 1173 and not completed until 1372, the tower had only a three-meter foundation set into unstable soil. The tower began to lean almost immediately and subsequent additions didn't help much. It is said that Benito Mussolini ordered the tower be straightened, but pouring additional concrete into the foundation only caused it to sink further. The Leaning Tower of Pisa has been leaning for more than 800 years now, making it as much an architectural marvel as a mistake.

Landscape Architects

At a Glance

Everyone enjoys attractively designed neighborhoods, public parks, college campuses, and golf courses. Landscape architects make these areas beautiful and useful. They decide where the buildings, roads, and walkways will go, and how the flower gardens and trees should be arranged. They create designs, estimate costs, and check that the plans are carried out correctly. Some landscape architects work on a variety of projects. Others specialize in a particular area, such as street and highway beautification, parks and playgrounds, or shopping centers. Increasingly, landscape architects are becoming involved with preserving and restoring natural environments and historical landscapes.

Data Bank

Education and Training: Bachelor's degree

Starting Salaries: $32,000

Average Earnings: $42,000–$71,000

Total Jobs Held: 25,000

Job Outlook: Above-average increase

Annual Job Openings: 1,000

Related Jobs: Architects, except landscape and naval; surveyors, cartographers, photogrammetrists, and surveying technicians; engineers; urban and regional planners; conservation scientists and foresters; biological scientists; medical scientists; environmental scientists and hydrologists; geoscientists

Personality Type: Artistic

Did You Know?

Before the widespread use of computers, architects had to draw their landscape designs by hand and build models piece by piece. Today, they use computer-aided design (CAD) systems and video simulations to let their clients see their ideas in full color and three dimensions. If the client wants to make a change, the architect can do it with the click of a mouse. Too bad it's not that easy at the actual construction site.

Career in Focus: *Park Design and Preservation*

Landscape architects who work for government agencies are often responsible for recreation planning and restoration in national parks and forests such as Glacier or Yellowstone. They must keep the natural environment intact for future generations while making it accessible for people to visit. For example, they may have to decide where to put a paved road that won't disrupt the wildlife.

Where and When

Though they are concerned with how to design the landscape, these architects still spend most of their time inside the office drawing plans and preparing models and reports. They do spend some time at the site doing tests and checking progress. Most work regular hours, and many are self-employed.

For More Information

* American Society of Landscape Architects, Career Information, 636 Eye St. NW, Washington, DC 20001-3736. Internet: www.asla.org

* Council of Landscape Architectural Registration Boards, 144 Church St. NW, Suite 201, Vienna, VA 22180-4550. Internet: www.clarb.org

Surveyors, Cartographers, Photogram-metrists, and Surveying Technicians

At a Glance

These workers measure and map the earth's surface. Surveyors are primarily responsible for establishing official land, airspace, and water boundaries. They also write descriptions for deeds, leases, and other legal documents and take measurements of construction sites. Cartographers prepare maps and charts in either digital or graphic form using information provided by geodetic surveys, aerial photographs, and satellite data. Surveying and mapping technicians assist these professionals by collecting data in the field and using it to calculate mapmaking information. Most of these workers use computers and software (such as GIS) to help them assemble, analyze, and display data.

Career in Focus:
Photogrammetrist

Photogrammetrists measure and analyze aerial and satellite photographs to help make detailed maps. They are especially needed to map areas that are inaccessible, difficult, or more costly to survey by other methods (mountain peaks or the South Pole, for example). Some states require photogrammetrists to be licensed as surveyors.

Where and When

These workers typically work 40-hour weeks and spend a lot of time outdoors. Demands for overtime tend to be seasonal. The work of surveyors and technicians often requires physical activity—some of it strenuous—and possible exposure to extreme weather conditions. Travel is usually required to get to survey sites or to present findings.

For More Information

* American Congress on Surveying and Mapping, Suite 403, 6 Montgomery Village Ave., Gaithersburg, MD 20879. Internet: www.acsm.net

* National Society of Professional Surveyors, Suite 403, 6 Montgomery Village Ave., Gaithersburg, MD 20879. Internet: www.acsm.net/nsps

* American Association of Geodetic Surveying (AAGS), Suite 403, 6 Montgomery Village Ave., Gaithersburg, MD 20879. Internet: www.acsm.net/aags

* ASPRS: Imaging and Geospatial Information Society, 5410 Grosvenor Ln., Suite 210, Bethesda, MD 20814-2160. Internet: www.asprs.org

Data Bank

Education and Training: Moderate-term on-the-job-training to bachelor's degree

Starting Salaries: $21,000

Average Earnings: $29,000–$51,000

Total Jobs Held: 132,000

Job Outlook: Average increase

Annual Job Openings: 14,000

Related Jobs: Engineers; architects, except landscape and naval; landscape architects; environmental scientists and hydrologists; geoscientists; urban and regional planners

Personality Type: Investigative; Conventional; Realistic

Did You Know?

Satellites are revolutionizing survey work. Surveyors can now use a Global Positioning System (GPS) to locate points on the earth and collect information from several satellites at once. Such receivers are also being placed in cars to help motorists, and they have been used widely by the military. And to think that a thousand years ago we thought the earth was flat.

Engineers

At a Glance

Engineers design machinery, buildings, and highways. They also develop new products and new ways of making them. Some engineers test the quality of products or supervise production in factories. They work in laboratories, factories, offices, and construction sites. Most engineers specialize to work in a particular industry or with particular materials: Aerospace engineers design, develop, and test aircraft, spacecraft, and missiles. Civil engineers design and supervise the construction of roads, buildings, airports, tunnels, dams, and bridges. Mechanical engineers research, develop, manufacture, and test tools, engines, and machines. Other specialties include agricultural, chemical, computer hardware, electrical, environmental, industrial, marine, materials, nuclear, and petroleum engineers. All engineers use computers extensively.

Data Bank

Education and Training: Bachelor's degree

Starting Salaries: $45,000

Average Earnings: $58,000–$90,000

Total Jobs Held: 1,450,000

Job Outlook: Average increase

Annual Job Openings: 111,000

Related Jobs: Architects, except landscape and naval; engineering and natural sciences managers; computer and information systems managers; computer programmers; computer software engineers; drafters; engineering technicians; sales engineers; science technicians

Personality Type: Enterprising; Investigative; Realistic

Did You Know?

Statistics show that each year the United States produces about 70,000 engineering graduates. This only includes those who graduate with a four-year degree and not those who graduate with degrees related to engineering such as computer scientists. Though that sounds like a lot, economists, educators, and theorists are worried that we aren't producing *enough* engineers to keep up with other countries like India and China. After all, a country needs engineers to keep its technological edge and stay innovative. So what are you waiting for?

Career in Focus: *Biomedical Engineer*

Working in one of the hottest fields in engineering, biomedical engineers develop devices and procedures that solve medical and health-related problems. They combine their knowledge of biology and medicine with engineering principles and practices. Biomedical engineers may also design devices used in various medical procedures, imaging systems such as magnetic resonance imaging (MRI), and devices for controlling body functions. This specialty combines a background in engineering with biomedical training.

Where and When

Engineers generally work in office buildings, laboratories, or industrial plants. They sometimes work outdoors onsite to monitor operations and solve problems. Though most work a standard 40-hour week, deadlines can cause them to work long hours.

For More Information

* JETS, 1420 King St., Suite 405, Alexandria, VA 22314-2794. Internet: www.jets.org

* Accreditation Board for Engineering and Technology, Inc., 111 Market Place, Suite 1050, Baltimore, MD 21202-4012. Internet: www.abet.org

* National Society of Professional Engineers, 1420 King St., Alexandria, VA 22314-2794. Internet: www.nspe.org

* American Society for Engineering Education, 1818 N St. NW, Suite 600, Washington, DC 20036-2479. Internet: www.asee.org

Drafters

At a Glance

Drafters prepare the technical drawings used to build everything from spacecraft to bridges. They start with the specifications, codes, and calculations previously made by engineers, surveyors, architects, or scientists. Then they produce detailed technical drawings with the information needed to create a finished product, including dimensions, materials, and procedures. Drafters use handbooks, tables, calculators, and computers to do their work.

Career in Focus: *Architectural Drafter*

Architectural drafters draw the features of buildings and other structures. These workers may specialize in a type of structure, such as residential (houses or apartments) or commercial (hospitals or department stores), or in a kind of material used, such as concrete, masonry, steel, or lumber. They make up about 43 percent of all drafters.

Where and When

Most drafters work 40 hours per week, usually in comfortable offices. Though a few may produce drawings manually, the majority use computers. Like other workers who spend long periods of time in front of a computer, drafters may be susceptible to eyestrain, back aches, and hand and wrist problems.

For More Information

* Accrediting Commission of Career Schools and Colleges of Technology, 2101 Wilson Blvd., Suite 302, Arlington, VA 22201. Internet: www.accsct.org
* American Design Drafting Association, 105 E. Main St., Newbern, TN 38059. Internet: www.adda.org

Data Bank

Education and Training: Vocational/technical training

Starting Salaries: $26,000

Average Earnings: $34,000–$53,000

Total Jobs Held: 230,000

Job Outlook: Little change

Annual Job Openings: 19,000

Related Jobs: Architects, except landscape and naval; landscape architects; commercial and industrial designers; engineers; engineering technicians; science technicians; surveyors, cartographers, photogrammetrists, and surveying technicians

Personality Type: Realistic

Did You Know?

Traditionally, drafters sat at drawing boards and used pencils and protractors to draw their designs manually. Most drafters today, however, use CADD systems (computer-aided design and drafting). Consequently, some drafters may be referred to as CADD operators. CADD systems use computers to create and store drawings, which lets drafters quickly prepare variations of a design. Despite the nearly universal use of CADD systems, manual drafting and sketching are still necessary in some cases.

Engineering Technicians

At a Glance

Engineering technicians use science, engineering principles, and math to solve problems in research and development, manufacturing, sales, construction, inspection, and maintenance. They help engineers and scientists with experiments and develop models of new equipment. Some supervise production workers or check the quality of products. In manufacturing, they may also assist in designing, developing, and producing new products. Like engineers, they specialize in an area such as aeronautics, mechanics, electronics, or chemicals.

Data Bank

Education and Training: Associate degree

Starting Salaries: $28,000

Average Earnings: $36,000–$57,000

Total Jobs Held: 533,000

Job Outlook: Average increase

Annual Job Openings: 55,000

Related Jobs: Science technicians; drafters; surveyors, cartographers, photogrammetrists, and surveying technicians; broadcast and sound engineering technicians and radio operators

Personality Type: Realistic

Did You Know?

In 1895, King C. Gillette, a Boston bottle-cap salesman, came up with an idea for a disposable razor blade. It took him eight years (and the help of engineering technicians) to develop the methods to mass-produce his razor for sale to the public. Today, the company he founded is worth millions, and most Americans have used his invention at one time or another. That or they're very hairy.

Career in Focus: *Mechanical Engineering Technician*

Mechanical engineering technicians help engineers design, develop, test, and manufacture machinery, products, and other equipment. They make sketches, record and analyze data, and report on their findings. In production, mechanical engineering technicians prepare layouts and drawings of the assembly process and of parts to be manufactured. They estimate labor costs, equipment life, and plant space. Some test and inspect machines and equipment or work with engineers to eliminate production problems.

Where and When

Engineering technicians tend to work at least 40 hours per week in offices, laboratories, plants, or construction sites. Some may be exposed to hazards from equipment, chemicals, or toxic materials.

For More Information

* JETS (Junior Engineering Technical Society) Guidance, 1420 King St., Suite 405, Alexandria, VA 22314-2794. Internet: www.jets.org

* Accreditation Board for Engineering and Technology, Inc., 111 Market Place, Suite 1050, Baltimore, MD 21202-4012. Internet: www.abet.org

* National Institute for Certification in Engineering Technologies, 1420 King St., Alexandria, VA 22314-2794. Internet: www.nicet.org

Agricultural and Food Scientists

At a Glance

Agricultural scientists study farm crops and animals and use the principles of biology, chemistry, physics, mathematics, and other sciences to solve problems in agriculture. They look for ways to control pests and weeds safely, increase crop yields with less labor, and save water and soil. They may specialize in plant, soil, or animal science. New research in genetics is opening up new ways for agricultural scientists to improve our food supply as well. Some agricultural scientists are consultants to business firms, private clients, or the government.

Career in Focus: *Food Scientist*

Food scientists usually work in the food processing industry, universities, or the federal government. They help meet consumer demand for foods that are healthy, safe, appetizing, and convenient. They also develop new or better ways of preserving, processing, packaging, storing, and delivering foods. Some food scientists engage in basic research, such as discovering new food sources, analyzing food products, or searching for substitutes for harmful additives. Other food scientists enforce government regulations, ensuring that sanitation, safety, and quality standards are met.

Where and When

Agricultural and food scientists tend to work in offices or laboratories. Specific work environments vary, from test kitchens to university labs. Soil and crop scientists spend much of their time outdoors doing research, and entomologists spend a lot of time hunting and studying insects in their natural habitats. These jobs generally allow for a great deal of independence. One out of every three of these workers is self-employed.

For More Information

* American Society of Agronomy, Crop Science Society of America, Soil Science Society of America, 677 S. Segoe Rd., Madison, WI 53711-1086. Internet: www.agronomy.org

* Food and Agricultural Careers for Tomorrow, Purdue University, 1140 Agricultural Administration Bldg., West Lafayette, IN 47907-1140.

Data Bank

Education and Training: Bachelor's degree

Starting Salaries: $30,000

Average Earnings: $38,000–$69,000

Total Jobs Held: 31,000

Job Outlook: Average increase

Annual Job Openings: 2,000

Related Jobs: Biological scientists; chemists and materials scientists; conservation scientists and foresters; farmers, ranchers, and agricultural managers; veterinarians; landscape architects

Personality Type: Investigative

Did You Know?

Did you know that the flavoring in a banana popsicle is actually isoamyl acetate? Or that the flavor in wintergreen gum is probably derived from methyl salicylate? Such are the discoveries of flavor scientists who use their knowledge of chemistry to recreate many natural flavors in artificial forms. In fact, some artificial flavors can even be safer than their natural versions because they don't contain the traces of toxins that natural flavor compounds do. Think about that the next time you enjoy some tasty isoamyl acetate-flavored pudding.

Biological Scientists

At a Glance

Biological scientists study living things and their environments. They do research, develop new medicines, and increase crop amounts. Some study specialty areas such as viruses, ocean life, plant life, or animal life. Many biological scientists work in research and development to find solutions to human health problems and to preserve the natural environment. Some conduct experiments using laboratory animals or greenhouse plants. Recent advances in biotechnology—especially in the field of genetics—have created research opportunities with commercial applications in the food industry, agriculture, and health care. Biological scientists may work in company, college, or government labs, or as high school biology teachers.

Data Bank

Education and Training: Doctoral degree

Starting Salaries: $33,000

Average Earnings: $45,000–$79,000

Total Jobs Held: 76,000

Job Outlook: Average increase

Annual Job Openings: 6,000

Related Jobs: Medical scientists, agricultural and food scientists, conservation scientists and foresters, physicians and surgeons, dentists, veterinarians

Personality Type: Investigative

Did You Know?

For those who believe we know all there is to know about the natural world, consider this: More than 6,000 new species of insects are described (discovered) each year. In total, there are about 900,000 known species of insects, and recent figures suggest that there are more than 200 million insects for every single human on the planet. If you want to become famous, one route might be to become an entomologist, travel to a tropical rainforest, and start looking under rocks and trees. The next new species of cockroach might be waiting for you.

Career in Focus: *Ecologist*

Ecologists study the relationships between living things and their environments. They examine the effects of population size, pollutants, rainfall, temperature, and altitude. Ecologists collect, study, and report data on the quality of air, food, soil, and water. This research is used by both corporate and government programs to help preserve the environment and maintain natural habitats.

Where and When

Biological scientists typically work regular hours in office and laboratory settings. Those who work with dangerous organisms or toxic chemicals follow strict safety procedures. Many biological scientists also spend time in the field doing research, which can require strenuous physical activity. Those working at colleges and universities must balance their research with their teaching responsibilities.

For More Information

* American Institute of Biological Sciences, 1444 I St. NW, Suite 200, Washington, DC 20005. Internet: www.aibs.org

* Federation of American Societies for Experimental Biology, 9650 Rockville Pike, Bethesda, MD 20814. Internet: www.faseb.org

* The Botanical Society of America, 4475 Castleman Ave., P.O. Box 299, St. Louis, MI 63166. Internet: www.botany.org

* American Society for Microbiology, Career Information–Education Department, 1752 N St. NW, Washington, DC 20036. Internet: www.asm.org

Medical Scientists

At a Glance

Medical scientists research diseases in order to improve human health. Most medical scientists do basic research to learn more about viruses, bacteria, and other infectious diseases. They then use this information to develop vaccines, medicines, and treatments. Medical scientists also attempt to discover ways to prevent health problems, such as finding a link between smoking and lung cancer. Recent research in genetics and advances in biotechnology have led to the discovery of important new drugs and treatments and opened up new avenues for research for these scientists. Medical scientists also engage in clinical investigation, technical writing, and drug application review. Some work in managerial, consulting, or administrative positions.

Career in Focus:
Epidemiologist

Epidemiologists investigate and describe the causes of disease, disability, and other health problems and develop means for prevention and control. Epidemiologists may study many different diseases, such as tuberculosis, influenza, or cholera, often focusing on epidemics. Research epidemiologists work at colleges and universities, medical schools, and research firms. Clinical epidemiologists work primarily in consulting roles at hospitals, informing the medical staff of infectious outbreaks and providing containment solutions. If you find infectious diseases interesting, this may be the job for you.

Where and When

Medical scientists typically work regular hours in offices, laboratories, clinics, or hospitals. Those who work with dangerous organisms, toxic chemicals, or infectious diseases follow strict safety procedures. Those working at colleges and universities must balance their research with their teaching responsibilities.

For More Information

* American Association of Pharmaceutical Scientists (AAPS), 2107 Wilson Blvd., Suite 700, Arlington, VA 22201.

* American Society for Microbiology, Career Information–Education Department, 1752 N St. NW, Washington, DC 20036-2804. Internet: www.asm.org

* Infectious Diseases Society of America, Guide to Training Programs, 66 Canal Center Plaza, Suite 600, Alexandria, VA 22314. Internet: www.idsociety.org

Data Bank

Education and Training: Doctoral degree

Starting Salaries: $33,000

Average Earnings: $45,000–$85,000

Total Jobs Held: 77,000

Job Outlook: Rapid increase

Annual Job Openings: 16,000

Related Jobs: Biological scientists, agricultural and food scientists, physicians and surgeons, dentists, veterinarians

Personality Type: Investigative

Did You Know?

Smallpox, typhoid fever, the bubonic plague. Though some of the diseases that have wreaked havoc on humanity have been all but eradicated, others continue to spring up in their place, such as Severe Acute Respiratory Syndrome (SARS) or the Avian flu. Medical scientists continue to research ways to control or eliminate infectious diseases, such as AIDS, a pandemic that has taken more than 25 million lives in the last 25 years.

Conservation Scientists and Foresters

At a Glance

Foresters and conservation scientists manage and protect natural resources such as water, wood, and wildlife. Foresters supervise the use of timber for lumber companies, protecting the forests and managing the harvesting of trees. They may also design campgrounds and recreation areas on public lands. Conservation scientists manage, improve, and protect the country's natural resources. They work with landowners and federal, state, and local governments to devise ways to use and improve the land without damaging the environment. A growing number are advising landowners and governments on recreational uses for the land as well. Soil conservationists specifically help farmers preserve soil, water, and other natural resources.

Data Bank

Education and Training: Bachelor's degree

Starting Salaries: $31,000

Average Earnings: $39,000–$65,000

Total Jobs Held: 32,000

Job Outlook: Little change

Annual Job Openings: 3,000

Related Jobs: Engineers; agricultural and food scientists; biological scientists; environmental scientists and hydrologists; geoscientists; farmers, ranchers, and agricultural managers

Personality Type: Investigative; Realistic

Did You Know?

Deforestation is an ongoing environmental concern for everyone, not just conservationists. According to the Food and Agriculture Organization of the United Nations, about 32 million acres of the world's forests are lost each year. The concern is not only for the loss of a valuable natural resource, but for the effect that it has on both the environment (including greenhouse gases) and the many species that call these forests home.

Career in Focus: *Range Manager*

Range managers—also called range conservationists, range ecologists, or range scientists—manage, improve, and protect rangelands. Rangelands cover hundreds of millions of acres of the United States and contain many natural resources, including grass and shrubs for animal grazing, wildlife habitats, water, and valuable mineral and energy resources. Range managers may inventory soils, plants, and animals; develop resource management plans; help to restore ecosystems; or simply assist in managing a ranch.

Where and When

Working conditions for foresters and conservationists vary considerably. They often split their time between field work and office work, though many spend most of their time outdoors. The work can be physically demanding, requiring extensive walking, sometimes in potentially dangerous environments.

For More Information

* Society of American Foresters, 5400 Grosvenor Lane, Bethesda, MD 20814-2198. Internet: www.safnet.org

* Society for Range Management, 445 Union Blvd., Suite 230, Lakewood, CO 80228-1259. Internet: www.rangelands.org

* The Wildlife Society, 5410 Grosvenor Lane, Suite 200, Bethesda, MD 20814-2197. Internet: www.wildlife.org/certification/index.cfm

Atmospheric Scientists

At a Glance

Atmospheric scientists, commonly called meteorologists, study the atmosphere (the blanket of air covering the earth) and its effects on our environment. The most well-known area of their work is weather forecasting. These meteorologists gather data from weather satellites, radars, sensors, and stations in many parts of the world. They study information on air pressure, temperature, humidity, and wind velocity, and then apply their knowledge of math and physics to make weather predictions. Atmospheric scientists also study trends in the earth's climate and apply their research to air-pollution control, agriculture, forestry, environmental studies, air and sea transportation, and defense. About 40 percent of these workers are employed by the federal government.

Career in Focus: *Climatologist*

Climatologists study changes in climate spanning hundreds or even millions of years. They collect, analyze, and interpret past records of wind, rainfall, sunshine, and temperature in specific areas or regions. Their studies are then used to design buildings, plan heating and cooling systems, and aid in farming.

Where and When

Atmospheric scientists often work nights, weekends, and holidays because weather stations operate around the clock. During weather emergencies meteorologists might work overtime. Some atmospheric scientists work in isolated or remote areas or spend time observing weather conditions from aircraft. Those involved in broadcasting must meet the constant deadlines for weather reports.

For More Information

* American Meteorological Society. Internet: www.ametsoc.org/AMS

Data Bank

Education and Training: Bachelor's degree

Starting Salaries: $35,000

Average Earnings: $52,000–$90,000

Total Jobs Held: 7,000

Job Outlook: Average increase

Annual Job Openings: 1,000

Related Jobs: Environmental scientists and hydrologists, geoscientists, physicists and astronomers, mathematicians, engineers

Personality Type: Investigative

Did You Know?

Though kids mainly count on them to spread the news about snow days, meteorologists are vital when it comes to predicting potential natural emergencies. Even with advanced warning from meteorologists, however, it is sometimes difficult to avoid the destruction caused by Mother Nature. In August of 2005, Hurricane Katrina touched down in Florida, Mississippi, Alabama, and Louisiana, with particularly devastating effects on the city of New Orleans. Doing at least $75 billion in damage, it is considered to be the most destructive hurricane in American history.

Chemists and Materials Scientists

At a Glance

Everything in our environment is composed of chemicals. Chemists and materials scientists look for and use new information about chemicals and other materials. They develop new paints, fibers, adhesives, and other products. They also develop processes that save energy and reduce pollution. Materials scientists study the structures and chemical properties of materials to develop new products or improve existing ones. Chemists work with life scientists to make new medicines. Chemists also work in production and quality control in chemical manufacturing plants. Chemists often specialize in a particular field such as organic chemistry, medicinal chemistry, or biochemistry. Many teach at colleges and universities.

Data Bank

Education and Training: Bachelor's degree

Starting Salaries: $34,000

Average Earnings: $44,000–$80,000

Total Jobs Held: 90,000

Job Outlook: Little change

Annual Job Openings: 5,000

Related Jobs: Agricultural and food scientists, biological scientists, medical scientists, engineers, physicists and astronomers, science technicians

Personality Type: Investigative

Did You Know?

When chemist Wallace Carothers began his work with Dupont in the 1930s, he might not have predicted that it would lead to panty hose and parachutes. Yet his work on polymerization (where small molecules unite to form large ones) led to the invention of nylon, a synthetic material which has been used in all kinds of products such as tires, tents, ropes, and ponchos—not to mention women's stockings.

Career in Focus: *Analytical Chemist*

Analytical chemists determine the structure, composition, and nature of substances by examining and identifying their various elements. These chemists help the pharmaceutical industry by identifying the compounds that the industry hopes to turn into drugs. Analytical chemists also identify the presence and concentration of chemical pollutants in air, water, and soil in order to help preserve the environment.

Where and When

Chemists and materials scientists typically work regular hours in office or laboratory settings. They may also do some of their work in a chemical plant or outdoors. They often have to work alongside engineers and other specialists. Proper safety precautions keep them from being exposed to harmful chemicals.

For More Information

❋ American Chemical Society, Education Division, 1155 16th St. NW, Washington, DC 20036. Internet: www.acs.org

Environmental Scientists and Hydrologists

At a Glance

Environmental scientists and hydrologists study the earth and humans' impact on it. Many are involved in water conservation and the preservation of natural resources. Environmental scientists conduct research to identify and eliminate sources of pollutants or hazards that affect people, wildlife, and their environments. They use their skills to design and monitor waste disposal sites, preserve water supplies, and reclaim contaminated land and water. Many environmental scientists and hydrologists work at consulting firms, helping businesses and government agencies comply with environmental policy. Environmental scientists also help identify how human behavior can be changed in the future to avoid problems.

Career in Focus: *Hydrologist*

Hydrologists study the distribution, circulation, and properties of water. Often, they specialize in either underground water or surface water. Hydrologists use sophisticated techniques and instruments to examine precipitation, its movement through the earth, and its return to the ocean and atmosphere. The work hydrologists do is important in flood control and environmental preservation.

Where and When

Entry-level environmental scientists and hydrologists spend most of their time in the field doing research, while more experienced workers spend the majority of their time in the office or laboratory. Those in the field may work in a variety of climates and conditions. The work often requires travel and physical activity. Those involved heavily in research are often under pressure to meet deadlines.

For More Information

* American Geological Institute, 4220 King St., Alexandria, VA 22302-1502. Internet: www.agiweb.org
* American Institute of Hydrology, 300 Village Green Circle, Suite #201, Smyrna, GA 30080. Internet: www.aihydro.org
* Marine Technology Society, 5565 Sterrett Place, Suite 108, Columbia, MD 21004. Internet: www.mtsociety.org

Data Bank

Education and Training: Master's degree

Starting Salaries: $32,000

Average Earnings: $41,000–$71,000

Total Jobs Held: 81,000

Job Outlook: Above-average increase

Annual Job Openings: 9,000

Related Jobs: Conservation scientists and foresters; atmospheric scientists; science and engineering technicians; physicists; chemists; engineers; surveyors, cartographers, photogrammetrists, and surveying technicians

Personality Type: Investigative

Did You Know?

Consider this: The average family goes through about 70 gallons of water per day washing clothes and dishes, taking showers, and flushing toilets. Americans as a whole drink more than one billion glasses of tap water per day. Hydrologists are constantly searching for greater supplies of fresh water and researching ways to make salt water usable to keep up with this demand.

Geoscientists

At a Glance

Geoscientists study the earth, focusing on its composition and geologic past and present. Many are involved in the search for natural resources such as groundwater, metals, and petroleum, while others concern themselves with cleaning up the environment. Geoscientists also study the evolution of life by analyzing plant and animal fossils. They often specialize in a particular field of study, such as volcanologists, who investigate volcanoes and try to predict their potential danger. Geophysicists use their knowledge of physics, math, and chemistry to study the earth's composition; atmosphere; oceans; and magnetic, electrical, and gravitational forces. Geoscientists spend a large part of their time in the field, identifying and examining rocks, conducting surveys, making field maps, and measuring the earth's gravity and magnetic field.

Data Bank

Education and Training: Master's degree

Starting Salaries: $34,000

Average Earnings: $44,000–$79,000

Total Jobs Held: 109,000

Job Outlook: Average increase

Annual Job Openings: 11,000

Related Jobs: Engineering technicians; science technicians; engineers; surveyors, cartographers, photogrammetrists, and surveying technicians; physicists and astronomers; chemists and materials scientists; atmospheric scientists; environmental scientists and hydrologists

Personality Type: Investigative

Did You Know?

One of the hottest fields in geology is seismology—the study of earthquakes. And one of the biggest seismology experiments in history continues in Parkfield, California. This small town is known for its regular pattern of earthquakes: For the last 150 years, Parkfield has experienced a magnitude 6 earthquake every 20 to 30 years. That's why seismologists from around the world set up monitors in Parkfield, waiting for a chance to measure the next one.

Career in Focus: *Oceanographer*

Oceanographers study the world's oceans and coastal waters. They study the motion and circulation of ocean waters, the physical and chemical properties of the oceans, and how these properties affect coastal areas, climate, and weather.

Where and When

Geoscientists divide their time between the office or laboratory and the field. Work at remote sites is common, and travel to some locations involves strenuous activity in a variety of weather conditions. Oceanographers may spend considerable time at sea. An increasing number of geoscientists do their research in foreign countries.

For More Information

* American Geological Institute, 4220 King St., Alexandria, VA 22302-1502. Internet: www.agiweb.org
* American Association of Petroleum Geologists, P.O. Box 979, Tulsa, OK 74101. Internet: www.aapg.org
* Marine Technology Society, 5565 Sterrett Place, Suite 108, Columbia, MD 21004. Internet: www.mtsociety.org

Physicists and Astronomers

At a Glance

Physicists study the matter that makes up the universe. They also study forces of nature such as gravity, motion, and the nature of energy, electromagnetism, and nuclear interactions. Some use their research to answer theoretical questions, such as the nature of time or origin of the universe. Others use their studies for practical matters, such as to design medical equipment, electronic devices, and lasers. Astronomers use the principles of physics and mathematics to study the moon, sun, planets, galaxies, and stars. Their knowledge is used in space flight and exploration, satellite communications, and navigation. A small number of astronomers work in museum planetariums. Most physicists and astronomers are involved in research of one kind or another, and many teach in colleges and universities.

Career in Focus: *Nuclear Physicist*

Because of the tremendous energy that is released through nuclear fission and fusion, physicists look for ways to harness that energy. They also study the effects of radiation, which has implications for modern medicine. Though some nuclear physicists do military research, the majority concentrate on finding safe and efficient ways to use nuclear reactions as an alternative energy resource. Of course you don't have to be a nuclear physicist to know that this job requires a lot of education.

Where and When

Physicists and astronomers typically work in laboratories and offices, though some may work away from home at national or international facilities. Astronomers may spend long periods of time in observatories, and their work often involves travel to remote locations and frequent night work (for obvious reasons).

For More Information

* American Institute of Physics, Career Services Division and Education and Employment Division, One Physics Ellipse, College Park, MD 20740-3843. Internet: www.aip.org

* The American Physical Society, One Physics Ellipse, College Park, MD 20740-3844. Internet: www.aps.org

Data Bank

Education and Training: Doctoral degree

Starting Salaries: 49,000

Average Earnings: $67,000–$113,000

Total Jobs Held: 16,000

Job Outlook: Little change

Annual Job Openings: 1,000

Related Jobs: Engineers, chemists and materials scientists, atmospheric scientists, environmental scientists and hydrologists, geoscientists, computer systems analysts, computer scientists and database administrators, computer programmers, mathematicians

Personality Type: Investigative

Did You Know?

In the early 1940s, physicists working at a secret U.S. defense lab in Los Alamos, New Mexico, made a scientific breakthrough. They split an atom, setting off a chain of events that led directly to the atomic bombs dropped by the U.S. during World War II on Hiroshima and Nagasaki, Japan. Several of those scientists later regretted their work on the bomb. For better or worse, those physicists assured their place in the history books and ushered in the atomic age.

Economists

At a Glance

Economists study how people use resources such as land, labor, raw materials, and machinery to produce goods and services. They monitor inflation, interest rates, and employment levels and research issues such as energy costs and business cycles. They use sampling and modeling techniques to make economic predictions. Economists working for corporations help predict consumer demand and sales of the firm's products. They also analyze the market and advise their company on how to handle the competition. Economists working in consulting or research firms collect data, analyze historical trends, and develop models to predict growth, inflation, unemployment, or interest rates. Their analyses and forecasts are frequently published in newspapers and journal articles. Economists in the federal government collect the majority of the economic data on the United States in order to estimate the economic effects of policy changes.

Did You Know?

The Federal Reserve is the central banking system of the United States. Its Board of Governors supervises banks and controls the amount of money in circulation. They also adjust the federal funds rate, which has a direct impact on the interest rates that the rest of us pay on loans. These interest rate changes are announced by the chairman of the board and have a significant impact on the economy. Because of this important power, even a whisper of activity by the Federal Reserve Board can cause the stock market to go up or down.

Career in Focus: *Labor Economist*

Labor economists study the supply and demand for labor and how wages are determined. These economists also try to explain the reasons for unemployment and the effects of changing demographic trends, such as an aging population or increasing immigration, on the economy. This information is especially useful to the government, which is constantly reviewing and changing its labor laws and policies.

Where and When

Economists typically work in comfortable office settings and spend much of their time doing research and writing reports. Most work under the stress of deadlines. Frequent travel may be required.

For More Information

* National Association for Business Economics, 1233 20th St. NW, Suite 505, Washington, DC 20036. Internet: www.nabe.com

Market and Survey Researchers

At a Glance

Market and survey researchers tell businesses the best ways to sell a product based on information they gather through interviews and questionnaires. Market research analysts are concerned with the potential sales of a product or service. By gathering data on competitors and examining prices, sales, and methods of marketing and distribution, they are able to predict future sales. They then provide the information needed to make decisions on the promotion, distribution, design, and pricing. They might also develop advertising brochures and commercials, sales plans, and product promotions such as rebates and giveaways. Market research analysts use a variety of methods for obtaining the data they need. They design telephone, mail, or Internet surveys and conduct some surveys as personal interviews. They may lead focus group discussions or set up booths in public places such as shopping malls.

Career in Focus: *Survey Researcher*

Survey researchers design and conduct surveys for a variety of clients, such as corporations, government agencies, and political candidates. The surveys collect information that is used for performing research, making funding or policy decisions, or improving customer satisfaction. Survey researchers may consult with economists, statisticians, or market research analysts to design surveys. They also may have to present survey results to clients.

Where and When

Market and survey researchers generally work a standard 40-hour week, though some overtime and travel may be required. The work is often done alone and involves extensive report writing, statistical analysis, and computer use.

For More Information

* Marketing Research Association, 110 National Dr., Glastonbury, CT 06033. Internet: www.mra-net.org
* Council of American Survey Research Organizations, 170 North Country Rd., Suite 4, Port Jefferson, NY 11777. Internet: www.casro.org

Data Bank

Education and Training: Master's degree

Starting Salaries: $29,000

Average Earnings: $39,000–$79,000

Total Jobs Held: 212,000

Job Outlook: Above-average increase

Annual Job Openings: 23,000

Related Jobs: Economists, psychologists, sociologists, statisticians, urban and regional planners

Personality Type: Investigative

Did You Know?

There's probably very little that hasn't been surveyed. Market research shows that dads prefer televisions over ties for Father's Day, that organic food is becoming more popular, and that (believe it or not) 60 percent of Americans are interested in traveling into outer space as a vacation. Yet despite numerous taste tests and millions of dollars in marketing research, America still hasn't decided whether it likes Coke or Pepsi better.

Psychologists

At a Glance

Psychologists study the way people think, feel, and act. They also work to understand, explain, and change people's behavior. They may conduct training programs, do market research, or provide counseling. Psychologists work with schools, businesses, and health-care centers to help people deal with stress and changes in their lives, such as divorce and aging.

Psychologists sometimes gather information through laboratory experiments, interviews, and clinical studies. Clinical psychologists—who make up the largest specialty—work most often in counseling centers, private practices, hospitals, or clinics. They help mentally and emotionally disturbed clients adjust to life and may assist medical patients in dealing with illnesses or injuries. Others help people deal with times of personal crisis or overcome addictions. Other focused fields of interest include neuropsychology, social psychology, and developmental psychology.

Data Bank

Education and Training: Master's degree to doctoral degree

Starting Salaries: $32,000

Average Earnings: $44,000–$76,000

Total Jobs Held: 179,000

Job Outlook: Above-average increase

Annual Job Openings: 11,000

Related Jobs: Counselors, physicians and surgeons, social workers, teachers–special education

Personality Type: Investigative; Social

Did You Know?

One hot avenue of research in psychology is pain management. Studies have shown that psychological factors such as mood, stress, and coping styles play important roles in increasing or decreasing levels of pain. Psychologists work with individuals who experience chronic pain to help them develop ways to manage their pain cycle. One technique, cognitive behavior therapy, involves substituting negative thoughts with more motivating ones that can lead to an increased activity level and improved functioning.

Career in Focus: *School Psychologist*

School psychologists help students in elementary and secondary schools. They work with teachers, parents, and school administrators to create safe, healthy, and supportive learning environments. They address learning and behavior problems, substance abuse, and classroom management strategies. They also assess gifted and talented students and students with learning disabilities to help determine the best way to educate them.

Where and When

Psychologists work in schools, clinics, and private offices. They often work evening or weekend hours to accommodate clients. Those employed in hospitals and health-care facilities often work in shifts.

For More Information

* American Psychological Association, Research Office and Education Directorate, 750 1st St. NE, Washington, DC 20002-4242. Internet: www.apa.org/students

* National Association of School Psychologists, 4340 East West Hwy., Suite 402, Bethesda, MD 20814. Internet: www.nasponline.org

* American Board of Professional Psychology, Inc., 300 Drayton St., 3rd Floor, Savannah, GA 31401. Internet: www.abpp.org

Urban and Regional Planners

At a Glance

Urban and regional planners develop programs that encourage growth in communities and regions. They make plans for the best use of land and study the area's schools, hospitals, parks, roads, and other facilities to see whether they meet the needs of the community. Planners may be involved in such issues as traffic congestion, public transportation, and the effects of growth and change on a community. They may help make plans to construct new school buildings or public housing. Some are involved in environmental issues ranging from pollution control to the location of new landfills. Planners also may be involved in legislation on environmental, social, and economic issues, such as sheltering the homeless, planning a new park, or meeting the demand for new prisons. Local governments employ the majority of urban and regional planners.

Career in Focus: *Housing Development Specialist*

Housing development specialists most often work for local governments. They are responsible for planning and developing affordable and assisted housing and revitalizing poor neighborhoods. They spend much of their time doing research and then reporting to other government departments and the legislature. They are also involved in the funding and oversight of approved projects.

Where and When

Urban and regional planners generally work a standard 40-hour week, though they may also attend evening or weekend meetings and hearings. Most work out of offices, though they travel often to inspect the regional and urban areas that concern them. They also work under the pressure of frequent deadlines and political interest groups.

For More Information

* American Planning Association, 1776 Massachusetts Ave. NW, Washington, DC 20036-1904. Internet: www.planning.org

* Association of Collegiate Schools of Planning, 6311 Mallard Trace, Tallahassee, FL 32312. Internet: www.acsp.org

Data Bank

Education and Training: Master's degree

Starting Salaries: $34,000

Average Earnings: $43,000–$69,000

Total Jobs Held: 32,000

Job Outlook: Average increase

Annual Job Openings: 3,000

Related Jobs: Architects, except landscape and naval; engineers; landscape architects

Personality Type: Investigative

Did You Know?

Some cities are planned to grow a certain way. Known as "planned communities" or "new towns," these cities are plotted in detail before the first house is built. Washington DC is, in fact, a planned community, as is the fairly successful city of Reston, Virginia. In 1994, the Disney Corporation built a planned community in Florida that's made to look like an old-fashioned town. It's called Celebration, and it's an easy drive from Disney World, though residents of Celebration do not get discounted tickets to the theme parks.

Social Scientists, Other

At a Glance

Social scientists study all aspects of society—from past events to human behavior and group relationships. Their research helps us understand different ways individuals and groups make decisions and respond to change, as well as suggest solutions to social, business, personal, governmental, and environmental problems. Anthropologists study the origin, development, and behavior of humans in order to analyze the customs, values, and social patterns of different cultures. Geographers study how physical geography affects politics and culture. Historians research, analyze, and interpret the past. Political scientists study the development and operation of political systems and public policy. Sociologists study society and social behavior by examining groups and their social, religious, political, and business organizations. All of these individuals are heavily involved in research.

Data Bank

Education and Training: Master's degree

Starting Salaries: $30,000

Average Earnings: $46,000–$80,000

Total Jobs Held: 57,000

Job Outlook: Average increase

Annual Job Openings: 3,000

Related Jobs: Economists; lawyers; statisticians; news analysts, reporters, and correspondents; social workers; psychologists; teachers; counselors; archivists, curators, and museum technicians

Personality Type: Investigative

Did You Know?

The Valley of the Kings in Egypt has been the site of many groundbreaking archaeological discoveries. Known for its tomb of King Tutankhamen (discovered in 1902), it was believed to have been fully explored. That is, until Egyptologist Kent Weeks began clearing out one of the outer tombs, which had been used as a dumping ground. There he found long corridors extending off into more than 120 rooms containing hundreds of artifacts. The discovery was made in 1995 and to this day archaeologists are still cataloguing everything they've found. There are always mysteries left to be uncovered.

Career in Focus: *Archaeologist*

Archaeologists recover evidence about past human cultures, such as the ruins of buildings, tools, pottery, and other objects. They study these artifacts to determine the history, customs, and living habits of earlier civilizations. Unlike Indiana Jones, most archaeologists spend most of their time at a dig site or in the library doing research and writing up their findings. Seldom, if ever, do they get to dodge bullets or boulders, and pits of poisonous snakes are uncommon.

Where and When

Most social scientists have regular work schedules and spend the majority of their time behind a desk. Sometimes they are part of a research team. Travel—including extensive international visits—is common. Some social scientists do fieldwork under rugged conditions involving strenuous physical exercise.

For More Information

* American Anthropological Association, 2200 Wilson Blvd., Suite 600, Arlington, VA 22201. Internet: www.aaanet.org

* Society for American Archaeology, 900 2nd St. NE, Suite 12, Washington, DC 20002-3560. Internet: www.saa.org

* Association of American Geographers, 1710 16th St. NW, Washington, DC 20009-3198. Internet: www.aag.org

* American Historical Association, 400 A St. SE, Washington, DC 20003-3889. Internet: www.historians.org

* American Sociological Association, 1307 New York Ave. NW, Suite 700, Washington, DC 20005-4712. Internet: www.asanet.org

Science Technicians

At a Glance

Science technicians use science and math to solve problems in research and development. They also invent and help improve products. They set up, operate, and maintain lab equipment; monitor experiments; and record results. Those working in production may be involved in ensuring quality by testing products for proper proportion of ingredients, for purity, or for strength and durability. Most technicians interpret data and devise solutions to problems under the direction of scientists. These technicians may specialize in agriculture, biology, chemistry, or other sciences, though their work tends to be more practical in nature than that of more traditional scientists.

Career in Focus: *Forensic Science Technician*

Forensic science technicians investigate crimes by collecting and analyzing physical evidence. Often, they specialize in areas such as DNA analysis or firearm examination. They perform tests on weapons or on substances such as fiber, glass, hair, tissue, and body fluids to determine their significance to the investigation. Forensic science technicians also prepare reports to document their findings, and they may provide information and expert opinion to investigators. When criminal cases come to trial, forensic science technicians often give testimony as expert witnesses to their findings.

Where and When

Science technicians can work in a wide variety of settings, though most work in a laboratory during regular hours. Some work irregular hours in order to monitor experiments, and some, such as agricultural technicians, do much of their work outdoors. Science technicians may be exposed to hazards from equipment, chemicals, or other toxic materials, though proper safety precautions all but eliminate these risks.

For More Information

* American Chemical Society, Education Division, Career Publications, 1155 16th St. NW, Washington, DC 20036. Internet: www.acs.org

* American Academy of Forensic Sciences, P.O. Box 669, Colorado Springs, CO, 80901. Internet: www.aafs.org

* Society of American Foresters, 5400 Grosvenor Ln., Bethesda, MD 20814. Internet: www.safnet.org

Data Bank

Education and Training: Associate degree

Starting Salaries: $22,000

Average Earnings: $29,000–$46,000

Total Jobs Held: 241,000

Job Outlook: Average increase

Annual Job Openings: 32,000

Related Jobs: Engineering technicians, broadcast and sound engineering technicians and radio operators, drafters, clinical laboratory technologists and technicians, diagnostic medical sonographers, radiologic technologists and technicians

Personality Type: Investigative; Realistic

Did You Know?

Undoubtedly one of the most useful innovations for forensic scientists and technicians to come about in the last few decades is DNA testing. Invented in 1985, DNA tests can be used to match potential suspects to blood, hair, saliva, or semen samples. Knowing that investigators will rely on this evidence, some criminals have planted fake DNA evidence (such as another person's blood or hair) at a crime scene to steer investigators and technicians the wrong way.

Counselors

At a Glance

Counselors help people with their problems, and the work they do depends on the people they serve. School counselors help students with personal, social, and behavioral problems. They also help students evaluate their abilities, interests, and talents in order to develop academic and career goals. School counselors may provide special services, including alcohol and drug prevention programs and conflict resolution classes. High school counselors specifically advise students regarding college admissions and financial aid. Career planning and placement counselors at colleges and universities help students decide on careers and find jobs. Rehabilitation counselors help people deal with the personal, social, and vocational effects of disabilities and addictions. Employment or vocational counselors help people decide what kinds of jobs they want and then help them find work. Mental health counselors work with individuals, families, and groups to address and treat mental and emotional disorders.

Data Bank

Education and Training: Bachelor's degree to master's degree

Starting Salaries: $23,000

Average Earnings: $29,000–$49,000

Total Jobs Held: 600,000

Job Outlook: Above-average increase

Annual Job Openings: 83,000

Related Jobs: Teachers; social and human service assistants; social workers; psychologists; physicians and surgeons; registered nurses; occupational therapists; human resources, training, and labor relations managers and specialists

Personality Type: Social

Did You Know?

As a society, we are not without our addictions. Whether it's alcoholism or nicotine, prescription drugs or gambling, statistics show that millions of people need help. And counselors are often the ones to provide it. Substance abuse counselors are trained to deal with a wide variety of issues, from drug addictions to eating disorders. Recently they have been given a new addiction to deal with: video games. While perhaps not as dangerous as some of the others, it is still a growing concern, and counselors are being educated to deal with this trend.

Career in Focus: *Marriage and Family Therapist*

Marriage and family therapists help individuals, families, or couples resolve emotional conflicts. They work to change people's perceptions and behaviors, enhance communication and understanding among family members, and help prevent family and individual problems. Marriage and family therapists also may perform research and teach college courses.

Where and When

Counselors tend to work standard hours, and school counselors often keep the same schedule as teachers (including the potential for summers off). Most work in office settings, though many therapists work evenings in order to counsel working clients. Dealing daily with the problems of others requires a lot of physical and emotional energy.

For More Information

* American Counseling Association, 5999 Stevenson Ave., Alexandria, VA 22304-3300. Internet: www.counseling.org

* American School Counselors Association, 1101 King St., Suite 625, Alexandria, VA 22314. Internet: www.schoolcounselor.org

* National Board for Certified Counselors, Inc., 3 Terrace Way, Suite D, Greensboro, NC 27403-3660. Internet: www.nbcc.org

Probation Officers and Correctional Treatment Specialists

At a Glance

Many people who are convicted of crimes are placed on probation instead of being sent to jail. Probation officers supervise these people, making sure they stay out of trouble. Probation and parole agencies also seek help from community organizations, such as churches, neighborhood groups, and local residents, to monitor the behavior of offenders. Probation officers may arrange for offenders to get substance abuse help or job training. They usually work with either adults or juveniles.

Parole officers and pretrial services officers perform many of the same duties as probation officers. The difference is that parole officers supervise offenders who have been released from prison, whereas probation officers work with those who are sentenced to probation instead of prison. Correctional treatment specialists work in jails, prisons, or parole or probation agencies. In jails and prisons, they evaluate the progress of inmates. In addition, they plan education and training programs to improve offenders' job skills and provide them with coping skills and counseling.

Career in Focus: *Prisoner-Classification Interviewer*

Some correctional specialists have the job of classifying incoming prisoners. These interviewers obtain social and criminal histories to help assign prisoners to appropriate work and other activities. They gather data, such as work history, school, criminal and military records, family background, habits, and religious beliefs. They also analyze the prisoner's social attitudes, mental capacity, character, and physical capabilities in order to prepare an admission summary.

Where and When

Some of the criminal offenders these individuals work with may be dangerous. In addition, probation officers and correctional treatment specialists may be assigned to work in high-crime areas or institutions where there is a risk of violence. Extensive travel may be necessary. Many of these workers may be required to carry a firearm for protection.

For More Information

* American Probation and Parole Association, P.O. Box 11910, Lexington, KY 40578. Internet: www.appa-net.org

Data Bank

Education and Training: Bachelor's degree

Starting Salaries: $26,000

Average Earnings: $32,000–$53,000

Total Jobs Held: 93,000

Job Outlook: Average increase

Annual Job Openings: 14,000

Related Jobs: Social workers, social and human service assistants, counselors, police and detectives, correctional officers

Personality Type: Social

Did You Know?

What happens when a man commits a crime in Ohio but is captured in Florida? Or a woman is convicted in Utah but will serve her sentence in Illinois? Some prisoners are simply handcuffed and put on a regular airplane with a guard, but prisoners who are too dangerous for commercial flights have their own airline. The U.S. Marshals Service operates a fleet of planes they use to transport prisoners. The Justice Prisoner and Alien Transportation System (JPATS) operates regular flights to 40 cities around the country. Security, we assume, is pretty tight.

Social and Human Service Assistants

At a Glance

This description encompass a wide range of job titles, from human service worker to case management aide to community outreach worker. Regardless of title, all social and human service assistants are in the business of helping people. They might work in a food bank, train mentally handicapped adults to do a job, or supervise groups of teenagers in a day program. They evaluate clients' needs, help them to get benefits, keep records, and file reports with social service agencies. They also arrange for transportation and escorts and provide emotional support. In group homes and government-supported housing programs, they assist adults who need supervision with personal hygiene and daily living skills. The amount of responsibility and supervision they are given varies a great deal.

Data Bank

Education and Training: Moderate-term on-the-job-training

Starting Salaries: $15,000

Average Earnings: $20,000–$32,000

Total Jobs Held: 352,000

Job Outlook: Rapid increase

Annual Job Openings: 61,000

Related Jobs: Social workers; clergy; counselors; childcare workers; occupational therapist assistants and aides; physical therapy assistants and aides; nursing, psychiatric, and home health aides

Personality Type: Social

Did You Know?

The boomers are getting old. This simple fact is important for human service assistants who are interested in working with the elderly. Not only are Americans living longer, but the post–World War II generation (known collectively as the baby boomers) is nearing retirement. That means they are also nearing the age when many of the services provided by human service assistants, especially those related to health care, become necessary. This will only increase the demand for individuals willing to work in group homes or provide in-home support.

Career in Focus: *Gerontology Aide*

Gerontology aides assist the elderly with their daily living arrangements. This can include helping them with their medication, assisting them in errands, or simply helping them maintain a high quality of life. Many work in nursing care centers, retirement communities, or hospitals. Others provide assistance to the elderly as a home health aide. America's increasing elderly population guarantees this will be a growing industry.

Where and When

Working conditions for these individuals vary. Some work in offices, clinics, or hospitals while others work in group homes, shelters, and day programs. Some clients can be dangerous, though agencies do everything they can to ensure workers' safety. The work can be both satisfying and emotionally draining. Turnover is high due to stress and relatively low pay.

For More Information

* National Organization for Human Services, 5601 Brodie Lane, Suite 620-215, Austin, TX 78745. Internet: www.nationalhumanservices.org

* Council for Standards in Human Services Education, Harrisburg Area Community College, Human Services Program, One HACC Dr., Harrisburg, PA 17110-2999.

Social Workers

At a Glance

Social workers help people find solutions to their problems and improve their lives. They might help a client find housing, a job, or health care. They deal with issues like child abuse, poverty, alcohol or drug abuse, and criminal behavior. They may work in hospitals, group homes, government agencies, or schools. Child, family, and school social workers provide services to help children function socially and psychologically and to improve family well-being. Some social workers assist single parents, arrange adoptions, or help find foster homes for children. In schools, they address such problems as teenage pregnancy, misbehavior, and truancy. Mental health and substance abuse social workers help individuals with mental illness or drug abuse problems. Medical and public health social workers provide people with the support needed to cope with chronic, acute, or terminal illnesses, such as Alzheimer's disease, cancer, or AIDS.

Career in Focus: *Social Work Planner and Policymaker*

Social work planners and policymakers develop the programs needed to address such issues as child abuse, homelessness, substance abuse, and poverty. These workers research and analyze policies and programs. They identify social problems and suggest solutions. They may help raise funds or write grants to support these programs. They are usually more involved in the legal and financial aspect of social services and thus spend less time working directly with people.

Where and When

Social workers usually work a standard 40-hour week, mostly in an office environment. They sometimes work evenings or weekends to meet with clients or handle emergencies. The work can be both internally gratifying and emotionally draining.

For More Information

* National Association of Social Workers, 750 First St. NE, Suite 700, Washington, DC 20002-4241. Internet: www.socialworkers.org
* Council on Social Work Education, 1725 Duke St., Suite 500, Alexandria, VA 22314-3457. Internet: www.cswe.org
* Association of Social Work Boards, 400 South Ridge Pkwy., Suite B, Culpeper, VA 22701. Internet: www.aswb.org

Data Bank

Education and Training: Bachelor's degree to master's degree

Starting Salaries: $23,000

Average Earnings: $29,000–$48,000

Total Jobs Held: 562,000

Job Outlook: Above-average increase

Annual Job Openings: 67,000

Related Jobs: Counselors, probation officers and correctional treatment specialists, psychologists, social and human services assistants

Personality Type: Social

Did You Know?

With turnover rates for social workers ranging anywhere from 20 percent to 100 percent depending on the state, there is no question that burnout is a huge problem for workers in this field. Low pay, huge caseloads, little room for advancement, and a lack of support all contribute to increased job stress. Yet agencies are starting to realize the toll this is taking on both their employees and their clients, and many have started initiatives to improve job satisfaction.

Court Reporters

At a Glance

These workers create written transcripts of speeches, conversations, legal proceedings, meetings, and other events where words are needed as records or legal proof. They make notes using shorthand or a stenotype machine. They also use audio recordings and computer voice translation software. They often help judges and attorneys access information, and they sometimes make suggestions regarding courtroom administration and procedure. Increasingly, court reporters are providing closed-captioning and real-time translating services to the deaf and hard-of-hearing community. Sometimes they type as fast as 200 words per minute, and because they are the only ones recording what is being said, they must be accurate.

Data Bank

Education and Training: Vocational/technical training

Starting Salaries: $24,000

Average Earnings: $30,000–$57,000

Total Jobs Held: 18,000

Job Outlook: Average increase

Annual Job Openings: 3,000

Related Jobs: Secretaries and administrative assistants; medical transcriptionists; receptionists and information clerks; human resources assistants, except payroll and timekeeping; paralegals and legal assistants; data entry and information processing workers

Personality Type: No data available

Did You Know?

Carpal tunnel syndrome is a painful condition that occurs when tendons in the wrist become inflamed. The syndrome is common among people who do lots of work using computer keyboards. In its worst form, it can be crippling. Health professionals recommend that individuals who are required to type for long periods of time take frequent breaks.

Career in Focus: *Stenocaptioner*

Court reporters who specialize in captioning (providing subtitles for) live television programming for people with hearing loss are commonly known as stenocaptioners. They work for television networks or cable stations captioning news, emergency broadcasts, sporting events, and other programming. In an emergency, such as a tornado or a hurricane, people's safety may depend on the accuracy of information provided in the form of captioning.

Where and When

Court reporters work in comfortable settings such as offices, courtrooms, and conventions. Many of them work from home as freelancers. As with any job that requires extensive keyboarding, court reporters are prone to backaches and eyestrain, and are especially susceptible to repetitive stress injuries such as carpal tunnel syndrome.

For More Information

* National Court Reporters Association, 8224 Old Courthouse Rd., Vienna, VA 22182. Internet: www.ncraonline.org

* United States Court Reporters Association, P.O. Box 465, Chicago, IL 60690-0465. Internet: www.uscra.org

* National Verbatim Reporters Association, 207 Third Ave., Hattiesburg, MS 39401. Internet: www.nvra.org

* American Association of Electronic Reporters and Transcribers, 23812 Rock Circle, Bothell, WA 98021-8573. Internet: www.aaert.org

Judges, Magistrates, and Other Judicial Workers

At a Glance

Judges, magistrates, and other judicial workers oversee trials and make sure that everyone follows the court rules. They preside over all types of cases, from traffic tickets to murder trials. All judicial workers must ensure that trials and hearings are conducted fairly and that the court protects the legal rights of all parties involved. Judges often hold pretrial hearings for cases where they determine whether there is enough evidence for a trial. In court cases without a jury, the judge decides the verdicts, imposes sentences, and awards compensation. All judges work for the government—either local, state, or federal. Traffic violations, misdemeanors, and small-claims cases constitute the bulk of the work of state court judges. Nearly all judges have law degrees.

Career in Focus: *Justice of the Peace*

In some states, the Justice of the Peace is a judge in a court with limited jurisdiction. They typically preside over cases involving misdemeanors, traffic violations, or petty crimes. They are often involved in small claims court proceedings. These proceedings tend to go much quicker than in other courts. A Justice of the Peace can also confer a civil union. Justices of the Peace normally don't require a law degree to be appointed.

Where and When

Judges, magistrates, and other judicial workers perform most of their duties in offices, law libraries, and courtrooms. Judges typically work a 40-hour week, though some overtime is required. Many judges work part-time in order to make room for other careers.

For More Information

* National Center for State Courts, 300 Newport Ave., Williamsburg, VA 23185-4147. Internet: www.ncsconline.org

* American Arbitration Association, 335 Madison Ave., Floor 10, New York, NY 10017-4605. Internet: www.adr.org

Data Bank

Education and Training: Bachelor's degree plus related work experience

Starting Salaries: $31,000

Average Earnings: $48,000–$111,000

Total Jobs Held: 48,000

Job Outlook: Little change

Annual Job Openings: 2,000

Related Jobs: Counselors, lawyers, paralegals and legal assistants, private detectives and investigators

Personality Type: Enterprising

Did You Know?

The United States Supreme Court is the highest court in the nation. It has ultimate authority to rule over cases that have been appealed to it. Most importantly, it is responsible for interpreting the U.S. Constitution, deciding how laws are interpreted, which in turn can have a drastic impact on the rest of us. There are only nine Supreme Court Justices, and each of them has to be appointed by the President. The only way a justice can lose his job is to resign or be impeached. Talk about job security.

Lawyers

At a Glance

Lawyers advise people about the law and their rights. They represent people in court, presenting evidence that supports a client's position, asking questions, and arguing their case. Lawyers must do research to support their cases. They must also have good reading, writing, and speaking skills. There are a number of areas that lawyers may specialize in. Trial lawyers must be able to think quickly and strategically and speak with authority. Most lawyers are in private practice, concentrating on criminal or civil law. In criminal law, lawyers represent individuals who have been charged with crimes. Attorneys dealing with civil law assist clients with personal lawsuits, wills, trusts, contracts, mortgages, titles, and leases. Other lawyers may specialize in bankruptcy, probate, or international law.

Data Bank

Education and Training: Professional degree

Starting Salaries: $47,000

Average Earnings: $68,000–$146,000+

Total Jobs Held: 735,000

Job Outlook: Average increase

Annual Job Openings: 40,000

Related Jobs: Paralegals and legal assistants; judges, magistrates, and other judicial workers

Personality Type: Enterprising

Did You Know?

Though the image we get of lawyers from television and movies suggest otherwise, the vast majority of lawsuits never go before a jury. Some surveys suggest that as few as two percent of lawsuits make it to trial, meaning the rest are settled out of court. Individuals interested in becoming lawyers should be aware that the majority of their time would be spent behind a desk and not in front of a jury.

Career in Focus: *Environmental Lawyer*

Lawyers specializing in environmental law may represent interest groups, waste disposal companies, or construction firms in their dealings with the U.S. Environmental Protection Agency (EPA) and other federal and state agencies. These lawyers help clients prepare and file for licenses and applications for approval. Those working for the government help ensure that companies keep up with environmental standards.

Where and When

Lawyers spend most of their time in offices, libraries, and courtrooms. They may have to travel to attend meetings, gather evidence, appear before courts, or meet with clients. They normally have structured work schedules, though they often work 50 hours or more per week.

For More Information

* American Bar Association, 321 North Clark St., Chicago, IL 60610. Internet: www.abanet.org

* National Association for Law Placement, 1025 Connecticut Ave. NW, Suite 1110, Washington, DC 20036. Internet: www.nalp.org

* Law School Admission Council, P.O. Box 40, Newtown, PA 18940. Internet: www.lsac.org

Paralegals and Legal Assistants

At a Glance

Paralegals and legal assistants help lawyers prepare their cases. They do research and write reports that lawyers use to present their arguments in court. Paralegals may help prepare the legal arguments and draft pleadings and motions to be filed with the court. They also obtain affidavits and assist attorneys during trials. Paralegals organize and track files of all important case documents. Some paralegals help lawyers draft contracts, mortgages, separation agreements, and wills. They also may assist in preparing tax returns and planning estates. Paralegals may meet with clients to get information about a case, but they do not argue cases in court, give legal advice, or set fees. Some paralegals have a wide variety of tasks, while others specialize in one area of the law, such as tax law or publishing law.

Career in Focus: *Community Legal-Services Provider*

Community legal-service programs are designed to provide legal assistance to those who could not otherwise afford it. Often federally funded, these programs employ lawyers and paralegals to help the poor, elderly, minorities, and middle-income families. They are often involved in consultation, and are dedicated to preserving the rights of all individuals, especially those who can't pay normal attorney fees.

Where and When

Like lawyers, paralegals and legal assistants spend the majority of their time in offices or libraries. Travel is occasionally required to do research. They are increasingly dependent upon computers and other technology to do their work. Most work a standard 40-hour week.

For More Information

* Standing Committee on Paralegals, American Bar Association, 321 North Clark St., Chicago, IL 60610. Internet: www.abanet.org/legalservices/paralegals

* National Association of Legal Assistants, Inc., 1516 South Boston St., Suite 200, Tulsa, OK 74119. Internet: www.nala.org

* National Federation of Paralegal Associations, 2517 Eastlake Ave. East, Suite 200, Seattle, WA 98102. Internet: www.paralegals.org

* American Association for Paralegal Education, 19 Mantua Rd., Mt. Royal, NJ 08061. Internet: www.aafpe.org

Data Bank

Education and Training: Associate degree to bachelor's degree

Starting Salaries: $26,000

Average Earnings: $33,000–$53,000

Total Jobs Held: 307,000

Job Outlook: Above-average increase

Annual Job Openings: 40,000

Related Jobs: Claims adjusters, appraisers, examiners, and investigators; occupational health and safety specialists and technicians

Personality Type: Enterprising

Did You Know?

The Latin phrase *pro bono* is actually short for *pro bono publico*, meaning "for the public good." Of course a more common translation would be "without charging a fee." The American Bar Association recommends that all lawyers offer at least 50 hours of pro bono service per year.

Archivists, Curators, and Museum Technicians

At a Glance

Archivists, curators, and museum technicians acquire and care for collections of books, records, art, and other items for libraries and museums. They also may work for governments, zoos, and universities. They catalogue, analyze, exhibit, and maintain valuable objects and collections for the benefit of researchers and the public. The items might include coins, stamps, plants, paintings, sculptures, or even animals. They plan exhibits, educational programs, and tours. Although some duties of archivists and curators are similar, the types of items they deal with differ: Curators usually handle objects such as sculptures, artifacts, and paintings, while archivists handle mainly records and documents. Today, an increasing part of a curator's duties involves fundraising and promotion.

Data Bank

Education and Training: Bachelor's degree to master's degree

Starting Salaries: $22,000

Average Earnings: $29,000–$52,000

Total Jobs Held: 26,000

Job Outlook: Average increase

Annual Job Openings: 4,000

Related Jobs: Artists and related workers; librarians; social scientists, other

Personality Type: Investigative; Artistic

Did You Know?

The national archives of the United States are held in the Smithsonian Institute in Washington, DC. The Smithsonian archives contain an estimated 7,000,000 photographs and about 50,000 cubic feet of paper documents. Add to this the Smithsonian libraries, which house more than 1.5 million books, and you have a lot of materials for the museums archivists and curators to take care of.

Career in Focus: *Conservator*

Conservators manage and preserve artifacts and works of art that require substantial historical, scientific, and archaeological research. They use X rays, chemical testing, microscopes, and other laboratory equipment to examine objects and determine their need for restoration and the appropriate method for preserving them. Conservators document their findings and treat items to preserve them or restore them. Conservators usually specialize in a particular group of objects such as books or paintings.

Where and When

Working conditions for these individuals vary. Many spend their time working with the public while others spend most of their time doing research or taking care of the collection. Curators who work for large libraries and museums may have to travel extensively to evaluate potential additions to the collection or organize exhibitions.

For More Information

* Society of American Archivists, 527 South Wells St., 5th floor, Chicago, IL 60607-3922. Internet: www.archivists.org

* American Association of Museums, 1575 Eye St. NW, Suite 400, Washington, DC 20005. Internet: www.aam-us.org

* American Institute for Conservation of Historic and Artistic Works, 1717 K St. NW, Suite 200, Washington, DC 20006. Internet: aic.stanford.edu

* Academy of Certified Archivists, 48 Howard St., Albany, NY 12207. Internet: www.certifiedarchivists.org

* National Association of Government Archivists and Records Administrators, 48 Howard St., Albany, NY 12207. Internet: www.nagara.org

Instructional Coordinators

At a Glance

Instructional coordinators help improve the quality of education in our classrooms. They evaluate how well a school or training program's curriculum meets students' needs. Based on their research and observations, they recommend instruction and curriculum improvements. They develop teaching materials, select textbooks, and train teachers. They also help bring new technology into the classroom. Instructional coordinators often specialize in a specific subject, such as language arts, math, or gifted and talented programs. Most work for school districts or independent consulting firms. Many instructional coordinators are former teachers and school administrators.

Career in Focus: *Curriculum Director*

Many educators are given the opportunity to choose their own books and resources. However, the constant pressure to meet standards often prompts a need for a standard curriculum to be used. The curriculum director or curriculum coordinator is responsible for selecting the textbooks, equipment, and instructional supplies for a school or even an entire district. The director or coordinator sets the guidelines for teachers to follow and helps them implement any changes in their classroom.

Where and When

Instructional coordinators usually work year round in offices or classrooms. Some may spend a majority of their time traveling between schools. Though the job of improving education can be gratifying, the task of meeting standards can be stressful. It is not uncommon for people in these jobs to work long hours.

For More Information

Information on requirements and job opportunities for instructional coordinators is available from local school systems and state departments of education.

Data Bank

Education and Training: Master's degree

Starting Salaries: $27,000

Average Earnings: $37,000–$67,000

Total Jobs Held: 117,000

Job Outlook: Rapid increase

Annual Job Openings: 15,000

Related Jobs: Teachers; education administrators; counselors; human resources, training, and labor relations managers and specialists

Personality Type: Social

Did You Know?

The No Child Left Behind Act of 2001 placed an increased emphasis on accountability, asking schools to focus on improving educational quality and student performance. This explains, in part, the increased need for instructional coordinators, especially those who specialize in reading, math, and science. In addition, the constant innovations in technology—especially with regards to computers and the Internet—suggests that more instructional coordinators will be needed to show teachers how to use that technology in their classrooms.

Librarians

At a Glance

Librarians help people find information. To do so, they must have knowledge of a wide variety of scholarly and public information sources. They follow trends related to publishing, computers, and the media in order to oversee the selection and organization of library materials. Librarians manage staff and develop and direct programs for the public, such as storytelling for children and book discussions for adults. They also conduct classes, publicize services, provide reference help, write grants, and oversee other administrative matters. Some manage other workers, prepare budgets, and order materials for their libraries. In large libraries, librarians often specialize in a single area, such as acquisitions, cataloguing, bibliography, reference, or administration.

Data Bank

Education and Training: Master's degree

Starting Salaries: $29,000

Average Earnings: $38,000–$59,000

Total Jobs Held: 159,000

Job Outlook: Little change

Annual Job Openings: 8,000

Related Jobs: Archivists, curators, and museum technicians; teachers; computer and information systems managers; computer scientists and database administrators

Personality Type: Artistic

Did You Know?

The Royal Library of Alexandria was one of the oldest and largest libraries in history. Founded in Egypt around 300 B.C., it was believed to hold anywhere from 40,000 to 700,000 books. Housed in several buildings, it was primarily a place of scholarly research and was visited by the likes of Euclid and Archimedes. The library fell victim to several fires and was almost completely destroyed by 400 A.D.

Career in Focus: *School Librarian*

In school library media centers, librarians—often called school media specialists—help teachers develop lessons, acquire materials for classroom instruction, and sometimes team-teach. They are involved in coordinating class research projects and often develop school-wide literacy programs. Because today's students are more comfortable with computers and the Internet, school librarians must be especially aware of changes in technology.

Where and When

Librarians spend most of their time at desks or in front of computers. Some may have to lift or carry heavy stacks of books. Some public and college librarians work weekends and evenings. As with all professions that involve extensive computer use, strain on the back, wrist, and eyes can be a hazard.

For More Information

* American Library Association, Office for Human Resource Development and Recruitment, 50 East Huron St., Chicago, IL 60611. Internet: www.ala.org

* Special Libraries Association, 331 South Patrick St., Alexandria, VA 22314. Internet: www.sla.org

* American Association of Law Libraries, 53 West Jackson Blvd., Suite 940, Chicago, IL 60604. Internet: www.aallnet.org

* Medical Library Association, 65 East Wacker Place, Suite 1900, Chicago, IL 60601. Internet: www.mlanet.org

* Human Resources Office, Library of Congress, 101 Independence Ave. SE, Washington, DC 20540-2231. Internet: www.loc.gov/hr

Library Technicians

At a Glance

Library technicians help librarians order, code, shelve, and organize library materials. They also help people find materials and information. Some maintain audiovisual equipment, prepare displays, and supervise other support staff. They answer questions, help patrons check out materials, and may prepare invoices or handle requests. They also handle technical services, such as entering catalogue information into the library's computer or instructing patrons in how to use the library's computer system. Some work in school libraries, helping students find information they need for research.

Career in Focus: *Bookmobile Technician*

To extend library services to more patrons, many libraries operate bookmobiles, often run by library technicians. The technicians take trucks stocked with books to designated sites on a regular schedule, frequently stopping at shopping centers, apartment complexes, schools, and nursing homes. Library technicians who drive bookmobiles are responsible for answering patrons' questions, receiving and checking out books, collecting fines, maintaining the book collection, shelving materials, and occasionally operating audiovisual equipment to show slides or films.

Where and When

Library technicians generally work at desks or computer terminals. Like other workers who spend long periods of time in front of a computer, they are susceptible to hand and wrist problems, back discomfort, and eyestrain. Those who work in school libraries work regular school hours, while others may work weekends, evenings, and even some holidays. Those who drive bookmobiles may have more unusual schedules.

For More Information

❊ American Library Association, Office for Human Resource Development and Recruitment, 50 East Huron St., Chicago, IL 60611. Internet: www.ala.org

❊ Human Resources Office, Library of Congress, 101 Independence Ave. SE, Washington, DC 20540-2231. Internet: www.loc.gov/hr

---

Data Bank

Education and Training: Short-term on-the-job training

Starting Salaries: $15,000

Average Earnings: $19,000–$33,000

Total Jobs Held: 122,000

Job Outlook: Average increase

Annual Job Openings: 25,000

Related Jobs: Library assistants, clerical; medical records and health information technicians

Personality Type: Conventional

Did You Know?

According to the American Library Association, there are approximately 117,500 libraries in the United States, employing nearly 400,000 workers. Though the job outlook for library-related occupations is about average, most individuals interested in working in a library shouldn't have to go far to find one.

Teacher Assistants

At a Glance

Teacher assistants—also called teacher aides—support classroom teachers, giving them more time for lesson planning and instruction. They help children in the classroom and school cafeteria or on the playground and field trips. Sometimes they pay special attention to individual students or small groups who need more help with a subject. They help teachers by grading papers, keeping attendance records, typing, filing, ordering supplies, helping out in the computer lab, or preparing class lessons. While most teacher assistants work in primary and secondary schools, others work in preschools and other child care centers. Teacher assistants also work with infants and toddlers who have developmental delays or other disabilities.

Data Bank

Education and Training: Short-term on-the-job training

Starting Salaries: $13,000

Average Earnings: $16,000–$25,000

Total Jobs Held: 1,296,000

Job Outlook: Average increase

Annual Job Openings: 252,000

Related Jobs: Teachers–preschool, kindergarten, elementary, middle, and secondary; teachers–special education; librarians; childcare workers; library technicians; library assistants, clerical; occupational therapist assistants and aides

Personality Type: Social

Did You Know?

Studies have shown that smaller class sizes generally produce better educational results. Still, there are many teachers with class sizes of 25 students or more due to budget and physical space constraints. While average student to teacher ratios range from 12 to 20 students per teacher depending on the state, there is no denying the impact that teacher assistants can have to help teachers manage large classes.

Career in Focus: *Special Education Teacher Assistant*

Many teacher assistants work extensively with special education students. As schools integrate special education students into general education classrooms, teacher assistants are increasingly needed to assist students with disabilities. Teacher assistants attend to a disabled student's physical needs. They also provide personal attention to students with other special needs, such as those who speak English as a second language or those who need remedial education.

Where and When

Most teacher assistants work in schools or preschools. They also work outdoors supervising recess, and spend much of their time standing, walking, or kneeling. Teacher assistants who work with special education students must often perform strenuous tasks including heavy lifting. About 4 out of every 10 teacher assistants work part-time, and most work a 40-hour week or less.

For More Information

* American Federation of Teachers, Paraprofessional and School Related Personnel Division, 555 New Jersey Ave. NW, Washington, DC 20001.

* National Education Association, Educational Support Personnel Division, 1201 16th Street, NW, Washington, DC 20036.

* National Resource Center for Paraprofessionals, 6526 Old Main Hill, Utah State University, Logan, UT 84322. Internet: www.nrcpara.org

Teachers–Adult Literacy and Remedial Education

At a Glance

Adult literacy and remedial education teachers teach basic skills courses, such as writing, reading, and math to adults and out-of-school youths. They also work with people who want to update their job skills or prepare for the GED (high school equivalency) exam. Traditionally, the students in adult education classes have been those who did not graduate high school or who passed through school without learning necessary skills. Increasingly, however, students in these classes are people whose native language is not English. Because the students often are at different levels, teachers must assess each student's abilities beforehand. They must often teach students effective study skills and give them the self-confidence they need to succeed academically as well.

Career in Focus: *ESOL Teacher*

ESOL teachers (teachers of English to speakers of other languages) help adults speak, listen, read, and write in English, often in the context of real-life situations. ESOL teachers teach adults who possess a wide range of abilities and who speak a variety of languages. More advanced students may concentrate on writing and conversational skills or focus on learning more academic or job-related communication skills.

Where and When

Many of these classes are held on days and at times to meet adult students' schedules, so evening and weekend work is common. A large number of these teachers work part-time, sometimes in addition to another full-time career. Most of the students are motivated to learn, which can make this job satisfying and rewarding.

For More Information

* The U.S. Department of Education, Office of Vocational and Adult Education, Potomac Center Plaza, 400 Maryland Ave. SW, Washington, DC 20202. Internet: www.ed.gov/about/offices/list/ovae/index.html

* The Center for Adult English Language Acquisition, 4646 40th St. NW, Washington, DC 20016. Internet: www.cal.org/caela

Data Bank

Education and Training: Bachelor's degree

Starting Salaries: $22,000

Average Earnings: $31,000–$54,000

Total Jobs Held: 98,000

Job Outlook: Average increase

Annual Job Openings: 27,000

Related Jobs: Teachers–preschool, kindergarten, elementary, middle, and secondary; teachers–special education; counselors; social workers

Personality Type: Social

Did You Know?

According to the U.S. Department of Education, ESL (English as a second language) programs are the fastest-growing adult education programs in the country, accounting for close to half of the total adult enrollment. The majority of these students are native Spanish speakers. Demand for ESL and ESOL teachers will be greatest in states with large populations of nonnative speakers, including California, Florida, Texas, and New York.

Teachers–Postsecondary

At a Glance

Postsecondary teachers work at colleges, community colleges, universities, and research facilities. They specialize in one field, such as history, physics, or journalism, and most have an advanced degree. College and university faculty teach and advise more than 16 million students. They prepare lectures, exercises, and laboratory experiments; grade exams and papers; and advise and work with students individually. Most research and write articles and books in addition to their teaching duties. Faculty members at universities and four-year colleges spend more of their time doing research, while those at two-year colleges spend most of their time teaching. Most faculty members also serve on committees that deal with departmental matters, academic issues, budgets, and hiring. Graduate teaching assistants assist faculty and staff at colleges and universities by performing teaching or teaching-related duties.

Data Bank

Education and Training: Work experience to professional degree

Starting Salaries: $25,000

Average Earnings: $34,000–$76,000

Total Jobs Held: 1,628,000

Job Outlook: Rapid increase

Annual Job Openings: 329,000

Related Jobs: Teachers–preschool, kindergarten, elementary, middle, and secondary; education administrators; librarians; counselors; writers and editors; public relations specialists; management analysts

Personality Type: Investigative; Artistic; Social

Did You Know?

The majority of universities and four-year colleges require their teachers to have a doctoral degree in their chosen field of study. Doctoral degrees generally take six years to complete. That's six years beyond a bachelor's degree, which means students graduating high school and wanting to teach at the college level can look forward to about 10 more years of schooling. Of course the rewards–tenure, long vacations, travel grants–are more than worth it for those who make it through and land a job.

Career in Focus: *Postsecondary Vocational Education Teacher*

Postsecondary vocational education teachers provide instruction for occupations that require specialized training but may not require a four-year degree, such as dental hygienist, X-ray technician, auto mechanic, and cosmetologist. Classes often are taught in an industrial or laboratory setting where students can get hands-on experience.

Where and When

Postsecondary teachers usually have flexible schedules and a great deal of freedom. Some teach night and weekend classes—especially at community colleges or schools with a lot of adult students. Most of these teachers work nine months out of the year and can take advantage of school holidays as well. Travel may be required to do research, and many postsecondary teachers experience some conflict between their responsibilities as teachers and as researchers.

For More Information

* Council of Graduate Schools, One Dupont Circle NW, Suite 430, Washington, DC 20036-1173. Internet: www.preparing-faculty.org

* Association for Career and Technical Education, 1410 King St., Alexandria, VA 22314. Internet: www.acteonline.org

Teachers—Preschool, Kindergarten, Elementary, Middle, and Secondary

At a Glance

Teachers plan lessons, prepare tests, grade papers, and write reports of students' progress. They encourage group learning and problem solving and prepare students for advanced education and the world of work. They meet with parents and school staff to talk about grades and problems. Preschool, kindergarten, and elementary school teachers introduce children to mathematics, language, science, and social studies. They use games, music, artwork, films, books, computers, and other tools to teach basic skills. Most elementary school teachers instruct one class of children in several subjects. Middle school teachers and secondary school teachers help students delve more deeply into subjects introduced in elementary school. Middle and secondary school teachers specialize in a specific subject, such as English, Spanish, mathematics, history, or biology. In addition to conducting classroom activities, teachers oversee study halls and homerooms, supervise extracurricular activities, and accompany students on field trips.

Career in Focus: *Vocational Education Teacher*

Vocational education teachers instruct and train mostly high school students to work in a wide variety of fields, such as health care, business, auto repair, communications, and, technology. They often teach courses that are in high demand by area employers, who may offer internships to students. Many vocational teachers play an active role in building and overseeing these partnerships.

Where and When

Teaching is considered one of the most frustrating and rewarding careers. Accountability standards, unruly students, heavy workloads, and a lack of control can lead to feelings of stress. Including duties performed outside of the class, such as lesson planning and grading, most teachers work more than 40 hours per week. The majority of them work a standard 10-month school year, though some work through the summer to supplement their income.

For More Information

* National Education Association, 1201 16th St. NW, Washington, DC 20036.
* National Council for Accreditation of Teacher Education, 2010 Massachusetts Ave. NW, Suite 500, Washington, DC 20036-1023. Internet: www.ncate.org
* National Center for Alternative Certification, 1901 Pennsylvania Ave NW, Suite 201, Washington, DC 20006. Internet: www.teach-now.org

Data Bank

Education and Training: Bachelor's degree

Starting Salaries: $28,000

Average Earnings: $34,000–$54,000

Total Jobs Held: 3,829,000

Job Outlook: Above-average increase

Annual Job Openings: 510,000

Related Jobs: Teachers—postsecondary; counselors; teacher assistants; education administrators; librarians; childcare workers; public relations specialists; social workers; athletes, coaches, umpires, and related workers

Personality Type: Social

Did You Know?

Although private schools certainly have their appeal, including smaller class sizes and more freedom for teachers to design their own classes, teacher turnover is actually higher in private schools than in public schools. In general, public schools pay better and offer solid benefit packages, but they also all require a teaching license. While licenses are recommended for most private school teaching positions, they aren't often required. Future teachers should weigh all the pros and cons before deciding whether to go public or private.

Teachers—Self-Enrichment Education

At a Glance

Self-enrichment teachers are usually specialists in a certain subject who are willing to share what they know with mostly adult students who are eager to learn. Some teach classes that provide students with life skills, such as personal finance, cooking, and time management classes. Others teach subjects purely for recreation, such as photography, painting, or ballroom dancing. Most self-enrichment classes are designed for individuals who just want to improve themselves, enrich their lives, or learn more about a topic. The courses seldom lead to a particular degree, and student attendance is voluntary. Some classes, such as pottery or sewing, may be largely hands-on. All self-enrichment teachers must prepare lessons beforehand and stay current in their fields. Many are self-employed.

Data Bank

Education and Training: Work experience

Starting Salaries: $16,000

Average Earnings: $23,000–$45,000

Total Jobs Held: 253,000

Job Outlook: Above-average increase

Annual Job Openings: 74,000

Related Jobs: Teachers—preschool, kindergarten, elementary, middle, and secondary; dancers and choreographers; artists and related workers; musicians, singers, and related workers; recreation workers; athletes, coaches, umpires, and related workers

Personality Type: Social

Did You Know?

"Lifelong learning" is a phrase growing in popularity. Retirees provide one of the larger groups of students in self-enrichment education because they have more time to take classes. The impending retirement of baby boomers should provide self-enrichment teachers increased opportunity to share their talents, whether it's working with wood or doing the cha-cha.

Career in Focus: *Art, Music, or Dance Instructor*

Many self-enrichment teachers provide one-on-one lessons to students or teach classes on their own as part of a studio, particularly in the arts. Whether it's teaching someone to play the piano, paint *a fresco*, or dance *en pointe*, most of these instructors teach subjects they are passionate about and skilled in. In the case of one-on-one instruction, the teacher may only work with each student for an hour or two per week. Many instructors work with the same students on a weekly basis for years, however, and find satisfaction in helping them mature and gain expertise.

Where and When

Few of these teachers are full-time salaried workers. Most either work part-time or are self-employed. Although pay for these jobs is generally low, most teachers enjoy sharing what they know with others, which leads to high job satisfaction. Many self-enrichment classes for adults are held in the evenings and on weekends. Those for children are almost always after school or on weekends. Most of the teaching is done in comfortable classroom, laboratory, or workshop settings.

For More Information

For information on employment of self-enrichment teachers, contact schools or local companies that offer self-enrichment programs.

Teachers–Special Education

At a Glance

Special education teachers work with students who have disabilities. Most work in elementary, middle, or high schools, but some work with toddlers and preschoolers. The majority work with children with mild to moderate disabilities, modifying the general curriculum to meet the child's individual needs. A small number of special education teachers work with students with mental retardation or autism, primarily teaching them life skills and basic literacy. Early identification of a child with special needs is an important part of a special education teacher's job. Special education teachers also help to develop an Individualized Education Program (IEP) for each special education student. The IEP sets personalized goals for each student and is tailored to the student's individual needs and ability. Special education teachers communicate frequently with parents, social workers, school psychologists, occupational and physical therapists, school administrators, and other teachers.

Career in Focus: *Inclusion Aide*

As schools become more inclusive, special education teachers and general education teachers are increasingly working together in general education classrooms. Inclusion aides provide one-to-one instruction for students with special needs as part of a general education classroom. They help general educators adapt class materials and teaching techniques to specifically meet the needs of students with disabilities.

Where and When

Although helping students with disabilities can be highly rewarding, the work is often emotionally and physically draining. Heavy workloads and lots of paperwork can lead to stress. The majority of special education teachers work a standard 10-month school schedule during regular school hours. Some heavy lifting may be required.

For More Information

* The Council for Exceptional Children, 1110 N. Glebe Rd., Suite 300, Arlington, VA 22201-5704. Internet: www.cec.sped.org

* National Center for Special Education Personnel and Related Service Providers, National Association of State Directors of Special Education, 1800 Diagonal Rd., Suite 320, Alexandria, VA 22314. Internet: www.personnelcenter.org

Data Bank

Education and Training: Bachelor's degree

Starting Salaries: $30,000

Average Earnings: $37,000–$58,000

Total Jobs Held: 441,000

Job Outlook: Above-average increase

Annual Job Openings: 37,000

Related Jobs: Psychologists; social workers; speech-language pathologists; audiologists; counselors; teacher assistants; occupational therapists; recreational therapists; teachers–preschool, kindergarten, elementary, middle, and secondary

Personality Type: Social

Did You Know?

Special education is not restricted to students with learning disabilities, though more and more students are being diagnosed with such disabilities. Special education covers classes for students with mental handicaps, physical disabilities, and emotional problems. It also includes classes for gifted and talented students. Special education classes spread from preschool and early-intervention programs to continuing education classes for disabled adults. It's a wide and growing field.

Artists and Related Workers

At a Glance

Artists communicate ideas, thoughts, or feelings through art. They might use oil paints, watercolors, pencils, clay, chalk, or even scrap metal to create their work. Art directors develop designs and review material for periodicals, newspapers, and other media. Craft artists hand-make a wide variety of objects that are sold either in their own studios, in retail outlets, or at arts-and-crafts shows. Craft artists work with many different materials, including ceramics, glass, wood, metal, and paper.

Visual artists are usually either graphic artists or fine artists. Graphic artists use art to meet the needs of business clients, such as stores, ad agencies, and publishing firms. Fine artists create artwork to sell and display in museums or galleries. More than half of all artists are self-employed and must use good business skills to be successful.

Data Bank

Education and Training: Long-term on-the-job training to bachelor's degree plus related work experience

Starting Salaries: $29,000

Average Earnings: $40,000–$74,000

Total Jobs Held: 200,000

Job Outlook: Average increase

Annual Job Openings: 29,000

Related Jobs: Architects, except landscape and naval; archivists, curators, and museum technicians; commercial and industrial designers; fashion designers; floral designers; graphic designers; interior designers; landscape architects; photographers; woodworkers; computer software engineers; desktop publishers

Personality Type: Artistic

Did You Know?

Scholars, artists, critics, and audiences have debated for centuries over what is and isn't art. Though most agree that art incorporates creativity, expression, and even a sense of beauty, it still holds true that one person's masterpiece is another person's garbage. One famous piece that called the definition of art into question was Marcel Duchamp's *Fountain*. Displayed in a museum in 1917, it was simply a urinal with "R. Mutt 1917" written on it. It has since been voted the "most influential artwork of the 20th century" by a panel of art world professionals.

Career in Focus: *Illustrator*

Illustrators create pictures for books, magazines, and other publications and for commercial products such as stationery, greeting cards, and calendars. Medical and scientific illustrators combine drawing skills with knowledge of biology or other sciences. Medical illustrators draw illustrations of human anatomy and surgical procedures. Scientific illustrators draw illustrations of animal and plant life, atomic and molecular structures, and geologic and planetary formations. Increasingly, illustrators are doing all their work directly on a computer.

Where and When

Most artists work in studios located in office buildings, warehouses, or in the privacy of their own home. Artists employed by publishing companies, advertising agencies, and design firms generally work a standard 40-hour workweek. Self-employed artists can set their own schedule, but spend much of their time meeting potential customers and building a reputation.

For More Information

* National Association of Schools of Art and Design, 11250 Roger Bacon Dr., Suite 21, Reston, VA 20190-5248. Internet: nasad.arts-accredit.org

* American Craft Council Library, 72 Spring St., 6th Floor, New York, NY 10012-4019. Internet: www.craftcouncil.org

* Society of Illustrators, 128 E. 63rd St., New York, NY 10021-7303. Internet: www.societyillustrators.org

* Association of Medical Illustrators, 245 First St., Suite 1800, Cambridge, MA 02142. Internet: www.ami.org

Commercial and Industrial Designers

At a Glance

These individuals are responsible for the look, feel, function, quality, and safety of most of the products we use everyday. They combine their knowledge of art, engineering, and business to create sketches and models that are then used in production. When creating a new design, they often begin by researching how the product will be used. Many designers use computer-aided design (CAD) tools to create and visualize the final product. Designers then present the designs and prototypes to their client or managers and incorporate any changes and suggestions. Often, commercial and industrial designers specialize in one product or another, from automobiles to appliances, toys to tools. Designers also work with engineers, accountants, and cost estimators to determine whether a product could be made safer, easier to use, or cheaper to produce.

Career in Focus: *Furniture Designer*

Commercial and industrial designers may specialize in any number of products. Furniture designers do exactly what their name suggests, designing everything from conference tables to microwave carts for industrial, commercial, and individual clients. Furniture designers must always balance the function of their design with its form or appearance. Sometimes the most beautiful chairs are the least comfortable and the ugliest couches offer the best naps. Being a furniture designer requires business skills as well. Many of them are self-employed.

Where and When

Working conditions vary. Designers employed by large corporations or design firms generally work regular hours in comfortable settings. Self-employed consultants and designers may work longer hours to meet deadlines. Some travel may be required to meet clients.

For More Information

* Industrial Designers Society of America, 45195 Business Court, Suite 250, Dulles, VA 20166-6717. Internet: www.idsa.org

* National Association of Schools of Art and Design, 11250 Roger Bacon Dr., Suite 21, Reston, VA 20190-5248. Internet: nasad.arts-accredit.org

Data Bank

Education and Training: Bachelor's degree

Starting Salaries: $29,000

Average Earnings: $39,000–$70,000

Total Jobs Held: 49,000

Job Outlook: Average increase

Annual Job Openings: 7,000

Related Jobs: Artists and related workers; architects, except landscape and naval; engineers; landscape architects; drafters; computer software engineers; desktop publishers; fashion designers; graphic designers; interior designers

Personality Type: Artistic

Did You Know?

Not all products are created on purpose. Post-it Notes—those colored, sticky pieces of paper—were created almost by accident. A researcher at 3M set out to make a stronger adhesive but ultimately only developed a weaker one that just barely stuck. Three years later, a fellow researcher at the company discovered he could coat scraps of paper with the stuff and use them as bookmarks. They would stick, but could be lifted off with ease. Now you can find them in almost every office.

Fashion Designers

At a Glance

Fashion designers create the clothing, shoes, and accessories worn by millions of people. They research fashion trends, sketch designs, select materials, create samples, and oversee the production of their items. The process from initial design to final production takes between 18 and 24 months. Once the design is finished and samples of the article are sewn, they are marketed to clothing retailers. Many designs are shown at fashion and trade shows a few times a year. Retailers will then place orders for the items they want to sell. Computer-aided design (CAD) is increasingly being used in the fashion design industry, meaning designers must be aware of trends in technology as well as trends in fashion.

Data Bank

Education and Training: Bachelor's degree

Starting Salaries: $28,000

Average Earnings: $41,000–$87,000

Total Jobs Held: 17,000

Job Outlook: Little change

Annual Job Openings: 2,000

Related Jobs: Artists and related workers; commercial and industrial designers; floral designers; graphic designers; interior designers; demonstrators, product promoters, and models; photographers; purchasing managers, buyers, and purchasing agents; retail salespersons; textile, apparel, and furnishing occupations

Personality Type: Artistic

Did You Know?

Two-thirds of fashion designers work in either New York or California, the fashion Meccas of the United States. This is an important consideration for anyone interested in pursuing fashion design as a career, especially given the cost of living in these states' major cities. Of course if you'd rather go international, you'll always have Paris.

Career in Focus: *Costume Designer*

Some fashion designers specialize in costume design for plays, movies, and television shows. The work of costume designers is similar to other fashion designers. Costume designers research the styles worn during the period in which the performance takes place or work with directors to select the right attire. They make sketches of designs, select fabric and other materials, and oversee the production of the costumes. They also must stay within the costume budget. At least they are given their own Academy Award category.

Where and When

Fashion designers generally work regular hours in comfortable settings. Freelancers who work on a contract basis must frequently adjust their schedules to meet their clients' needs. Regardless of their work setting, all fashion designers must occasionally work long hours in order to meet deadlines or prepare for fashion shows. Travel can be frequent.

For More Information

* National Association of Schools of Art and Design, 11250 Roger Bacon Dr., Suite 21, Reston, VA 20190-5248. Internet: nasad.arts-accredit.org

* Fashion Group International, 8 West 40th St., 7th Floor, New York, NY 10018. Internet: www.fgi.org

Floral Designers

At a Glance

Floral designers use flowers, greenery, ribbons, and containers to produce arrangements for decoration and special occasions. They are skilled at making bouquets, corsages, table centerpieces, and wreaths. Most work independently or in small shops creating designs for special events such as weddings and funerals. Others work in the wholesale floral business or in the floral departments in grocery stores. Some designers also assist interior designers in creating live or silk floral displays for hotels, restaurants, and private residences. Self-employed floral designers must handle the various aspects of running their own businesses, such as selecting and purchasing flowers, hiring and supervising staff, and maintaining financial records. Floral designers often work under deadlines (the flowers need to be fresh after all) and must have a good sense of visual design.

Career in Focus: *Wedding Florist*

Because of the wide variety of designs involved—from boutonnières to the bride's bouquet—some florists choose to focus only on weddings. The average cost of wedding flowers ranges from $500 to $1,500, though at more elaborate weddings they can cost as much as $5,000 or $10,000. As long as people continue to get married (and spend lots of money on weddings), floral designers will always have some job security.

Where and When

Most floral designers work in comfortable settings, though work outdoors is sometimes required. Designers may have to make frequent trips to deliver or pick up flowers or to set up arrangements. Because fresh flowers are perishable, orders cannot be completed too far in advance. Many designers often work long hours before or during holidays, plus nights and weekends to complete large orders for weddings and other events. They can be susceptible to allergic reactions from flower pollens.

For More Information

* American Institute of Floral Designers, 720 Light St., Baltimore, MD 21230. Internet: www.aifd.org
* Society of American Florists, 1601 Duke St., Alexandria, VA 22314. Internet: www.safnow.org

Data Bank

Education and Training: Moderate-term on-the-job training

Starting Salaries: $14,000

Average Earnings: $17,000–$26,000

Total Jobs Held: 98,000

Job Outlook: Average increase

Annual Job Openings: 14,000

Related Jobs: Artists and related workers; commercial and industrial designers; fashion designers; graphic designers; interior designers; landscape architects

Personality Type: Artistic

Did You Know?

Can you guess what the biggest holiday is for floral designers? Despite the dramatic increase in the sale of roses in February, it's not Valentine's Day. And though geraniums are common in May, it's not Mother's Day either. It's Christmas. In fact, flowers are becoming more and more popular as a holiday gift.

Graphic Designers

At a Glance

Otherwise known as graphic artists, these designers decide the best way to communicate a message in print, film, or electronic media. Some graphic designers develop the layout of newspapers, journals, and magazines, while others work in advertising, designing packaging and logos and making signs. Perhaps the hottest trend in graphic designing is developing material for Web pages and other interactive multimedia environments. In creating their designs, graphic artists first gather relevant information by meeting with clients or art directors. Graphic designers then prepare sketches or layouts to illustrate the vision for the design. Finally, they present the completed design to their clients or to the art director for approval. Graphic designers use computer software to assist in their designs and so are expected to be familiar with the latest technology.

Data Bank

Education and Training: Bachelor's degree

Starting Salaries: $23,000

Average Earnings: $29,000–$51,000

Total Jobs Held: 228,000

Job Outlook: Average increase

Annual Job Openings: 35,000

Related Jobs: Artists and related workers; commercial and industrial designers; fashion designers; floral designers; interior designers; computer software engineers; drafters; desktop publishers; advertising, marketing, promotions, public relations, and sales managers; photographers; writers and editors

Personality Type: Artistic

Did You Know?

The Nike "Swoosh" is one of the most recognizable symbols in the world and can be found on hats, shirts, socks, towels, bags, posters, and of course, shoes. The logo was originally created by a graphic design student named Carolyn Davidson, who sold it to the company founder, Phil Knight, for a modest sum of $35. Rumor has it that Mr. Knight wasn't thrilled with the design, but went with it anyway. Since then the "Swoosh" has become an icon, and Davidson has been justly rewarded for her contributions to the company.

Career in Focus: *Graphic Designer–Marketing*

Marketing and advertising departments are one of the chief employers of graphic designers. These designers develop catalogs and brochures, create print and Web-based graphics, create promotional and event materials, and design Web sites. The job requires a mix of artistic vision and business savvy. Those with degrees or experience in both marketing and design should have the best chances at such jobs.

Where and When

Graphic designers employed by large advertising, publishing, or design firms usually work regular hours in comfortable settings. Freelancers or those working at smaller firms may frequently adjust their schedules to meet their clients' needs. They also may work longer hours in smaller, more congested environments. Designers frequently spend a lot of time in front of a computer, which can result in strain on the eyes, back, and wrists.

For More Information

* National Association of Schools of Art and Design, 11250 Roger Bacon Dr., Suite 21, Reston, VA 20190-5248. Internet: nasad.arts-accredit.org

* American Institute of Graphic Arts, 164 Fifth Ave., New York, NY 10010. Internet: www.aiga.org

* Art Directors Club, 106 West 29th St., New York, NY 10001. Internet: www.adcglobal.org

Interior Designers

At a Glance

These workers design and arrange the physical space within buildings, whether it's a home, hospital, theater, restaurant, or office. They experiment with colors, textures, furniture, lighting, and space to create a safe, functional, and pleasing atmosphere. Traditionally, most interior designers focused on decorating: choosing a style and colors, and then selecting appropriate furniture, floor and window coverings, artwork, and lighting. However, an increasing number of designers are becoming involved in the architectural details, helping to determine the location of windows, stairways, escalators, and walkways. Designers frequently work with architects, electricians, and building contractors to ensure that their designs are safe and meet construction requirements.

Career in Focus: *In-Store Designer*

Those who work as in-store designers for furniture or home and garden stores offer their design services in addition to selling the store's products. In-store designers help customers select a style and color scheme that fits their needs or find suitable accessories and lighting. However, in-store designers rarely visit a customer's home or business and are limited in using only their store's products.

Where and When

Interior designers employed by large corporations or firms usually work regular hours in comfortable settings. Those in smaller firms or who work on a freelance basis may have irregular schedules and work in more cramped environments. Interior designers may work under stress to meet deadlines, stay under budget, and please clients.

For More Information

* American Society of Interior Designers, 608 Massachusetts Ave. NE, Washington, DC 20002-6006. Internet: www.asid.org
* Foundation for Interior Design Education Research, 146 Monroe Center NW, Suite 1318, Grand Rapids, MI 49503-2822. Internet: www.fider.org
* National Association of Schools of Art and Design, 11250 Roger Bacon Dr., Suite 21, Reston, VA 20190-5248. Internet: nasad.arts-accredit.org
* National Council for Interior Design Qualification, 1200 18th St. NW, Suite 1001, Washington, DC 20036-2506. Internet: www.ncidq.org

Data Bank

Education and Training: Bachelor's degree

Starting Salaries: $23,000

Average Earnings: $31,000–$56,000

Total Jobs Held: 65,000

Job Outlook: Average increase

Annual Job Openings: 10,000

Related Jobs: Artists and related workers; architects, except landscape and naval; commercial and industrial designers; fashion designers; floral designers; graphic designers; landscape architects

Personality Type: Artistic

Did You Know?

Three areas of design that are becoming increasingly popular are ergonomic design, elder design, and environmental—or green—design. Ergonomic design involves designing work spaces and furniture that emphasize good posture and minimize muscle strain on the body. Elder design involves planning interiors to aid in the movement of the elderly and disabled, such as widening passageways to accommodate wheelchairs. Green design involves selecting furniture and carpets that are free of chemicals and using construction materials that are energy efficient. So your environmentally conscious grandfather with bad posture can now have the living room of his dreams.

Actors, Producers, and Directors

At a Glance

Actors, producers, and directors make words come alive through plays, TV shows, and films. Actors perform in stage, radio, television, video, or movie productions. They also work in nightclubs, theme parks, commercials, and training and educational films. Directors are responsible for the creative decisions in a production. They interpret scripts, advise set and costume designers, audition and select cast members, conduct rehearsals, and direct the work of cast and crew. Producers arrange the financing and decide the size of the production and the budget. Directors and producers often work under tight deadlines and stressful conditions. Although the most famous actors, producers, and directors work in film or network television, far more work in local or regional television studios, theaters, or film production companies preparing independent, small-scale productions.

Data Bank

Education and Training: Long-term on-the-job training to bachelor's degree plus related work experience

Starting Salaries: $22,000

Average Earnings: $37,000–$85,000 (for producers and directors only)

Total Jobs Held: 83,000

Job Outlook: Average increase

Annual Job Openings: 22,000

Related Jobs: Announcers; dancers and choreographers; musicians, singers, and related workers; writers and editors; fashion designers; set and exhibit designers; top executives

Personality Type: Artistic; Enterprising; Realistic

Did You Know?

Actors have some of the best-paying and worst-paying jobs in the country. While movie stars can make upwards of $20 million per picture, many extras barely make minimum wage. The key is to speak up for yourself—literally. Motion picture and television actors with speaking parts are guaranteed a minimum daily rate of $716. Of course, once the production is done filming, these actors aren't guaranteed anything. For most it is an uphill struggle, and it's rare to find an actor who doesn't have another job on the side.

Career in Focus: *Talent Director*

Sometimes called casting directors, talent directors audition and interview performers in order to select the most appropriate person for parts in stage, television, radio, or film productions. They arrange screen tests and find and hire extras, stand-ins, and photo and stunt doubles. They also negotiate contracts and maintain talent files.

Where and When

All of these individuals work under the constant pressure of deadlines and schedules. Many of them are under pressure to find their next job as well. Acting assignments are usually short-term, which often results in periods of unemployment. Actors and directors usually work long, irregular hours when filming or performing. Extensive travel may be necessary for those filming or recording in other locations or touring with a show.

For More Information

* National Association of Schools of Theater, 11250 Roger Bacon Dr., Suite 21, Reston, VA 20190. Internet: nast.arts-accredit.org

* Actors Equity Association, 165 West 46th St., New York, NY 10036. Internet: www.actorsequity.org

* Screen Actors Guild, 5757 Wilshire Blvd., Los Angeles, CA 90036-3600. Internet: www.sag.org

* American Federation of Television and Radio Artists– Screen Actors Guild, 4340 East-West Hwy., Suite 204, Bethesda, MD 20814-4411. Internet: www.aftra.org or www.sag.org

Athletes, Coaches, Umpires, and Related Workers

At a Glance

Athletes compete in organized sports events to entertain spectators. They spend many hours each day practicing and improving teamwork under the guidance of a coach. Because competition is intense and job security is questionable, many athletes train year round to stay in peak physical condition. Coaches organize, lead, teach, and referee indoor and outdoor games. Along with refining athletes' skills, coaches are responsible for instilling good sportsmanship, a competitive spirit, and teamwork, and for managing their teams. During competition, coaches may call specific plays and substitute players. Umpires, referees, and other sports officials officiate at competitive athletic and sporting events. They observe the play and make sure everyone follows the established rules and regulations.

Career in Focus: *Sports Instructor*

Sports instructors train professional and nonprofessional athletes on a one-to-one basis. They organize, instruct, and lead athletes in indoor and outdoor sports such as bowling, tennis, golf, and swimming. Because activities are as diverse as weight lifting, gymnastics, scuba diving, and karate, instructors tend to specialize in one or a few activities. Like coaches, sports instructors also may hold daily practice sessions and be responsible for equipment and supplies.

Where and When

Because of the intense physical nature of most sports, professional athletes are highly prone to injury. Athletes, coaches, and sports officials work irregular hours, often working weekends, evenings, and holidays. They may work longer hours during the regular season, but will continue to practice in the off-season as well. Travel by bus or airplane can be frequent. Sports officials regularly encounter verbal abuse by fans, coaches, and players.

For More Information

* National Association of Sports Officials, 2017 Lathrop Ave., Racine, WI 53405. Internet: www.naso.org
* Professional Tennis Registry, P.O. Box 4739, Hilton Head Island, SC 29938. Internet: www.ptrtennis.org
* U.S. Professional Tennis Association, 3535 Briarpark Dr., Suite One, Houston, TX 77042. Internet: www.uspta.org

Data Bank

Education and Training: Long-term on-the-job training

Starting Salaries: $13,000

Average Earnings: $18,000–$43,000 (for coaches, umpires, and related workers only)

Total Jobs Held: 211,000

Job Outlook: Above-average increase

Annual Job Openings: 75,000

Related Jobs: Dietitians and nutritionists; physical therapists; recreation workers; fitness workers; recreational therapists; teachers–preschool, kindergarten, elementary, middle, and secondary

Personality Type: Enterprising

Did You Know?

We are a sports-loving nation. Many who participate in amateur sports dream of becoming paid professional athletes, coaches, or sports officials, but very few beat the odds of making a living from it. Only about 1 out of every 5,000 high school athletes ever signs a professional sports contract. Those athletes who do make it to professional levels find that careers are short and jobs are insecure. Even though the chances of employment as a professional athlete are slim, there are many opportunities for at least a part-time job as a coach, instructor, referee, or umpire in amateur athletics or in high school, college, or university sports.

Dancers and Choreographers

At a Glance

Dancers express ideas and tell stories through the movement of their bodies. Dance styles include classical ballet, modern dance, tap, jazz, and different folk dances. Dancers perform in musicals, operas, TV shows, movies, music videos, and commercials. Dancers must be strong, coordinated, and dedicated. Choreographers create dances and teach dancers. In addition, choreographers usually are involved in auditioning performers. They may work for one company or on a freelance basis. Those who operate their own studios must have good business skills.

Data Bank

Education and Training: Long-term on-the-job training to related work experience

Starting Salaries: $8,000

Average Earnings: $21,000–$48,000 (for choreographers only)

Total Jobs Held: 19,000

Job Outlook: Average increase

Annual Job Openings: 8,000

Related Jobs: Actors, producers, and directors; musicians, singers, and related workers; set and exhibit designers; fashion designers; barbers, cosmetologists, and other personal appearance workers; athletes, coaches, umpires, and related workers

Personality Type: Artistic

Did You Know?

To dance *en pointe* means to dance on the tips of one's toes, and it is a notoriously difficult skill to master. *Pointe* ballet training traditionally starts at the age of 12, although regular ballet classes usually start much earlier. Most dancers have their first professional auditions by the time they are 17 or 18. But the training and practice for professional ballet dancers never ends. By the time they are 30, most ballet dancers are done with their performing days and move into teaching and choreography.

Career in Focus: *Dance Instructor*

While the opportunities to dance on Broadway may be few, thousands of kids across the country enroll in dance classes each year. Dance instructors primarily teach children and youth from kindergarten up through high school various forms of dance, including ballet, tap, and jazz. They are responsible for creating a safe and fun environment for the participants as well as for coordinating performances and working with parents. Many dance instructors work out of studios, school, or gyms.

Where and When

Dancing is strenuous exercise. Few dancers can continue performing in their forties or fifties due to the stress on the body. Daily rehearsals require long hours, and many dance companies usually tour for part of the year. Dancers in musical productions spend much of their time on the road, and others work in nightclubs or on cruise ships.

For More Information

* National Association of Schools of Dance, 11250 Roger Bacon Dr., Suite 21, Reston, VA 20190. Internet: nasd.arts-accredit.org

* Dance/USA, 1156 15th St. NW, Suite 820, Washington, DC 20005. Internet: www.danceusa.org

Musicians, Singers, and Related Workers

At a Glance

Musicians and singers play instruments and perform vocal music. They may perform alone or in groups, before live audiences or in recording studios. Venues may include nightclubs, concert halls, and theaters. Regardless of the setting, musicians and singers spend considerable time practicing. Music directors conduct, direct, plan, and lead instrumental or vocal performances by musical groups such as orchestras, choirs, and glee clubs. Conductors specifically lead instrumental music groups, such as symphony orchestras, dance bands, and show bands. These leaders audition and select musicians, choose appropriate music, and direct rehearsals and performances. Composers create original music such as symphonies, operas, sonatas, radio and television jingles, film scores, and popular songs. Most musicians work nights and weekends and must travel to perform. Because it's so hard to support themselves with music, many take other jobs as well.

Career in Focus: *Arranger*

Arrangers adapt musical compositions to a particular style for orchestras, bands, choral groups, or individuals. For example, a piece written specifically for a full orchestra may be adapted to be played by a small band, or another piece written for a musical may be changed to become a pop song. Many arrangers use computer software to make changes.

Where and When

Working conditions vary dramatically. Musicians typically perform at night and on weekends. Those who work in nightclubs or perform solo or in small groups may travel extensively. The stress of constantly looking for work leads many musicians to find full-time jobs in other occupations while working part-time as musicians. Most professional singers work in cities with major recording studios such as New York, Los Angeles, Chicago, and Nashville. Composers and conductors may hold positions as teachers in high schools and colleges as well.

For More Information

* National Association of Schools of Music, 11250 Roger Bacon Dr., Suite 21, Reston, VA 20190. Internet: nasm.arts-accredit.org

Data Bank

Education and Training: Long-term on-the-job training to master's degree

Starting Salaries: Varies tremendously

Average Earnings: $24,000–$51,000 (for music directors and composers only)

Total Jobs Held: 249,000

Job Outlook: Average increase

Annual Job Openings: 48,000

Related Jobs: Precision instrument and equipment repairers; actors, producers, and directors; announcers; dancers and choreographers

Personality Type: Artistic

Did You Know?

If you want to be a singer but can't find a job in Nashville or New York, consider the Caribbean. Cruise ships hire hundreds of entertainers each year for everything from lounge acts to big musical productions. It won't pay as much as a recording contract, but you get to travel to exotic places and the food is plentiful. And believe it or not, there are books, trade magazines, and Web sites dedicated to helping performers land jobs on cruise ships.

Announcers

At a Glance

Radio announcers (or disc jockeys) plan and perform radio programs. They may choose and play music, interview guests, and write program material. Television announcers and newscasters prepare and present the news, weather, and sports, although most specialize in one of these areas. When emergency situations arise, newscasters must be there to cover them. Show hosts may specialize in a certain area of interest, such as politics, personal finance, sports, or health. Most announcers help prepare the program's content, interview guests, and discuss issues with viewers, listeners, or the studio audience. Some announcers provide commentary for the audience during sporting events, at parades, and on other special occasions. Announcers may make promotional appearances and do remote broadcasts for their stations.

Data Bank

Education and Training: Moderate-term on-the-job training to associate degree

Starting Salaries: $13,000

Average Earnings: $17,000–$38,000

Total Jobs Held: 69,000

Job Outlook: Declining

Annual Job Openings: 10,000

Related Jobs: News analysts, reporters, and correspondents; interpreters and translators; actors, producers, and directors; musicians, singers, and related workers; broadcast and sound engineering technicians and radio operators; public-relations specialists; writers and editors

Personality Type: Artistic; Social

Did You Know?

There were several famous radio announcers before Rush Limbaugh and Howard Stern took to the air. Most notable was a man by the name of Robert Smith who became famous as a disc jockey in the 1960s and '70s for his gravelly voice and his signature howl. Taking the name "Wolfman Jack," Smith created an on-air persona that was known worldwide. He was also noted for playing whatever music he wanted, regardless of the ethnicity of the performer, which caused quite a bit of scandal in those racially turbulent decades.

Career in Focus: *Mobile Disc Jockey*

Some DJs announce and play music at clubs, dances, restaurants, weddings, private parties, and other special occasions. They generally have their own equipment, including a huge library of music, and they rent their services out on a job-by-job basis. At special events, they may act as an MC (Master of Ceremonies), keeping the guests informed about everything from the cutting of the cake at a wedding to the last call at the bar.

Where and When

Most announcers work in well-lighted, comfortable, soundproof studios. Most radio and television stations broadcast for 24 hours a day, so announcers can expect to work unusual schedules.

For More Information

* National Association of Broadcasters, 1771 N St. NW, Washington, DC 20036. Internet: www.nab.org

Broadcast and Sound Engineering Technicians and Radio Operators

At a Glance

Broadcast and sound engineering technicians and radio operators set up, operate, and maintain the electrical and electronic equipment involved in almost any radio or television broadcast, concert, musical recording, or movie. They operate, install, and repair microphones, TV cameras, digital recorders, projectors, monitors, mixing boards, and antennas. Many technicians also work in program production. The transition to digital recording, editing, and broadcasting has greatly changed this work, making it much easier for these operators and technicians to do their jobs, though it has forced them to learn more computer skills.

Career in Focus: *Sound Engineering Technician*

Sound engineering technicians operate machines and equipment to record, synchronize, mix, or reproduce music, voices, or sound effects in recording studios, sporting arenas, theater productions, or movie and video productions. More specifically, sound mixers or re-recording mixers produce soundtracks for movies or television programs. After filming or recording is complete, these workers may use a process called "dubbing" to insert sounds.

Where and When

This work is usually done indoors in comfortable environments. Those broadcasting news from locations outside the studio may have to work in all types of weather. Technicians may also be required to climb poles or towers and do heavy lifting. Evening, weekend, and holiday work is common because most stations are on the air most hours of the day, seven days a week. Technicians, especially those who work on motion pictures, may be required to travel extensively.

For More Information

* National Association of Broadcasters, 1771 N St. NW, Washington, DC 20036. Internet: www.nab.org
* Society of Broadcast Engineers, 9247 North Meridian St., Suite 305, Indianapolis, IN 46260. Internet: www.sbe.org
* InfoComm International, 11242 Waples Mill Rd., Suite 200, Fairfax, VA 22030. Internet: www.infocomm.org

Data Bank

Education and Training: Moderate-term on-the-job training to associate degree

Starting Salaries: $18,000

Average Earnings: $24,000–$47,000

Total Jobs Held: 95,000

Job Outlook: Average increase

Annual Job Openings: 11,000

Related Jobs: Engineering technicians; science technicians; electrical and electronics installers and repairers; computer support specialists and systems administrators; communications equipment operators

Personality Type: Conventional; Realistic

Did You Know?

Did you ever wonder how a moviemaker got a certain sound—maybe the hum of a spacecraft engine or the blast of a star exploding? The soundtrack in a movie is made by sound mixers, using everything from explosives to cabbage to corn flakes. Take the movie *Star Wars*. The sound of a TIE Fighter soaring by was actually just an altered elephant roar, and the sound of a laser blast is simply the bang of a hammer on an antenna tower wire.

Interpreters and Translators

At a Glance

Interpreters and translators convert spoken and written words from one language into another. They must thoroughly understand the subject in order to convert information from one language, known as the source language, into another, the target language. In addition, they must remain sensitive to the cultures associated with those languages. While interpreters often work into *and* from both languages, translators generally work only *into* their native language. For interpreters, strong research and analytical skills, mental dexterity, and a good memory are important. Translators, who convert written materials from one language into another, must have excellent writing and analytical ability, plus good editing skills. Interpreters and translators may specialize in one of several fields, including conference interpreters, travel guides, and literary translators.

Data Bank

Education and Training: Long-term on-the-job training

Starting Salaries: $20,000

Average Earnings: $27,000–$46,000

Total Jobs Held: 31,000

Job Outlook: Above-average increase

Annual Job Openings: 4,000

Related Jobs: Teachers, announcers, writers and editors, computer software engineers, court reporters, medical transcriptionists

Personality Type: Artistic

Did You Know?

One out of every five Americans speaks a language other than English at home. That's more than 50 million people. You can imagine the growing need for people who can translate and interpret between English and these other languages. In fact, many businesses and government agencies have an urgent need for translators to help them communicate with their customers both at home and abroad.

Career in Focus: *Sign Language Interpreter*

Sign language interpreters help people who are deaf or hard of hearing communicate with people who can hear. Sign language interpreters must be fluent in English and in American Sign Language (ASL), which combines signing, finger spelling, and specific body language. ASL has its own grammatical rules, sentence structure, and idioms. Thus sign language interpreting involves more than simply replacing a word of spoken English with a sign representing that word.

Where and When

Interpreters work in a variety of settings, such as hospitals, conference centers, and courtrooms. They are often required to travel to wherever their services are needed. Some work in a school setting or in call centers in urban areas. Translators often work in office settings or from their own home. Many interpreters and translators freelance.

For More Information

* American Translators Association, 225 Reinekers Ln., Suite 590, Alexandria, VA 22314. Internet: www.atanet.org

* The Translators and Interpreters Guild, 962 Wayne Ave., Suite 500, Silver Spring, MD 20910. Internet: www.ttig.org

* American Literary Translators Association, The University of Texas at Dallas, Box 830688 Mail Station JO51, Richardson, TX 75083-0688. Internet: www.literarytranslators.org

* Registry of Interpreters for the Deaf, 333 Commerce St., Alexandria, VA 22314. Internet: www.rid.org

News Analysts, Reporters, and Correspondents

At a Glance

News analysts, reporters, and correspondents gather information and write articles or deliver reports about local, state, national, and international events. News analysts—also called newscasters or news anchors—interpret and broadcast news received from various sources. News anchors present news stories and introduce videotaped news or live transmissions from on-the-scene reporters. Newscasters at large stations and networks usually specialize in a particular type of news, such as sports or weather. In covering a story, reporters investigate leads, look at documents, observe events at the scene, and interview people. Reporters take notes and may take photographs or shoot videos. Radio and television reporters often report "live" from the scene of crimes or disasters. Commentators or columnists interpret the news or offer opinions to readers, viewers, or listeners.

Career in Focus: *News Correspondent*

News correspondents report on news occurring in the U.S. and foreign cities where they are stationed. The job requires more than just a willingness to travel. Correspondents must be comfortable with other cultures and often speak more than one language. They report from dangerous locations and often risk their lives to get the story right. Covering everything from wars and political uprisings to fires and floods, correspondents are often in more danger than most other reporters and analysts.

Where and When

The work of news analysts, reporters, and correspondents is often hectic. Deadlines provide constant stress because broadcasts are sometimes aired with little or no time for preparation. Most work in large, noisy rooms. Working hours vary dramatically, and travel can be quite frequent.

For More Information

- National Association of Broadcasters, 1771 N St. NW, Washington, DC 20036. Internet: www.nab.org
- Dow Jones Newspaper Fund, Inc., P.O. Box 300, Princeton, NJ 08543-0300.
- Newspaper Guild, Research and Information Department, 501 Third St. NW, Suite 250, Washington, DC 20001.

Data Bank

Education and Training: Bachelor's degree

Starting Salaries: $19,000

Average Earnings: $24,000–$54,000

Total Jobs Held: 64,000

Job Outlook: Little change

Annual Job Openings: 5,000

Related Jobs: Writers and editors, public relations specialists, announcers, interpreters and translators

Personality Type: Artistic

Did You Know?

Though every precaution is taken to ensure their safety, war correspondents often find themselves in potentially deadly situations. The war in Iraq, begun in March of 2003, had claimed the lives of 131 journalists and media specialists three years later. That's more than the number of journalists killed in the entire Vietnam conflict.

Photographers

At a Glance

Photographers use cameras to record people, places, and events on film. Their images often paint a picture or tell a story. Commercial photographers take pictures of various subjects, such as buildings, models, merchandise, and landscapes. These photographs are then used in books, reports, advertisements, and catalogs. Portrait photographers work in studios, taking pictures of people for special occasions. Some specialize in weddings, religious ceremonies, or school photographs. Many work on location. News photographers—also called photojournalists—photograph newsworthy people, places, and sporting, political, and community events for newspapers, journals, magazines, or television. Today, most photographers use digital cameras instead of traditional film cameras.

Data Bank

Education and Training: Long-term on-the-job training

Starting Salaries: $15,000

Average Earnings: $18,000–$37,000

Total Jobs Held: 129,000

Job Outlook: Average increase

Annual Job Openings: 23,000

Related Jobs: Architects, except landscape and naval; artists and related workers; commercial and industrial designers; fashion designers; graphic designers; news analysts, reporters, and correspondents; television, video, and motion picture camera operators and editors

Personality Type: Artistic

Did You Know?

The Pulitzer Prize is the most distinguished award in journalism. In addition to awards for reporting, commentary, and even cartoons, the Pulitzer committee gives two awards for photography: one for breaking-news photography and another for feature photography. Many of the most haunting and tragic images that help us to remember history have won the award.

Career in Focus: *Scientific Photographer*

Scientific photographers take pictures to illustrate or record scientific or medical phenomena. Their images are used for measurement or analysis or to accompany reports, articles, and other research. They use infrared, time-lapse, ultraviolet, and other kinds of specialized photography to take pictures that a normal camera can't. They might photograph a virus attacking a cell or the moons of Saturn. They typically possess additional knowledge in areas such as engineering, medicine, biology, or chemistry.

Where and When

Working conditions for photographers vary. Those employed by studios usually work a standard 40-hour week. On the flipside, photojournalists must be able to go to work on a moment's notice. News photographers especially can work in uncomfortable and dangerous surroundings. They also work under strict deadlines. Most photographers spend only a small portion of their time taking the photographs—more often they are developing or editing those pictures.

For More Information

* Professional Photographers of America, Inc., 229 Peachtree St. NE, Suite 2200, Atlanta, GA 30303.

* National Press Photographers Association, Inc., 3200 Croasdaile Dr., Suite 306, Durham, NC 27705. Internet: www.nppa.org

* American Society of Media Photographers, Inc., 150 North Second St., Philadelphia, PA 19106. Internet: www.asmp.org

Public Relations Specialists

At a Glance

Public relations specialists serve as advocates for businesses, nonprofit associations, universities, hospitals, and other organizations. They work to present a good public image of their clients. Their job is to spread the clients' good news far and wide and to put a positive "spin" on the bad news. Public relations specialists do more than "tell the organization's story." They must understand the attitudes and concerns of community, consumer, employee, and public interest groups and maintain cooperative relationships with them. They write press releases and speeches and set up "photo opportunities" of their clients doing good things.

Career in Focus: *Press Secretary*

In government, public relations specialists are also called press secretaries, information officers, public affairs specialists, or communication specialists. Their job is to keep the public informed about the activities of agencies and officials. For example, public affairs specialists in the U.S. Department of State keep the public informed of the government's positions on foreign issues. A press secretary for a member of Congress keeps potential voters aware of the representative's accomplishments (especially as elections get closer).

Where and When

Public relations specialists generally work a standard 40-hour workweek, but overtime is common, especially if there is an emergency or crisis. Public relations offices are busy places, and workers are commonly under pressure to meet deadlines, give speeches, and attend meetings.

For More Information

* Public Relations Society of America, Inc., 33 Maiden Lane, New York, NY 10038-5150. Internet: www.prsa.org
* International Association of Business Communicators, One Hallidie Plaza, Suite 600, San Francisco, CA 94102.

Data Bank

Education and Training: Bachelor's degree

Starting Salaries: $26,000

Average Earnings: $34,000–$62,000

Total Jobs Held: 188,000

Job Outlook: Above-average increase

Annual Job Openings: 38,000

Related Jobs: Advertising, marketing, promotions, public relations, and sales managers; demonstrators, product promoters, and models; news analysts, reporters, and correspondents; lawyers; market and survey researchers; sales representatives, wholesale and manufacturing

Personality Type: Enterprising

Did You Know?

When people are being skeptical, they might refer to a public relations specialist as a "spin doctor." The phrase originated in the 1980s and refers most often to government press secretaries and public affairs specialists, though it can apply to anyone in public relations who tries to give a persuasive slant to information. Though people disagree whether the origin of the phrase goes back to "spinning a yarn" or the "spin" you might put on a ball when playing pool, the idea is that the public doesn't get the whole truth—just the prettiest version of it.

Television, Video, and Motion Picture Camera Operators and Editors

At a Glance

Television, video, and motion picture camera operators produce images that tell a story, inform or entertain an audience, or record an event. Camera operators work behind the scenes on TV shows, documentaries, motion pictures, and industrial films. They shoot the film you see on screen, sometimes from high up on scaffolding or flat on the ground. Producing successful images requires choosing interesting material, selecting appropriate equipment, and applying a good eye and a steady hand to ensure smooth, natural movement of the camera. Film and video editors edit soundtracks, film, and video for the motion picture, cable, and television industries. Making commercial-quality movies and videos requires both creativity and technical expertise.

Data Bank

Education and Training: Moderate-term on-the-job training to bachelor's degree

Starting Salaries: $18,000

Average Earnings: $29,000–$64,000

Total Jobs Held: 48,000

Job Outlook: Average increase

Annual Job Openings: 7,000

Related Jobs: Artists and related workers, broadcast and sound engineering technicians and radio operators, photographers, graphic designers

Personality Type: Artistic

Did You Know?

Film editors are responsible for taking reels of footage and cutting the best parts together to make a story that audiences can enjoy in the span of an evening or afternoon. But that isn't always the case. Several movies have been produced that eclipse even the five-hour mark. According to the *Guinness Book of World Records*, the longest movie ever made is *The Cure for Insomnia*. At 87 hours long, it consists primarily of a poet reading his epic 5,000-page poem in its entirety. Whether the film needed a good editor is debatable, but it certainly needs an intermission or two.

Career in Focus: *Director of Photography*

The director of photography (also called a cinematographer) on a film set is responsible for planning and coordinating the actual filming of a motion picture. The DP, as they are called for short, determines the lighting requirements and other kinds of equipment needed, decides on the right camera angles, distance, and depth of focus, and then instructs camera operators during the filming process. The DP also views the film after processing in order to make any adjustments.

Where and When

Conditions for these workers vary considerably. Those employed by television and cable networks and advertising agencies usually work a standard 40-hour week, though production schedules may require them to work overtime. Those who work in the movie industry face long, irregular hours. They may have to travel extensively to film on location.

For More Information

* International Cinematographer's Guild, 80 Eighth Avenue, 14th Floor, New York, NY 10011.

* National Association of Broadcast Employees and Technicians, 501 Third Street, NW, 6th Floor, Washington, DC 20001. Internet: www.nabetcwa.org/

Writers and Editors

At a Glance

Writers write novels and nonfiction books, articles, movies, plays, poems, and ads. Nonfiction writers must establish their credibility through strong research and the use of appropriate sources. Freelance writers sell their work to publishers, manufacturing firms, public relations departments, or advertising agencies. Sometimes, they contract with publishers to write a book or an article. Editors choose the stories and books that publishing houses will print. Magazine editors choose articles for publication and assign stories to writers. They review, rewrite, and edit the work of writers, and may also do original writing themselves. Most writers and editors regularly use personal computers, desktop or electronic publishing systems, and scanners.

Career in Focus: *Technical Writer*

Technical writers put technical information into easily understandable language. They prepare operating and maintenance manuals, catalogs, parts lists, assembly instructions, sales promotion materials, and project proposals. They plan and edit technical materials and oversee the preparation of illustrations, photographs, diagrams, and charts. Many technical writers work directly with engineers and should have some knowledge of the product or process they are writing about.

Where and When

Environments range from offices to laboratories to noisy newsrooms. Many writers and editors work from home or on the road. Freelance writers and editors enjoy flexible hours and creative freedom, but are also usually working under deadlines and are often unsure where their next paycheck will come from. Due to these deadlines, overtime or evening and weekend hours are common. The extensive computer and keyboard work can cause back pain, eyestrain, and fatigue.

For More Information

* Society for Technical Communication, Inc., 901 N. Stuart St., Suite 904, Arlington, VA 22203. Internet: www.stc.org

Data Bank

Education and Training: Bachelor's degree

Starting Salaries: $26,000

Average Earnings: $36,000–$65,000

Total Jobs Held: 319,000

Job Outlook: Average increase

Annual Job Openings: 35,000

Related Jobs: News analysts, reporters, and correspondents; interpreters and translators; announcers; public relations specialists

Personality Type: Artistic

Did You Know?

One of America's all-time best-selling authors, Stephen King sold his first novel, *Carrie,* to the publishers at Doubleday for a $2,500 advance. The paperback rights were later sold for $400,000, proving that every writer needs to start somewhere.

Audiologists

At a Glance

Audiologists work with people who have hearing, balance, and other ear problems. They examine individuals of all ages and identify those with the symptoms of hearing loss and other problems using audiometers, computers, and other testing devices. They assess the nature and extent of the problems and help patients manage them. Treatment may include examining and cleaning the ear canal, fitting for hearing aids, and programming cochlear implants. In hearing clinics, audiologists may develop and carry out treatment programs. In other settings, audiologists may work with other health and education providers as part of a team.

Data Bank

Education and Training: Master's degree

Starting Salaries: $35,000

Average Earnings: $44,000–$66,000

Total Jobs Held: 10,000

Job Outlook: Average

Annual Job Openings: Less than 500

Related Jobs: Occupational therapists, optometrists, physical therapists, psychologists, recreational therapists, counselors, speech-language pathologists

Personality Type: Social

Did You Know?

One of the most common side effects of aging is hearing loss. In the United States, it's estimated that only 5 percent of children have some degree of hearing loss, but that it affects as much as 80 percent of adults over the age of 65. It also has been shown to affect men more frequently than women. Studies show that as people age, they particularly lose their ability to hear high-pitched noises, which many elderly husbands use as an excuse for not listening to their wives.

Career in Focus: *Clinic Director*

Directors of speech-and-hearing clinics oversee the daily operations of their programs. They consult with medical and professional staff of other departments to coordinate joint patient care. They conduct conferences and plan training programs to maintain the proficiency of their staff. They also decide whether to use new methods and equipment to meet patients' needs. They often set the work schedule for personnel, and may coordinate research projects to develop new approaches to therapy.

Where and When

Audiologists usually work in clean, comfortable surroundings. While the job is not physically demanding, it does require intense concentration. Most full-time audiologists work a 40-hour week, which may include some weekends and evenings to meet the needs of patients.

For More Information

* American Academy of Audiology, 11730 Plaza America Dr., Suite 300, Reston, VA 20190. Internet: www.audiology.org

* American Speech-Language-Hearing Association, 10801 Rockville Pike, Rockville, MD 20852. Internet: www.asha.org

* American Board of Audiology, 11730 Plaza America Dr., Suite 300, Reston, VA 20190. Internet: www.americanboardofaudiology.org

Chiropractors

At a Glance

Chiropractors help people who have problems with their muscles, nerves, or skeleton, especially the spine. Chiropractors believe that problems with these systems keep the body from functioning normally and lowers its resistance to disease. Like other medical professionals, they examine patients, order tests, and take X rays. Chiropractors provide natural health treatments and rely on the body's inherent healing abilities, without the use of drugs or surgery. They primarily treat patients by massaging or adjusting the spinal column. Some chiropractors use water, light, ultrasound, electric, acupuncture, and heat therapy. They may also apply supports such as straps and braces. Well over half of all chiropractors are self-employed.

Career in Focus: *Chiropractic Assistant*

Chiropractic assistants are involved in both patient and office management. They may interview new patients, teach them about treatments, perform exams, or take X rays. They also may be responsible for answering the phone and making appointments, handling billing, and keeping track of patient files. They generally do not treat patients, though those studying to become a licensed chiropractor can learn a great deal by being an assistant.

Where and When

Chiropractors work in clean, comfortable offices and generally work a standard 40-hour week. Solo practitioners set their own hours but may work evenings and weekends to accommodate patients. Like most health practitioners, chiropractors are on their feet for most of the day.

For More Information

* American Chiropractic Association, 1701 Clarendon Blvd., Arlington, VA 22209. Internet: www.acatoday.org

* International Chiropractors Association, 1110 North Glebe Rd., Suite 1000, Arlington, VA 22201. Internet: www.chiropractic.org

* Council on Chiropractic Education, 8049 North 85th Way, Scottsdale, AZ 85258-4321. Internet: www.cce-usa.org

* Federation of Chiropractic Licensing Boards, 5401 W. 10th St., Suite 101, Greeley, CO 80634-4400. Internet: www.fclb.org

Data Bank

Education and Training: Professional degree

Starting Salaries: $34,000

Average Earnings: $46,000–$103,000

Total Jobs Held: 53,000

Job Outlook: Above-average increase

Annual Job Openings: 4,000

Related Jobs: Athletic trainers, massage therapists, occupational therapists, physical therapists, physicians and surgeons, podiatrists, veterinarians

Personality Type: Investigative

Did You Know?

Headaches can result from poor posture, tension, or a misalignment of the spinal cord. Using massage, heat therapy, and realignment exercises and techniques, chiropractors can help people who suffer from persistent or chronic headaches. They also teach people how to prevent headaches in the first place. Whether the bill for your treatment gives you a new headache is a different story.

Dentists

At a Glance

Dentists remove decay, fill cavities, examine X rays, and straighten and repair teeth. They also perform corrective surgery on gums and supporting bones to treat gum diseases. Dentists extract teeth and make models and measurements for dentures to replace missing teeth. They provide instruction on diet, brushing, flossing, and other aspects of dental care. They also administer anesthetics and write prescriptions for antibiotics and other medications. Dentists use a variety of equipment, including drills, probes, forceps, brushes, and scalpels. They wear masks, gloves, and safety glasses to protect themselves and their patients from infectious diseases. Many are self-employed. Most are general practitioners, handling a variety of dental needs, though there are several specialties ranging from those who specialize in root canals to those who focus on replacing lost teeth.

Data Bank

Education and Training: Professional degree

Starting Salaries: $57,000

Average Earnings: $91,000–$146,000+

Total Jobs Held: 150,000

Job Outlook: Average increase

Annual Job Openings: 8,000

Related Jobs: Chiropractors, optometrists, physicians and surgeons, podiatrists, psychologists, veterinarians

Personality Type: Investigative

Did You Know?

Dentists have been practicing for nearly 7,000 years, although treatments have changed dramatically over the millennia. In ancient Babylon, for example, "dentists" used worms, prayers, and herbs to treat tooth decay. In the Middle Ages, dentists were considered the first surgeons—although about all they could do was remove teeth, which they did to treat nearly every condition you can think of, and without the use of anesthetics (unless brandy counts).

Career in Focus: *Orthodontist*

As children grow, their teeth may form improperly, which can cause problems later in life. That's when they need to see an orthodontist. Orthodontists are the largest group of dental specialists (and the ones most feared by kids). They specialize in straightening teeth by applying pressure to them with braces, space fillers, or retainers. Thankfully, technology has dramatically improved the appearance of such devices, making kids a little less afraid of braces (though parents still fear paying for them).

Where and When

Dentists work four or five days a week, though many work evenings and weekends to accommodate their patients' schedules. Most own their own business and work alone or with a small staff or a partner. They take every precaution to keep their work environment clean and safe.

For More Information

* American Dental Association, Commission on Dental Accreditation, 211 E. Chicago Ave., Chicago, IL 60611. Internet: www.ada.org

* American Dental Education Association, 1400 K St. NW, Suite 1100, Washington, DC 20005. Internet: www.adea.org

Dietitians and Nutritionists

At a Glance

Dietitians and nutritionists plan, prepare, and serve meals in clinics, schools, nursing homes, and hospitals. They help prevent and treat illnesses by teaching clients to eat properly. Some specialize in helping overweight or critically ill patients, or in caring for kidney or diabetic patients. In addition, clinical dietitians in nursing care facilities, small hospitals, or correctional facilities may manage the food service department. Some are self-employed and act as consultants. Increased public interest in nutrition has led to job opportunities in food manufacturing and marketing. In these areas, dietitians analyze foods, prepare literature for distribution, or report on issues such as nutritional content.

Career in Focus: *Community Dietitian*

Community dietitians counsel the public on nutritional practices designed to prevent disease and promote health. Working in places such as public health clinics, home health agencies, and health maintenance organizations, community dietitians evaluate individual needs, develop nutritional care plans, and instruct people on how to eat properly. Dietitians working in home health agencies also provide instruction on grocery shopping and food preparation to the elderly, individuals with special needs, and children.

Where and When

Dietitians and nutritionists generally work a regular 40-hour week, though about one in four works part-time. They usually work in clean, comfortable settings, though those involved directly in food preparation work in warm, busy kitchens. Most of them are on their feet for much of the workday.

For More Information

✳ The American Dietetic Association, 120 South Riverside Plaza, Suite 2000, Chicago, IL 60606-6995. Internet: www.eatright.org

Data Bank

Education and Training: Bachelor's degree

Starting Salaries: $28,000

Average Earnings: $37,000–$55,000

Total Jobs Held: 50,000

Job Outlook: Above-average increase

Annual Job Openings: 4,000

Related Jobs: Food service managers, registered nurses

Personality Type: Investigative

Did You Know?

According to the National Health and Nutrition Examination Survey, more than 60 percent of American adults are overweight, and more than 30 percent of them are obese. Obesity has become the number one risk factor for many diseases in the United States, including heart disease. Dietitians and nutritionists are on the frontlines battling this trend by educating Americans on how to eat healthy.

Occupational Therapists

At a Glance

Occupational therapists help individuals who have mental, physical, developmental, or emotional disabilities to become independent and productive in their work and daily life. Occupational therapists assist clients in performing activities of all types, ranging from using a computer to caring for daily needs such as dressing, cooking, and eating. They may help a patient learn to use a wheelchair or develop a new skill. They also help patients find jobs. They usually work in hospitals, schools, or rehab centers, and some provide home health care as well.

Data Bank

Education and Training: Master's degree

Starting Salaries: $37,000

Average Earnings: $48,000–$70,000

Total Jobs Held: 92,000

Job Outlook: Rapid increase

Annual Job Openings: 7,000

Related Jobs: Audiologists, chiropractors, physical therapists, recreational therapists, rehabilitation counselors, respiratory therapists, speech-language pathologists

Personality Type: Social

Did You Know?

Beginning in 2007, a master's degree or higher will be the minimum education requirement in order to be a licensed therapist. In addition to a master's degree, individuals must pass a national certification exam to become a registered occupational therapist.

Career in Focus: *School Occupational Therapist*

Occupational therapists may work exclusively with individuals in a particular age group or with particular disabilities. In schools, for example, therapists evaluate children's abilities, recommend and provide therapy, modify classroom equipment, and help children participate in school activities. A therapist may work with children individually, lead small groups in the classroom, consult with a teacher, or serve on a committee.

Where and When

Occupational therapists generally work a 40-hour week, though more than 25 percent of them work part-time. The work can be exhausting; therapists are on their feet much of the time, and some lifting and moving may be required.

For More Information

✳ American Occupational Therapy Association, 4720 Montgomery Lane, Bethesda, MD 20824-1220. Internet: www.aota.org

Optometrists

At a Glance

Optometrists examine people's eyes to diagnose vision problems and eye diseases. They prescribe glasses and contact lenses. They also prescribe drugs to treat some eye diseases. Optometrists often provide preoperative and postoperative care to cataract patients, as well as to patients who have had laser vision or other eye surgery. Some optometrists work especially with the elderly or children. Others develop ways to protect workers' eyes from on-the-job strain or injury. A few teach optometry, perform research, or do consulting.

Career in Focus:
Ophthalmologist

Ophthalmologists are physicians who perform eye surgery, as well as diagnose and treat eye diseases and injuries. Like optometrists, they also examine eyes and prescribe eyeglasses and contact lenses; however, the education requirements for becoming an ophthalmologist are more intense. For more information about the requirements and earnings for ophthalmologists and other physicians see the section on physicians and surgeons.

Where and When

Optometrists work in clean, comfortable offices and labs. Most work a 40-hour week, though many work weekends and evenings to meet the needs of their patients. Most are self-employed in their own private practice.

For More Information

* Association of Schools and Colleges of Optometry, 6110 Executive Blvd., Suite 510, Rockville, MD 20852. Internet: www.opted.org

* American Optometric Association, Educational Services, 243 North Lindbergh Blvd., St. Louis, MO 63141. Internet: www.aoanet.org

Data Bank

Education and Training: Professional degree

Starting Salaries: $42,000

Average Earnings: $64,000–$115,000

Total Jobs Held: 34,000

Job Outlook: Above-average increase

Annual Job Openings: 2,000

Related Jobs: Chiropractors, dentists, physicians and surgeons, podiatrists, psychologists, veterinarians

Personality Type: Investigative

Did You Know?

Famous American inventor Benjamin Franklin was both near-sighted and far-sighted. Tired of having to switch back and forth between two pairs of glasses, he invented bifocals in 1784. The top half of the lenses allowed him to see far away, and the bottom half allowed him to see up close. He soon became recognizable by his glasses alone, and many depictions of him show him with his invention perched on his nose.

Pharmacists

At a Glance

Pharmacists measure and sell medication prescribed by physicians and provide information to patients about the medications and their use. They also provide information about over-the-counter drugs and make recommendations to patients. Pharmacists must understand the use, effects, and composition of drugs in order to inform patients about reactions and possible side effects. Most pharmacists work in a community setting, such as a retail drugstore, or in a health-care facility, such as a hospital, nursing home, or mental health institution. Most pharmacists keep confidential records of patients' drug therapies to prevent harmful interactions. Pharmacists are responsible for the accuracy of every prescription that is filled, but they often rely upon pharmacy technicians and pharmacy aides to assist them in dispensing drugs.

Data Bank

Education and Training: Professional degree

Starting Salaries: $61,000

Average Earnings: $79,000–$103,000

Total Jobs Held: 230,000

Job Outlook: Above-average increase

Annual Job Openings: 16,000

Related Jobs: Pharmacy technicians, pharmacy aides, biological scientists, medical scientists, chemists and materials scientists, physicians and surgeons

Personality Type: Investigative

Did You Know?

Though statistics vary, current studies suggest that Americans fill more than 3.5 billion prescriptions per year, which is an average of 14 prescriptions per person. While this certainly provides added job security for pharmacists, it has led some physicians and policy makers to wonder if we aren't overmedicated as a society. It has also led some people to consider alternative cures to their ailments such as acupuncture or herbal medicines.

Career in Focus: *Geriatric Pharmacist*

Geriatric pharmacy is an area experiencing rapid job growth. These pharmacists specialize in administering drug regiments to the elderly in hospitals, nursing homes, assisted-living facilities, and home care settings. Because many of today's elderly are taking more than one prescription drug, these pharmacists must be particularly aware of possible drug interactions.

Where and When

Pharmacists work in clean, well-ventilated areas. Because many of the medications need to be kept sterile or are dangerous, pharmacists wear gloves and masks and use other special equipment. Some pharmacists may work extended hours, nights, or weekends, and they tend to spend a lot of time on their feet. About one in five works part-time.

For More Information

* American Association of Colleges of Pharmacy, 1426 Prince St., Alexandria, VA 22314. Internet: www.aacp.org

* American Society of Health-System Pharmacists, 7272 Wisconsin Ave., Bethesda, MD 20814. Internet: www.ashp.org

* Academy of Managed Care Pharmacy, 100 North Pitt St., Suite 400, Alexandria, VA 22314. Internet: www.amcp.org

* American Pharmacists Association, 2215 Constitution Ave. NW, Washington, DC 20037-2985. Internet: www.aphanet.org

Physical Therapists

At a Glance

Physical therapists work with accident victims, stroke patients, and people with disabilities to restore function, improve mobility, and relieve pain. They also promote overall fitness and health. Treatment often includes exercise for patients who lack flexibility, strength, or endurance. Therapists may also use electricity, heat, or cold to relieve pain, reduce swelling, or increase flexibility. Therapists sometimes teach patients to use assistive devices, such as crutches, prostheses, and wheelchairs. They often show patients exercises to do at home to speed up their recovery.

Career in Focus: *Orthopedic Therapist*

While some physical therapists treat a wide range of ailments, others specialize in areas such as pediatrics, geriatrics, or neurology. One of the most common forms of physical therapy is orthopedic therapy. It is designed to help patients who have problems or limitations with their muscles, ligaments, tendons, and bones. This could include people with arthritis, those recovering from surgery or sports-related injuries, or people with spinal dysfunction that restricts their muscle control. Several hospitals and institutes across the country have programs specializing in orthopedic therapy.

Where and When

Physical therapists work in hospitals, clinics, and private offices. Some of them treat patients in their own homes. Most work a standard 40-hour week, though one in four works part-time. The job can be physically demanding as therapists must stoop, kneel, crouch, and stand for long periods, in addition to lifting patients and helping them move.

For More Information

✳ American Physical Therapy Association, 1111 North Fairfax St., Alexandria, VA 22314-1488. Internet: www.apta.org

Data Bank

Education and Training: Master's degree

Starting Salaries: $42,000

Average Earnings: $52,000–$75,000

Total Jobs Held: 155,000

Job Outlook: Rapid increase

Annual Job Openings: 13,000

Related Jobs: Audiologists, chiropractors, occupational therapists, recreational therapists, counselors, respiratory therapists, speech-language pathologists

Personality Type: Social

Did You Know?

You've probably heard of limb reattachment—where a hand, arm, foot, or leg that has been cut off is replaced—but have you ever heard of a limb transplant? This somewhat controversial procedure first began in 1998 and involves taking someone else's limb and attaching it to the patient. Such procedures are dangerous, as the body may reject the new tissue, which can cause a serious infection. In order to avoid rejection, patients with transplants of any kind must take drugs to suppress a reaction. Those with transplanted limbs must also undergo rigorous physical therapy as well, often for several hours every day.

Physician Assistants

At a Glance

Physician assistants always work under the supervision of a physician. They handle many of the routine but time-consuming tasks physicians do, such as taking medical records, examining patients, ordering X rays and tests, and making diagnoses. They also treat minor injuries by suturing, splinting, and casting. In most states, physician assistants may prescribe medications. PAs also may order medical supplies or equipment and supervise other technicians and assistants. PAs may be the principal care providers in rural or inner city clinics, where a physician is present for only one or two days each week.

Data Bank

Education and Training: Bachelor's degree

Starting Salaries: $37,000

Average Earnings: $59,000–$87,000

Total Jobs Held: 62,000

Job Outlook: Rapid increase

Annual Job Openings: 10,000

Related Jobs: Audiologists, occupational therapists, physical therapists, registered nurses, speech-language pathologists

Personality Type: Investigative

Did You Know?

According to CNN's *Money Magazine*, physician assistant is one of the fastest-growing fields in the nation. Combined with the relatively high pay, this makes it one of the more desirable jobs around. The rising cost of health care is forcing hospitals and clinics to use more and more PAs in order to cut down the cost of hiring full-fledged physicians. Plus the education requirements for becoming a PA are not nearly as rigorous as the requirements to be a doctor.

Career in Focus: *Surgical Physician Assistant*

Physician assistants specializing in surgery provide preoperative and postoperative care and may work as first or second assistants during major surgery, helping with the prepping, positioning, and transportation of the patient as well. They are often responsible for providing labs and records to the surgeon, managing patient issues during preop, and organizing follow-up care. These are in addition to the duties they share with other physician assistants.

Where and When

Physician assistants spend much of their time standing or walking, and their schedules vary considerable. Those working at hospitals may work weekends, nights, or early mornings and may also be on call. Most physician assistants in clinics usually work a 40-hour week.

For More Information

* American Academy of Physician Assistants Information Center, 950 North Washington St., Alexandria, VA 22314-1552. Internet: www.aapa.org

* National Commission on Certification of Physician Assistants, Inc., 12000 Findley Rd., Suite 200, Duluth, GA 30097. Internet: www.nccpa.net

Physicians and Surgeons

At a Glance

Physicians help people who are sick or have been hurt. They examine patients, perform tests, diagnose illnesses, prescribe and administer treatments, and teach people about health care. Family and general practitioners are often the first point of contact for people seeking health care. Acting as the traditional family doctor, they treat a wide range of ailments and injuries. General internists diagnose and provide treatment for diseases and injuries of internal organs such as the stomach or liver. General pediatricians are concerned with the health of infants, children, and teenagers. Obstetricians and gynecologists focus on women's health. They also provide care related to pregnancy and the reproductive system. Psychiatrists assess and treat mental illnesses through a combination of therapy, hospitalization, and medication. Surgeons perform operations on patients with life-threatening illness and injuries. Most physicians work in hospitals, clinics, and private practice.

Career in Focus:
Anesthesiologist

Anesthesiologists focus on the care of surgical patients and pain relief. Anesthesiologists are responsible for maintaining the patient's heart rate, body temperature, blood pressure, and breathing throughout surgery, while at the same time administering medications for pain. They often work outside of the operating room as well, providing pain relief in the intensive care unit, during labor and delivery, and for those who suffer from chronic pain.

Where and When

Many physicians work in small private offices or clinics, often assisted by a staff. More and more physicians are practicing in groups or health care organizations as part of a team, which allows for more time off. Most physicians work long, irregular hours, and travel can be quite frequent.

For More Information

* Association of American Medical Colleges, Section for Student Services, 2450 N St. NW, Washington, DC 20037-1126. Internet: www.aamc.org

* American Association of Colleges of Osteopathic Medicine, 5550 Friendship Blvd., Suite 310, Chevy Chase, MD 20815-7231. Internet: www.aacom.org

* American Medical Association, 515 N. State St., Chicago, IL 60610. Internet: www.ama-assn.org

Data Bank

Education and Training: Professional degree

Starting Salaries: $67,000

Average Earnings: $80,000–$146,000+

Total Jobs Held: 4,536,000

Job Outlook: Above-average increase

Annual Job Openings: 41,000

Related Jobs: Chiropractors, dentists, optometrists, physician assistants, podiatrists, registered nurses, veterinarians

Personality Type: Investigative

Did You Know?

One-third of full-time physicians worked 60 or more hours per week in 2004, and only 8 percent worked part-time. Physicians have been known to work long shifts and go for 20 hours or more without sleep. They are often on call as well, making a doctor's workweek one of the most demanding of any job on the market.

Podiatrists

At a Glance

Podiatrists diagnose and treat diseases and injuries of the foot and lower leg. They may treat corns, calluses, ingrown toenails, bunions, heel spurs, and arch problems. They also treat ankle and foot injuries, deformities, and infections. They take care of foot problems caused by diseases such as diabetes or arthritis. They prescribe medications, set fractures, perform surgery, and order physical therapy. They also fit for corrective shoe inserts, make plaster casts, and design custom-made shoes.

Data Bank

Education and Training: Professional degree

Starting Salaries: $42,000

Average Earnings: $67,000–$146,000+

Total Jobs Held: 10,000

Job Outlook: Average increase

Annual Job Openings: 1,000

Related Jobs: Athletic trainers, chiropractors, massage therapists, occupational therapists, physical therapists, physicians and surgeons

Personality Type: Social

Did You Know?

The human foot is a complex structure. It contains 26 bones plus muscles, nerves, ligaments, and blood vessels. The 52 total bones in the feet make up about one-fourth of all the bones in the human body. As people become more physically active across all age groups, openings for podiatrists will continue to grow. (Although you still have to be willing to handle other people's feet all day, which not everybody is up for.)

Career in Focus: *Orthotic Practitioner*

These certified specialists examine patients and assess their needs for orthotics—mechanical devices designed to help control or correct limb movements. They examine patients, decide what kind of devices are necessary, fit and adjust the devices, and instruct patients on their use. Because many foot problems are cured by inserts and special shoes, orthotic practitioners spend much of their time doing the work of podiatrists.

Where and When

Podiatrists spend most of their time in their own offices, though they may also visit patients in nursing homes or perform surgery at hospitals. Those who work in private practice set their own hours, but still may work evenings and weekends to accommodate patients.

For More Information

* American Podiatric Medical Association, 9312 Old Georgetown Rd., Bethesda, MD 20814-1621. Internet: www.apma.org

* American Association of Colleges of Podiatric Medicine, 15850 Crabbs Branch Way, Suite 320, Rockville, MD 20855-2622. Internet: www.aacpm.org

Radiation Therapists

At a Glance

Radiation therapists use machines to administer radiation treatment to cancer patients. The machines, called linear accelerators, project high-energy X rays that shrink and sometimes destroy cancerous cells. Therapists both advise patients and perform the treatment. Because many patients are under stress, it is important for the therapist to maintain a positive attitude and provide emotional support. Treatment can take anywhere from 10 to 30 minutes and is usually administered once a day, five days a week, for a period of several weeks. Radiation therapists most often work in hospitals and cancer treatment centers.

Career in Focus: *Dosimetrist*

A dosimetrist is a technician who calculates the amount of radiation that will be needed for treating each patient. The process involves complex mathematical calculations. They often prepare the treatment devices and work closely with the radiation oncologist (the physician) and the radiation therapist to ensure that the patient is getting just the right amount of treatment. After each session, the dosimetrist reviews records to ensure that the treatment plan is working and keep unwanted side effects to a minimum.

Where and When

Radiation therapists work in clean, well-ventilated environments, and great care is taken to limit their exposure to dangerous levels of radiation. They work on their feet most of the time, and may be required to do considerable lifting and maneuvering in order to get patients on and off treatment tables. Unlike other medical professionals, therapists generally only work a 40-hour week, mostly during the day.

For More Information

* American Registry of Radiologic Technologists, 1255 Northland Dr., St. Paul, MN 55120-1155. Internet: www.arrt.org/web

* American Society of Radiologic Technologists, 15000 Central Ave., SE, Albuquerque, NM 87123-3917. Internet: www.asrt.org

Data Bank

Education and Training: Associate degree

Starting Salaries: $39,000

Average Earnings: $51,000–$74,000

Total Jobs Held: 15,000

Job Outlook: Above-average increase

Annual Job Openings: 1,000

Related Jobs: Radiation technologists and technicians, diagnostic medical sonographers, nuclear medicine technicians, dental hygienists, respiratory therapists, registered nurses, physicians and surgeons.

Personality Type: Social

Did You Know?

Cancer is the cause of death for nearly 500,000 people per year and more than a million new cases are discovered each year, according to the American Cancer Society. Yet most cancers are preventable with exercise and a healthy diet, not to mention routine checkups. And, of course, it pays not to smoke, as a third of cancer cases are the result of tobacco use.

Recreational Therapists

At a Glance

Recreational therapists help people with disabilities or illnesses improve their health and well-being. They teach patients games, arts and crafts, dance, music, and sports activities and take them on community outings. These activities help patients regain skills they've lost because of illness or injury, and also improve their state of mind. More specifically, recreational therapy helps individuals reduce depression, stress, and anxiety. It also helps them recover basic motor functioning and reasoning abilities. Recreational therapy helps people build confidence so that they can enjoy greater independence. In addition, therapists teach people how to use community resources. They work closely with medical staff in hospitals and nursing homes, and are careful to document each patient's progress.

Data Bank

Education and Training: Bachelor's degree

Starting Salaries: $20,000

Average Earnings: $26,000–$43,000

Total Jobs Held: 24,000

Job Outlook: Little change

Annual Job Openings: 3,000

Related Jobs: Occupational therapists, physical therapists, recreation workers, rehabilitation counselors

Personality Type: Social

Did You Know?

Individuals in nursing homes account for less than ten percent of the total population over the age of 65. The majority of retirees will spend the rest of their lives in their own homes (or their Florida condos). Yet many of them will still take advantage of some of the services recreational therapists offer through community outreach programs.

Career in Focus: *Community-Based Recreational Therapist*

Community-based recreational therapists may work in park and recreation departments, special-education programs for school districts, or programs for older adults and people with disabilities. In these programs, therapists use activities and outings to develop specific skills, while providing opportunities for exercise, creativity, and fun.

Where and When

Recreational therapists work primarily in special activity rooms, though they spend some time in offices planning activities and doing paperwork. They may be required to travel locally, and often accompany their clients to public areas such as swimming pools and theaters. Therapists often lift and carry heavy equipment, and can lead recreational activities that require physical exercise. They sometimes work evenings, weekends, and holidays.

For More Information

* American Therapeutic Recreation Association, 1414 Prince St., Suite 204, Alexandria, VA 22314-2853. Internet: www.atra-tr.org

* National Therapeutic Recreation Society, 22377 Belmont Ridge Rd., Ashburn, VA 20148-4501. Internet: www.nrpa.org

* National Council for Therapeutic Recreation Certification, 7 Elmwood Dr., New City, NY 10956. Internet: www.nctrc.org

Registered Nurses

At a Glance

Registered nurses (RNs) care for the sick and injured and help people stay healthy. In clinics, hospitals, and nursing homes, they provide much of the day-to-day care for patients. Under a doctor's supervision, they take patient histories, help perform tests, give treatments and medications, and help with patient follow-up and rehabilitation. RNs teach patients and their families how to manage their illness or injury, including post-treatment home care needs, diet and exercise programs, and self-administration of medication. RNs also might run general health screening or immunization clinics, blood drives, and public seminars on health issues.

Career in Focus: *Nurse Practitioner*

Most RNs work as staff nurses, providing critical health-care services along with physicians and surgeons. However, some RNs choose to become nurse practitioners, who work independently or in collaboration with physicians. Nurse practitioners provide basic health care to patients and increasingly serve as primary care providers as well. The most common areas of specialty for nurse practitioners include family practice, adult practice, women's health, and pediatrics. In most states, nurse practitioners can prescribe medications.

Where and When

Registered nurses have demanding jobs. They may spend considerable time walking and standing, and they are often required to work nights, weekends, and holidays (in addition to being on call). Nurses also confront health hazards because of the conditions they treat and the equipment they use, though strict guidelines help guard against potential dangers.

For More Information

⁕ National League for Nursing, 61 Broadway, New York, NY 10006. Internet: www.nln.org

⁕ American Association of Colleges of Nursing, 1 Dupont Circle NW, Suite 530, Washington, DC 20036. Internet: www.aacn.nche.edu

⁕ American Nurses Association, 8515 Georgia Ave., Suite 400, Silver Spring, MD 20910. Internet: nursingworld.org

⁕ National Council of State Boards of Nursing, 111 E. Wacker Dr., Suite 2900, Chicago, IL 60611. Internet: www.ncsbn.org

Data Bank

Education and Training: Associate degree

Starting Salaries: $37,000

Average Earnings: $46,000–$67,000

Total Jobs Held: 2,394,000

Job Outlook: Rapid increase

Annual Job Openings: 229,000

Related Jobs: Emergency medical technicians and paramedics; licensed practical and licensed vocational nurses; massage therapists; medical and health services managers; nursing, psychiatric, and home health aides; occupational therapists; physical therapists; physician assistants; respiratory therapists; social workers

Personality Type: Social

Did You Know?

Nurses save lives. Though this might seem obvious, studies have been done to show the effect that nurses have on overall patient care. According to several studies, hospitals with more registered nurses have lower death rates following surgeries than those with fewer nurses. That's because it's often a nurse who notices whether a patient has a bad reaction to a drug, complications from surgery, or other problems. After all, nurses are the medical professionals that patients are in contact with most.

Respiratory Therapists

At a Glance

Respiratory therapists evaluate, treat, and care for patients with breathing problems, from premature babies to heart attack victims. They perform tests, connect patients to machines that help them breathe, and teach patients how to use these machines at home. Respiratory therapists provide temporary relief to patients with chronic asthma or emphysema. They also provide emergency care to patients who are victims of a heart attack, stroke, drowning, or shock. Therapists may also help in surgery by removing mucus from a patient's lungs so that he or she can breathe more easily. In some hospitals, therapists perform tasks that fall outside their traditional role, such as disease prevention, case management, and polysomnography—the diagnosis of breathing disorders during sleep.

Data Bank

Education and Training: Vocational/technical training to associate degree

Starting Salaries: $31,000

Average Earnings: $38,000–$52,000

Total Jobs Held: 119,000

Job Outlook: Above-average increase

Annual Job Openings: 9,000

Related Jobs: Registered nurses, occupational therapists, physical therapists, radiation therapists

Personality Type: Investigative

Did You Know?

While we don't recommend going without it for any length of time, it's true that too much oxygen can be harmful. Though it is rare, pulmonary oxygen toxicity occurs when an individual takes in too much oxygen. The lungs can begin to bleed internally and then thicken and scar, sometimes causing irreversible damage. Therefore, respiratory therapists are careful to ensure that a patient is getting just the right amount of oxygen.

Career in Focus: *Respiratory Therapy Technician*

Respiratory therapy technicians follow specific care procedures under the direction of respiratory therapists and physicians. In clinical practice, many of the daily duties of therapists and technicians overlap. Furthermore, the two have the same education and training requirements. However, therapists generally have greater responsibility than technicians. It is likely that an individual may start as a technician and work his or her way up to the level of therapist.

Where and When

Respiratory therapists generally work 40 hours per week, though those hours may include evenings, nights, and weekends. They often spend long periods standing and walking. In emergency situations they are required to be cool under pressure. Those employed in home health care must travel frequently.

For More Information

✴ American Association for Respiratory Care, 9425 N. MacArthur Blvd., Suite 100, Irving, TX 75063-4706. Internet: www.aarc.org

✴ Commission on Accreditation for Allied Health Education Programs, 35 East Wacker Dr., Suite 1970, Chicago, IL 60601. Internet: www.caahep.org

✴ National Board for Respiratory Care, Inc., 8310 Nieman Rd., Lenexa, KS 66214-1579. Internet: www.nbrc.org

Speech-Language Pathologists

At a Glance

Speech-language pathologists, also called speech therapists, help people who cannot produce speech sounds clearly and those with speech rhythm and fluency problems, such as stuttering. They help people with voice disorders or problems understanding language. They may work with people who wish to improve their communication skills or people with attention, memory, and problem-solving disorders. They may also work with people who have swallowing difficulties. Speech-language pathologists use assessments such as standardized tests and other special instruments to diagnose the nature of the problem. They then develop a plan of care tailored to each patient's needs. They may teach sign language to nonspeaking patients as well.

Career in Focus: *School Speech Therapist*

Most speech-language pathologists provide clinical services to individuals with communication problems. Speech-language pathologists in schools, however, also collaborate with teachers, interpreters, other school personnel, and parents to develop and run programs, provide counseling, and support classroom activities. They may work with one particular student or several, helping them function normally in a regular classroom environment.

Where and When

Speech-language pathologists usually work in comfortable surroundings, in hospital rooms or classrooms, or in a client's home. The job requires intense concentration and can be emotionally demanding. Most pathologists work 40 hours per week, though one in five works part-time.

For More Information

* American Speech-Language-Hearing Association, 10801 Rockville Pike, Rockville, MD 20852. Internet: www.asha.org

Data Bank

Education and Training: Master's degree

Starting Salaries: $35,000

Average Earnings: $44,000–$69,000

Total Jobs Held: 96,000

Job Outlook: Average increase

Annual Job Openings: 5,000

Related Jobs: Audiologists, occupational therapists, optometrists, physical therapists, psychologists, recreational therapists

Personality Type: Social

Did You Know?

Researchers have found that people who stutter can often speak and sing more smoothly as part of a group, such as when reciting the Pledge of Allegiance. Scientists used this fact to invent a device that helps people who stutter. It looks like a small hearing aid that is worn in the ear. The aid makes it sound to the person like he or she is speaking in a group, so he or she can speak more fluently.

Veterinarians

At a Glance

Veterinarians care for pets, farm animals, zoo residents, and laboratory animals. They diagnose health problems, treat injuries, prescribe medicine, perform surgery, and vaccinate animals against diseases such as rabies. They also advise owners about animal feeding, behavior, and breeding. Some veterinarians use their skills to protect humans against diseases carried by animals and conduct clinical research on human and animal health problems. A small number of veterinarians work exclusively with large animals, mostly horses or cows. These veterinarians test for and vaccinate against diseases and consult with farm or ranch owners and managers regarding animal production, feeding, and housing issues. Veterinarians euthanize (put to sleep) animals when necessary.

Data Bank

Education and Training: Professional degree

Starting Salaries: $39,000

Average Earnings: $54,000–$91,000

Total Jobs Held: 61,000

Job Outlook: Average increase

Annual Job Openings: 8,000

Related Jobs: Chiropractors, dentists, optometrists, physicians and surgeons, podiatrists, biological scientists, medical scientists, animal care and service workers, veterinary technologists and technicians

Personality Type: Investigative

Did You Know?

Veterinarians contribute to human as well as animal health. They work with physicians and scientists researching ways to prevent and treat various human health problems. For example, veterinarians contributed greatly in conquering malaria and yellow fever, solved the mystery of botulism, produced a medicine used to treat people with heart disease, and developed surgical techniques.

Career in Focus: *Small-Animal Practitioner*

More than half of all clinical veterinarians are small-animal practitioners. They usually care for companion animals, such as dogs and cats, but they also treat birds, reptiles, rabbits, and other animals that can be kept as pets. Most work out of their own clinic and supervise a staff of assistants and technicians as well.

Where and When

Most veterinarians treat animals in private clinics or hospitals and work 50 hours or more per week. They may work nights and weekends. Those treating large animals travel to farms or ranches to see their patients. The work environment can be noisy, and veterinarians run the risk of being bitten, kicked, or scratched by hurt or frightened animals.

For More Information

* American Veterinary Medical Association, 1931 N. Meacham Rd., Suite 100, Schaumburg, IL 60173-4360. Internet: www.avma.org

* Association of American Veterinary Medical Colleges, 1101 Vermont Ave. NW, Suite 710, Washington, DC 20005. Internet: www.aavmc.org

Athletic Trainers

At a Glance

Athletic trainers specialize in the prevention and treatment of injuries to the muscular and skeletal system. These injuries are most often caused by playing sports, training, or exercising. Athletic trainers are often the first heath-care providers on the scene when these injuries occur, and therefore must provide immediate care when needed. They are also heavily involved in the rehabilitation process. Athletic trainers work under the supervision of a licensed physician and in cooperation with other health-care providers. Athletic trainers also may have administrative responsibilities. These may include regular meetings with an athletic director to deal with budgets, purchasing, policy implementation, and other business-related issues.

Career in Focus: *School Athletic Trainer*

Athletic trainers are as much teachers as they are treaters. Their first mission is to prevent injuries from ever occurring. Those who are more interested in the teaching aspect, however, should consider working as an athletic trainer in a high school or college. They will not only have the opportunity to assist athletes at all levels, but are often given the chance to teach classes in health, physical education, or a sport or activity that interests them.

Where and When

Athletic trainers work both indoors and outdoors, and their job may require extensive exercise. Schedules vary dramatically, especially for those who work and travel with college and professional sports teams. Those in high school settings who also teach can expect to work 50 to 60 hours per week or more.

For More Information

* National Athletic Trainers' Association, 2952 Stemmons Freeway, Dallas, TX 75247. Internet: www.nata.org

* Board of Certification, Inc., 4223 South 143rd Circle, Omaha, NE 68137. Internet: www.bocatc.org

Data Bank

Education and Training: Bachelor's degree

Starting Salaries: $21,000

Average Earnings: $27,000–$43,000

Total Jobs Held: 15,000

Job Outlook: Rapid increase

Annual Job Openings: 1,000

Related Jobs: Emergency medical technicians and paramedics, physical therapists, physician assistants, registered nurses, licensed practical and licensed vocational nurses, recreational therapists, occupational therapists, respiratory therapists

Personality Type: Social

Did You Know?

What is the most dangerous sport? According to some studies, the two most dangerous sports are football and cheerleading. People who are surveyed often say rugby. Statistics show that more injuries are caused from bicycling and basketball. And this doesn't count extreme sports like cave diving or BASE jumping off of a skyscraper. All sports provide some degree of risk, and as our culture becomes more active, that risk only increases. Good news—in a way—for athletic trainers looking for job security.

Cardiovascular Technologists and Technicians

At a Glance

These workers help doctors diagnose and treat heart and blood vessel diseases. They administer a variety of tests, check the results, prepare patients for procedures, and sometimes assist in surgery. Those specializing in surgical procedures are called cardiology technologists. They help physicians guide a small tube, or catheter, through a patient's artery to determine whether a problem exists and to help treat it. Cardiovascular technologists who specialize in echocardiography run tests using ultrasound. Those who use ultrasound to examine the heart chambers, valves, and vessels are referred to as cardiac sonographers. Vascular technologists help physicians diagnosis disorders affecting circulation. All of these workers may also schedule patient appointments, type doctors' reports, keep patient files, and care for equipment.

Data Bank

Education and Training: Associate degree

Starting Salaries: $22,000

Average Earnings: $29,000–$52,000

Total Jobs Held: 45,000

Job Outlook: Rapid increase

Annual Job Openings: 5,000

Related Jobs: Diagnostic medical sonographers, nuclear medicine technologists, radiation therapists, radiologic technologists and technicians, respiratory therapists

Personality Type: Investigative

Did You Know?

One out of every five deaths in the United States is caused by coronary heart disease (CHD), and Americans only continue to increase their risk. The good news is that CHD is mostly preventable with a balanced diet and daily exercise. Though it is a prescription that has been repeated over and over in television ads and news reports, the statistics show that people still aren't hearing it. As a result, we are unfortunately keeping cardiovascular technologists busier than ever.

Career in Focus: *Cardiographic Technician*

Cardiovascular technicians who specialize in electrocardiograms (EKGs) and stress testing are known as cardiographic technicians, or EKG technicians. An EKG traces electrical impulses transmitted by the heart. By examining these readings, doctors and specialists can determine whether the person has a heart condition and decide on a treatment. Stress tests involve monitoring the patient's EKG as they exercise, usually walking on a treadmill at increasing speeds, to examine the effects of physical activity on the heart.

Where and When

Technologists and technicians usually work a standard 40-hour week, though it might include evenings and weekends. They may also be on call. They spend a lot of time walking or standing, and some heavy lifting may be involved. Because many cardiovascular problems are life-threatening, the job can be stressful and emotionally draining.

For More Information

* Alliance of Cardiovascular Professionals, Thalia Landing Offices, Bldg. 2, 4356 Bonney Rd., Suite 103, Virginia Beach, VA 23452-1200. Internet: www.acp-online.org

* Society for Vascular Ultrasound, 4601 Presidents Dr., Suite 260, Lanham, MD 20706-4381. Internet: www.svunet.org

* American Society of Echocardiography, 1500 Sunday Dr., Suite 102, Raleigh, NC 27607. Internet: www.asecho.org

Clinical Laboratory Technologists and Technicians

At a Glance

These workers perform medical tests to help detect, diagnose, and treat diseases. They match blood types, test for drug levels, and look for abnormal cells, bacteria, and parasites. They analyze test results of body fluids and cells and send the results to doctors to aid in diagnoses and treatment. They use automated equipment and computerized instruments capable of performing a number of tests at the same time. They also use microscopes, cell counters, and other sophisticated laboratory equipment.

Career in Focus: *Blood Bank Technologist*

Blood bank technologists collect, type, and prepare blood and its components for transfusions. They are responsible for finding any abnormalities in the blood that might cause problems in a transfusion. They are also involved in selecting blood donors, performing screening, preparing blood for storage, and confirming tests to ensure patient safety. They may work at a hospital or a blood bank.

Where and When

In large hospitals or labs, these individuals may work day, evening, or night shifts, including weekends and holidays. In some facilities, laboratory personnel are on call several nights per week in case of emergency. Clinical laboratory personnel are trained to work with dangerous samples and infectious diseases. They follow strict procedures for keeping their environment sterile and safe.

For More Information

* National Accrediting Agency for Clinical Laboratory Sciences, 8410 W. Bryn Mawr Ave., Suite 670, Chicago, IL 60631. Internet: www.naacls.org

* American Association of Bioanalysts, Board of Registry, 906 Olive St., Suite 1200, St. Louis, MO 63101-1434. Internet: www.aab.org

* American Society for Clinical Pathology, 2100 West Harrison St., Chicago, IL 60612. Internet: www.ascp.org

* National Credentialing Agency for Laboratory Personnel, P.O. Box 15945, Lenexa, KS 66285. Internet: www.nca-info.org

* American Society for Clinical Laboratory Science, 6701 Democracy Blvd., Suite 300, Bethesda, MD 20817. Internet: www.ascls.org

Data Bank

Education and Training: Associate degree to bachelor's degree

Starting Salaries: $27,000

Average Earnings: $33,000–$48,000

Total Jobs Held: 303,000

Job Outlook: Above-average increase

Annual Job Openings: 28,000

Related Jobs: Chemists and materials scientists, science technicians, veterinary technologists and technicians

Personality Type: Investigative; Realistic

Did You Know?

Though different people are credited with inventing the microscope (some say it was Galileo, others say Zacharias Janssen), most agree that it was Anton van Leeuwenhoek who first used it for biological study, looking at everything from bacteria to blood. But while his single-lens microscopes magnified up to 270 times, current electron microscopes can maginify up to two million times. Take that, ancient scientists.

Dental Hygienists

At a Glance

Dental hygienists examine patients' teeth and gums to find disease. They help dentists by cleaning patients' teeth, taking and developing X rays, and applying fluoride treatments and sealants. They teach patients how to brush and floss correctly. Hygienists sometimes work chairside with the dentist during treatment. Dental hygienists use hand and rotary instruments and ultrasonics to clean and polish teeth, syringes to administer local anesthetics, and models of teeth to explain oral hygiene.

Data Bank

Education and Training: Associate degree

Starting Salaries: $38,000

Average Earnings: $49,000–$71,000

Total Jobs Held: 158,000

Job Outlook: Rapid increase

Annual Job Openings: 17,000

Related Jobs: Dental assistants, medical assistants, occupational therapist assistants and aides, physical therapist assistants and aides, physician assistants, registered nurses

Personality Type: Social

Did You Know?

Ancient Egyptians had their own toothpaste made of ox hooves and burnt eggshells, among other things. Later toothpastes used oyster shells, charcoal, and honey. The 19th century saw common additions of brick, chalk, and salt. It wasn't until the 20th century that the fluoride toothpaste we use today was invented. As for flavors, one can only imagine what ox hooves taste like, though ancient peoples were known to chew on mint leaves to freshen their breath at least.

Career in Focus: *Advanced Dental Hygienist*

Even though the job titles are the same, state regulations that define what dental hygienists can do vary considerably. As a result, some dental hygienists have a wider variety of tasks to perform than others, and thus more responsibility. In some states, for example, hygienists administer anesthetics; place and carve filling materials, temporary fillings, and periodontal dressings; remove sutures; and smooth and polish metal restorations. For lack of a better title, we'll just call these workers *advanced* dental hygienists.

Where and When

Dental hygienists generally have flexible schedules, though some may work evenings and weekends. They work in clean, well-lighted offices. Important safety precautions are taken to ensure their safety, including the use of surgical masks, gloves, and safety glasses.

For More Information

* Division of Education, American Dental Hygienists Association, 444 N. Michigan Ave., Suite 3400, Chicago, IL 60611. Internet: www.adha.org

* Commission on Dental Accreditation, American Dental Association, 211 E. Chicago Ave., Suite 1814, Chicago, IL 60611. Internet: www.ada.org

Diagnostic Medical Sonographers

At a Glance

Sonography, or ultrasonography, is the use of sound waves to generate an image for diagnosing various medical conditions. Sonographers use special machines called transducers to look for signs of unhealthy tissue. They take measurements and analyze the results to prepare reports for physicians. Doctors use these results to find tumors, check growing fetuses, and make medical decisions. In addition to working directly with patients, diagnostic medical sonographers keep patient records and adjust and maintain equipment. They also may prepare work schedules, evaluate equipment purchases, or manage an entire diagnostic imaging department.

Career in Focus: *Obstetric and Gynecologic Sonographer*

Obstetric and gynecologic sonographers specialize in the study of the female reproductive system. Included in this field is one of the more well-known uses of sonography: examining the fetus of a pregnant woman to track the baby's growth and health. Advances in sonography have helped doctors improve the quality of prenatal care dramatically, including treating a baby for illnesses and medical problems before it is even born.

Where and When

Sonographers work about 40 hours per week, though they may work evenings and weekends and may also be on call. A growing number of sonographers work as contract employees and may have to travel to different hospitals. Sonographers are on their feet for long periods and may have to lift and turn patients.

For More Information

* Society of Diagnostic Medical Sonography, 2745 Dallas Pkwy., Suite 350, Plano, TX 75093-8730. Internet: www.sdms.org

* American Registry for Diagnostic Medical Sonography, 51 Monroe St., Plaza East 1, Rockville, MD 20850-2400. Internet: www.ardms.org

* Joint Review Committee on Education in Diagnostic Medical Sonography, 2025 Woodlane Dr., St. Paul, MN 55125-2998. Internet: www.jrcdms.org

Data Bank

Education and Training: Associate degree

Starting Salaries: $38,000

Average Earnings: $47,000–$64,000

Total Jobs Held: 42,000

Job Outlook: Rapid increase

Annual Job Openings: 5,000

Related Jobs: Cardiovascular technologists and technicians, clinical laboratory technologists and technicians, nuclear medicine technologists, radiologic technologists and technicians, respiratory therapists

Personality Type: No data available

Did You Know?

What makes ultrasound ultra? Ultrasound is actually any sound whose frequency is high enough to be outside the range of human hearing (over 20,000 Hz). But just because we can't hear it doesn't mean it goes unheard. Animals with sensitive hearing, such as dogs, mice, dolphins, and bats, can hear ultrasounds. So unless you want to confuse it, don't take your pet poodle to an ultrasound appointment with you.

Emergency Medical Technicians and Paramedics

At a Glance

Automobile accidents, heart attacks, drownings, childbirth, and gunshot wounds all require immediate medical attention. Emergency medical technicians (EMTs) and paramedics drive ambulances and provide emergency medical care on the scene and on the way to the hospital. In an emergency, EMTs and paramedics typically are dispatched by a 911 operator and often work with police and fire department personnel. They give appropriate emergency care and, when necessary, transport the patient. Usually, one EMT or paramedic drives while the other monitors the patient's vital signs and gives additional care as needed. Some EMTs work as part of the flight crew of helicopters that transport critically ill or injured patients to hospital trauma centers.

Data Bank

Education and Training: Vocational/technical training

Starting Salaries: $16,000

Average Earnings: $20,000–$34,000

Total Jobs Held: 192,000

Job Outlook: Rapid increase

Annual Job Openings: 21,000

Related Jobs: Air traffic controllers, firefighting occupations, physician assistants, police and detectives, registered nurses

Personality Type: Social

Did You Know?

Though its origins may date back to Napoleon and horse-drawn carts filled with wounded soldiers, the Emergency Medical Service (EMS) system as we know it today is relatively new. The movement for it began in the 1960s and gained wider acceptance in the decades to come (yes, there were people opposed to the idea of an emergency medical service system). Before the 1960s, patients were often transported in vehicles owned and operated by mortuary services rather than ambulances. Modified station wagons were a popular choice.

Career in Focus: *Paramedic*

Beyond the general duties discussed above, the specific responsibilities of EMTs depend on their level of qualification and training. The National Registry of Emergency Medical Technicians registers emergency medical service providers at four levels. The highest level, the EMT-Paramedics (EMT-4), provide the most extensive prehospital care. In addition to giving intravenous fluids, using defibrillators to give lifesaving shocks to a stopped heart, and opening a patient's airway, paramedics may also administer drugs, interpret electrocardiograms (EKGs), and use monitors and other complex equipment.

Where and When

EMTs and paramedics work both indoors and out, in all types of weather. They do considerable kneeling, bending, and heavy lifting, and they may be exposed to diseases, as well as violence from patients. Because many of the situations are life or death, the work can be stressful and challenging. Many work more than 50 hours per week, and some of them are on call for extended periods.

For More Information

* National Association of Emergency Medical Technicians, P.O. Box 1400, Clinton, MS 39060-1400. Internet: www.naemt.org

* National Registry of Emergency Medical Technicians, Rocco V. Morando Bldg., 6610 Busch Blvd., P.O. Box 29233, Columbus, OH 43229. Internet: www.nremt.org

Licensed Practical and Licensed Vocational Nurses

At a Glance

Licensed practical nurses (LPNs) and Licensed Vocational Nurses (LVNs)—as LPNs are known in Texas and California—take care of sick, injured, and disabled people. They are supervised by physicians or registered nurses. Most LPNs provide basic bedside care, taking vital signs such as temperature, blood pressure, and pulse. They also prepare and give injections, monitor catheters, apply dressings, and treat bedsores. LPNs monitor their patients and report reactions to medications or treatments. They collect samples for testing, perform routine laboratory tests, feed patients, and record food and fluid intake and output. To help keep patients comfortable, LPNs assist with bathing, dressing, and personal hygiene. In states where the law allows, they may administer medication.

Career in Focus: *Nursing Care Facility LPN*

About 25 percent of LPNs work in nursing care facilities. Their responsibilities are much the same as those nurses working in hospitals, though they generally spend more time with their residents and get to know them better. LPNs in nursing care facilities help determine residents' needs, develop care plans, and supervise other nursing aides.

Where and When

Most LPNs work 40-hour weeks, but they often work nights, weekends, and holidays. They stand for long periods of time and sometimes must help patients move. LPNs may face hazards from chemicals, radiation, and infectious diseases. They often have heavy workloads and spend much of their time interacting directly with patients.

For More Information

* National Association for Practical Nurse Education and Service, Inc., P.O. Box 25647, Alexandria, VA 22313. Internet: www.napnes.org

* National League for Nursing, 61 Broadway, New York, NY 10006. Internet: www.nln.org

* National Federation of Licensed Practical Nurses, Inc., 605 Poole Dr., Garner, NC 27529. Internet: www.nflpn.org

* National Council of State Boards of Nursing, 111 East Wacker Dr., Suite 2900, Chicago, IL 60611. Internet: www.ncsbn.org

Data Bank

Education and Training: Vocational/technical training

Starting Salaries: $24,000

Average Earnings: $30,000–$42,000

Total Jobs Held: 726,000

Job Outlook: Average increase

Annual Job Openings: 84,000

Related Jobs: Emergency medical technicians and paramedics; medical assistants; nursing, psychiatric, and home health aides; registered nurses; social and human service assistants; surgical technologists

Personality Type: Social

Did You Know?

Some LPNs work as private-duty nurses. Instead of working for a hospital, clinic, or nursing care facility, these nurses provide in-home care to patients. They may work 8 to 12 hours per day caring for a single patient. In some cases, their duties involve cooking meals and caring for other members of the patient's family as well. At night, most return to their own homes and families, but some actually live with their patients' families while they provide care.

Medical Records and Health Information Technicians

At a Glance

These workers organize and keep track of patients' medical records, including medical histories, exam results, reports of X rays and laboratory tests, and treatment plans. They make sure all the right forms have been signed, input the information into a computer file, and code the information so that it can be pulled up easily. Some technicians also use computer programs to analyze data to improve patient care, control costs, or use in legal actions or research studies. Health information technicians must be computer literate and pay close attention to details.

Data Bank

Education and Training: Associate degree

Starting Salaries: $18,000

Average Earnings: $21,000–$34,000

Total Jobs Held: 159,000

Job Outlook: Rapid increase

Annual Job Openings: 14,000

Related Jobs: Medical transcriptionists

Personality Type: Conventional

Did You Know?

What happens if someone gets a hold of your medical records? If your family has a history of cancer, for example, a business might decide not to hire you because you are at risk for high medical bills. Or an insurance company might decide not to sign you up. Thankfully, the Federal Health Insurance Portability and Accountability Act (HIPAA) sets a national standard for privacy of health information. But HIPAA only applies to medical records kept by health care providers and insurance companies—and only if they maintain and transmit records in electronic form.

Career in Focus: *Medical Record Coder*

Some medical records and health information technicians specialize in coding patients' medical information for insurance purposes. Technicians who specialize in coding are often called health information coders or medical record coders. These technicians assign a code to each diagnosis and procedure. They consult manuals and also rely on their knowledge of diseases. Technicians then use computer software to assign the patient to one of several hundred "diagnosis-related groups," or DRGs. These programs determine the amount for which the hospital will be reimbursed if the patient is covered by insurance.

Where and When

These technicians usually work a 40-hour week. In hospitals where health information departments are open around the clock, technicians may work day, evening, and night shifts. They work in comfortable offices and have little contact with patients. They spend long periods of time in front of a computer and are susceptible to eyestrain and muscle fatigue.

For More Information

* American Health Information Management Association, 233 N. Michigan Ave., Suite 2150, Chicago, IL 60601-5800. Internet: www.ahima.org

* American Academy of Professional Coders, P.O. Box 45855, Salt Lake City, UT 84145-0855.

* National Cancer Registrars Association, 1340 Braddock Pl., #203, Alexandria, VA 22314. Internet: www.ncra-usa.org

Nuclear Medicine Technologists

At a Glance

Nuclear medicine technologists give radioactive drugs to patients. These drugs help doctors diagnose and treat diseases. Using a camera, the technologist follows the drug as it enters the patient's body and records the drug's effects using magnetic resonance imaging (MRI). Abnormal areas show higher-than-expected or lower-than-expected concentrations of radioactivity. The images are produced on a computer screen or on film for a physician to interpret. Technologists must keep accurate, detailed patient records.

Career in Focus: *Chief Technologist*

Chief technologists in nuclear medicine assign workers to prepare treatments, perform research studies and conduct laboratory tests, and monitor procedures to ensure accuracy. They develop guidelines for new procedures and train department workers in the use of equipment. They also implement safety procedures. This is all in addition to performing the regular duties of a nuclear medicine technologist when needed.

Where and When

Nuclear medicine technologists typically work a 40-hour week, though this might include evening or weekend hours. In addition, they may be on call on a rotational basis. Technologists are on their feet most of the day and are often required to lift and turn patients. Though the potential for radiation exposure exists, it is kept to a minimum through protective devices and strict safety guidelines.

For More Information

⁕ Society of Nuclear Medicine Technologists, 1850 Samuel Morse Dr., Reston, VA 20190-5316. Internet: www.snm.org

⁕ American Society of Radiologic Technologists, 15000 Central Ave. SE, Albuquerque, NM 87123-3917. Internet: www.asrt.org

⁕ American Registry of Radiologic Technologists, 1255 Northland Dr., St. Paul, MN 55120-1155. Internet: www.arrt.org

⁕ Nuclear Medicine Technology Certification Board, 2970 Clairmont Rd., Suite 935, Atlanta, GA 30329-4421. Internet: www.nmtcb.org

Data Bank

Education and Training: Associate degree

Starting Salaries: $42,000

Average Earnings: $51,000–$70,000

Total Jobs Held: 18,000

Job Outlook: Above-average increase

Annual Job Openings: 2,000

Related Jobs: Cardiovascular technologists and technicians, clinical laboratory technologists and technicians, diagnostic medical sonographers, radiation therapists, radiologic technologists and technicians, respiratory therapists

Personality Type: Investigative

Did You Know?

The work of nuclear medicine technologists is highly related to that of radiologic technologists and technicians and medical sonographers. So related, in fact, that many schools offer one-year certificate programs for individuals with an associate degree in one of these other two fields, letting them specialize in nuclear medicine. Whether you would rather work with X rays, sound waves, or radioactive elements may just be a matter of personal preference, though specialists in nuclear medicine do make more money on average.

Occupational Health and Safety Specialists and Technicians

At a Glance

Also known as occupational health and safety inspectors, these specialists and technicians help keep workplaces safe and workers healthy. Nearly half work for federal, state, or local government agencies to enforce rules on health and safety. The rest work for companies to ensure that their workplaces are operating safely. They analyze work environments and design programs to control, eliminate, and prevent disease or injury caused by chemical, physical, radiological, and biological factors. They may conduct inspections and inform the management about areas that may not be in compliance with laws and policies. They advise management on the cost and effectiveness of safety and health programs. Occupational health and safety technicians collect data on work environments and help run and evaluate programs designed to limit risks to workers.

Data Bank

Education and Training: Associate degree to master's degree

Starting Salaries: $29,000

Average Earnings: $39,000–$66,000

Total Jobs Held: 52,000

Job Outlook: Average increase

Annual Job Openings: 4,000

Related Jobs: Agricultural inspectors, construction and building inspectors, correctional officers, financial examiners, fire inspectors, police and detectives, transportation inspectors

Personality Type: Social

Did You Know?

On September 11, 2001, the U.S. suffered the most devastating terrorist attack in history. Months later, New York occupational health and safety inspectors were still working at the scene of the World Trade Center collapse, testing air and soil samples and collecting blood samples from rescue and cleanup workers. Their findings were grim. Firefighters, paramedics, construction workers, and others who spent much time at Ground Zero showed signs of asbestos poisoning—which means that the 9/11 attacks might be claiming more victims for years to come.

Career in Focus: *Environmental Protection Officer*

Environmental protection officers evaluate and coordinate programs that impact the environment, such as storing and handling hazardous waste or cleaning up contaminated soil or water. Many of them work for the federal government, though most companies who deal with hazardous wastes and chemicals have their own inspectors to make sure they are following the rules.

Where and When

Occupational health and safety specialists and technicians work in a variety of environments. Their jobs often require fieldwork, so they may travel frequently and work long, irregular hours. In addition, they may be exposed to the same potentially hazardous conditions as industrial employees.

For More Information

* American Industrial Hygiene Association, 2700 Prosperity Ave., Suite 250, Fairfax, VA 22031. Internet: www.aiha.org

* American Society of Safety Engineers, 1800 E Oakton St., Des Plaines, IL 60018. Internet: www.asse.org

* Board of Certified Safety Professionals, 208 Burwash Ave., Savoy, IL 61874. Internet: www.bcsp.org

* Council on Certification of Health, Environmental, and Safety Technologists, 208 Burwash Ave., Savoy, IL 61874. Internet: www.cchest.org

Opticians, Dispensing

At a Glance

Dispensing opticians work for optometrists, making glasses and contact lenses according to the doctors' orders. They also keep customer records, track inventory, and help customers find frames that fit them well. They write up work orders that include the prescription for lenses and information on their size, material, color, and style. After the glasses are made, dispensing opticians verify that the lenses have been ground to specifications. Then they may reshape or bend the frame so that the eyeglasses fit the customer properly. Some also fix, adjust, and refit broken frames. After additional education and training, dispensing opticians may specialize in fitting contacts, artificial eyes, or cosmetic shells to cover blemished eyes.

Career in Focus: *Laboratory Technician*

Laboratory technicians cut, grind, edge, and finish lenses according to specifications provided by the optometrist. They then insert the lenses into frames to produce finished glasses. However, some dispensing opticians do this work themselves. For more information about this job and other technicians in the health care fields, see the entry on medical, dental, and ophthalmic laboratory technicians.

Where and When

Dispensing opticians work indoors in comfortable surroundings. They may work in medical offices or stores, and they spend a fair amount of time on their feet. Most work 40 hours per week, but those who work in stores may work evenings and weekends.

For More Information

* National Academy of Opticianry, 8401 Corporate Dr., Suite 605, Landover, MD 20785. Telephone (toll-free): 800-229-4828. Internet: www.nao.org

* Commission on Opticianry Accreditation, 8665 Sudley Rd., #341, Manassas, VA 20110.

* American Board of Opticianry, 6506 Loisdale Rd., Suite 209, Springfield, VA 22150. Internet: www.abo.org

* National Contact Lens Examiners, 6506 Loisdale Rd., Suite 209, Springfield, VA 22150. Internet: www.abo-ncle.org/

Data Bank

Education and Training: Long-term on-the-job training

Starting Salaries: $17,000

Average Earnings: $22,000–$37,000

Total Jobs Held: 66,000

Job Outlook: Average increase

Annual Job Openings: 6,000

Related Jobs: Jewelers and precious stone and metal workers, locksmiths and safe repairers, orthotists and prosthetists, precision instrument and equipment repairers

Personality Type: Enterprising

Did You Know?

While Lasik eye surgery is a relatively new phenomenon, eye surgery itself is ancient. Long before glasses were invented, ancient surgeons were removing cataracts from people's eyes. Evidence indicates that this surgery was performed in India more than 3,000 years ago—though the evidence doesn't say whether the patient was knocked unconscious first.

Pharmacy Technicians

At a Glance

Pharmacy technicians help licensed pharmacists provide medicines and other health-care products to patients. In pharmacies they help prepare medications. They receive prescriptions or refills from patients and verify that the information on the prescription is complete and accurate. To prepare the prescription, technicians must retrieve, count, pour, measure, and sometimes mix the medication. They then prepare the prescription labels. After the prescription is filled, technicians price and file the prescription, which must be checked by a pharmacist before it is given to the patient. Technicians may establish and maintain patient profiles, prepare insurance claim forms, and stock and take inventory of medications. They may also handle telephone calls, work the cash register, and perform other clerical duties.

Data Bank

Education and Training: Moderate-term on-the-job training

Starting Salaries: $17,000

Average Earnings: $20,000–$30,000

Total Jobs Held: 258,000

Job Outlook: Rapid increase

Annual Job Openings: 35,000

Related Jobs: Pharmacists, pharmacy aides, dental assistants, licensed practical and licensed vocational nurses, medical transcriptionists, medical records and health information technicians, occupational therapist assistants and aides, physical therapist assistants and aides, surgical technologists

Personality Type: Conventional

Did You Know?

It's a good time to be a pharmacy technician. As the population ages, demand for prescription drugs will increase dramatically (the older you get, the fuller your medicine chest). Advances in science and research will increase the number of medications available on the market. Add to this the fact that insurers, pharmacies, and health systems will attempt to keep costs down by hiring technicians over pharmacists, and you have a field with tremendous potential for job growth.

Career in Focus: *Pharmacy Technician–Non-Retail*

In hospitals, nursing homes, and assisted-living facilities, pharmacy technicians have added responsibilities. In addition to other technician responsibilities, they may also read patients' charts and prepare and deliver the medicine to patients. Still, the pharmacist must check the order before it is delivered. Technicians also may assemble a 24-hour supply of medicine for every patient or client. The job requires close attention to detail.

Where and When

Pharmacy technicians work in clean, comfortable environments. Most of their workday is spent on their feet, and they may do some lifting. They may be required to work evenings, nights, weekends, and holidays, particularly in facilities that are open 24 hours a day, such as hospitals and some retail pharmacies.

For More Information

* Pharmacy Technician Certification Board, 2215 Constitution Ave. NW, Washington DC 20037-2985. Internet: www.ptcb.org

* American Society of Health-System Pharmacists, 7272 Wisconsin Ave., Bethesda, MD 20814. Internet: www.ashp.org

* National Pharmacy Technician Association, P.O. Box 683148, Houston, TX 77268. Internet: www.pharmacytechnician.org

Radiologic Technologists and Technicians

At a Glance

Radiologic technologists and technicians work in hospitals and clinics. They operate the machines that take X rays or magnetic resolution pictures of people's bones and internal organs for diagnosing medical problems. Some specialize in diagnostic imaging technologies, such as computerized tomography (CT) and magnetic resonance imaging (MRI). Radiologic technologists and technicians must follow physicians' orders precisely. They must also conform to regulations concerning the use of radiation in order to protect themselves, their patients, and their co-workers from unnecessary exposure. In addition to preparing patients and taking pictures, radiologic technologists and technicians keep patient records and adjust and maintain equipment.

Career in Focus: *CT Technologist*

Experienced radiographers may perform more complex imaging procedures. Some radiographers, called CT technologists, operate CT scanners to produce cross-sectional images of patients. CT stands for computerized tomography, and uses several X rays to create a three-dimensional image. In addition to operating the equipment and recording the images, CT technologists may schedule patients for procedures and provide training to new technologists. They often have to calm patients who are nervous about being scanned.

Where and When

Radiologic technologists and technicians work about 40 hours per week, though some may work evenings or weekends or be on call. They are on their feet for long periods and may be required to lift and position disabled patients. Radiation hazards are minimized by using shielding devices and badges that monitor the amount of radiation in the area.

For More Information

* American Society of Radiologic Technologists, 15000 Central Ave. SE, Albuquerque, NM 87123-3917. Internet: www.asrt.org

* Joint Review Committee on Education in Radiologic Technology, 20 N. Wacker Dr., Suite 2850, Chicago, IL 60606-3182. Internet: www.jrcert.org

* American Registry of Radiologic Technologists, 1255 Northland Dr., St. Paul, MN 55120-1155. Internet: www.arrt.org

Data Bank

Education and Training: Associate degree

Starting Salaries: $30,000

Average Earnings: $38,000–$55,000

Total Jobs Held: 182,000

Job Outlook: Above-average increase

Annual Job Openings: 17,000

Related Jobs: Cardiovascular technologists and technicians, clinical laboratory technologists and technicians, diagnostic medical sonographers, nuclear medicine technologists, respiratory therapists

Personality Type: Realistic

Did You Know?

The first X ray ever taken was by a German scientist named Conrad Roentgen, who discovered them quite by accident. He called them X rays (rather than Roentgen rays as his colleagues suggested) because the type of radiation was unknown. The first X ray of the human body was actually a picture of his wife's hand, ring and all.

Surgical Technologists

At a Glance

Surgical technologists assist in operations under the supervision of surgeons and registered nurses. They set up equipment, prepare patients for surgery, and take patients to and from the operating room. They help the surgical team "scrub" and put on gloves, masks, and surgical clothing. During an operation, they help with supplies and instruments and operate lights and equipment. Surgical technologists help prepare, care for, and dispose of specimens taken for laboratory analysis and help apply dressings. After the operation, they restock the operating room. Surgical technicians must be able to stay calm and steady in stressful circumstances.

Data Bank

Education and Training: Vocational/technical training

Starting Salaries: $24,000

Average Earnings: $29,000–$42,000

Total Jobs Held: 84,000

Job Outlook: Rapid increase

Annual Job Openings: 12,000

Related Jobs: Dental assistants, licensed practical and licensed vocational nurses, clinical laboratory technologists and technicians, medical assistants

Personality Type: Realistic

Did You Know?

Would you believe that one of the oldest forms of surgery, in fact one of the first acts of practiced medicine, was brain surgery? Scientists have uncovered evidence of brain surgery dating as far back as 7,000 B.C. (using bronze and rock instruments). The Egyptians, Greeks, and Romans all produced writings discussing brain surgery, and some even had notable surgeons. To top it all, research also shows that many of these operations were actually successful.

Career in Focus: *First Assistant*

With additional training, some technologists advance to first assistants. These vital members of the surgical team help with retracting, sponging, suturing, cauterizing, and closing and treating wounds. In other words, they spend more of their time getting their hands dirty. The increased responsibility generally comes with a pay increase as well.

Where and When

Surgical technologists work in clean, comfortable environments. They must stand for long periods and pay close attention to detail. They may be exposed to communicable diseases and must be prepared for the sights and smells of the operating room. Most work a 40-hour week, though they may be on call or work nights, weekends, and holidays.

For More Information

☀ Association of Surgical Technologists, 6 West Dry Creek Circle, Littleton, CO 80120. Internet: www.ast.org

☀ Liaison Council on Certification for the Surgical Technologist, 6 West Dry Creek Circle, Suite 100, Littleton, CO 80120. Internet: www.lcc-st.org

Veterinary Technologists and Technicians

At a Glance

Veterinary technologists and technicians perform many of the same duties for a veterinarian that a nurse would for a physician. For example, they may perform laboratory tests, assist with cleaning teeth, or take blood samples. Some veterinary technicians obtain and record case histories, expose and develop X rays, and provide specialized nursing care. Experienced veterinary technicians may discuss a pet's condition with its owners and train new clinic personnel. Veterinary technologists and technicians assisting small-animal practitioners usually care for companion animals, such as cats and dogs, but also may help with mice, rats, sheep, pigs, cattle, monkeys, birds, fish, and frogs. Some veterinary technologists vaccinate newly admitted animals.

Career in Focus: *Veterinary Research Technologist*

Besides working in private clinics and animal hospitals, veterinary technologists and technicians may work in research facilities. There they may administer medications; prepare samples for laboratory examinations; and record information on an animal's diet, weight, medications, and signs of pain and distress. Some may be required to sterilize laboratory and surgical equipment and provide routine postoperative care.

Where and When

Some of this work can be unpleasant and physically demanding or dangerous, even for animal lovers. These workers may be required to clean cages and restrain animals, risking exposure to bites and scratches. Those who witness abused or unwanted animals may experience emotional stress, and those who work for humane societies and animal shelters often have to deal with the public. In research centers, night shifts are not uncommon.

For More Information

* American Association for Laboratory Animal Science, 9190 Crestwyn Hills Dr., Memphis, TN 38125. Internet: www.aalas.org

* American Veterinary Medical Association, 1931 N. Meacham Rd., Suite 100, Schaumburg, IL 60173-4360. Internet: www.avma.org

Data Bank

Education and Training: Associate degree

Starting Salaries: $18,000

Average Earnings: $21,000–$32,000

Total Jobs Held: 60,000

Job Outlook: Rapid increase

Annual Job Openings: 9,000

Related Jobs: Animal care and service workers, veterinarians

Personality Type: No data available

Did You Know?

Veterinary technologists and technicians often have to help put sick or dangerous animals to sleep. This is usually done by means of a lethal injection, which provides a quick and almost pain-free death. Even knowing that it is usually the kindest thing that can be done for an animal in distress, it can still be emotionally trying. These workers often help the pet's owners deal with the loss as well.

Service Occupations

Dental Assistants

At a Glance

Dental assistants help dentists examine and treat patients. They make patients as comfortable as possible, prepare them for treatment, and obtain their records. Assistants hand instruments to dentists and keep patients' mouths dry and clear by using suction or other devices. Assistants also sterilize instruments and equipment, and they teach patients how to take proper care of their teeth. Those with lab duties clean removable dentures and make temporary crowns for teeth.

Data Bank

Education and Training: Moderate-term on-the-job training

Starting Salaries: $19,000

Average Earnings: $24,000–$35,000

Total Jobs Held: 267,000

Job Outlook: Rapid increase

Annual Job Openings: 45,000

Related Jobs: Medical assistants, occupational therapist assistants and aides, pharmacy aides, pharmacy technicians, physical therapist assistants and aides

Personality Type: Social

Did You Know?

Most assistants learn their skills from on-the-job training. However, an increasing number are being trained in dental-assistant programs offered by community and junior colleges, trade schools, and technical schools. Most programs take a year or less to complete, though all require a high school diploma.

Career in Focus: *Dentist Office Assistant*

In some dentists' offices, dental assistants are responsible for a wide variety of tasks, from suctioning saliva to scheduling a filling. In other offices they might specialize. Dental assistants with primarily office duties spend little time by the dentist chair. Instead, they schedule appointments, keep patient records, handle billing, and order supplies.

Where and When

Dental assistants work in clean, comfortable environments. Those who work chairside must wear gloves, masks, and eyewear to protect themselves and their patients from infectious diseases. Their work schedule may include weekends or evenings to accommodate patients' needs.

For More Information

* Commission on Dental Accreditation, American Dental Association, 211 East Chicago Ave., Suite 1814, Chicago, IL 60611. Internet: www.ada.org

* Dental Assisting National Board, Inc., 676 North Saint Clair St., Suite 1880, Chicago, IL 60611. Internet: www.danb.org

* American Dental Assistants Association, 35 East Wacker Dr., Suite 1730, Chicago, IL 60601. Internet: www.dentalassistant.org

Massage Therapists

At a Glance

These therapists use massage to treat muscle pain and fatigue, relieve stress, rehabilitate sport injuries, and promote general health. Some massage therapy is done simply for relaxation and rejuvenation. Massage therapists can specialize in 80 different types of massage, including Swedish massage, deep tissue massage, acupressure, and sports massage. A massage can be as long as two hours or as short as five minutes. Some therapists work in hospitals, nursing homes, or sports facilities, although a good number operate out of private offices or travel to homes and businesses. Massage can be a delicate issue for some clients. For this reason—and also for general business risks—about half of all massage therapists have liability insurance.

Career in Focus: *Sports Massage Therapist*

One area where massage therapy is commonplace is the world of sports. Sports massage therapists specialize in the kinds of massage most beneficial to athletes. Because athletes tend to overwork their muscles, the build-up of tension can cause joint, ligament, tendon, and muscle problems that can affect the athlete's performance. Sports massage therapists are trained to detect potential problems in the muscles and work them out. The services they provide are key to preventing more serious injuries.

Where and When

Massage therapists work in a wide variety of settings, from offices to hospitals, nursing homes to shopping malls. Many travel to clients' homes and offices. The work can be physically demanding, and therapists spend the majority of their time on their feet. Because of these demands, most therapists work less than 40 hours per week.

For More Information

* Associated Bodywork & Massage Professionals, 1271 Sugarbush Dr., Evergreen, CO 80439.

* American Massage Therapy Association, 500 Davis St., Suite 900, Evanston, IL 60201. Internet: www.amtamassage.org

* Commission on Massage Therapy Accreditation, 1007 Church St., Suite 302, Evanston, IL 60201. Internet: www.comta.org

* Accrediting Commission of Career Schools and Colleges of Technology, 2101 Wilson Blvd., Suite 302, Arlington, VA 22201. Internet: www.accsct.org

Data Bank

Education and Training: Vocational/technical training

Starting Salaries: $15,000

Average Earnings: $21,000–$52,000

Total Jobs Held: 97,000

Job Outlook: Above-average increase

Annual Job Openings: 12,000

Related Jobs: Physical therapists, physical therapist assistants and aides, chiropractors

Personality Type: No data available

Did You Know?

Massage has been around for 5,000 years. Ancient Chinese texts from about 3,000 B.C. discuss the merits of moving energy around the body. The medical benefits of what they called "friction" were first documented in Western culture by the Greek physician Hippocrates around 400 B.C. Since then the techniques have varied considerably, but much of the philosophy behind the practice has remained the same.

Medical Assistants

At a Glance

Medical assistants help keep a doctor's office running smoothly. They should not be confused with physician assistants, who examine, diagnose, and treat patients under the direct supervision of a physician. Medical assistants answer phones, greet patients, schedule appointments, arrange for tests, handle billing, and file records. Clinical duties vary according to state law and include taking medical histories, recording vital signs, explaining procedures, preparing patients for examination, and assisting the physician during the exam. Medical assistants also may arrange equipment, purchase and maintain supplies, and keep waiting and examining rooms neat and clean.

Data Bank

Education and Training: Moderate-term on-the-job training

Starting Salaries: $18,000

Average Earnings: $21,000–$30,000

Total Jobs Held: 387,000

Job Outlook: Rapid increase

Annual Job Openings: 93,000

Related Jobs: Dental assistants, medical records and health information technicians, occupational therapist assistants and aides, pharmacy aides, physical therapist assistants and aides

Personality Type: Social

Did You Know?

This is projected to be one of the fastest-growing occupations over the next 8–10 years. Why? It's because medical assistants are able to handle both clerical and clinical duties—answering phones and taking pulses. Because of an increasing need to give them more responsibilities, medical assistants with some formal training or certification will have the best job prospects.

Career in Focus: *Ophthalmic Medical Assistant*

Ophthalmic medical assistants are specialized assistants who have additional duties. They help ophthalmologists provide eye care. They might measure and record vision and test eye muscle function. They show patients how to insert, remove, and care for contact lenses. They also apply eye dressings. Under the direction of the physician, ophthalmic medical assistants may administer eye medications. They also maintain instruments and may assist the ophthalmologist in surgery.

Where and When

Medical assistants work in clean, comfortable environments. They are in constant contact with people and must handle several responsibilities at once. Most work 40 hours per week. Many work evenings and weekends.

For More Information

* American Association of Medical Assistants, 20 North Wacker Dr., Suite 1575, Chicago, IL 60606. Internet: www.aama-ntl.org

* American Medical Technologists, 710 Higgins Rd., Park Ridge, IL 60068-5765.

* Joint Commission on Allied Health Personnel in Ophthalmology, 2025 Woodlane Dr., St. Paul, MN 55125-2998. Internet: www.jcahpo.org/newsite/index.htm

* American Society of Podiatric Medical Assistants, 2124 South Austin Blvd., Cicero, IL 60804. Internet: www.aspma.org

* Commission on Accreditation of Allied Health Education Programs, 1361 Park St., Clearwater, FL 33756. Internet: www.caahep.org

Medical Transcriptionists

At a Glance

Medical transcriptionists listen to recordings made by doctors and transcribe them into documents such as discharge summaries, medical histories, progress notes, and various reports. Such documents eventually become part of patients' permanent files and must be accurate. Using a foot pedal to pause the tape when necessary, transcriptionists type the material into a computer, editing it for grammar and clarity. To transcribe clearly and effectively, medical transcriptionists must understand medical terminology, anatomy and physiology, medical procedures, and other medical jargon.

Career in Focus: *Physician's Office Transcriptionist*

Because the need for transcription may be limited on a given day, medical transcriptionists who work in physicians' offices may have other duties. They may receive patients, schedule appointments, answer the phone, and handle incoming and outgoing mail.

Where and When

Medical transcriptionists work in comfortable settings in hospitals and doctors' offices. Many are subcontracted out and telecommute from home. Like other jobs that require extended typing and computer use, these workers can suffer wrist, back, neck, or eye problems. Many work 40-hour weeks, though those who are self-employed may work irregular hours.

For More Information

* American Association for Medical Transcription, 100 Sycamore Ave., Modesto, CA 95354-0550. Internet: www.aamt.org

Data Bank

Education and Training: Vocational/technical training

Starting Salaries: $20,000

Average Earnings: $25,000–$35,000

Total Jobs Held: 105,000

Job Outlook: Above-average increase

Annual Job Openings: 20,000

Related Jobs: Court reporters; human resources assistants, except payroll and time-keeping; receptionists and information clerks; secretaries and administrative assistants; medical assistants; medical records and health information technicians

Personality Type: No data available

Did You Know?

Do you know what it means to have chronic stromal inflammation or what the squamous metaplasia of the trigone is? Neither do we, but we aren't medical transcriptionists either. The job isn't simply a matter of being a fast typist. In order to check for errors, medical transcriptionists need to know medical terminology and procedures. That's why most employers prefer transcriptionists who have completed a two-year associate degree or a one-year certification program.

Nursing, Psychiatric, and Home Health Aides

At a Glance

Nursing and psychiatric aides care for physically or mentally ill, injured, or disabled individuals in hospitals, nursing homes, and mental health clinics. Home health aides care for patients in the patient's home. All of these workers feed, bathe, and dress patients, help them get in and out of bed, take vital signs, and set up equipment. They report any changes to doctors or nurses. Aides employed in nursing care facilities often are the primary caregivers, having far more contact with residents than other members of the staff. Most home health aides work with elderly or disabled persons who need more care than family or friends can provide. Some help discharged hospital patients who have relatively short-term needs.

Data Bank

Education and Training: Short-term on-the-job training

Starting Salaries: $15,000

Average Earnings: $18,000–$25,000

Total Jobs Held: 2,138,000

Job Outlook: Rapid increase

Annual Job Openings: 487,000

Related Jobs: Childcare workers, licensed practical and licensed vocational nurses, medical assistants, occupational therapist assistants and aides, personal and home care aides, physical therapist assistants and aides, registered nurses

Personality Type: Social

Did You Know?

The education and training requirements for being an aide are minimal—a high school degree is usually sufficient. Being an aide is a good stepping-stone to better paying jobs. Experience as an aide can help people decide whether to pursue a career in health care. Then with some additional training or education they often become nurses or medical assistants.

Career in Focus: Psychiatric Aide

Psychiatric aides care for mentally impaired or emotionally disturbed individuals. They work under a team that may include psychiatrists, psychologists, psychiatric nurses, social workers, and therapists. In addition to helping patients dress, bathe, and eat, psychiatric aides lead them in activities such as playing cards or taking field trips. Because they have such close contact, psychiatric aides can have a great deal of influence on their patients' outlook and treatment.

Where and When

Most aides work 40 hours per week, though many work evenings, nights, weekends, and holidays. About one in four work part-time. They spend much of their time standing and walking and may have to lift and move patients as well. Some of the work can be unpleasant or stressful. While the work can be emotionally demanding, many aides get satisfaction from helping those in need.

For More Information

Information about employment opportunities may be obtained from local hospitals, nursing care facilities, home health care agencies, psychiatric facilities, state boards of nursing, and local offices of the state employment service.

Occupational Therapist Assistants and Aides

At a Glance

Occupational therapist assistants and aides help therapists in clinics, rehab centers, nursing homes, and home health care programs. The ultimate goal is to improve clients' quality of life and ability to perform daily activities. Assistants help injured patients regain use of damaged muscles. They might help patients learn to use wheelchairs or other devices. They also help mentally disabled patients with living skills such as cooking and keeping a checkbook. The assistant is responsible for reporting the client's progress to the therapist and helping him or her decide on the best course of action.

Career in Focus: *Occupational Therapist Aide*

Occupational therapist aides typically prepare materials and assemble equipment used during treatment. They are also responsible for a range of office tasks, including scheduling appointments, answering the telephone, ordering supplies, and filling out insurance forms or other paperwork. Aides are not licensed, so the law does not allow them to perform as wide a range of tasks as occupational therapist assistants.

Where and When

These assistants and aides work in a variety of settings. Many offices and clinics have evening and weekend hours to meet patients' personal schedules. These workers are often required to lift and help move patients, and the constant kneeling, stooping, and standing require the assistant or aide to be in good shape.

For More Information

❋ American Occupational Therapy Association, 4720 Montgomery Lane, Bethesda, MD 20824-1220. Internet: www.aota.org

Data Bank

Education and Training: Short-term on-the-job training to associate degree

Starting Salaries: $24,000

Average Earnings: $30,000–$44,000

Total Jobs Held: 26,000

Job Outlook: Rapid increase

Annual Job Openings: 2,000

Related Jobs: Occupational therapists, dental assistants, medical assistants, pharmacy aides, pharmacy technicians, physical therapist assistants and aides

Personality Type: Social

Did You Know?

Though the principles behind it had been around for centuries, the formal practice behind occupational therapy is less than a century old. The National Society for the Promotion of Occupational Therapy was founded in 1917 to help World War I veterans recover from their injuries and reenter the workforce. The momentum behind OT (as it is called) increased again after World War II. America's need to help its returning veterans has helped transform the occupational therapy industry into what it is today.

Pharmacy Aides

At a Glance

Pharmacy aides help licensed pharmacists by answering phones, stocking shelves, cleaning pharmacy equipment, and running the cash register. They also maintain patient files, prepare insurance papers, and take inventory of medicines and supplies. They must keep accurate records to avoid dangerous drug interactions. In addition, because many people have medical insurance to help pay for prescriptions, pharmacy aides communicate with third-party insurance providers to obtain payment. Pharmacy aides are different from pharmacy technicians, who perform more complex tasks involved in filling prescriptions.

Data Bank

Education and Training: Short-term on-the-job training

Starting Salaries: $13,000

Average Earnings: $16,000–$23,000

Total Jobs Held: 50,000

Job Outlook: Average increase

Annual Job Openings: 9,000

Related Jobs: Pharmacy technicians, cashiers, stock clerks and order fillers, dental assistants, licensed practical and licensed vocational nurses, medical transcriptionists, medical records and health information technicians, occupational therapist assistants and aides, physical therapist assistants and aides, surgical technologists

Personality Type: No data available

Did You Know?

There is no question that most prescription drugs are dangerous if abused. But the same is true for many over-the-counter drugs as well. Recent studies show that 1 out of every 11 teenagers has used cough medicine to get "high," which can be harmful and even fatal. In fact, the drug pseudoephedrine used to be found in many over-the-counter cold medicines until it was discovered that drug dealers were using it to make methamphetamine, a dangerous narcotic. Before the drugs were taken off the market, pharmacy aides were told to be on the lookout for anyone stockpiling boxes of Sudafed.

Career in Focus: *Pharmacy Aide–Retail*

There aren't many varieties of pharmacy aides—nearly all share the same basic job description. The variety comes in where an aide works. Those who work in hospitals and clinics may have different work schedules, benefits, and sometimes responsibilities than those working in drug stores or grocery stores. In fact, retail pharmacies account for 80 percent of the pharmacy aide workforce. Being an aide is a good entry-level job for someone hoping to later pursue a career in pharmacy, though more education and training would be required.

Where and When

Pharmacy aides work in clean, comfortable environments. Most of their workday is spent on their feet, and they are often required to lift heavy boxes or use stepladders. They work the same hours as pharmacists, though that often includes evenings and weekends.

For More Information

For information on employment opportunities, contact local employers or local offices of the state employment service.

Physical Therapist Assistants and Aides

At a Glance

Physical therapist assistants and aides help physical therapists care for patients in hospitals, nursing homes, and home health care programs. They help patients recovering from injuries or disease improve their mobility, relieve pain, and regain muscle use. They may help with exercises, traction, ultrasound, and electrical stimulation. They also may give massages and apply hot/cold packs. Physical therapist assistants record the patient's responses to treatment and report the results to the physical therapist.

Career in Focus: *Physical Therapist Aide*

Physical therapist aides help make therapy sessions productive. They usually are responsible for keeping the treatment area clean and organized and for preparing for each patient's therapy. Because they are not licensed, aides do not perform the clinical tasks of a physical therapist assistant. Instead, the duties of aides include some clerical tasks, such as ordering supplies, answering the phone, and filling out insurance forms.

Where and When

These assistants and aides generally work in offices and clinics, and many have evening and weekend hours. About 30 percent work part-time. Like physical therapists, their assistants and aides need moderate strength to assist patients with their treatment. Lifting, kneeling, stooping, and standing for long periods of time are all part of the job.

For More Information

✳ The American Physical Therapy Association, 1111 North Fairfax St., Alexandria, VA 22314-1488. Internet: www.apta.org

Data Bank

Education and Training: Short-term on-the-job training to associate degree

Starting Salaries: $20,000

Average Earnings: $26,000–$38,000

Total Jobs Held: 102,000

Job Outlook: Rapid increase

Annual Job Openings: 12,000

Related Jobs: Physical therapists, dental assistants, medical assistants, occupational therapist assistants and aides, pharmacy aides, pharmacy technicians, social and human service assistants

Personality Type: Social

Did You Know?

When LeBron James pulls a muscle, who does he turn to for help? A sports medicine specialist is a physical therapist specializing in sports-related injuries. These workers help athletes prepare for competition, and they are available during sporting events to help in emergencies. After an injury or illness, they work with an athlete to help him or her rebuild muscle tone and agility. Of course with LeBron's salary, he could probably hire the Surgeon General if he wanted to.

Correctional Officers

At a Glance

Correctional officers guard people who are awaiting trial and those who have been convicted and sentenced to serve time. They keep order and enforce rules in jails or prisons. They also assign and supervise inmates' work, help inmates with personal problems, and report any bad behavior. Sometimes, officers must search inmates and their living quarters for weapons or drugs, settle disputes between inmates, and enforce discipline. If necessary, they help law enforcement authorities investigate crimes. Some correctional officers oversee individuals being held by the U.S. Immigration and Naturalization Service pending release or deportation. Others work for correctional institutions that are run by private for-profit organizations. Most of the jails in the United States are operated by county governments, with about three-quarters of all jails under the jurisdiction of an elected sheriff.

Data Bank

Education and Training: Moderate-term on-the-job training to related work experience

Starting Salaries: $23,000

Average Earnings: $28,000–$46,000

Total Jobs Held: 485,000

Job Outlook: Little change

Annual Job Openings: 58,000

Related Jobs: Security guards and gaming surveillance officers, police and detectives, probation officers and correctional treatment specialists

Personality Type: Realistic; Social

Did You Know?

Most correctional officers are employed in state and federal prisons, watching over about 1.4 million offenders. Correctional officers in local jails admit and process about 12 million people per year, with about 700,000 offenders in jail at any given time. When individuals are first arrested, the jail staff may not know their true identity or criminal record, and violent detainees may be placed alongside everyone else. This is the most dangerous phase of the incarceration process.

Career in Focus: *Bailiff*

Bailiffs, also known as marshals or court officers, maintain safety and order in courtrooms. Their duties include enforcing courtroom rules, assisting judges, guarding juries from outside contact, delivering court documents, and providing general security for courthouses.

Where and When

Obviously working in a correctional institution can be stressful and hazardous. Each year correctional officers are injured in confrontations with inmates. Some prisons can be overcrowded, hot, and noisy. Most correctional officers work 40 hours per week on rotating shifts. However, night, weekend, and holiday work is common. Some officers may carry firearms for protection.

For More Information

* American Correctional Association, 4380 Forbes Blvd., Lanham, MD 20706. Internet: www.aca.org

* American Jail Association, 1135 Professional Ct., Hagerstown, MD 21740.

* Information on entrance requirements, training, and career opportunities for correctional officers at the federal level may be obtained from the Federal Bureau of Prisons. Internet: www.bop.gov

Fire Fighting Occupations

At a Glance

Every year, fires and other emergencies take thousands of lives and destroy billions of dollars worth of property. Fire fighters help protect the public against these dangers. They are frequently the first emergency personnel at the scene. They put out fires, rescue victims, treat injuries, and attempt to salvage the contents of buildings. Because fighting fires is dangerous, it requires organization and teamwork. Fire fighters sometimes remain at the site of a disaster for several days, rescuing trapped survivors and assisting with medical treatment. In fact, 65 percent of all fire departments provide emergency medical service. Some specialize in fighting forest fires. Elite fire fighters, called smoke jumpers, parachute from airplanes to reach otherwise inaccessible areas. Between alarms, fire fighters clean and maintain equipment, conduct practice drills and fire inspections, and participate in physical fitness activities.

Career in Focus: *Fire Inspector*

Most fire departments have a fire prevention division, usually headed by a fire marshal and staffed by fire inspectors. These individuals conduct inspections of structures to prevent fires and ensure fire codes are met. They also work with developers to approve plans for new buildings. Some of them speak on these subjects in schools and before assemblies to help educate the public about fire hazards.

Where and When

While fire fighters spend much of their time at stations, their working conditions can change on a moment's notice. Fire fighting involves risk of death or injury from cave-ins; traffic accidents; exposure to flames and smoke; and contact with poisonous, flammable, or explosive gases. They wear heavy protective gear, and the work is incredibly demanding, both emotionally and physically. Most work more than 50 hours per week and many work extra-long shifts with several days off in between.

For More Information

* International Association of Fire Fighters, 1750 New York Ave. NW, Washington, DC 20006. Internet: www.iaff.org
* U.S. Fire Administration, 16825 South Seton Ave., Emmitsburg, MD 21727. Internet: www.usfa.fema.gov
* National Fire Academy, 16825 South Seton Ave., Emmitsburg, MD 21727. Internet: www.usfa.fema.gov/nfa/index.htm

---

Data Bank

Education and Training: Moderate-term on-the-job training to bachelor's degree

Starting Salaries: $23,000

Average Earnings: $32,000–$55,000

Total Jobs Held: 353,000

Job Outlook: Above-average increase

Annual Job Openings: 25,000

Related Jobs: Emergency medical technicians and paramedics, police and detectives

Personality Type: Conventional; Realistic; Investigative

Did You Know?

Firefighting is one of the most dangerous jobs in the U.S. economy. Each year about a hundred fire fighters lose their lives in the line of duty. On September 11, 2001, more than 300 fire fighters died attempting to rescue victims. Individuals in this profession are so committed to helping others that they are willing to risk their lives everyday.

Police and Detectives

At a Glance

Police, detectives, and special agents protect people from crime and violence. They patrol highways, issue traffic tickets, and help accident victims. They also collect evidence and investigate crimes. Uniformed police officers maintain regular patrols and respond to calls for service. They may direct traffic at the scene of an accident, investigate a burglary, or give first aid to an accident victim. During their shift, they may identify, pursue, and arrest suspected criminals; resolve problems within the community; and enforce traffic laws. Sheriffs and deputy sheriffs enforce the law on the county level. State police officers arrest criminals statewide and patrol highways to enforce motor vehicle laws. Regardless of job duties or location, police officers and detectives at all levels must write reports and maintain accurate records.

Did You Know?

Federal Bureau of Investigation (FBI) agents are the federal government's main detectives, responsible for investigating violations of federal law and national security. The FBI investigates organized crime, public corruption, fraud, bribery, civil rights violations, bank robbery, extortion, kidnapping, terrorism, espionage, drug trafficking, and other violations. Other government positions with related job skills and responsibilities include U.S. Drug Enforcement Administration (DEA) agents, U.S. marshals and deputy marshals, Federal Air Marshals, and U.S. Secret Service special agents.

Career in Focus: *Detective*

Detectives are investigators who gather facts and collect evidence for criminal cases. They conduct interviews, examine records, observe the activities of suspects, and participate in raids or arrests. Detectives usually specialize in investigating one kind of crime, such as homicide or fraud. They are assigned cases on a rotating basis and work on them until an arrest and conviction occurs or until the case is dropped.

Where and When

This line of work can obviously be very dangerous and stressful. Law enforcement officers witness death and suffering. Most of these individuals work 40-hour weeks, though paid overtime is common and shift work is a necessity. Nearly all officers are expected to be armed at all times. The jobs of some federal agents require extensive travel.

For More Information

* National Sheriffs' Association, 1450 Duke St., Alexandria, VA 22314. Internet: www.sheriffs.org

* Information about employment as an FBI Special Agent is available from the nearest state FBI office. Internet: www.fbi.gov

* Secret Service Personnel Division. Internet: www.treas.gov/usss

* Information about employment as a DEA Special Agent is available from the nearest DEA office. Internet: www.usdoj.gov/dea

* U.S. Marshals Service, Human Resources Division—Law Enforcement Recruiting, Washington, DC 20530-1000. Internet: www.usmarshals.gov

Private Detectives and Investigators

At a Glance

Private detectives and investigators work for lawyers, insurance companies, businesses, and individuals. They gather information for trials, track down people who owe companies money, search for missing persons, and conduct background checks. They also investigate computer crimes and are sometimes hired to prove or disprove infidelity. Corporate investigators conduct internal and external investigations for corporations, looking for things such as drug use in the workplace or theft of company assets. Financial investigators may be hired to develop confidential profiles of individuals involved in large financial transactions. All of these investigators may spend long hours doing surveillance, hunting for clues, and interviewing people, though much of a private detective's work can now be done via computer.

Career in Focus: *Store Detective*

Detectives who work for retail stores or hotels are responsible for preventing theft. Store detectives arrest anyone attempting to steal merchandise or destroy store property. Store detectives also conduct periodic inspections of stock areas, dressing rooms, and restrooms, and sometimes assist in opening and closing the store. They may prepare security reports for management and testify in court against people they catch.

Where and When

Private detectives and investigators often work irregular hours in order to conduct surveillance and interviews. Though much of the time is spent behind a desk, working conditions outside of the office vary considerably. Some of this work involves possible confrontation, making the job stressful and dangerous. For this reason, some detectives and investigators are licensed to carry handguns.

For More Information

＊ National Association of Legal Investigators, 908 21st St., Sacramento, CA 95814-3118. Internet: www.nalionline.org

---

Data Bank

Education and Training: Work experience

Starting Salaries: $19,000

Average Earnings: $24,000–$44,000

Total Jobs Held: 43,000

Job Outlook: Average increase

Annual Job Openings: 7,000

Related Jobs: Bill and account collectors; claims adjusters, appraisers, examiners, and investigators; police and detectives; security guards and gaming surveillance officers; accountants and auditors; financial analysts and personal finance advisors

Personality Type: Enterprising

Did You Know?

Watching Humphrey Bogart or *Magnum P.I.* gives the impression that being a private detective is an action-packed career full of mischief and mayhem, but it is seldom that exciting. Most private detectives spend the majority of their time on the phone, running computer searches, recording statements, or watching people from afar. They prefer avoiding confrontation, and they don't all wear trench coats.

Security Guards and Gaming Surveillance Officers

At a Glance

Security guards, who are also called security officers, patrol and inspect property to protect against fire, theft, and vandalism. They use radios and telephones to call for assistance from police, fire, or emergency medical services when necessary. They also may interview witnesses or victims, prepare case reports, and testify in court. The security guard's job responsibilities vary with the employer. In office buildings, banks, and hospitals, for example, guards maintain order and protect the property, staff, and customers. At air, sea, and rail terminals, guards protect people and freight, and they screen passengers and baggage using metal detectors and high-tech equipment. Guards working at universities, parks, and sports stadiums perform crowd control and direct traffic. All security officers must use good judgment and common sense.

Data Bank

Education and Training: Short-term on-the-job training to related work experience

Starting Salaries: $15,000

Average Earnings: $18,000–$28,000

Total Jobs Held: 1,156,000

Job Outlook: Average increase

Annual Job Openings: 285,000

Related Jobs: Correctional officers, police and detectives, private detectives and investigators

Personality Type: Social

Did You Know?

Imagine having to put on a bulletproof vest every time you got out of your car. Well, if it's an armored car carrying hundreds of thousands, even millions of dollars in cash, it might be worth it. When an armored car arrives at the door of a business, an armed guard enters, signs for the money, and returns to the truck with the valuables in hand. Carrying money just the few steps between the truck and the door can be extremely hazardous. Just hope you never have to stop and change a flat tire.

Career in Focus: *Gaming Surveillance Officer*

Gaming surveillance officers act as security agents for casino managers and patrons. Using primarily audio and video equipment, they observe casino operations for irregular activities, such as cheating or theft, by either employees or patrons. They keep recordings that are sometimes used as evidence in police investigations. So don't go counting cards the next time you're in Vegas. You are being watched, after all.

Where and When

Most security guards and gaming surveillance officers spend most of their time on their feet or behind a desk. While the work is usually routine, guards must be constantly on alert. They usually work in shifts, though most still work a standard 40-hour week.

For More Information

Further information about work opportunities for guards is available from local security and guard firms and state employment service offices. Information about licensing requirements for guards may be obtained from the state licensing commission or the state police department.

Chefs, Cooks, and Food Preparation Workers

At a Glance

Chefs, cooks, and food preparation workers prepare a wide range of foods—from soups, snacks, and salads to entrees, side dishes, and desserts—in a variety of restaurants and other food services establishments. Chefs and cooks create recipes and prepare meals. Food preparation workers perform more routine tasks: They peel and cut vegetables, trim meat, prepare poultry, and perform other duties such as keeping work areas clean and monitoring ovens. Executive chefs and head cooks coordinate the work of the kitchen staff and direct the preparation of meals. They determine serving sizes, plan menus, order food supplies, and oversee kitchen operations. Private household cooks (or personal chefs) plan and prepare meals in private homes according to the client's tastes or dietary needs. They order groceries and supplies, clean the kitchen, and wash dishes. They also may serve meals.

Career in Focus: *Research Chef*

Research chefs combine cooking skills with knowledge of food science to develop recipes, test new formulas, and experiment with the flavors and appeal of foods. They also may test new products and equipment for chain restaurants, food growers, manufacturers, and marketers. The education requirements for research chefs tend to be higher than other chefs, however, and often include a college degree.

Where and When

Working conditions for chefs, cooks, and food preparation workers vary considerable, from large, air-conditioned kitchens to cramped, steamy ones. These workers spend most of their time on their feet and are usually under constant pressure to keep up with orders. Job hazards include slips and falls, cuts, and burns. Work hours can vary from early morning shifts to late nights, including holidays and weekends. Part-time work is very common.

For More Information

* National Restaurant Association, 1200 17th St. NW, Washington, DC 20036-3097. Internet: www.restaurant.org
* American Culinary Federation, 180 Center Place Way, St. Augustine, FL 32095. Internet: www.acfchefs.org
* American Personal Chef Association, 4572 Delaware St., San Diego, CA 92116.

Data Bank

Education and Training: Short-term on-the-job training to related work experience

Starting Salaries: $13,000

Average Earnings: $15,000–$22,000

Total Jobs Held: 3,122,000

Job Outlook: Average increase

Annual Job Openings: 844,000

Related Jobs: Food processing occupations, food service managers, food and beverage serving and related workers

Personality Type: Enterprising; Realistic

Did You Know?

While traditional colleges and universities do offer degrees in hospitality or the culinary arts, many chefs and cooks prefer to attend independent cooking schools and culinary arts institutes. There they can focus on their training and earn their certification much faster. The American Culinary Federation accredits more than 100 formal training programs, including the prestigious Le Cordon Bleu schools, which will teach you how to make more than chicken cordon bleu (like veal cordon bleu, for example).

Food and Beverage Serving and Related Workers

At a Glance

These workers deal with customers in restaurants, coffee shops, and other places that serve food. Most work as part of a team, helping to improve customer service. Waiters and waitresses, the largest group of these workers, take customers' orders, serve food and beverages, prepare bills, and sometimes accept payment. Their specific duties vary considerably depending on the establishment. Hosts and hostesses welcome guests, maintain reservation or waiting lists, and assign guests to tables. Dining room and cafeteria attendants and helpers assist waiters, waitresses, and bartenders by cleaning tables, removing dirty dishes, and keeping serving areas stocked with supplies. Counter attendants take orders and serve food in cafeterias, coffee shops, and carryout eateries.

Data Bank

Education and Training: Short-term on-the-job training

Starting Salaries: $12,000

Average Earnings: $13,000–$18,000

Total Jobs Held: 6,830,000

Job Outlook: Average increase

Annual Job Openings: 2,359,000

Related Jobs: Flight attendants, gaming services occupations, retail salespersons

Personality Type: Social; Enterprising; Realistic

Did You Know?

Working in a restaurant is a time-honored first job for many people. About 25 percent of these workers are 16 to 19 years old. That's about six times the proportion for all workers. In fact, about one in ten Americans will end up working at a McDonald's at some point in their lives. The variable schedules make it an ideal job for high-school and college students, and if the tips are good, it can help pay the tuition.

Career in Focus: *Bartender*

Bartenders fill drink orders. Bartenders must know a wide range of drink recipes and be able to mix drinks accurately, quickly, and without waste. Besides mixing and serving drinks, bartenders stock and prepare garnishes; maintain an adequate supply of ice, glasses, and other bar supplies; and keep the bar area clean for customers. Bartenders should be friendly and enjoy talking with customers. They also need to know when a patron has had one too many.

Where and When

Food and beverage service workers spend most of their time on their feet and are often under pressure to serve customers quickly. Part-time work is more common among these workers than in almost any other occupation. In fact, half of all waiters and waitresses work part-time. Because of long dining hours, work schedules vary and often include weekends and holidays.

For More Information

* National Restaurant Association, 1200 17th St. NW, Washington, DC 20036-3097. Internet: www.restaurant.org

* International Council on Hotel, Restaurant, and Institutional Education, 2613 North Parham Rd., 2nd Floor, Richmond, VA 23294. Internet: www.chrie.org

Building Cleaning Workers

At a Glance

Building cleaning workers include janitors, maids, housekeepers, window washers, and rug shampooers. They keep office buildings, hospitals, stores, hotels, and residences clean and in good condition. Some do only cleaning, while others have a wide range of duties. Janitors and cleaners perform a variety tasks. In addition to general cleaning they may fix leaky faucets, empty trash cans, do painting and carpentry, mow lawns, and see that heating and air-conditioning equipment works properly. Maids and housekeeping cleaners perform light cleaning duties to keep private households, hotels, restaurants, or hospitals clean and orderly. Those in private households dust and polish furniture; sweep, mop, and wax floors; vacuum; and clean ovens, refrigerators, and bathrooms. They also may wash dishes and clothes and change and make beds.

Career in Focus: *Cleaning Supervisor*

Cleaning supervisors coordinate, schedule, and supervise the activities of janitors and cleaners. They assign tasks and inspect areas to see that work has been done properly. They also manage supplies and equipment. Supervisors screen and hire job applicants; train new and experienced employees; and recommend promotions, transfers, or dismissals. Some also perform cleaning duties as the need arises.

Where and When

Most of these workers perform their duties in the evening, though some, such as school and hospital custodians, work in the daytime. Most full-time building cleaners work 40 hours per week. Both indoor and outdoor work is common. Janitors may suffer cuts, bruises, and burns from machines, hand tools, and chemicals. Many cleaning tasks require constant bending, stooping, and stretching, which can result in back injuries and sprains.

For More Information

* Information about janitorial jobs may be obtained from state employment service offices.

* International Executive Housekeepers Association, Inc., 1001 Eastwind Dr., Suite 301, Westerville, OH 43081-3361. Internet: www.ieha.org

Data Bank

Education and Training: Short-term on-the-job training to related work experience

Starting Salaries: $13,000

Average Earnings: $16,000–$25,000

Total Jobs Held: 4,032,000

Job Outlook: Average increase

Annual Job Openings: 863,000

Related Jobs: Pest control workers, general maintenance and repair workers, grounds maintenance workers

Personality Type: Realistic; Enterprising

Did You Know?

Families are becoming more and more pressed for time. Between soccer practice, school meetings, and ballet, families with single parents or two working parents are finding it difficult to keep the house clean. This is good news for those who clean residential properties, many of whom are self-employed.

Grounds Maintenance Workers

At a Glance

Grounds maintenance workers care for lawns, trees, gardens, and other plants and keep the grounds free of litter. They may prune, feed, and water gardens and cut, fertilize, and water lawns at private homes and public places. In addition to caring for sod, plants, and trees, they rake and mulch leaves and clear snow from walkways and parking lots. They maintain and repair sidewalks, parking lots, pools, fountains, fences, and benches. They also maintain athletic fields, golf courses, cemeteries, and parks. Some care for indoor gardens and plants in malls, hotels, and botanical gardens. They may specialize in using pesticides, often working for chemical lawn service companies. Tree trimmers and pruners cut away dead or excess branches from trees or shrubs either to maintain rights-of-way for roads, sidewalks, or utilities or to improve the appearance and health of trees. Grounds maintenance workers use handtools such as shovels and saws, as well as power lawnmowers, chain saws, snowblowers, and electric clippers.

Data Bank

Education and Training: Short-term on-the-job training to related work experience

Starting Salaries: $16,000

Average Earnings: $18,000–$29,000

Total Jobs Held: 1,467,000

Job Outlook: Above-average increase

Annual Job Openings: 279,000

Related Jobs: Agricultural workers; farmers, ranchers, and agricultural managers; forest, conservation, and logging workers; landscape architects; biological scientists

Personality Type: Enterprising; Realistic

Did You Know?

Groundskeepers don't always work with Mother Nature. Groundskeepers who are responsible for keeping athletic fields in top condition may work with artificial turf (or Astroturf) instead. Instead of mowing, watering, and fertilizing it, they vacuum and disinfect it to prevent bacteria from growing. In addition, like worn carpet, they sometimes must remove the turf and replace the cushioning pad underneath it as well.

Career in Focus: *Greenskeeper*

Workers who maintain golf courses are called greenskeepers. Greenskeepers do many of the same things as other groundskeepers, spending a great deal of time mowing and trimming. In addition, greenskeepers periodically relocate the holes on putting greens to eliminate uneven wear of the turf and to add interest and challenge to the game. Greenskeepers also keep canopies, benches, ball washers, and tee markers repaired and freshly painted.

Where and When

Many of these jobs are only in demand in the spring, summer, and fall. Most of the work is done outdoors in all kinds of weather. The work is physically demanding and repetitive, involving lots of bending, lifting, pushing, and shoveling. Those who work with pesticides, fertilizers, and other chemicals, as well as dangerous equipment such as chainsaws, must exercise safety precautions.

For More Information

* Tree Care Industry Association, 3 Perimeter Rd., Unit I, Manchester, NH 03103-3341. Internet: www.TreeCareIndustry.org

* Professional Landcare Network, 950 Herndon Parkway, Suite 450, Herndon, VA 20170-5528. Internet: www.landcarenetwork.org

* Professional Grounds Management Association, 720 Light St., Baltimore, MD 21230-3850. Internet: www.pgms.org

Pest Control Workers

At a Glance

Unwanted creatures that infest households, buildings, or surrounding areas are pests that can pose serious risks to human health and safety. Pest control workers find and exterminate roaches, rats, mice, spiders, termites, ants, bees, and many other pests. They use chemicals, poisonous fumes, traps, and electrical equipment. They travel to homes and offices, often crawling and climbing into tight places. Because many of the chemicals they use pose a threat to other living creatures and the environment, all pest control workers are licensed according to state and federal law.

Career in Focus: *Pest Control Supervisor*

Also known as operators, pest control supervisors manage service technicians and certified applicators. While they are licensed to apply pesticides, they usually are more involved in running the business. Supervisors are responsible for ensuring that employees obey rules regarding pesticide use, and they must resolve any problems that arise with government officials or angry customers. Most states require each pest control establishment to have a supervisor. Self-employed pest control workers usually fill that position themselves.

Where and When

Pest control workers often wear heavy protective gear and spend much of their time kneeling, bending, reaching, and crawling, sometimes in dark, restrictive areas. They often work evenings and weekends, and about 25 percent of them work more than 40 hours per week. Despite the training and the precautions taken by pest control workers, pesticides still pose a health risk.

For More Information

Private employment agencies and state employment services offices have information about available job opportunities.

Data Bank

Education and Training: Moderate-term on-the-job training

Starting Salaries: $17,000

Average Earnings: $22,000–$34,000

Total Jobs Held: 68,000

Job Outlook: Above-average increase

Annual Job Openings: 4,000

Related Jobs: Building cleaning workers; grounds maintenance workers; carpenters; electricians; heating, air-conditioning, and refrigeration mechanics and installers

Personality Type: Realistic

Did You Know?

Pest control workers use a combination of techniques, known as "integrated pest management." This involves ensuring there is proper sanitation; creating physical barriers; setting traps; and using baits, some of which destroy the pests, and others that prevent them from reproducing. Integrated pest management is becoming popular for several reasons. First, it cuts down on the amount of pesticides used. Second, some pests are becoming more resistant to pesticides and thus require a more comprehensive solution. How else are you going to take out those mutated, hard-to-kill super-roaches?

Animal Care and Service Workers

At a Glance

Animal care and service workers feed, water, bathe, and exercise animals in clinics, kennels, and zoos. They play with the animals, watch them for illness or injury, and clean and repair their cages. Kennel staff care for cats and dogs. They may also sell pet food and supplies, assist in obedience training, and help with breeding. Caretakers in animal shelters perform a variety of duties. In addition to meeting the basic needs of the animals, caretakers also keep health and admittance records. Some vaccinate newly admitted animals and euthanize (painlessly put to death) seriously ill, severely injured, or unwanted animals. Stable workers groom, exercise, and care for horses. In zoos, keepers prepare the diets and clean the enclosures of animals. Keepers also may answer questions and ensure that the public behaves responsibly. Animal trainers train animals for riding, security, performance, obedience, or assisting persons with disabilities.

Data Bank

Education and Training: Short-term on-the-job training to moderate-term on-the-job training

Starting Salaries: $13,000

Average Earnings: $15,000–$23,000

Total Jobs Held: 172,000

Job Outlook: Above-average increase

Annual Job Openings: 34,000

Related Jobs: Farmers, ranchers, and agricultural managers; agricultural workers; veterinarians; veterinary technologists and technicians; veterinary assistants; biological scientists; medical scientists

Personality Type: Realistic; Social

Did You Know?

An adult lion can eat as much as 40 pounds of meat in one sitting. An adult elephant usually eats between 300 and 600 pounds of vegetables per day. Feeding the animals in a zoo can be a challenge. Zookeepers must know what kind of food the animals need, how much they need, and when to feed them. Exotic animals, such as the koala, which only eats eucalyptus, might need foods that must be specially ordered or grown.

Career in Focus: *Groomer*

Animal caretakers who specialize in grooming or maintaining a pet's appearance (usually a dog or cat) are called groomers. Groomers also answer telephones and schedule appointments. Some groomers work in kennels, veterinary clinics, animal shelters, or pet-supply stores. Others run their own business, typically at a salon, or increasingly, by making house calls. Such mobile services are growing rapidly as they offer convenience for pet owners and flexible hours for groomers.

Where and When

This work may be unpleasant (cleaning cages), physically and emotionally demanding (putting a cat to sleep), and dangerous (convincing a crocodile to get a vaccination). The work often involves kneeling, crawling, bending, and heavy lifting. Those working with humane societies and animal shelters often deal with the public, which may have its own challenges. Work conditions vary—much of it may be outdoors, and hours are irregular. Still, animal lovers find a lot of satisfaction in these careers.

For More Information

* Humane Society of the United States, 2100 L St. NW, Washington, DC 20037-1598. Internet: www.hsus.org

* National Animal Control Association, P.O. Box 148 0851, Kansas City, MO 64148-0851. Internet: www.nacanet.org

* American Boarding Kennels Association, 1702. East Pikes Peak Ave., Colorado Springs, CO 80909.

Barbers, Cosmetologists, and Other Personal Appearance Workers

At a Glance

These workers—also called hairdressers and hairstylists—help people look their best. They cut, shampoo, style, color, and perm hair. They may fit customers for hairpieces, shave male customers, and give facial massages or advice on makeup. In addition to working with clients, personal appearance workers are expected to clean their work areas and instruments. They may make appointments and keep records. A growing number actively sell hair care products and other cosmetic supplies. Those who operate their own salons have managerial duties that may include hiring, supervising, and firing workers, as well as keeping inventory, ordering supplies, and arranging for advertising.

Career in Focus: *Manicurist and Pedicurist*

A number of workers offer specialized services. Manicurists and pedicurists work exclusively on nails and provide manicures, pedicures, coloring, and nail extensions to clients. They may also treat nails to repair them or improve their strength, as well as provide hand massages. Many of these workers are self-employed.

Where and When

These workers are on their feet most of their shift in clean, pleasant surroundings. Prolonged exposure to some hair and nail chemicals can cause irritation, so protective clothing is usually worn. Work schedules are variable, often including evenings and weekends.

For More Information

* National Accrediting Commission of Cosmetology Arts and Sciences, 4401 Ford Ave., Suite 1300, Alexandria, VA 22302. Internet: www.naccas.org
* National Cosmetology Association, 401 N. Michigan Ave., 22nd floor, Chicago, IL 60611. Internet: www.ncacares.org

Data Bank

Education and Training: Short-term on-the-job training to vocational/technical training

Starting Salaries: $13,000

Average Earnings: $16,000–$27,000

Total Jobs Held: 789,000

Job Outlook: Average increase

Annual Job Openings: 87,000

Related Jobs: Massage therapists, fitness workers

Personality Type: Realistic; Enterprising; Artistic

Did You Know?

Entrepreneurship is alive and well in the personal appearance industry. Nearly half of all barbers, cosmetologists, and other personal appearance workers are self-employed. Many own their own salons, but those who can't afford it can lease booth space or a chair from another salon's owner. Self-employed stylists with a good reputation can usually charge much more than someone working out of a chain establishment.

Child Care Workers

At a Glance

Child care workers nurture and care for children under the age of five. They also may work with older children in before- and after-school situations. Those caring for infants and toddlers may change diapers, heat bottles, teach basic skills, and rock children to sleep. Those caring for preschoolers serve meals, play games, read stories, and organize activities to help the children socialize and learn new skills. These workers are responsible for helping children grow physically, emotionally, intellectually, and socially. They help children explore individual interests, develop independence, build self-esteem, and learn how to get along with others. Those working at before- and after-school programs watch over school-aged children during the gap between school hours and their parents' work hours. They help students with their homework or engage them in other activities.

Data Bank

Education and Training: Short-term on-the-job training

Starting Salaries: $12,000

Average Earnings: $14,000–$21,000

Total Jobs Held: 1,280,000

Job Outlook: Average increase

Annual Job Openings: 439,000

Related Jobs: Teacher assistants; teachers–preschool, kindergarten, elementary, middle, and secondary; and teachers–special education

Personality Type: Social

Did You Know?

Research suggests that 75 percent of human brain development occurs in the first 3–5 years. Whether it's learning how to drink out of a cup, forming a first sentence, or learning shapes and colors, the pace at which toddlers and preschoolers learn is startling. Child care workers have a tremendous responsibility when it comes to shaping a young mind, and many of them enjoy the process.

Career in Focus: *Nanny*

While many child care workers work out of their own homes, some work directly out of the parents' home. Nannies work full or part time for a single family, usually when both parents are working or in single-parent homes. They generally take care of children from birth to age 10 or 12, tending to the child's early education, nutrition, health, and other needs. They may also perform the duties of a house-keeper, including cleaning and laundry. Because they generally spend so much time with one or two children, they often develop close bonds and are sometimes treated as part of the family.

Where and When

Child care work can be physically and emotionally demanding. Workers stand, walk, bend, stoop, and lift to attend to each child's interests and needs. Work hours vary, though child care is usually open year round. Most centers employ both full-time and part-time staff. A third of all child care workers run childcare services out of their homes.

For More Information

* National Child Care Information Center, 243 Church St. NW, 2nd floor, Vienna, VA 22180. Internet: www.nccic.org

* National Child Care Association, 1016 Rosser St., Conyers, GA 30012. Internet: www.nccanet.org

* International Nanny Association, 191 Clarksville Rd., Princeton Junction, NJ 08550-3111. Telephone (toll-free): 888-878-1477. Internet: www.nanny.org

Fitness Workers

At a Glance

Fitness workers help people exercise and get healthy. They teach proper exercise methods and activities including cardiovascular exercise, strength training, and stretching. They work in commercial and nonprofit health clubs, country clubs, hospitals, universities, resorts, and clients' homes. Personal trainers work one-on-one with individuals to help them reach their fitness goals. Group exercise instructors, on the other hand, lead sessions focusing on a particular activity like yoga or aerobics. Naturally these workers must be in good shape. They are sometimes required to do other tasks, such as tending the front desk, signing up new members, giving tours, and supervising the weight training and cardiovascular equipment areas.

Career in Focus: *Fitness Director*

Fitness directors oversee the daily programs of a health club or fitness center. They create and maintain programs to meet the needs of the club's members, including new member orientations, fitness assessments, and workout incentive programs. They also select fitness equipment; coordinate personal training and group exercise programs; and hire, train, and supervise fitness staff.

Where and When

Most of these workers spend their time indoors at fitness centers and health clubs. Hours vary but may include evenings, weekends, and even holidays. Naturally the physical exercise required presents some risk for injury. Fitness workers generally have the freedom to design their own classes and their clients' routines.

For More Information

* American Council on Exercise, 4851 Paramount Dr., San Diego, CA 92123. Internet: www.acefitness.org

* American College of Sports Medicine, P.O. Box 1440, Indianapolis, IN 46206-1440. Internet: www.acsm.org

* National Academy of Sports Medicine, 26632 Agoura Rd., Calabasas, CA 91302. Internet: www.nasm.org

* National Strength and Conditioning Association Certification Commission, 3333 Landmark Circle, Lincoln, NE 68504. Internet: www.nsca-cc.org

Data Bank

Education and Training: Vocational/technical training

Starting Salaries: $15,000

Average Earnings: $18,000–$40,000

Total Jobs Held: 205,000

Job Outlook: Rapid increase

Annual Job Openings: 50,000

Related Jobs: Athletes, coaches, umpires, and related workers

Personality Type: Social

Did You Know?

Yoga began as a spiritual practice in India more than 7,000 years ago. However, in Western culture, it is much more popular as a form of exercise designed to improve health, reduce stress, and keep fit. The interest in yoga has exploded in recent years, and many programs have sprung up to train yoga instructors. For more information, visit the Yoga Alliance at www.yogaalliance.org.

Flight Attendants

At a Glance

Flight attendants help keep airline passengers safe and comfortable. In an emergency, they help passengers react calmly and quickly. They also stock the plane with food, drinks, blankets, first-aid kits, and other supplies. Before takeoff they greet passengers, check their tickets, help them store their baggage, and instruct them on safety procedures. During the flight, they serve food and drinks and answer questions. They may administer first aid to passengers who become injured or ill. All flight attendants must be able to remain calm in emergencies.

Data Bank

Education and Training: Long-term on-the-job training

Starting Salaries: $23,000

Average Earnings: $32,000–$71,000

Total Jobs Held: 102,000

Job Outlook: Average increase

Annual Job Openings: 7,000

Related Jobs: Emergency medical technicians and paramedics, fire fighting occupations

Personality Type: Enterprising

Did You Know?

Being a flight attendant is hard work, but it does have its benefits. Attendants receive discounted travel on many airlines (often between 50 and 90 percent) and sometimes travel free on their company airline. They are often granted 10–15 days off each month, and the benefits packages for flight attendants are usually good. Not to mention it provides the possibility of meeting rock stars, athletes, and politicians (the ones who don't own their own jet, at least).

Career in Focus: *Lead Flight Attendant*

Lead, or first, flight attendants oversee the work of the other attendants aboard the aircraft, while performing most of the same duties. They are responsible for coordinating and directing all in-flight services on board and ensuring that each flight attendant has a working knowledge of his or her position. Lead flight attendants tend to be better paid for their added responsibilities. They usually earn the position through years of experience.

Where and When

Flight attendants may be expected to work evenings, nights, weekends, and holidays. Most work a maximum of 12 hours a day, and attendants usually work anywhere from 65 to 90 hours a month. When they are away from their home base, the airline provides accommodations. The work can be strenuous and tiring. Flight attendants spend most of their time on their feet, and must often deal with demanding, nervous, or irritated passengers. Contrary to what Hollywood might suggest, flight attendants do not have to deal with snakes on their planes.

For More Information

* Association of Flight Attendants, 501 Third St. NW, Washington, DC 20001. Internet: www.afanet.org

Gaming Service Occupations

At a Glance

Legalized gambling in the United States today includes casino gaming, state lotteries, betting on contests such as horse or dog racing, and charitable gaming, all of which provide unique job opportunities. Most gaming services workers are employed by casinos. Some positions are concerned with supervision, surveillance, and investigation. Others involve working with the games or patrons themselves, such as tending slot machines, handling money, and dealing cards. Supervisors oversee the gaming tables and workers. Slot attendants watch over the slot machines, making sure everything is working smoothly. Gaming and sportsbook writers and runners run games such as bingo and keno, in addition to taking bets on sporting events. All gaming workers must be licensed and have good customer-relations skills.

Career in Focus: *Gaming Dealer*

Gaming dealers operate table games such as craps, blackjack, and roulette. Standing or sitting behind the table, dealers provide dice, deal cards to players, or run the equipment. Some dealers also watch the patrons for cheating. Dealers determine winners, calculate and pay winning bets, and collect losing bets. Most gaming dealers are competent in at least two games, usually blackjack and craps. All gaming dealers must be skilled in customer service to ensure that patrons are having a good time, even when they are losing.

Where and When

Casino work can be physically demanding. Most workers stand for long periods, and some may be required to do heavy lifting. Smoking is still permitted in many casinos, which can also be noisy and chaotic places. In addition, casinos are generally open 24 hours a day, 7 days a week, so a variety of shifts are possible.

For More Information

* American Gaming Association, 555 13th St. NW, Suite 1010 East, Washington, DC 20004. Internet: www.americangaming.org

Data Bank

Education and Training: Work experience to vocational/technical training

Starting Salaries: $14,000

Average Earnings: $17,000–$24,000

Total Jobs Held: 177,000

Job Outlook: Above-average increase

Annual Job Openings: 47,000

Related Jobs: Security guards and gaming surveillance officers, sales worker supervisors, cashiers, retail salespersons, gaming cage workers, tellers

Personality Type: Enterprising

Did You Know?

Don't want or can't afford to go to college? Try dealing school. These are schools all across the country that teach students how to run games like blackjack, poker, craps, and roulette. Programs generally take between three and six weeks, and some even offer job placement assistance. Places like the Casino Career Institute in New Jersey or the Casino College in California can teach you everything you need to know. Naturally the majority of dealing schools are in Las Vegas.

Personal and Home Care Aides

At a Glance

Home health and personal care aides help elderly, disabled, and seriously ill patients live at home instead of in a nursing home. Others help recently discharged hospital patients who have relatively short-term needs. They clean, do laundry, prepare meals, and help with personal hygiene. Some accompany clients to doctors' appointments or on other errands. Personal and home care aides provide instruction and psychological support to their patients. They may advise families and patients on nutrition, cleanliness, and household tasks. Aides keep records of each patient's condition and progress. They often work with registered nurses, therapists, and other medical staff to ensure the best possible care.

Data Bank

Education and Training: Short-term on-the-job training

Starting Salaries: $12,000

Average Earnings: $14,000–$21,000

Total Jobs Held: 701,000

Job Outlook: Rapid increase

Annual Job Openings: 230,000

Related Jobs: Childcare workers; nursing, psychiatric, and home health aides; occupational therapist assistants and aides; physical therapist assistants and aides; social and human services assistants

Personality Type: Social

Did You Know?

Many people require some form of assistance to help them with their daily routines, but increasingly that assistance doesn't have to be human. We all know about seeing-eye dogs, but what about trained monkeys? Today, many people who are wheelchair-bound have trained monkeys who help them live independently. These little animals perform simple household tasks, fetch items for their owners, and are even trained to call for help in an emergency.

Career in Focus: *Personal Aide for the Blind*

Personal and home health care aides perform a variety of duties depending on the level of care and assistance needed. While some individuals may only need help cooking and cleaning, others may need help bathing and grooming. Those aides who work with blind individuals may provide transportation; assist in dressing, cooking, and moving around; or teach their clients how to use specialized equipment.

Where and When

Working conditions vary. Aides may go to the same home every day for months, even years, or they may work with a client for only a week. Aides sometimes visit four or five clients on the same day. The stress of the job often varies with the personality and mood of the client. Most aides work independently, and some work weekends and evenings to accommodate their clients' needs. Some heavy lifting and moving may be required.

For More Information

Information about employment opportunities may be obtained from local hospitals, nursing care facilities, home health care agencies, residential mental health facilities, social assistance agencies, and local offices of the state employment service.

Recreation Workers

At a Glance

Recreation workers often work as camp counselors or coaches, organizing leisure activities at parks, health clubs, camps, tourist sites, community centers, and theme parks. They may also work in state and national parks, health clubs, or even on cruise ships. Activities vary but often include dance, drama, crafts, games, and sports. They organize events and direct participants, teach people how to use recreation equipment, and schedule the use of facilities. Directors develop and manage recreation programs in parks, playgrounds, and other settings. Directors usually serve as technical advisors to state and local recreation and park commissions and may be responsible for budgets.

Career in Focus: *Camp Counselor*

Camp counselors lead and instruct children and teenagers in activities such as swimming, hiking, horseback riding, and camping. In addition, counselors teach subjects such as archery, boating, music, drama, gymnastics, tennis, and computers. In resident camps, counselors also provide guidance and supervise daily living. This often makes an ideal summer job for high school and college students, especially those who want long-term careers helping people or working with kids.

Where and When

The setting for recreation workers can range from a woodland park to an urban playground to a cruise ship on the Caribbean. Regardless of setting, most recreation work is physically demanding, requiring workers to spend the majority of their time on their feet. Many recreation workers work a 40-hour week, though night and weekend hours are common and schedules vary tremendously. Many of these jobs are seasonal as well.

For More Information

* National Recreation and Park Association, Division of Professional Services, 22377 Belmont Ridge Rd., Ashburn, VA 20148-4501. Internet: www.nrpa.org

* American Camping Association, 5000 State Road 67 North, Martinsville, IN 46151-7902. Internet: www.acacamps.org

Data Bank

Education and Training: Work experience to bachelor's degree

Starting Salaries: $13,000

Average Earnings: $16,000–$26,000

Total Jobs Held: 310,000

Job Outlook: Average increase

Annual Job Openings: 69,000

Related Jobs: Counselors, probation officers and correctional treatment specialists, psychologists, recreational therapists, social workers

Personality Type: Social

Did You Know?

People from all walks of life can get a taste of the wilderness with Outward Bound expeditions. Teenagers, senior citizens, school groups, and business groups can take two-week treks into the mountains. There, they go hiking, white-water rafting, rock climbing, and backcountry skiing. Outward Bound trainers help the adventurers build their self-confidence and their teamwork, while making sure they are safe.

Sales and Related Occupations

Advertising Sales Agents

At a Glance

Advertising sales agents do exactly what the name suggests—they sell advertising, including space in publications, signs and billboards, and television and radio time. Some work with businesses to decide what forms of advertising will work best for them. Others work for media companies to sell the space they have for advertising. In fact, most of the revenue for magazines, newspapers, and broadcasters is generated from advertising. Sales agents gather background information and explain how specific types of advertising will help promote a client's products or services. They prepare an advertising proposal, which includes sample advertisements and estimates of the cost. Advertising sales agents serve as the main contact between the client and the firm. They also analyze sales statistics, prepare reports, and handle the scheduling of their appointments. The good ones read about new and existing products and monitor the prices and products of their competitors.

Data Bank

Education and Training: Moderate-term on-the-job training

Starting Salaries: $20,000

Average Earnings: $29,000–$62,000

Total Jobs Held: 154,000

Job Outlook: Average increase

Annual Job Openings: 24,000

Related Jobs: Advertising, marketing, promotions, public relations, and sales managers; insurance sales agents; real estate brokers and sales agents; sales engineers; sales representatives, wholesale and manufacturing; securities, commodities, and financial services sales agents

Personality Type: Enterprising

Did You Know?

Advertising is everywhere. It's on our radios and televisions, in our magazines and newspapers, on billboards, on our shirts and shoes, in our schools, as part of our movie previews, and now as part of our bodies. Some advertisers pay individuals to wear temporary tattoos on their foreheads pitching a particular product. Some people have even gone so far as to sell their forehead space on eBay.

Career in Focus: *Local Sales Agent*

Local sales agents work for local publications (such as a newspaper) or radio and television stations. They are generally responsible for sales in a specific territory. For these sales agents, obtaining new accounts is an important part of the job, and they may spend much of their time visiting advertisers and current clients. They are often under constant pressure to meet quotas.

Where and When

Because income and job security are often dependent on the worker's results, selling can be stressful. The need to meet monthly quotas often causes sales agents to work more than 40 hours per week, though most have the freedom to set their own schedule. More and more of an advertising sales agent's business can be done over the phone and Internet, making telecommuting more popular.

For More Information

* The Newspaper Association of America, 1921 Gallows Rd., Suite 600, Vienna, VA 22182. Internet: www.naa.org

Cashiers

At a Glance

Supermarkets, department stores, gasoline service stations, movie theaters, restaurants, and many other businesses employ cashiers. Cashiers add up customers' bills, take their money, and give change. They also fill out charge forms for credit cards, give receipts, and handle returns and exchanges. Cashiers are responsible for the money they collect during their shift, and they cannot leave their cash drawers without permission from their supervisor. At the end of the day they compare the cash in their drawers with their sales totals. In many establishments, repeated shortages are grounds for dismissal. Cashiers use cash registers, scanners, and computers regularly.

Career in Focus: *Booth Cashier*

In casinos, booth cashiers exchange coins, chips, and tokens and may issue payoffs. They may also operate a booth in the slot-machine area or count and audit money in drawers. Unlike most cashiers in stores, booth cashiers in casinos generally operate behind protective enclosures and are at much less risk for robbery.

Where and When

Cashiers spend most of their day on their feet, doing repetitive work in mostly comfortable environments. The job requires constant interaction with the public, which can sometimes be stressful. In addition, most places employing cashiers are open nights and weekends, which means schedules may vary. Being a cashier can also be dangerous work: Cashiers' risk from robberies and homicides is much higher than most other occupations.

For More Information

* National Retail Federation, 325 7th St. NW, Suite 1100, Washington, DC 20004. Internet: www.nrf.com
* Food Marketing Institute, 655 15th St. NW, Washington, DC 20005.
* National Association of Convenience Stores, 1605 King St., Alexandria, VA 22314-2792. Internet: www.nacsonline.com
* United Food and Commercial Workers International Union, Education Office, 1775 K St. NW, Washington, DC 20006-1502. Internet: www.ufcw.org

Data Bank

Education and Training: Short-term on-the-job training

Starting Salaries: $12,000

Average Earnings: $14,000–$19,000

Total Jobs Held: 3,499,000

Job Outlook: Little change

Annual Job Openings: 1,222,000

Related Jobs: Tellers, counter and rental clerks, food and beverage serving and related workers, gaming cage workers, Postal Service workers, retail salespersons

Personality Type: Conventional

Did You Know?

Cashiers used to have to look at the price tag of an item and ring it up manually (and still do in some stores). In 1974, however, the business of cashiering changed forever. That was the year the first U.P.C. (Uniform Product Code) scanner was installed at a Marsh Supermarket in Troy, Ohio. The first product to have a bar code: a pack of Wrigley's gum. Now advances in scanner and checkout technology could begin to put cashiers out of business. More and more grocery stores are using new self-checkout lanes where customers scan, bag, and pay for their items themselves.

Counter and Rental Clerks

At a Glance

Whether they are renting out videos, taking in laundry to be dry-cleaned, or handing out musty-smelling bowling shoes, the job duties of counter and rental clerks are similar. They take orders, figure out fees, receive payment, and accept returns. They answer questions about what kinds of items are in stock and how much they cost. They must know about the company's products, services, and policies. Some fill out forms and tickets by hand, but most use computers and scanners.

Data Bank

Education and Training: Short-term on-the-job training

Starting Salaries: $13,000

Average Earnings: $15,000–$26,000

Total Jobs Held: 451,000

Job Outlook: Above-average increase

Annual Job Openings: 126,000

Related Jobs: Tellers, cashiers, food and beverage serving and related workers, gaming cage workers, Postal Service workers, retail salespersons

Personality Type: Conventional

Did You Know?

With more than 6,000 stores in operation, Blockbuster Video is one of the largest employers of rental clerks in the country. In fact, about one in every four rental clerks works at a video store, and Blockbuster is far and away the leader in that market. Unfortunately, Internet piracy and the relatively low cost of buying DVDs could cause some video rental stores to close rather than hire new employees.

Career in Focus: *Car Rental Clerk*

Depending on the type of establishment, counter and rental clerks may have more specific job duties. In the car rental industry, these workers inform customers about the features of different types of automobiles and about daily and weekly rental costs. They also ensure that customers meet age and other requirements for renting cars, inform customers about potential insurance needs, and indicate when and in what condition the cars must be returned.

Where and When

Counter and rental clerks typically work in comfortable environments, though they are often on their feet for much of the day. They may sometimes be required to move, lift, and carry heavy equipment. Many work nights and weekends for the convenience of customers, and more than half are on part-time schedules. The job requires constant interaction with the public, which can be stressful for some and enjoyable for others.

For More Information

* American Rental Association, 1900 19th St., Moline, IL 61265. Internet: www.ararental.org

* International Fabricare Institute, 14700 Sweitzer Lane, Laurel, MD 20707. Internet: www.ifi.org

Demonstrators, Product Promoters, and Models

At a Glance

Demonstrators, product promoters, and models create public interest in products such as clothing, cosmetics, food, and housewares. Demonstrators show products to customers, either in retail stores or in private homes. Product promoters try to convince stores to carry new products. They may set up displays in stores or host special events to show off their products. Some demonstrations are intended to generate immediate sales through impulse buying, while others are designed to generate future sales and increase brand awareness. Demonstrations and product promotions are conducted in stores, shopping malls, trade shows, and outdoor fairs. A demonstrator's presentation may include visuals, models, case studies, testimonials, test results, and surveys.

Career in Focus: *Model*

Models pose for photos or as subjects for paintings or sculptures. They display clothing for a variety of audiences and in various types of media. They model accessories, such as handbags, shoes, and jewelry, and promote beauty products, including fragrances and cosmetics. The most successful models, called supermodels, hold celebrity status and often use their image to sell other products (including *lots* of calendars). Almost all models work through agents who provide a link between models and clients.

Where and When

More than half of all demonstrators, product promoters, and models work part-time, and many positions last six months or less. Demonstrators may work long hours while standing and walking, and many of them travel frequently. Models may have demanding schedules and travel frequently as well.

For More Information

For information about modeling schools and agencies in your area, contact a local consumer affairs organization such as the Better Business Bureau.

Data Bank

Education and Training: Moderate-term on-the-job training

Starting Salaries: $15,000

Average Earnings: $17,000–$27,000

Total Jobs Held: 120,000

Job Outlook: Average increase

Annual Job Openings: 33,000

Related Jobs: Actors, producers, and directors; insurance sales agents; real estate brokers and sales agents; retail salespersons; sales representatives, wholesale and manufacturing; reservation and transportation ticket agents and travel clerks

Personality Type: Enterprising; Artistic

Did You Know?

Nearly everyone recognizes Kate Moss and Tyra Banks, but how about Ellen Sirot? You might not recognize her name or face, but you might recognize her hands. They've been photographed holding everything from soft drinks to cell phones. She's a hand model, and she makes a living showing off her slim wrists, tapering fingers, and healthy nails. The modeling industry uses foot models, leg models, hair models, and even lip models. You don't always have to have a pretty face to be a model; sometimes good lookin' toes are enough.

Insurance Sales Agents

At a Glance

Insurance agents sell insurance policies to people and businesses, protecting them against losses. Common policies include health, life, and car insurance. Insurance agents and brokers help people choose the policies that best meet their needs. Captive agents work for a single insurance company, while insurance brokers and independent agents sell insurance for several different companies. All of these workers prepare reports, maintain records, and seek out new clients. In the event of a loss, they help policyholders settle their insurance claims. Increasingly, some are also offering their clients financial advice. The Internet has made the insurance industry much more efficient, reducing the amount of time agents spend actively seeking new clients and allowing them to take on more work.

Did You Know?

People buy insurance to protect their assets. But not all assets are cars or houses. The famous insurance group Lloyd's of London has issued some odd insurance policies in recent years. Some of these policies include accident insurance for Russian cosmonauts traveling to the MIR space station; coverage in case of a crocodile attack; and insuring a famous model's legs, a singer's vocal chords, and a food critic's taste buds. Another insurance company, Goodfellow Rebecca Ingrams Pearson, even offers insurance protection in case of alien abduction.

Career in Focus: *Life Insurance Agent*

Life insurance agents specialize in selling policies that pay beneficiaries when a policyholder dies. The policy can be designed to provide retirement income, funds for the education of children, or other benefits. Selling life insurance can be difficult: The money is only paid out under certain conditions, and if you are the person being covered, odds are you won't be around to spend it.

Where and When

Most insurance sales agents work out of small offices, but much of their time may be spent traveling to meet with clients or to investigate insurance claims. Agents usually set their own hours, though most work at least 40 hours per week, and some can work as many as 60.

For More Information

❋ Independent Insurance Agents of America, 127 S. Peyton St., Alexandria, VA 22314. Internet: www.iiaa.org

❋ Insurance Vocational Education Student Training (InVEST), 127 S. Peyton St., Alexandria, VA 22314. Internet: www.investprogram.org

❋ National Association of Health Underwriters, 2000 N. 14th St., Suite 450, Arlington, VA 22201. Internet: www.nahu.org

❋ Insurance Information Institute, 110 William St., New York, NY 10038. Internet: www.iii.org

❋ The American Institute for Chartered Property and Casualty Underwriters/Insurance Institute of America, 720 Providence Rd., P.O. Box 3016, Malvern, PA 19355-0716. Internet: www.aicpcu.org

Real Estate Brokers and Sales Agents

At a Glance

Real estate agents and brokers help people buy and sell homes and rental properties. Real estate agents show homes, help buyers get financing, and make sure the contract conditions are met. Brokers may sell houses and rent and manage properties. Both know which neighborhoods will best fit clients' needs and budgets. They are familiar with local zoning and tax laws and know where to obtain financing. Agents and brokers also help in price negotiations between buyers and sellers.

Agents and brokers spend lots of time obtaining listings—agreements by owners to place properties for sale with the firm. After the property is sold, both the agent who sold it and the agent who obtained the listing receive a portion of the profit.

Career in Focus: *Real Estate Broker–Nonresidential*

Most real estate brokers and sales agents sell houses. However, a small number—usually employed in large or specialized firms—sell commercial, industrial, agricultural, or other types of real estate. Each specialty requires knowledge of that particular type of property. For example, selling or leasing business property requires an understanding of leasing practices, business trends, and the location of the property. Likewise, agents who sell or lease industrial properties must know about the region's transportation, utilities, and labor supply.

Where and When

Most real estate brokers and sales agents work out of their home or office, though much of their time is spent meeting with clients, showing properties, or doing research. They often work more than 40 hours per week, and evenings and weekends are common. However, they also get to set their own schedule.

For More Information

* National Association of Realtors, 430 North Michigan Ave., Chicago, IL 60611. Internet: www.realtor.org

---

Data Bank

Education and Training: Work experience to vocational/technical training

Starting Salaries: $19,000

Average Earnings: $28,000–$72,000

Total Jobs Held: 459,000

Job Outlook: Average increase

Annual Job Openings: 53,000

Related Jobs: Insurance sales agents; retail salespersons; sales representatives, wholesale and manufacturing; securities, commodities, and financial services sales agents; property, real estate, and community association managers

Personality Type: Enterprising

Did You Know?

Real estate sales agents often don't have the privilege of a steady paycheck. Not only is the housing market seasonal (more people buy in the spring and summer), but it is highly sensitive to swings in the economy. When economic activity declines and interest rates go up, people are much less likely to buy a new home. This means real estate brokers and sales agents may be eating filet mignon one month and Spam-on-toast the next.

Retail Salespersons

At a Glance

Consumers spend millions of dollars every day on merchandise and often form their impression of a store based on its employees. That's why retailers stress the importance of providing courteous and efficient service. Retail salespersons help customers choose and buy all kinds of items, from sweaters and makeup to lumber and plumbing. Their primary job is to interest customers in the products they are selling. They describe a product's features, demonstrate its use, or show various models and colors. They also fill out sales checks, take payment, bag purchases, and give change and receipts. Most sales workers are responsible for keeping track of the money in their cash registers. In addition, they may help stock shelves, mark price tags, take inventory, and prepare displays.

Data Bank

Education and Training: Short-term on-the-job training

Starting Salaries: $13,000

Average Earnings: $16,000–$26,000

Total Jobs Held: 4,256,000

Job Outlook: Average increase

Annual Job Openings: 1,350,000

Related Jobs: Sales representatives, wholesale and manufacturing; securities, commodities, and financial services sales agents; counter and rental clerks; real estate brokers and sales agents; purchasing managers, buyers, and purchasing agents; insurance sales agents; sales engineers; cashiers

Personality Type: Enterprising

Did You Know?

Internet sales have exploded in the last few years. Whether they are buying a book from Amazon or a plane ticket to Tahiti, more and more people are shopping online. Contrary to expectations, however, this has not decreased the need for retail salespersons. Retail salespersons provide a specialized service that Internet services can't: face-to-face human interaction with a smile.

Career in Focus: *Automobile Salesperson*

For some sales jobs, particularly those involving expensive items, retail salespersons need special knowledge or skills. Salespersons who sell automobiles must be able to explain the features of various models, the manufacturers' specifications, the types of options and financing available, and the warranty. They frequently negotiate or "haggle" with the consumer for the price, and they spend more time than most other retail salespersons filling out paperwork. Many of them work at least partly on commission and make considerably more than most other workers in retail sales.

Where and When

Most salespersons in retail work in clean, comfortable stores. They often stand for the majority of their time. Some may work outdoors selling cars, plants, or construction materials. Most salespersons work evenings and weekends, and they may not be allowed to take vacation during the holiday season.

For More Information

* National Retail Federation, 325 7th St. NW, Suite 1100, Washington, DC 20004. Internet: www.nrf.com

* Retail, Wholesale, and Department Store Union, 30 East 29th St., 4th Floor, New York, NY 10016.

* National Automobile Dealers Association, Public Relations Department, 8400 Westpark Dr., McLean, VA 22102-3591. Internet: www.nada.org

Sales Engineers

At a Glance

Sales engineers work for companies that produce complex products, such as chemicals or technical tools. Sales engineers work with the production or research and development departments of their companies, or with independent sales firms, to determine how products and services could be designed or modified to suit customers' needs. Selling is an important part of the job, but sales engineers also help their customers learn to use the products they buy. They also may help companies produce better materials based on customer feedback. Most sales engineers have a bachelor's degree in engineering, and many have previous work experience in an engineering specialty.

Career in Focus: *Technical Sales Engineer*

Technology is constantly changing, and it can be difficult for businesses to keep up. Technical sales engineers combine their technical knowledge with sales experience to find products that will meet each client's technology needs, whether it's a new computer mainframe or the control systems of an airplane. Those sales engineers who specialize in keeping up with innovations in technology should have good job prospects over the next ten years.

Where and When

Many sales engineers work more than 40 hours per week to satisfy their clients' needs. Some may be required to travel extensively, often for days or weeks at a time. Though hours may be long and irregular, many sales engineers have the freedom to set their own schedules.

For More Information

* Manufacturers' Agents National Association, P.O. Box 3467, Laguna Hills, CA 92654-3467. Internet: www.manaonline.org

* Manufacturers' Representatives Educational Research Foundation, P.O. Box 247, Geneva, IL 60134. Internet: www.mrerf.org

Data Bank

Education and Training: Bachelor's degree

Starting Salaries: $41,000

Average Earnings: $56,000–$95,000

Total Jobs Held: 74,000

Job Outlook: Average increase

Annual Job Openings: 8,000

Related Jobs: Advertising, marketing, promotions, public relations, and sales managers; engineers; insurance sales agents; purchasing managers, buyers, and purchasing agents; real estate brokers and sales agents; sales representatives, wholesale and manufacturing; securities, commodities, and financial services sales agents

Personality Type: Enterprising

Did You Know?

Why does an engineer become a salesman? Given that the vast majority of sales engineers have a bachelor's degree in engineering, one might wonder why they pursue a career with so much focus on selling and all the pressures that come with it. Some do it for the added challenge, others because it allows them to pursue two interests at once, and still others because of the larger paycheck that commissions and bonuses bring in. Sales engineers get to experience the best and the worst of two worlds.

Sales Representatives, Wholesale and Manufacturing

At a Glance

These sales representatives sell products to manufacturers, wholesale and retail stores, construction contractors, government agencies, and other institutions. They answer questions about their products and show how the products can meet clients' needs. Sales representatives may help install new equipment and train employees to use it. They also take orders and resolve problems or complaints about the merchandise. Sales representatives follow leads from other clients, participate in trade shows and conferences, and may visit potential clients unannounced.

Data Bank

Education and Training: Moderate-term on-the-job training

Starting Salaries: $25,000

Average Earnings: $36,000–$72,000

Total Jobs Held: 1,851,000

Job Outlook: Average increase

Annual Job Openings: 216,000

Related Jobs: Advertising, marketing, promotions, public relations, and sales managers; insurance sales agents; purchasing managers, buyers, and purchasing agents; real estate brokers and sales agents; retail salespersons; sales engineers; securities, commodities, and financial services sales agents

Personality Type: Enterprising

Did You Know?

While the minimum requirement to become a sales representative is on-the-job training, more and more companies are looking for college graduates. Firms selling complex, technical products especially look for individuals with a degree in a technical field. There are also several certification programs available. Though either of these routes will increase your chances of landing a career in this field, some companies will still hire non-college graduates, provided they have sales experience and the right personality.

Career in Focus: *Manufacturers' Agent*

Manufacturers' agents are self-employed sales workers or independent firms who contract their services to all types of manufacturing companies. Manufacturers' agents might sell several similar products made by different manufacturers. They also take orders and resolve any problems with the merchandise. Manufacturers' agents who operate a sales agency also must manage their business. This requires organizational and general business skills, as well as knowledge of accounting, marketing, and administration.

Where and When

Sales representatives with large territories travel considerably. Because of the travel and the nature of the work, many sales representatives work more than 40 hours per week. Though the hours are long and irregular, most sales representatives have the freedom to set their own schedule. Sales representatives are under constant pressure to make their clients happy, expand their client base, and meet sales goals.

For More Information

✳ Manufacturers' Agents National Association, One Spectrum Pointe, Suite 150, Lake Forest, CA 92630. Internet: www.manaonline.org

✳ Manufacturers' Representatives Educational Research Foundation, P.O. Box 247, Geneva, IL 60134. Internet: www.mrerf.org

Sales Worker Supervisors

At a Glance

Sales worker supervisors oversee the work of retail salespersons, cashiers, customer service representatives, stock clerks and order fillers, and others. They work in all kinds of businesses—dress shops, toy stores, department stores, and bakeries, just to name a few. They hire, train, and supervise workers and set the work schedule. They order supplies, make bank deposits, and often wait on customers themselves. In retail establishments, supervisors ensure that customers receive satisfactory service. They also deal with complaints, and sometimes handle purchasing, budgeting, and accounting. All sales worker supervisors must have good management skills.

Career in Focus: *Sales Worker Supervisor–Nonretail*

Supervisors in nonretail establishments supervise and coordinate the activities of sales workers who sell industrial products, automobiles, or services such as advertising or Internet service. They may prepare budgets, make hiring and firing decisions, create sales-incentive programs, assign sales territories, and approve sales contracts. They generally have less direct contact with customers than the sales workers they supervise, though they often deal with problems and complaints.

Where and When

Sales worker supervisors in retail spend a majority of their time on the sales floor (and on their feet). Most supervisors have offices as well. Work hours vary because work schedules depend on customer's needs. Most supervisors work at least 40 hours per week, and long irregular hours, evenings, and weekends are common.

For More Information

* National Retail Federation, 325 7th St. NW, Suite 1100, Washington, DC 20004.

* International Food Service Distributors Association, 201 Park Washington Ct., Falls Church, VA 22046-4521. Internet: www.ifdaonline.org

* National Automobile Dealers Association, Public Relations Dept., 8400 Westpark Dr., McLean, VA 22102-3591. Internet: www.nada.org

* National Association of Convenience Stores, 1600 Duke St., Alexandria, VA 22314-3436.

Data Bank

Education and Training: Related work experience

Starting Salaries: $22,000

Average Earnings: $30,000–$53,000

Total Jobs Held: 2,183,000

Job Outlook: Little change

Annual Job Openings: 267,000

Related Jobs: Financial managers, food service managers, lodging managers, medical and health services managers

Personality Type: Enterprising

Did You Know?

Many sales worker supervisors are promoted from within. Most begin their careers on the sales floor and work their way up the ladder through years of service, establishing a record of success. Promotion generally occurs more quickly in larger companies, though this can sometimes result in relocation. Those who become sales worker supervisors often use that experience to later start their own business. In fact, 36 percent of all supervisors are self-employed.

Securities, Commodities, and Financial Services Sales Agents

At a Glance

Securities and commodities sales agents—also called brokers, account executives, or financial consultants—buy and sell stocks, bonds, and other financial products for clients who want to invest in the stock market. They explain the advantages and disadvantages of different investments. They also supply the latest price quotes on any securities and information on the financial positions of the corporations issuing the securities. In addition, many agents provide advice on investments, insurance, tax planning, estate planning, and other financial matters. Most securities and commodities sales agents help individual investors. Others specialize in institutional investors, such as banks. The most important part of a sales representative's job is finding clients and building a customer base.

Data Bank

Education and Training: Bachelor's degree

Starting Salaries: $29,000

Average Earnings: $42,000–$124,000

Total Jobs Held: 281,000

Job Outlook: Average increase

Annual Job Openings: 37,000

Related Jobs: Insurance sales agents, real estate brokers and sales agents, financial analysts and personal financial advisors

Personality Type: Enterprising

Did You Know?

Have you heard of the Dow Jones Industrial Average or the *Wall Street Journal*? The same person was the driving force behind both. Charles Dow published the first daily paper that gave financial information about companies. That paper grew into the *Wall Street Journal*. Dow also developed the first stock market average, which became the Dow Jones Industrial Average. Interestingly, Charles Dow never finished high school, though the vast majority of agents working on Wall Street today have a college degree.

Career in Focus: *Financial Service Sales Agent*

Financial service sales agents usually work for banks. They contact potential customers to sell their bank's services, which might include loans, mutual funds, deposit accounts, retirement planning, and other investment services. They also may ask businesses to participate in consumer credit card programs. Financial services sales agents who serve all the financial needs of a single person or business often are called private bankers.

Where and When

Though most securities and commodities sales agents work in comfortable offices, they are almost always working under stressful conditions. Sales activity fluctuates daily, and sales agents have to constantly keep up with these shifts. Most of them work a standard 40-hour week, though beginning sales agents may spend more time meeting potential customers. Many accommodate customers by meeting with them in the evenings or on weekends.

For More Information

＊ Securities Industry and Financial Markets Association, 120 Broadway, New York, NY 10271. Internet: www.sia.com

Travel Agents

At a Glance

Travel agents make hotel, airline, car-rental, and cruise reservations for people and businesses. They also plan group tours and conferences. They tell clients which documents they will need for foreign travel and help them plan their trip. They must be up-to-date on cultural and political issues, restaurants, and tourist attractions. Travel agents consult published and computer-based sources for information on departure and arrival times, fares, and hotel ratings and accommodations. They may also visit hotels, resorts, and restaurants so that they can base recommendations on their own travel experiences. Many cruise lines, resorts, and specialty travel groups use travel agents to promote travel packages to millions of people every year.

Career in Focus: *Adventure Travel Agent*

While the majority of travel agents plan getaways to the Bahamas or family cruises, some specialize in more exotic and unusual destinations. Whether it's planning a climb up Mount Kilimanjaro or tracking gorillas through the Bwindi Impenetrable Forest, there are agents out there who specialize in exotic trips. These agents not only plan complex (and sometimes risky) vacations, many of them also act as tour guides. Most are experts at the activity in question, such as mountain climbing, or on the kind of vacation, such as an African safari. The trips they offer tend to be all-inclusive and *very* expensive.

Where and When

Travel agents spend most of their time behind their desks in comfortable office environments. Pressure and hours may increase during peak vacation periods and holidays. Advances in computer systems and telecommunications make it easier than ever for travel agents to work from home.

For More Information

* American Society of Travel Agents, Education Department, 1101 King St., Alexandria, VA 22314. Internet: www.travelsense.org

* The Travel Institute, 148 Linden St., Suite 305, Wellesley, MA 02482. Internet: www.thetravelinstitute.com

Data Bank

Education and Training: Vocational/technical training

Starting Salaries: $17,000

Average Earnings: $22,000–$36,000

Total Jobs Held: 103,000

Job Outlook: Declining

Annual Job Openings: 4,000

Related Jobs: Reservation and transportation ticket agents and travel clerks

Personality Type: Enterprising

Did You Know?

Two important factors have contributed to the decline in the number of travel agent jobs. First, airlines have stopped offering commissions to travel agencies. But perhaps even more powerful is the effect of the Internet. Travel accommodations account for a large percent of online business, and many people find it easier to just point-and-click to get plane tickets and hotel reservations. However, because some people want more information or want someone else to do the work, travel agents who specialize in specific destinations or luxury travel will have an easier time combating the competition offered by the Internet.

Office and Administrative Support Occupations

Bill and Account Collectors

At a Glance

These workers keep track of accounts that are overdue and try to collect payment on them. Some are employed by third-party collection agencies. Others work directly for companies like stores, hospitals, or banks. First they track down and notify customers who owe money. Where feasible, they offer the customer advice on how to pay off the debts. If a customer fails to respond, collectors notify the credit department of the establishment. In more extreme cases, collectors may initiate repossession proceedings, disconnect the customer's service, or hand the account over to an attorney for legal action. Collectors use computers and special software to keep track of clients. They spend a lot of time on the phone and must have good communication skills.

Data Bank

Education and Training: Short-term on-the-job training

Starting Salaries: $19,000

Average Earnings: $23,000–$35,000

Total Jobs Held: 456,000

Job Outlook: Above-average increase

Annual Job Openings: 85,000

Related Jobs: Credit authorizers, checkers, and clerks; loan officers; interviewers

Personality Type: Conventional

Did You Know?

According to American Consumer Credit Counseling, about half of all credit card holders pay only their minimum monthly balance. Given that there are more than a billion credit and retail cards in North America, that means some potentially big bills getting even bigger. The United States is a nation that relies on credit for its spending, and thus a nation that relies on its bill collectors to make sure lenders and companies get that money back.

Career in Focus: *Skip Tracer*

When customers move without leaving a forwarding address, collectors may check with the post office, telephone companies, credit bureaus, or former neighbors to obtain the new address. The attempt to find the new address is called "skip tracing," and some collectors specialize in this kind of research. New computer systems assist in tracing by automatically tracking when customers change their contact information on any of their open accounts. Skip tracers are like private investigators in some respects, except they track down missing persons who would usually prefer to *stay* missing.

Where and When

Bill and account collectors work in a comfortable office or call-center environment. They spend most of their time on the phone. The work can be stressful as some customers get confrontational when asked about debts and overdue payments. Bill and account collectors often have to work evenings and weekends, when it is easier to reach people at home. Most still work a 40-hour week.

For More Information

* ACA International, The Association of Credit and Collection Professionals, P.O. Box 390106, Minneapolis, MN 55439. Internet: www.acainternational.org

Billing and Posting Clerks and Machine Operators

At a Glance

Billing and posting clerks keep records of customers' charges and payments. They calculate the total amount due from a customer and prepare a detailed bill showing any new charges and payments. In accounting, law, consulting, and similar firms, billing clerks calculate client fees based on the time required to perform the task. They keep track of the accumulated hours and the type of job performed. Computers and specialized billing software allow many clerks to calculate charges and prepare bills in one step. Computer software also allows bills to be sent electronically, saving the additional step of printing. In offices that are not automated, billing machine operators print the bill on a machine to send to the customer.

Career in Focus: *Medical Billing Clerk*

Hospital bills can be long and complex (not to mention terrifying). These clerks are responsible for ensuring the accuracy of those bills. A hospital's billing clerk may need to contact an insurance company to determine what items will be reimbursed and for how much. In addition, regulations put in place by the federal government require that all hospital records, including invoices, be kept confidential. Because of the complexity of medical bills, medical billing clerks may need additional training. A number of two-year colleges offer certificate programs in medical billing, which cover basic biology, anatomy, and physiology, in addition to training in coding and billing software.

Where and When

Billing clerks typically work in comfortable office environments, though a growing number work at home. Most work 40 hours per week, although one in seven works part-time. The extended computer use can cause eye and muscle strain, headaches, backaches, and repetitive motion injuries like carpal tunnel syndrome.

For More Information

Information on employment opportunities for billing clerks is available from local offices of the state employment service.

Data Bank

Education and Training: Moderate-term on-the-job training

Starting Salaries: $19,000

Average Earnings: $23,000–$34,000

Total Jobs Held: 523,000

Job Outlook: Little change

Annual Job Openings: 70,000

Related Jobs: Payroll and timekeeping clerks; bookkeeping, accounting, and auditing clerks; tellers; order clerks

Personality Type: Conventional

Did You Know?

In college, "cramming" usually just means studying for an exam. In the world of bills and invoices, "cramming" refers to unexplained charges—usually on phone bills and often initiated by scam artists offering free contests or services. Crammers charge people for services they didn't want or get, and the costs often show up as "miscellaneous charges" on the bill. Billing clerks are usually the first people to get blamed for these charges, and often they must calm down irate customers before they can fully investigate the matter.

Bookkeeping, Accounting, and Auditing Clerks

At a Glance

Bookkeeping and accounting clerks keep records of all the money their company spends and receives. They might be full-charge bookkeepers who maintain an entire company's books, or clerks who handle specific accounts. All of these clerks make numerous computations each day and must be comfortable using computers. They prepare reports, post bank deposits, and pay bills. They also may handle payroll, make purchases, prepare invoices, and keep track of overdue accounts. In small establishments, bookkeeping clerks handle all financial transactions and recordkeeping. They produce financial statements and prepare reports and summaries for supervisors and managers. In large offices and accounting departments, accounting clerks have more specialized tasks. Most bookkeeping, accounting, and auditing clerks use specialized accounting software to do their work.

Data Bank

Education and Training: Moderate-term on-the-job training

Starting Salaries: $19,000

Average Earnings: $24,000–$36,000

Total Jobs Held: 2,046,000

Job Outlook: Little change

Annual Job Openings: 291,000

Related Jobs: Bill and account collectors; billing and posting clerks and machine operators; brokerage clerks; credit authorizers, checkers, and clerks; payroll and timekeeping clerks; procurement clerks; tellers

Personality Type: Conventional

Did You Know?

The history of financial record keeping goes back thousands of years, but the history of modern bookkeeping begins in Italy in the 1400s with a mathematician named Fra Luca Pacioli. His book was the first to detail the debit/credit system still used by accountants today. Luca Pacioli is considered the Father of Accounting. We don't know who the Mother is.

Career in Focus: *Auditing Clerk*

Auditing clerks verify records of transactions posted by other workers *within* a company. They check figures, postings, and documents for accuracy. They also correct or note errors for accountants or other workers to adjust. The work is crucial to ensure that the company is operating within the boundaries of local, state, and federal law.

Where and When

Bookkeeping, accounting, and auditing clerks work in comfortable office settings. They typically work a 40-hour week, though many choose to work part-time. They may work longer hours at the end of the fiscal year, during tax time, or when audits are performed. Having to sit and use a computer for extended periods can cause eye and muscle strain, head and backaches, and hand and wrist problems.

For More Information

* ACA International, The Association of Credit and Collection Professionals, P.O. Box 390106, Minneapolis, MN 55439. Internet: www.acainternational.org

Gaming Cage Workers

At a Glance

Gaming cage workers, also called cage cashiers, work in casinos and other gaming establishments. The "cage" they work in is the central depository for money, chips, and paperwork. They do checks on people who want to open a casino credit account and sell gambling chips, tokens, and tickets. They use cash registers, adding machines, and computers. At the end of their shift, cage cashiers must balance their books. Because gaming establishments are closely watched, cage workers must follow a number of rules and regulations related to handling money. For example, they must report all large cash transactions to the Internal Revenue Service for tax purposes.

Career in Focus: *Gaming Cage Workers—Riverboats and Cruises*

While there isn't a lot of variety in the career of a gaming cage worker, there is some variety in terms of location. While the majority of cage cashiers work in Las Vegas and Atlantic City, gaming establishments are popping up all across the nation, and not always on land. Riverboats and large cruise ships offer gambling as well. Gaming cage workers working on cruise ships may be away for long periods of time.

Where and When

Gaming cage workers stand for long periods, often doing repetitive work. The casino atmosphere exposes workers to cigarette, cigar, and pipe smoke, in addition to noise pollution. Because most casinos are open around the clock, cage workers are expected to work in shifts, including nights, weekends, and holidays.

For More Information

✳ American Gaming Association, 555 13th St. NW, Suite 1010 East, Washington, DC 20004. Internet: www.americangaming.org

Data Bank

Education and Training: Short-term on-the-job training

Starting Salaries: $16,000

Average Earnings: $19,000–$27,000

Total Jobs Held: 20,000

Job Outlook: Average increase

Annual Job Openings: 2,000

Related Jobs: Credit authorizers, checkers, and clerks; gaming service occupations; sales worker supervisors; cashiers; retail salespersons; tellers

Personality Type: No data available

Did You Know?

Las Vegas pulls in more than 30 billion dollars a year in revenue from tourists. More than 7 billion of that comes from gambling. Gaming cage workers are used to seeing big dollar amounts taken in and cashed out. To them, thousands of dollars won or lost is just part of a day's work.

Payroll and Timekeeping Clerks

At a Glance

Payroll and timekeeping clerks make sure workers get their paychecks on time and for the right amount. Payroll clerks figure a worker's pay by adding up the hours worked and subtracting taxes, insurance, and other deductions. If inaccuracies occur, these workers research and correct the records. Payroll clerks record changes in employees' addresses; close out files when workers retire, resign, or transfer; and advise employees on income tax withholding. They also issue and record adjustments to workers' pay. Payroll clerks follow changes in tax and deduction laws. They also prepare and mail earnings and tax-withholding statements.

Data Bank

Education and Training: Moderate-term on-the-job training

Starting Salaries: $20,000

Average Earnings: $25,000–$38,000

Total Jobs Held: 214,000

Job Outlook: Average increase

Annual Job Openings: 36,000

Related Jobs: Bill and account collectors; billing and posting clerks and machine operators; bookkeeping, accounting, and auditing clerks; gaming cage workers; procurement clerks; tellers

Personality Type: Conventional

Did You Know?

Computers have had a tremendous impact on this field. Well over half of all companies use some kind of software to record hours worked and calculate payroll. While this doesn't eliminate the need for payroll and timekeeping clerks, it does force them to expand their skills. Also, many companies are now outsourcing the payroll function, suggesting that the best employment opportunities will be with independent companies who specialize in payroll, including those who do accounting and tax preparation.

Career in Focus: *Timekeeping Clerk*

Timekeeping clerks distribute and collect timecards each pay period. These workers review employee work charts, timesheets, and timecards to ensure that information is properly recorded and authorized. In companies that bill for staff time, such as law or accounting firms, timekeeping clerks make sure that clients are properly billed. In addition, timekeeping clerks are responsible for informing managers and other employees about changes in payroll policies.

Where and When

Payroll and timekeeping clerks generally work in comfortable office settings. They usually work 35–40 hours per week. They often face the stress of meeting deadlines.

For More Information

✻ American Payroll Association, 660 North Main Ave., Suite 100, San Antonio, TX 78205-1217. Internet: www.americanpayroll.org

✻ WorldatWork, 14040 N. Northsight Blvd., Scottsdale, AZ 85260. Internet: www.worldatwork.org

Procurement Clerks

At a Glance

Procurement clerks order the supplies and materials companies need to stay in business. They keep track of orders, making sure they arrive on schedule and at the right price. These clerks perform inventory checks, keep spreadsheets, and place orders when stocks are short. They prepare and mail purchase orders and resolve any problems. When the shipment arrives, procurement clerks make sure the purchase order and shipment match. They may have additional clerical duties as well. They work in just about every industry in companies of all sizes.

Career in Focus: *Inventory Control*

Some purchasing departments, particularly in small companies, are responsible for overseeing the organization's inventory control system. At these organizations, procurement clerks monitor in-house inventory movement and complete transfer forms for bookkeeping purposes. They may keep inventory spreadsheets and place orders when materials on hand are insufficient.

Where and When

Procurement clerks usually work a standard 40-hour week in comfortable office environments. However, they spend most of their time in front of computers, which can cause eyestrain, headaches, backaches, and hand and wrist problems.

For More Information

Information on employment opportunities for procurement clerks is available from local offices of the state employment service.

Data Bank

Education and Training: Short-term on-the-job training

Starting Salaries: $20,000

Average Earnings: $26,000–$39,000

Total Jobs Held: 74,000

Job Outlook: Declining

Annual Job Openings: 10,000

Related Jobs: Purchasing managers, buyers, and purchasing agents; order clerks; file clerks; secretaries and administrative assistants; receptionists and information clerks

Personality Type: Conventional

Did You Know?

Automation is having a profound effect on this occupation. Orders for goods now can be placed electronically when supplies are low. For example, computers in cash registers record purchases and automatically reorder goods when supplies reach a certain level. Of course, some companies will always need a real human being to order inventory, but there are fewer today than yesterday (procurement clerks, that is, not human beings).

Tellers

At a Glance

Tellers make up approximately one-fourth of bank employees and conduct most of a bank's routine transactions. They cash checks, make deposits and withdrawals, and accept loan payments. They also may sell savings bonds, accept payment for utility bills and charge cards, and sell travelers' checks. Some tellers specialize in handling foreign currencies or commercial or business accounts. They all use computers to keep records. Tellers end the workday by accurately balancing their cash drawers with the day's receipts. Tellers are also frequently trained to identify sales opportunities. They explain the bank's products and services and then refer interested customers to appropriate sales personnel.

Data Bank

Education and Training: Short-term on-the-job training

Starting Salaries: $16,000

Average Earnings: $19,000–$25,000

Total Jobs Held: 558,000

Job Outlook: Little change

Annual Job Openings: 108,000

Related Jobs: Bill and account collectors; billing and posting clerks and machine operators; bookkeeping, accounting, and auditing clerks; gaming cage workers; brokerage clerks; credit authorizers, checkers, and clerks

Personality Type: Conventional

Did You Know?

Despite the wide variety of safety precautions in place, from security guards to silent alarms, a bank robbery occurs every 50 minutes on average in the United States according to an FBI study. The robberies are seldom worth the risk, however, as most robbers get away with less than $5,000. And just so you know, more bank robberies happen on Friday than any other day of the week. Maybe you should start cashing your paycheck on Monday instead.

Career in Focus: *Head Teller*

In most banks, head tellers are responsible for the other tellers. They set work schedules, ensure that the proper procedures are followed, and act as mentors to less experienced tellers. They may manage the vault and oversee large cash transactions. Head tellers may deal with the more difficult customer problems, and they perform the typical duties of a teller as needed. The added responsibility usually comes with higher pay.

Where and When

Tellers work in a comfortable office-type environment. They may experience eye and muscle strain, backaches, headaches, and hand and wrist injuries due to extensive computer use. Many work regular business hours, 40 hours per week, though a substantial number work part-time. Some evenings and weekends may be required, but banks are usually closed on Sundays and holidays.

For More Information

✳ Bank Administration Institute, 1 North Franklin St., Chicago, IL 60606.

Brokerage Clerks

At a Glance

Brokerage clerks record the sale and purchase of stocks, bonds, and other investments. Most workers assist stock brokers, for whom they take calls from clients, write up order tickets, and process paperwork. A significant and growing number of brokerage clerks use custom-designed software programs to process transactions more quickly. Some of these jobs are more clerical and require only a high school diploma, while others are considered entry-level positions for which a bachelor's degree is needed.

Career in Focus: *Broker's Assistant*

Broker's assistants, also called sales assistants, typically assist two brokers, for whom they write up order tickets, process paperwork, record purchases and sales, and inform clients of changes to their accounts. All broker's assistants must be knowledgeable about investment products so that they can communicate clearly with clients. Those with a "Series 7" license can even make recommendations to clients at the instruction of the broker. This license, issued by the National Association of Securities Dealers (NASD), allows them to provide advice on investments to the public.

Where and When

Brokerage clerks work in comfortable office environments. They generally work a standard 40-hour week, though overtime is common during busy periods. Work flow is fairly regular, though the pace can become hectic when sales activity increases.

For More Information

State employment service offices and agencies can provide information about job openings for brokerage clerks.

Data Bank

Education and Training: Moderate-term on-the-job training

Starting Salaries: $23,000

Average Earnings: $29,000–$45,000

Total Jobs Held: 75,000

Job Outlook: Little change

Annual Job Openings: 17,000

Related Jobs: Bill and account collectors; billing and posting clerks and machine operators; bookkeeping, accounting, and auditing clerks; order clerks; tellers

Personality Type: Conventional

Did You Know?

There's Wall Street the street, and then there's Wall Street the idea. Originally, Wall Street in New York City was the city's financial center and home to the New York Stock Exchange. However, today most of New York's financial institutions aren't even located on the street. The name has taken on new meaning and now encompasses pretty much all of the United States' financial markets and institutions, whether they are in New York or not.

Credit Authorizers, Checkers, and Clerks

At a Glance

Credit clerks collect and confirm information that people give when they apply for credit. Sometimes they verify employment or financial information in order to process the application. Credit checkers investigate the credit history of a person or business prior to giving them a loan. Credit authorizers approve charges against customers' existing accounts. Most charges are approved automatically by computer. However, when accounts are past due, over their limit, invalid, or questionable, authorizers are asked to research the customers' records and payment histories and quickly decide whether to approve new charges. All of these workers spend much of their day on the telephone or on the Internet obtaining information from credit bureaus, employers, banks, credit institutions, and other sources to determine an applicants' ability to repay what they borrow or charge.

Data Bank

Education and Training: Short-term on-the-job training

Starting Salaries: $19,000

Average Earnings: $23,000–$37,000

Total Jobs Held: 67,000

Job Outlook: Declining

Annual Job Openings: 5,000

Related Jobs: Bill and account collectors, loan officers, insurance underwriters

Personality Type: Conventional

Did You Know?

Credit card authorizers are trained to look for unusual charges on a statement (such as a $3,000 wire transfer from a different state than the card holder lives in). Identity theft—when someone uses another person's personal information for his or her own financial gain—is the most common form of credit card fraud. Many credit card companies have insurance against this, though the Internet and online shopping has made policing credit card fraud even tougher.

Career in Focus: *Credit Investigator*

Credit investigators are hired by credit reporting agencies and bureaus to update and verify information for credit reports. In other words, a credit card *company* might have their credit *checker* contact a credit *investigator* at a credit *reporting agency* to ask about the credit *history* of a potential credit card *customer* (try saying that ten times fast). Not only do businesses ask for credit reports, but individuals often obtain their own reports to make sure there are no errors in their credit history.

Where and When

Credit authorizers and clerks work in comfortable, quiet areas. They may sit for long periods of time in front of a computer screen, which can cause eyestrain, backaches, and headaches. They usually work a standard 40-hour week, though overtime is possible during busy periods such as the holiday shopping season. During those periods, companies may hire temporary workers as well.

For More Information

State employment service offices and agencies can provide information about job openings for credit authorizers, checkers, and clerks.

Customer Service Representatives

At a Glance

These representatives work directly with customers, answering questions, taking orders, and solving problems. They make sure customers are satisfied. They may handle billing mistakes, arrange for customers to have services switched on or off, and listen to lots of complaints. In handling customers' complaints, customer service representatives attempt to resolve the problem according to guidelines established by the company. In some cases, they are required to follow up with a customer until an issue is resolved. Some customer service representatives even help people decide what types of products or services would best suit their needs. Many work for banks, insurance companies, and utilities, such as electric, gas, or cable companies. These workers spend a lot of time on the phone or replying to e-mail.

Career in Focus: *Customer Service in Insurance*

Customer service representatives in insurance interact with agents, other insurance companies, and policyholders. They handle much of the paperwork related to insurance policies, such as applications and renewals. They answer questions regarding policy coverage and help with reporting claims. Although they know as much as insurance agents about insurance products and have the credentials required to sell products and make changes to policies, they are not responsible for actively seeking potential customers.

Where and When

Customer service representatives tend to work in clean, comfortable environments, usually in their own workstation or cubicle. Many of these positions require early morning, evening, or late night shifts as well as weekend or holiday work. The work may be repetitive and stressful, and conversations may be monitored by supervisors. For nearly all of these workers, dealing with irate customers can be difficult. Nearly one out of every five customer service representatives works part-time.

For More Information

State employment service offices can provide information about employment opportunities for customer service representatives.

Data Bank

Education and Training: Moderate-term on-the-job training

Starting Salaries: $18,000

Average Earnings: $22,000–$35,000

Total Jobs Held: 2,063,000

Job Outlook: Above-average increase

Annual Job Openings: 510,000

Related Jobs: Tellers; insurance sales agents; securities, commodities, and financial services sales agents; retail salespersons; computer support specialists; gaming services occupations

Personality Type: Conventional

Did You Know?

The customer wasn't always "always right." In fact, the phrase, "the customer is always right," wasn't coined until the early 1900s, when it became the working policy of American entrepreneur Harry Selfridge in his department stores. Since then, the idea has become the mantra of customer service representatives. However, many customer service representatives can probably make you a list of the customers who have been wrong (though the customers were probably *told* they were right anyway).

File Clerks

At a Glance

File clerks sort, store, retrieve, and update office records. They examine and code incoming information and then store it in a paper file or enter the information into a computer file (often doing both). When someone in the company needs information from a file, the clerk retrieves it. In order for records to be useful, they must be up-to-date and accurate. File clerks ensure that new information is added to files in a timely manner and may discard outdated materials. When records cannot be found, file clerks attempt to locate them. In many small offices, file clerks often have additional responsibilities, such as entering data, performing word processing, sorting mail, and operating copy or fax machines.

Data Bank

Education and Training: Short-term on-the-job training

Starting Salaries: $14,000

Average Earnings: $17,000–$27,000

Total Jobs Held: 255,000

Job Outlook: Declining

Annual Job Openings: 50,000

Related Jobs: Receptionists and information clerks, stock clerks and order fillers

Personality Type: Conventional

Did You Know?

The digital age is taking its toll on this job. Most files are now stored digitally and can be retrieved electronically, thus reducing the demand for clerks. Those job opportunities that are available are usually to replace workers who have left to pursue other interests. Individuals with keyboarding and other secretarial skills and who are familiar with a wide variety of computer software and office equipment should have the best job opportunities.

Career in Focus: *File Clerk in Health Care*

If there is one area where maintaining accurate files is a necessity, it is the health care industry. In fact, health care facilities employ one out of every four file clerks. The job description for these workers is much the same as for other file clerks, except that the laws regulating the use and storage of medical files are tougher. Not to mention the effect a lost or mismanaged file might have on a patient ("What do you mean he has a heart condition? I didn't see that in his records!"). In hospitals and clinics, file clerks may work closely with medical records and health information technicians.

Where and When

File clerks tend to work in clean, well-lit, and relatively quiet areas. The work may involve a lot of standing, walking, reaching, pulling, and bending. Long periods in front of a computer screen can cause eyestrain, headaches, and backaches.

For More Information

State employment service offices and agencies can provide information about job openings for file clerks.

Hotel, Motel, and Resort Desk Clerks

At a Glance

Hotel, motel, and resort desk clerks help guests check in and out using computers to assign rooms. They answer questions about the local area and the establishment itself. They keep records of room assignments and collect payment from guests, explaining any charges. Clerks also report problems with guest rooms or public facilities to members of the housekeeping or maintenance staff. In smaller inns and motels, desk clerks often are responsible for all front-office operations, information, and services. For example, they may perform the work of a bookkeeper, cashier, laundry attendant, and telephone switchboard operator.

Career in Focus: *Concierge*

While not specifically a member of the front desk, the concierge has many of the same responsibilities. They answer questions, give directions, and make recommendations or reservations for shows, activities, or restaurants. A concierge must be knowledgeable about hotel services, local establishments and venues, and transportation options. Concierges must stay up-to-date with present and future events planned in the city and the hotel. Sometimes they are asked to satisfy special requests made by hotel guests and to resolve customer complaints.

Where and When

Hotels and motels operate around the clock, making night and weekend work a necessity. Only about half of all desk clerks work 35–40 hours per week—the rest work fewer, making this an attractive job for part-timers. Most clerks work in comfortable environments, though they frequently have to deal with angry guests.

For More Information

❋ Educational Institute of the American Hotel and Lodging Association, 800 N. Magnolia Ave., Suite 1800, Orlando, FL 32803. Internet: www.ei-ahma.org

---

Data Bank

Education and Training: Short-term on-the-job training

Starting Salaries: $13,000

Average Earnings: $15,000–$21,000

Total Jobs Held: 195,000

Job Outlook: Average increase

Annual Job Openings: 62,000

Related Jobs: Counter and rental clerks, customer service representatives, receptionists and information clerks, retail salespersons

Personality Type: Conventional

Did You Know?

You've no doubt heard of haunted houses (and maybe been in one), but what about haunted hotels? Supposedly there are hundreds of them all around the United States. Some of the more famous include the Myrtles Plantation in Louisiana, the Queen Mary Hotel in California, and the Stanley Hotel in Colorado, which served as inspiration for Steven King's *The Shining*. So in addition to angry guests, some hotel desk clerks may have to deal with restless spirits as well.

Human Resources Assistants, Except Payroll and Timekeeping

At a Glance

Human resources assistants work with job applicants and newly hired workers. They explain company rules, dress codes, pay policies, and benefits. They also maintain employee records and notify employees of job openings in the company. On a daily basis, these assistants answer questions about employee absences and job performance. When an employee receives a promotion or switches health insurance plans, the human resources assistant updates the appropriate form. When conflicts arise at work, human resources workers help solve them. In small organizations, some human resources assistants perform a variety of other clerical duties, including answering telephone, sending out announcements of job openings, and handing out applications. Some human resources assistants are involved in the hiring process directly.

Data Bank

Education and Training: Short-term on-the-job training

Starting Salaries: $21,000

Average Earnings: $27,000–$40,000

Total Jobs Held: 172,000

Job Outlook: Average increase

Annual Job Openings: 28,000

Related Jobs: Bookkeeping, accounting, and auditing clerks; communications equipment operators; customer service representatives; data entry and information processing workers; order clerks; receptionists and information clerks; secretaries and administrative assistants; stock clerks and order fillers

Personality Type: Conventional

Did You Know?

Statistics show that health care costs are rising at the fastest rate the nation has ever seen. Because many employers offer health insurance as part of their benefit plan, this puts an added pressure on human resources to seek out the best plan available. Unfortunately, many companies are finding that they can't keep up with the rising costs and are shifting those additional costs back to their employees.

Career in Focus: *Assignment Clerk*

In some companies, human resources assistants have specific job titles. Assignment clerks notify a company's existing employees of upcoming job vacancies, identify applicants who qualify for the vacancies, and assign qualified workers to various positions. When job applications are returned, these clerks review and verify the information using personnel records. Because companies aren't always filling vacancies, assignment clerks often have other responsibilities as well.

Where and When

Human resources assistants usually work in comfortable office settings. The majority work 35–40 hours per week. Those who spend long periods of time at a computer can experience headache, backache, and eyestrain.

For More Information

* Society for Human Resource Management, 1800 Duke St., Alexandria, VA 22314. Internet: www.shrm.org

Interviewers

At a Glance

Interviewers obtain information from individuals and businesses. This information is used to open bank accounts, obtain loans, participate in consumer surveys, receive government aid, or provide data for other purposes. Interviewers verify this information by mail, telephone, or in person. Admitting interviewers get financial and medical information before admitting patients to a hospital. Interviewing clerks who conduct market research ask prepared questions, record the responses, and forward the results to management. New accounts clerks help people fill out bank account or charge card applications. Almost all interviewers use computers or similar devices to enter the responses to questions, and all of them must have good people skills.

Career in Focus: *Loan Interviewer*

Loan interviewers and clerks review the credit history of applicants for loans and credit cards. These workers spend much of their day on the telephone, gathering information from credit bureaus, employers, banks, credit institutions, and other sources to determine an applicant's ability to pay back a loan. Mortgage loans are the primary type of loan handled by loan clerks, who also may have to order appraisals of the property, set up escrow accounts, and help transfer the title. Loan interviewers interview potential borrowers, help them fill out applications for loans, and verify the information on the application.

Where and When

Most interviewers work in clean, comfortable environments. While the majority work 35–40 hours per week, some evening and weekend work may be required. Interviewers may conduct surveys on the street, in shopping malls, or going door to door.

For More Information

* Mortgage Bankers Association, 1919 Pennsylvania Ave. NW, Washington, DC 20006-3404. Internet: www.mortgagebankers.org

Data Bank

Education and Training: Short-term on-the-job training to moderate-term on-the-job training

Starting Salaries: $19,000

Average Earnings: $23,000–$36,000

Total Jobs Held: 515,000

Job Outlook: Little change

Annual Job Openings: 89,000

Related Jobs: Procurement clerks, customer service representatives, bill and account collectors

Personality Type: Conventional; Social

Did You Know?

Loan clerks and interviewers make up about 40 percent of all workers in this field, and most of their time is spent determining whether a person qualifies for a mortgage. Much of that decision is based on credit reports. A credit score above 720 is considered good, and a score below 600 is considered poor. Most lending companies view anyone with a credit score below 620 to be high risk. It is estimated that the majority of Americans have a credit score above 670.

Library Assistants, Clerical

At a Glance

Library assistants help librarians by working at the checkout desk, issuing library cards, and repairing books. They file books when they are returned or left out and collect overdue book fines. They may provide special help to students looking for assignment materials. They also answer patrons' questions and refer those they cannot answer to a librarian. Because nearly all library catalogues are computerized, library assistants must be comfortable using computers.

Data Bank

Education and Training: Short-term on-the-job training

Starting Salaries: $13,000

Average Earnings: $16,000–$27,000

Total Jobs Held: 109,000

Job Outlook: Average increase

Annual Job Openings: 26,000

Related Jobs: File clerks; human resources assistants, except payroll and timekeeping; order clerks; receptionists and information clerks; reservation and transportation ticket agents and travel clerks; librarians; library technicians

Personality Type: Conventional

Did You Know?

Today, many cities across the country owe their free public libraries to one man: Andrew Carnegie. Carnegie was poor when he came to the United States from Scotland. In America, however, he made millions of dollars in the steel industry. When he sold his interest in the industry, he gave most of his fortune away to charity, including funds for the creation of more public libraries. In total, there are more than 2,500 Carnegie libraries in the United States.

Career in Focus: *Braille-and-Talking-Books Clerk*

Some library assistants specialize in helping patrons who have vision problems. They review the borrower's list of desired reading material; locate those materials from the library's collection of large-type or Braille volumes, cassettes, and DVDs; and then help the borrower check out.

Where and When

Library assistants generally work at desks or computer terminals. Their work with computers can cause headaches or eyestrain, and much of the work might be considered repetitive or boring (such as shelving materials). However, many in this field enjoy helping patrons find what they need. Library assistants in schools work regular school hours. Those in public libraries may work weekends, evenings, and some holidays. More than half of all assistants work part-time, making the job ideal for retirees and students.

For More Information

* Council on Library/Media Technology, P.O. Box 42048, Mesa, AZ 85274-2048. Internet: colt.ucr.edu
* American Library Association, 50 East Huron St., Chicago, IL 60611. Internet: www.ala.org/hrdr

Order Clerks

At a Glance

Order clerks receive and fill requests for machine parts, movie rentals, clothing, food, and all kinds of other items. After completing the order, they send it to the proper department to be filled. An increasing number of order clerks work for catalog companies and online retailers, receiving orders from customers by telephone, fax, mail, or e-mail. Some order clerks—especially those in industrial settings—must be able to give price estimates for entire jobs, not just single parts. Others must be able to take special orders, give expected arrival dates, prepare contracts, and handle complaints. Clerks review orders and fill in missing information. Clerks also notify customers of delays in filling the order.

Career in Focus: *Inside Order Clerk*

Orders for materials, merchandise, or services can come from inside or outside of an organization. In large companies, inside order clerks receive orders from other workers in the same company or from salespersons in the field. In an automobile manufacturing company, for example, an inside order clerk may have to order parts and equipment from the company's warehouses to fill requests from various plants and departments.

Where and When

Order clerks work a standard 40-hour week, and most work in clean, comfortable, and relatively quiet environments. Prolonged periods of time in front of computers can cause eyestrain, back problems, and headaches. Overtime may be possible during the holiday season or other times when sales volume is high.

For More Information

State employment service offices and agencies can provide information about job openings for order clerks.

Data Bank

Education and Training: Short-term on-the-job training

Starting Salaries: $16,000

Average Earnings: $20,000–$33,000

Total Jobs Held: 293,000

Job Outlook: Declining

Annual Job Openings: 48,000

Related Jobs: Stock clerks and order fillers; hotel, motel, and resort desk clerks

Personality Type: Conventional

Did You Know?

This job has been hit hard by advances in technology. Automated systems make placing orders easy and convenient, and the growth of Internet ordering and automated phone menus means fewer jobs for the living and breathing. Although job growth is expected to decline, there will still be openings because of turnover, especially during the holiday season when the Eddie Bauer sweater and Hickory Farms holiday sausage orders start rolling in.

Receptionists and Information Clerks

At a Glance

Receptionists greet customers on the phone and in person and refer them to the proper person or department. Making a good impression is an important part of this job. Some receptionists are responsible for the coordination of all mail into and out of the office as well. In addition, they contribute to security by monitoring visitor access. When they are not busy with callers, most receptionists perform a variety of office duties, including opening and sorting mail, transmitting and delivering faxes, updating appointment calendars, and performing basic bookkeeping, word processing, and filing.

Data Bank

Education and Training: Short-term on-the-job training

Starting Salaries: $15,000

Average Earnings: $18,000–$27,000

Total Jobs Held: 1,133,000

Job Outlook: Above-average increase

Annual Job Openings: 299,000

Related Jobs: Dispatchers, secretaries and administrative assistants, customer service representatives

Personality Type: Conventional

Did You Know?

While this job may not have the best pay or the most perks, it does have its own day. The second Wednesday in May is the unofficial National Receptionists Day. Employers are urged to treat their receptionists to lunch or buy them flowers or candy. This is not to be confused with Administrative Professionals Day, which is celebrated during the last week of April.

Career in Focus: *Medical Receptionist*

Receptionists in hospitals and doctors' offices perform most of the same duties as any other receptionist. In addition, they are expected to gather patients' personal and financial information and direct them to the proper waiting rooms. They answer questions regarding charges and insurance coverage, schedule patient appointments, explain clinic or hospital policy, schedule hospital admissions, pull patient charts, and even code diagnoses and procedures. Some schools offer special certification or two-year degree programs for medical receptionists.

Where and When

Receptionists usually work in areas that are designed to make a good impression, so they are usually clean, comfortable, and relatively quiet. The work can be tiring, repetitious, and stressful, especially for those who answer the phone all day and encounter angry callers. The majority work a standard 40-hour week.

For More Information

State employment offices can provide information on job openings for receptionists.

Reservation and Transportation Ticket Agents and Travel Clerks

At a Glance

Reservation and transportation ticket agents make and confirm travel and hotel reservations, answer questions about rates and routes, and sell tickets. These clerks and agents might work for travel clubs, airlines, hotels, or other businesses. Most reservation agents work for large hotel chains or airlines, helping people to plan trips. They usually work in large call centers, answering telephone or e-mail inquiries and offering information about travel arrangements. Transportation ticket agents work in airports, train stations, and bus stations, selling tickets, assigning seats to passengers, and checking baggage.

Career in Focus: *Travel Counselor*

Many travel clerks are employed by membership organizations, such as automobile clubs. These workers, sometimes called member services counselors or travel counselors, help members plan trips. They offer travel suggestions, such as the best route, points of interest, restaurants, and overnight accommodations. In some cases, they make rental car, hotel, and restaurant reservations for club members.

Where and When

Work spaces tend to be clean and well lit, though they can also be crowded and noisy. The work may be repetitive and stressful, especially for those who must meet quotas for calls answered or reservations made. Difficult customers are an additional hazard of the job. Many agents spend most of their time on their feet and may be required to lift heavy baggage. Most work a standard 40-hour week, though evenings, late nights, weekends, and holidays are common.

For More Information

* Air Transport Association of America, 1301 Pennsylvania Ave. NW, Suite 1100, Washington, DC 20004-1707.

Data Bank

Education and Training: Short-term on-the-job training

Starting Salaries: $18,000

Average Earnings: $22,000–$39,000

Total Jobs Held: 163,000

Job Outlook: Little change

Annual Job Openings: 30,000

Related Jobs: Hotel, motel, and resort desk clerks; travel agents; flight attendants; counter and rental clerks; order clerks; customer service representatives; receptionists and information clerks

Personality Type: Conventional

Did You Know?

Six out of every ten ticket agents and travel clerks work for airlines. Most airlines have their own extensive training programs, which can last several weeks. Because of the increased training required and the increased responsibility compared to other agents, those in the airline industry generally have higher salaries. However, due to increased security measures, numerous flight delays, and the general stress of travel, airline employees are bound to encounter angry passengers as well.

Cargo and Freight Agents

At a Glance

Cargo and freight agents work for air and railroad carriers, trucking services, and department stores. They sort cargo by destination, determine shipping rates, and then track the shipments. They take orders from customers and arrange for pickup of items or delivery to loading platforms. They also check on missing or damaged items. For imported or exported freight, they verify that the proper customs paperwork is in order. Cargo and freight agents often track shipments electronically using bar codes and computers, and they must be able to answer customers' questions on the status of their shipments.

Data Bank

Education and Training: Moderate-term on-the-job training

Starting Salaries: $21,000

Average Earnings: $27,000–$45,000

Total Jobs Held: 70,000

Job Outlook: Declining

Annual Job Openings: 12,000

Related Jobs: Couriers and messengers; shipping, receiving, and traffic clerks; weighers, measurers, checkers, and samplers, recordkeeping; truck drivers and driver/sales workers; postal service workers

Personality Type: Conventional

Did You Know?

While cargo traffic is expected to increase, the number of jobs for cargo and freight agents will decrease. Technology has improved the process of tracking shipments to the point of cutting jobs in this part of the economy. The use of bar codes, online forms, and Internet tracking procedures make it possible to automate most of this process, which explains the decline in the number of new jobs.

Career in Focus: *Transportation Agent*

Cargo and freight agents working in airline services are sometimes called transportation agents. They oversee and assist in the movement of freight, mail, baggage, and passengers through airline terminals. They report the arrival of air freight and record data on the airplane's flight papers. They oversee or participate in loading cargo, and they may be required to operate a forklift or other heavy machinery.

Where and When

Cargo and freight agents work in a variety of businesses and industries. Some may work in warehouses or stockrooms, others in cold storage rooms or outside on loading platforms. Most jobs require frequent standing, bending, walking, and stretching. The work can by physically strenuous, even with the automated devices used to lift heavy materials. While the typical workweek is Monday through Friday, evening and weekend hours are common.

For More Information

Information about job opportunities may be obtained from local employers and local offices of the state employment service.

Couriers and Messengers

At a Glance

Messengers and couriers drive, walk, or ride bicycles to pick up and deliver letters and packages that must be delivered quickly—usually within a single city. Most work for courier services, although some work for law firms and many others are self-employed. By sending an item by courier or messenger, the sender ensures that it reaches its destination the same day or even within the hour. Couriers and messengers also deliver very important items such as legal or financial documents, passports, airline tickets, or medical samples. Some messengers are paid by how many deliveries they make and how far they travel.

Career in Focus: *Medical Courier*

Although e-mail and fax machines can deliver information faster than couriers and messengers, some things, such as medical samples, simply can't be faxed. (Imagine trying to send a liver tissue sample through a fax machine.) Medical couriers are trained to handle medical samples and specimens, keeping them safe as they deliver them from one medical facility to another. Some work within hospitals or health care networks, while others work for special medical courier services. Such companies generally have specialized insurance plans in case something (or part of some*body*) should get lost or damaged in delivery.

Where and When

Couriers and messengers spend most of their time on their own making deliveries. They are sometimes required to lift heavy loads and are exposed to all weather conditions. The pressure to make as many deliveries as possible in a given day can be stressful. The typical workweek is Monday through Friday, though evening and weekend hours are common.

For More Information

Information about job opportunities may be obtained from local employers and offices of the state employment service.

Data Bank

Education and Training: Short-term on-the-job training

Starting Salaries: $14,000

Average Earnings: $17,000–$26,000

Total Jobs Held: 147,000

Job Outlook: Declining

Annual Job Openings: 24,000

Related Jobs: Postal Service workers; truck drivers and driver/sales workers; shipping, receiving, and traffic clerks; cargo and freight agents

Personality Type: Realistic

Did You Know?

If you have a desire to act or sing and want to be a messenger as well, there is a job for you. Believe it or not, there are a few companies out there who still specialize in delivering "singing telegrams." First started by Western Union in 1933, the "singing telegram" involves a performer, often dressed in costume, delivering a message in song or rhyme. Whereas telegrams were first designed to inform people of emergencies or death, the singing variety tend to be given as gifts on happy occasions such as birthdays and anniversaries.

Dispatchers

At a Glance

Dispatchers schedule and dispatch workers, equipment, or service vehicles. They keep records, logs, and schedules of the calls that they receive, the vehicles that they monitor, and the actions they take. They prepare detailed reports on all activities occurring during their shifts. Many dispatchers use computer-aided dispatch systems. The work of dispatchers varies greatly, depending on the industry. Dispatchers in public safety receive emergency calls; find out where help is needed and how serious the situation is; and send police, firefighters, or ambulances to the scene. Dispatchers in transportation coordinate arrivals and departures of shipments to meet specific time schedules.

Data Bank

Education and Training: Moderate-term on-the-job training

Starting Salaries: $19,000

Average Earnings: $24,000–$40,000

Total Jobs Held: 266,000

Job Outlook: Average increase

Annual Job Openings: 31,000

Related Jobs: Air traffic controllers, communications equipment operators, customer service representatives, reservation and transportation ticket agents and travel clerks

Personality Type: Conventional; Social

Did You Know?

Not only do emergency dispatchers direct emergency services to accident scenes, they sometimes play a direct role in saving lives. 911 operators tell children how to help a sick or injured parent, give instructions for helping people who are in shock, and help callers prevent someone from losing too much blood before help arrives. Emergency dispatchers never know what will happen when they go to work, but they can be sure that they will make a difference in people's lives.

Career in Focus: *Truck Dispatcher*

Many dispatchers work in the transportation industry, coordinating deliveries, pick-ups, and service calls for everything from taxicabs to tow trucks. Truck dispatchers work for local and long-distance trucking companies, coordinating the movement of trucks and freight between cities. They receive customers' requests for pickup and delivery of freight, consolidate freight orders into truckloads for specific destinations, assign drivers and trucks, and draw up routes and schedules.

Where and When

The work of dispatchers can be hectic, especially for those who work in public safety. Many of the people who call in are afraid, anxious, or abusive. Dispatchers sit for long periods, often using computers. As a result, they can experience significant eyestrain, headaches, and back discomfort. Most work a 40-hour week, though alternative work schedules are necessary to accommodate round-the-clock operations.

For More Information

* Association of Public Safety Communications Officials, International, 351 N. Williamson Blvd., Daytona Beach, FL 32114-1112. Internet: www.apco911.org

* International Municipal Signal Association (IMSA), P.O. Box 359, 165 E. Union St., Newark, NY 14513-0539. Internet: www.IMSAsafety.org

Meter Readers, Utilities

At a Glance

Meter readers check electric, gas, water, or steam meters at businesses and houses and record how much has been used. They also inspect the meters for damage and contact repair workers if needed. They may turn off services if the customer does not pay the bill and turn on services for new customers. Meter readers check for abnormal readings that might indicate an unauthorized connection. These workers usually keep records showing which meters they have worked on and what work was done.

Career in Focus: *AMR Technician*

Automated Reader Systems (AMR) are replacing the work of meter readers across the country. These systems allow meters to be monitored and billed from a central location. However, someone has to watch over the system itself: the AMR technician. These workers record data from residential, industrial, and commercial customers using electronic remote reading device mounted in a company vehicle. At the end of the day they upload the data and review their reports. They also are involved in troubleshooting and maintaining the monitoring equipment, and they are sometimes involved in customer service.

Where and When

Meter readers usually work about 40 hours per week, though they work outdoors in all types of weather. The typical workweek is Monday through Friday.

For More Information

Information about job opportunities may be obtained from local employers and offices of the state employment service.

Data Bank

Education and Training: Short-term on-the-job training

Starting Salaries: $19,000

Average Earnings: $23,000–$38,000

Total Jobs Held: 50,000

Job Outlook: Declining

Annual Job Openings: 8,000

Related Jobs: Power plant operators, distributors, and dispatchers

Personality Type: Conventional

Did You Know?

The price you pay for gas, water, and electricity may not always be equal to the amount you used. If a meter reader can't access your meter on the appointed day, the company simply estimates how much gas, water, or electricity you probably used and bills you for that amount instead. These estimates might be over or under the actual use, but they are generally evened out during the next billing cycle.

Postal Service Workers

At a Glance

Each week, the U.S. Postal Service delivers billions of pieces of mail. Postal workers at post offices sort mail for delivery, sell stamps, weigh packages, certify and insure mail, and help customers file claims for damaged packages. Mail carriers deliver the mail to homes and businesses on foot or by car in all kinds of weather. They pick up mail from homes and businesses on their route as well. Carriers also collect money for postage-due and COD (cash-on-delivery) fees and obtain signed receipts for registered, certified, and insured mail.

Data Bank

Education and Training: Short-term on-the-job training

Starting Salaries: $30,000

Average Earnings: $38,000–$51,000

Total Jobs Held: 619,000

Job Outlook: Little change

Annual Job Openings: 34,000

Related Jobs: Cashiers; counter and rental clerks; file clerks; shipping, receiving, and traffic clerks; couriers and messengers; truck drivers and driver/sales workers; inspectors, testers, sorters, samplers, and weighers; material moving occupations

Personality Type: Conventional

Did You Know?

According to the U.S. Postal Service, about 14 percent of the nation's population moves every year, resulting in more than 45 million address changes. That's a lot of movement to keep track of. Combine that with mail being held and forwarded, and the fact that the post office delivers *billions* of pieces of mail *each week*, and it's a wonder that anything ends up in the right mailbox.

Career in Focus: *Mail Sorter*

Mail sorters, processors, and processing machine operators prepare incoming and outgoing mail for distribution. They load and unload postal trucks and move mail around a processing center with forklifts, tractors, or hand-pushed carts. They also load and operate mail processing, sorting, and canceling machinery. The largest volume of mail is sorted during the evening hours.

Where and When

Window clerks work in clean, well-lit environments. They have frequent contact with the public, often have to deal with angry customers, and stand for long periods of time. Mail sorters are required to move heavy sacks of mail and engage in tiring and repetitive work. Many work nights and weekends. Most mail carriers work early in the morning, and overtime hours are frequent. Most of the work is done independently, although it is mostly outdoors in all kinds of weather. Not to mention the dog attacks. Seriously.

For More Information

Local post offices and state employment service offices can provide details about specific employment opportunities for postal service workers.

Production, Planning, and Expediting Clerks

At a Glance

These clerks coordinate the flow of information, work, and materials within or among offices. They set and review schedules, estimate costs, keep inventory of materials, inspect and assemble materials, and order supplies. Production and planning clerks schedule, monitor, and chart production. They compile reports on the progress of work and on production problems. In addition, they may route and deliver parts to ensure that production quotas are met and that merchandise is delivered on the date promised. Most of these clerks work in manufacturing companies or in wholesale trade or grocery stores.

Career in Focus: *Expediting Clerk*

Expediting clerks ensure that merchandise, supplies, and equipment reach their destination on time. They communicate with transportation companies to prevent delays, and they may arrange for the distribution of material after it arrives. Expediting clerks may inspect products for quality and quantity to ensure they meet specifications.

Where and When

Production, planning, and expediting clerks typically work 40 hours per week, Monday through Friday. Like many other administrative support positions, they tend to work in comfortable environments, though long periods sitting and using a computer can cause backaches and eyestrain.

For More Information

Information about job opportunities may be obtained from local employers and offices of the state employment service.

Data Bank

Education and Training: Short-term on-the-job training

Starting Salaries: $22,000

Average Earnings: $29,000–$48,000

Total Jobs Held: 292,000

Job Outlook: Little change

Annual Job Openings: 24,000

Related Jobs: Cargo and freight agents; shipping, receiving, and traffic clerks; stock clerks and order fillers; weighers, measurers, checkers, and samplers, recordkeeping

Personality Type: Conventional

Did You Know?

Most of these jobs are entry level and only require a high school diploma. However, being such an integral part of the production process allows these clerks the opportunity to get to know the company and how it works. Those who find that the company is a good fit will likely be able to advance into supervisory positions.

Shipping, Receiving, and Traffic Clerks

At a Glance

Shipping, receiving, and traffic clerks keep records of all goods shipped and received. In smaller companies, a clerk also prepares shipments and accepts deliveries. Shipping clerks keep records on all outgoing shipments. Sometimes they fill the order themselves, obtaining merchandise from the stockroom and wrapping or packing the goods themselves. They also address and label packages, compute freight or postal rates, and record the weight and cost of each shipment. They may be responsible for directing the workers who load products onto trucks. Receiving clerks check materials coming into the warehouse, make sure they are in good condition, and send them to the right departments. In many companies, receiving clerks use hand-held scanners to record barcodes on incoming products.

Data Bank

Education and Training: Short-term on-the-job training

Starting Salaries: $16,000

Average Earnings: $20,000–$32,000

Total Jobs Held: 751,000

Job Outlook: Little change

Annual Job Openings: 121,000

Related Jobs: Stock clerks and order fillers; production, planning, and expediting clerks; cargo and freight agents; postal service workers

Personality Type: Conventional

Did You Know?

Today's warehouses may look like something out of yesterday's science fiction novels. Computerized conveyor belts, robots, computer-directed trucks, and automated data storage systems are commonplace, not to mention the hand-held scanners used by the clerks who monitor all of these gadgets and machines. Despite all the automation, a human being is still needed to make sure everything in the shipment checks out . . . and to keep the robots from taking over the world.

Career in Focus: *Traffic Clerk*

Traffic clerks keep track of shipments in transit. They maintain records on the destination, weight, and charges of all incoming and outgoing freight. The information they gather is used by the accounting department or other departments. Traffic clerks also keep a file of claims for overcharges and for damage to goods in transit.

Where and When

Most of these jobs require frequent standing, bending, walking, and stretching. Some lifting and carrying of smaller items may also be necessary. Most work a typical 40-hour week, Monday through Friday, though evening and weekend hours may be required for some jobs.

For More Information

Information about job opportunities may be obtained from local employers and offices of the state employment service.

Stock Clerks and Order Fillers

At a Glance

Stock clerks receive, unpack, and check materials into the stockroom. They keep records of items and report damaged or spoiled products. They sort, organize, and mark items with identifying codes so that they can be located quickly and easily. They then bring items to the sales floor and stock shelves. In smaller companies, they also may perform tasks usually handled by shipping and receiving clerks. Many stock clerks work for department or grocery stores. All stock clerks and order fillers may be required to lift cartons of various sizes.

Career in Focus: *Order Filler*

Order fillers primarily work in wholesale and retail sales. They take customers' orders and either hold the merchandise until the customers can pick it up or ship it to them. Order fillers are responsible for computing prices, completing order receipts, and keeping records of outgoing orders. They also may be responsible for requesting additional materials, supplies, and equipment. The continued rise of online shopping should increase the need for order fillers in companies that sell over the Internet.

Where and When

Most of these jobs require frequent standing, bending, walking, carrying, and stretching. Some heavy lifting may also be involved. They typically work 40 hours per week, Monday through Friday, though evening and weekend hours are common.

For More Information

Information about job opportunities may be obtained from local employers and offices of the state employment service.

Data Bank

Education and Training: Short-term on-the-job training

Starting Salaries: $14,000

Average Earnings: $16,000–$26,000

Total Jobs Held: 1,566,000

Job Outlook: Declining

Annual Job Openings: 351,000

Related Jobs: Shipping, receiving, and traffic clerks; production, planning, and expediting clerks; cargo and freight agents; procurement clerks

Personality Type: Conventional; Realistic

Did You Know?

Stock clerks aren't allowed to just throw any product anywhere. In fact, most products at your local grocery store compete for the best shelf spaces, with some companies insisting that their products go in certain places. The next time you walk down the cereal aisle, compare where the sugary kids' cereals are located (usually on the lower shelves) versus the more healthy adult cereals (more towards the top). Just like in real estate, stocking and selling groceries is about location, location, location.

Weighers, Measurers, Checkers, and Samplers, Recordkeeping

At a Glance

Just as the job titles imply, these workers weigh, measure, and check materials, supplies, and equipment to keep records. Most of their duties are clerical. They make sure that the amounts, quality, and value of things the company is buying matches what was ordered and paid for. They prepare reports on warehouse inventory levels and on the use of parts. They use weight scales, counting tools, tally sheets, computers, and calculators in their work. They may also issue receipts for the products when needed or requested.

Career in Focus: *Quality Control Checker*

Most manufacturing and retail industries have a quality control system in place to make sure the products they make meet certain standards. For example, quality control checkers in the clothing industry examine clothes for defects. They look for unfinished edges, broken buttons, loose threads or stitches, or incorrect packaging. They then record the number and type of defects for each worker and return the rejected part or garment to the appropriate department to be reworked.

Where and When

Weighers, measures, checkers, and samplers work in a wide variety of businesses and industries. Some work in warehouses, stockrooms, or shipping rooms that might not be temperature controlled. Others may spend time outdoors where they are exposed to the weather. Most work a standard 40-hour week, though shift work is common.

For More Information

Information about job opportunities may be obtained from local employers and offices of the state employment service.

Data Bank

Education and Training: Short-term on-the-job training

Starting Salaries: $16,000

Average Earnings: $20,000–$33,000

Total Jobs Held: 88,000

Job Outlook: Declining

Annual Job Openings: 7,000

Related Jobs: Cargo and freight agents; production, planning, and expediting clerks; shipping, receiving, and traffic clerks; stock clerks and order fillers; procurement clerks

Personality Type: Conventional

Did You Know?

Many government agencies are in place to ensure that the products we use are safe. The U.S. Consumer Product Safety Commission is responsible for informing everyone about product recalls—when companies ask customers to return products for replacement, repair, or refund because they are unsafe. Whether it's because of a fingertip amputation hazard caused by a sofa bed or a circular saw blade that suddenly and unexpectedly detaches itself, it's always a good idea to keep track of the recalls on the products you buy. Thankfully measurers and checkers catch most of these defects before the products ever make it onto the market.

Communication Equipment Operators

At a Glance

Most of these individuals work as switchboard operators for a wide variety of businesses, such as offices, hospitals, and hotels. They route incoming and outgoing phone calls to the appropriate person. They also may handle other clerical duties, such as supplying information, taking messages, and announcing visitors. Directory assistance operators provide callers with information such as telephone numbers or area codes, though automated systems now handle many of these responsibilities. General communications equipment operators often work in offices, usually wearing portable headgear that frees their hands for typing.

Career in Focus: *Central Office Operator*

When callers dial "0," they usually reach a central office operator. Most of these operators work for telephone companies, and many of their responsibilities (such as placing long-distance calls) have now been automated. Not everything is handled by a computer, however. Callers still need a central office operator for placing person-to-person calls or interrupting busy lines in case of an emergency. When natural disasters occur, central office operators provide emergency phone contacts. They also assist callers who are having difficulty with automated phone systems.

Where and When

Most communications equipment operators work in pleasant, comfortable surroundings. They spend much of their time working at computers, which can cause eyestrain, back discomfort, and wrist injuries. Most work a standard 40-hour week, though they often work a variety of shifts. Entry-level phone operators often have less desirable schedules, working late evenings and weekends. This work can be repetitive and stressful.

For More Information

* Communications Workers of America, 501 3rd St. NW, Washington, DC 20001.

* International Brotherhood of Electrical Workers, Telecommunications Department, 1125 15th St. NW, Room 807, Washington, DC 20005.

* International Association of Administrative Professionals, 10502 NW Ambassador Dr., PO Box 20404, Kansas City, MO 64195-0404.

Data Bank

Education and Training: Short-term on-the-job training

Starting Salaries: $16,000

Average Earnings: $19,000–$29,000

Total Jobs Held: 256,000

Job Outlook: Declining

Annual Job Openings: 38,000

Related Jobs: Dispatchers; hotel, motel, and resort desk clerks; customer service representatives; receptionists and information clerks; reservation and transportation ticket agents and travel clerks

Personality Type: Conventional

Did You Know?

Telephone operators used to be almost all female. In fact, in 1970, AT&T settled a class action lawsuit that claimed that it discriminated against men in its hiring practices for the job. While the job is now wide open to both men and women, it turns out that computers are getting most of the work. Still, it seems that even most of the recorded voices you hear on automated menus are female—perhaps as a throwback to women's dominance in this career.

Computer Operators

At a Glance

Computer operators supervise computer hardware systems and keep them working smoothly and securely. They may work with mainframes, minicomputers, or networks of personal computers. Computer operators must anticipate problems and take preventative action, as well as solve problems that occur during operations. On a daily basis, they might check the computer's controls and load tapes, paper, and disks as needed. Operators also maintain logbooks that list each job that is run and events, such as machine malfunctions, that occur during their shift. In addition, computer operators may help programmers and systems analysts test and debug new programs.

Data Bank

Education and Training: Moderate-term on-the-job training

Starting Salaries: $19,000

Average Earnings: $25,000–$41,000

Total Jobs Held: 149,000

Job Outlook: Declining

Annual Job Openings: 13,000

Related Jobs: Computer software engineers; computer programmers; computer support specialists and systems administrators; computer systems analysts, database administrators, and computer scientists; data entry and information processing workers; secretaries and administrative assistants

Personality Type: Conventional

Did You Know?

Did you know the first computer was designed more than 175 years ago? In 1830, a British mathematician named Charles Babbage designed a machine he called an "analytical engine," which performed basic logic and computing tasks. There was no electricity then, so it ran on steam. It also weighed 15 tons and was 8 feet high. Charles Babbage is called the father of computing, though we wonder what he would think of a Palm Pilot if he were alive today to see it.

Career in Focus: *Computer Operations Manager*

Computer operators rank among the most rapidly declining occupations. Because of advances in technology, many of the duties these operators used to perform are no longer necessary. The result is that fewer operators are needed, but they need to perform more highly skilled work. Someone who brings more skills to the table, such as a computer operations manager, has a better chance of finding a job in this field. Computer operations managers coordinate all of the activities of workers involved in computer operations. They plan and develop policies and procedures for using computer systems, and work to resolve problems and ensure that a company's computer systems are safe and efficient.

Where and When

Most computer operators work in comfortable rooms. Because many organizations use their computers around the clock, evening, night, and weekend shifts are common. Spending long periods of time in front of a computer can cause eyestrain, backaches, and hand and wrist problems.

For More Information

* Association for Computer Operations Management (AFCOM), 722 E. Chapman Ave., Orange, CA 92860. Internet: www.afcom.com

Data Entry and Information Processing Workers

At a Glance

We live in the "Information Age." Data entry and information processing workers efficiently handle all of that incoming and outgoing information. By keying in text, entering data into a computer, operating a variety of office machines, and performing other clerical duties, these workers help organizations keep up with the data flow. Information processing workers set up and type reports, letters, manuscripts, and mailing labels. They may have other office duties as well, such as filing, answering telephones, and sorting mail. Sometimes they also proofread and edit documents.

Career in Focus: *Data Entry Keyer*

Data entry keyers usually input lists of items, numbers, or other data into computers or complete forms that appear on a computer screen. They also may edit current information or proofread new entries into a database for accuracy. Some examples of data sources include customers' personal information, medical records, and membership lists. Data entry keyers may work with non-keyboard forms of data entry as well, such as scanners and electronically transmitted files.

Where and When

Data entry and information processing workers usually work 40-hour weeks in clean office environments. They do sit for long periods of time, however, and are susceptible to eyestrain, neck and back injuries, and carpal tunnel syndrome. To combat these conditions, many offices have exercise breaks and specially designed keyboards. They also have workstations that can be used while standing to give the data entry worker's behind a break as well.

For More Information

Information about job opportunities may be obtained from local employers and offices of the state employment service.

Data Bank

Education and Training: Moderate-term on-the-job training

Starting Salaries: $17,000

Average Earnings: $21,000–$31,000

Total Jobs Held: 524,000

Job Outlook: Declining

Annual Job Openings: 115,000

Related Jobs: Dispatchers, communications equipment operators, court reporters, medical records and health information technicians, secretaries and administrative assistants, computer operators

Personality Type: Conventional

Did You Know?

Anyone interested in a career in this field must type at least 50 words per minute accurately. Of course for some people that's nothing. World record holder Stella Pajunas typed 216 words in one minute back in 1946. Over a one-hour span, Margaret Hamma averaged 149 words per minute. One way to learn to type faster is by typing to music. Start with something moderately slow (like a love song), and then work up to faster and faster beats.

Desktop Publishers

At a Glance

Desktop publishers use computers to format text, photos, charts, and other graphics in order to produce newsletters, magazines, calendars, business cards, newspapers, and books. Depending on the project, desktop publishers may write and edit text, create graphics, convert photographs and drawings into digital images, and design page layouts. They may also create proposals, develop presentations and advertising campaigns, and translate electronic information onto film. Using specialized software, an entire newspaper, catalog, or book can be created on the screen exactly as it will appear in print. Most desktop publishers work for newspapers or in companies that handle commercial printing. This is one of the fastest-growing jobs in the United States.

Data Bank

Education and Training: Vocational/technical training

Starting Salaries: $19,000

Average Earnings: $25,000–$43,000

Total Jobs Held: 34,000

Job Outlook: Above-average increase

Annual Job Openings: 8,000

Related Jobs: Artists and related workers; commercial and industrial designers; news analysts, reporters, and correspondents; prepress technicians and workers; public relations specialists; writers and editors

Personality Type: Realistic

Did You Know?

One of the keys to landing a job as a desktop publisher is a degree in graphic arts, graphic communications, or graphic design. Both associate and bachelor's degree programs teach everything from typography, to packaging, to Web site design. Many employers prefer these graduates because their training helps them learn the company's processes and software faster.

Career in Focus: *Web Publications Designer*

Although desktop publishers must be familiar with a variety of computer applications, most of them use computers to produce materials on real paper. Web publications designers, on the other hand, specialize in creating, formatting, and developing materials for the Internet. These may be anything from online newsletters to Web-based instructional materials. Like all desktop publishing jobs, this career combines a love of creative arts and a love of (or at least a tolerance for) computers.

Where and When

Desktop publishers typically work in comfortable office environments. Most work a standard 40-hour week, though some night shifts, weekends, and holidays may be required. The job can be stressful given the pressure of deadlines and tight work schedules. Like others who work in front of a computer for extended periods, desktop publishers are susceptible to eyestrain, back discomfort, and wrist problems.

For More Information

❋ Graphic Communications Council, 1899 Preston White Dr., Reston, VA 20191-4367. Internet: www.makeyourmark.org

❋ Graphic Arts Information Network, 200 Deer Run Rd., Sewickley, PA 15143. Internet: www.gain.org

Office and Administrative Support Worker Supervisors and Managers

At a Glance

All organizations need office and administrative support to operate efficiently. These supervisors and managers make sure their employees work up to expectations. If supplies are low or equipment needs to be repaired, they order new supplies or contract with a repair service. They train new employees, plan their work, and check their progress. They evaluate their employees' work habits and recommend pay raises and promotions. If a worker is performing inadequately, the supervisor discusses the problem with the employee to improve his or her performance. If the situation does not improve, the supervisor may recommend a transfer, demotion, or dismissal. Office and administrative support supervisors and managers usually interview and evaluate prospective employees as well. These workers can be found in nearly every part of the economy.

Career in Focus: *First-Line Supervisor–Customer Service*

Customer service representatives represent more than two million members of the workforce. These employees generally work under a supervisor. First-line supervisors coordinate the activities of their employees. They plan and prepare work schedules; evaluate workers' performance; hire, train, and discharge workers; and perform many of the same functions as other supervisors. However, being on the front line of customer service means these managers have to interact with customers as well, often answering questions or dealing with complaints.

Where and When

Office and administrative support supervisors and managers usually work in clean, well-lit offices. Most work a standard 40-hour week, but those working for organizations that operate around the clock may have to work nights, weekends, and holidays. Shifts are often assigned on the basis of seniority.

For More Information

* National Management Association, 2210 Arbor Blvd., Dayton, OH 45439. Internet: www.nma1.org
* International Association of Administrative Professionals, 10502 NW Ambassador Dr., P.O. Box 20404, Kansas City, MO 64195-0404. Internet: www.iaap-hq.org

Data Bank

Education and Training: Work experience

Starting Salaries: $25,000

Average Earnings: $33,000–$55,000

Total Jobs Held: 1,482,000

Job Outlook: Little change

Annual Job Openings: 167,000

Related Jobs: Bookkeeping, accounting, and auditing clerks; cashiers; communications equipment operators; customer service representatives; data entry and information processing workers; office clerks, general; receptionists and information clerks; stock clerks and order fillers; order clerks; tellers

Personality Type: Enterprising

Did You Know?

Perhaps the most dreaded task of any manager or supervisor is to dismiss an employee. Over the years we have developed a number of euphemisms to make it sound less harsh than it usually is: Employees are let go, laid off, made redundant, and downsized as companies retrench, de-layer, or right-size themselves. Seldom is anyone "fired" or "terminated" anymore, unless they did something unethical. Regardless of what you call it, it isn't an easy thing for supervisors to do, and it's certainly not easy for the person on the other end.

Office Clerks, General

At a Glance

General office clerks work in all kinds of businesses, from doctors' offices to banks, from big law firms to small companies. Clerks' duties vary by industry and level of experience. These workers generally file, type, keep records, prepare mailings, and proofread documents. Depending on the organization, they may sort checks, keep payroll records, take inventory, access information, or fill orders. Part-time and temporary positions are common in this field.

Data Bank

Education and Training: Short-term on-the-job training

Starting Salaries: $15,000

Average Earnings: $18,000–$29,000

Total Jobs Held: 3,138,000

Job Outlook: Little change

Annual Job Openings: 695,000

Related Jobs: Bookkeeping, accounting, and auditing clerks; communications equipment operators; customer service representatives; data entry and information processing workers; order clerks; receptionists and information clerks; secretaries and administrative assistants; stock clerks and order fillers; tellers

Personality Type: Conventional

Did You Know?

Don't let the job outlook data fool you. While employment of office clerks will grow more slowly than average over the next ten years, the number of job openings is still huge, primarily because of high turnover. Those who know how to use basic office equipment—computers, telephones, fax machines, copiers, and scanners—and have good communication skills will have the best opportunities.

Career in Focus: *Senior Office Clerk*

When is an office clerk more than an office clerk? When he gets promoted to senior clerk. Despite the fact that office clerk is traditionally an entry-level job, there *is* room for advancement. Senior office clerks are generally responsible for more complicated or sensitive work tasks, such as maintaining financial records, setting up spreadsheets, or handling customer complaints. In addition, senior clerks may be expected to monitor and direct the work of lower-level clerks.

Where and When

Most office clerks work in comfortable office settings. Those who are full-time work a standard 40-hour week, though some work shifts or overtime during busy periods. About 16 percent of clerks work part-time.

For More Information

* International Association of Administrative Professionals, 10502 NW Ambassador Dr., P.O. Box 20404, Kansas City, MO 64195-0404. Internet: www.iaap-hq.org

Secretaries and Administrative Assistants

At a Glance

Secretaries and administrative assistants help keep offices organized and running smoothly. In their role as information and communication managers, they schedule appointments, maintain files, type correspondence, greet visitors, and answer telephone calls. They also may manage projects, conduct research, and send out company information by telephone, mail, and e-mail. They work with office equipment such as computers, fax machines, and copiers. In addition, secretaries and administrative assistants do tasks previously handled by managers and professionals: create spreadsheets; manage databases; and create presentations, reports, and other documents. They may supervise clerks and other office workers as well.

Career in Focus: *Legal Secretary*

In addition to many of the tasks performed by other kinds of secretaries, legal secretaries have special job responsibilities. For example, they prepare correspondence and legal papers such as complaints, motions, responses, and subpoenas under the supervision of an attorney or a paralegal. They also may review legal journals and assist with legal research, such as verifying quotes and citations in legal briefs.

Where and When

Secretaries and administrative assistants work in schools, hospitals, government agencies, and legal, medical, and corporate offices. Their jobs often involve sitting for long periods in front of a computer, which can cause eyestrain, stress, backaches, and wrist problems. Though one in five secretaries works part-time, the majority work a standard 40-hour week.

For More Information

* International Association of Administrative Professionals, 10502 NW Ambassador Dr., P.O. Box 20404, Kansas City, MO 64195-0404. Internet: www.iaap-hq.org

* Legal Secretaries International, Inc. Internet: www.legalsecretaries.org

* National Association of Legal Secretaries, Inc., 314 East Third St., Suite 210, Tulsa, OK 74120. Internet: www.nals.org

---

Data Bank

Education and Training: Moderate-term on-the-job training to vocational/technical training

Starting Salaries: $20,000

Average Earnings: $25,000–$39,000

Total Jobs Held: 4,126,000

Job Outlook: Little change

Annual Job Openings: 545,000

Related Jobs: Bookkeeping, accounting, and auditing clerks; receptionists and information clerks; court reporters; human resources assistants, except payroll and timekeeping; computer operators; data entry and information processing workers; paralegals and legal assistants; medical assistants; medical records and health information technicians

Personality Type: Conventional

Did You Know?

In the past, people thought of secretaries as low-level gophers: young women who typed, answered phones, and made coffee. Today's reality is much different. Changes in organization and technology have prompted secretaries and administrative assistants to assume responsibilities formally reserved for managers and professional staff. A secretary now acts as a kind of junior executive, the keeper of the office schedules and key information.

Farming, Fishing, and Forestry Occupations

Agricultural Workers

At a Glance

Agricultural workers plant, harvest, grade, and sort farm products. They work with food crops, animals, trees, and plants in farms, nurseries, and slaughterhouses. They may work indoors or outdoors, in all kinds of working conditions. Farmworkers grow grains, fruits, vegetables, nuts, and other crops. They also operate heavy machinery for plowing, harvesting, and sorting. Nursery and greenhouse workers grow trees, plants, and flowers in controlled environments. Graders and sorters examine agricultural products and classify them according to quality or size. Animal breeders select and breed animals using their knowledge of genetics and animal science to produce offspring with desired characteristics, such as chickens that lay more eggs and pigs that produce leaner meat. Farming is one of the most dangerous jobs in the United States.

Data Bank

Education and Training: Short-term on-the-job training to related work experience

Starting Salaries: $13,000

Average Earnings: $15,000–$20,000

Total Jobs Held: 835,000

Job Outlook: Declining

Annual Job Openings: 160,000

Related Jobs: Fishers and fishing vessel operators; forest, conservation, and logging workers; grounds maintenance workers; animal care and service workers; veterinary technologists; veterinarians

Personality Type: Realistic

Did You Know?

Many of the laborers working in farms today are migrant farmworkers; they move from one farm to the next to keep up with various harvests. Many times the entire family works on the farm, though children must be 12 years old according to federal law. Most migrant farmworkers struggle to find permanent housing, and the pay is quite low. About two-thirds of these workers are immigrants, and their life expectancy of around 50 years is much less than that of the average American.

Career in Focus: *Agricultural Inspector*

Agricultural inspectors are employed by federal and state governments to enforce laws and regulations governing the health, quality, and safety of the food we eat. Inspectors also make sure that the facilities and equipment meet quality standards as well. They ensure that the meat we eat is free of harmful ingredients or bacteria and inspect livestock to help determine the effectiveness of medication and feeding programs. Some inspectors weigh and inspect agricultural shipments leaving and entering the country.

Where and When

Much of this work takes place outdoors on farms and ranches, or indoors in nurseries and factories. The work tends to be physically demanding, especially for farmworkers, and much of it is seasonal in nature. Many farmers work six or seven days per week, and many farmworkers must migrate from one location to the next to keep a steady paycheck. Inspectors also work long, irregular hours, sometimes in extreme conditions. Agricultural workers involved in crop production risk exposure to pesticides and other hazardous chemicals.

For More Information

✳ National FFA Organization, The National FFA Center, Attention: Career Information Requests, P.O. Box 68690, Indianapolis, IN 46268-0960. Internet: www.ffa.org

✳ Growing New Farmers Consortium, c/o New England Small Farm Institute, P.O. Box 11, Belchertown, MA 01007.

Fishers and Fishing Vessel Operators

At a Glance

Fishers and fishing vessel operators catch and trap fish and seafood for the country's restaurants and grocery stores. The boat's captain plans and oversees the fishing, hires crew members, and arranges for the day's catch to be sold. The first mate is the captain's assistant and is in charge when the captain is not on duty. The deckhands carry out the sailing and fishing operations. Large fishing vessels that operate in deep water may have facilities on board where the fish are processed and prepared for sale. Fishers on small boats work in relatively shallow waters, often in sight of land. A very small proportion of commercial fishing is conducted as diving operations. Although most fishers are involved in commercial fishing, some captains and deckhands use their fishing expertise for sport or recreational purposes, often hiring themselves out as guides to tourists.

Career in Focus: *Boatswain*

The boatswain is a highly experienced deckhand who supervises the other deckhands as they carry out the sailing and fishing operations. Before departure, the boatswain directs the deckhands to load equipment and supplies. When necessary, boatswains repair fishing gear, equipment, nets, and accessories. Their supervisory roles usually earn them a slightly better percentage of the sale of the catch.

Where and When

Fishers and fishing vessel operators work under some of the most hazardous conditions of any occupation. Storms, fog, wind, potentially dangerous gear, slippery decks, and a host of other problems make this job one of the most dangerous. In addition, the work is physically demanding and requires workers to be away from home for weeks or even months. The job can be seasonal as well.

For More Information

* Marine Technology Society, 5565 Sterrett Place, Suite 108, Columbia, MD 21044. Internet: www.mtsociety.org
* Licensing and Evaluation Branch, National Maritime Center, 4200 Wilson Blvd., Suite 630, Arlington, VA 22203-1804.

Data Bank

Education and Training: Moderate-term on-the-job training
Starting Salaries: $14,000
Average Earnings: $18,000–$37,000
Total Jobs Held: 38,000
Job Outlook: Declining
Annual Job Openings: 6,000
Related Jobs: Water transportation occupations
Personality Type: Realistic

Did You Know?

American fisheries are in a state of recovery. Destruction of natural habitats and excessive fish harvesting have dramatically hampered the fishing industry. As a result of government regulations designed to replenish the number of fish naturally, many fishers are forced to limit their catches, which in turn means limited paychecks. For these reasons, and because of the dangerous and seasonal nature of the job, many fishers and fishing vessel operators are leaving the occupation.

Forest, Conservation, and Logging Workers

At a Glance

Managing and harvesting our nation's forests and woodlands requires many different kinds of workers. Forestry and conservation workers help develop and protect forests by planting new trees, fighting the pests and diseases that attack trees, and helping to control soil erosion. Some forest workers are employed on tree farms, where they plant, cultivate, and harvest many different kinds of trees. Timber cutters and loggers cut down thousands of acres of forest each year for the timber that is used for wood and paper products. The timber-cutting and logging process is carried out by a variety of workers who make up a logging crew. Fallers cut down trees, buckers trim off the tops and branches and cut the resulting logs into specified lengths, and choke setters fasten steel cables around logs to be dragged by tractors, just to name a few. These jobs can be dangerous.

Data Bank

Education and Training: Moderate-term on-the-job training

Starting Salaries: $17,000

Average Earnings: $22,000–$34,000

Total Jobs Held: 91,000

Job Outlook: Little change

Annual Job Openings: 17,000

Related Jobs: Conservation scientists and foresters, grounds maintenance workers, material moving operators

Personality Type: Realistic

Did You Know?

The paper that you are holding comes at a cost. Logging is dangerous work. In fact, in 1997, logging surpassed fishing as the most dangerous job in the nation. Every year more than 100 workers lose their lives in this industry, despite all of the safety precautions that are taken.

Career in Focus: *Log Grader*

Log graders inspect logs for defects, measure logs to determine their volume, and estimate their value on the market. These workers often use hand-held computers to enter data about individual trees. Later, the data can be downloaded or sent from the scaling area to a central computer for processing.

Where and When

These jobs are physically demanding. Workers spend all their time outdoors in all kinds of weather, and some commute long distances from their homes to logging sites. Most logging occupations involve lifting and climbing. Workers wear hardhats, eye and ear protection, safety clothing, and boots.

For More Information

* Forest Resources Association, Inc., 600 Jefferson Plaza, Suite 350, Rockville, MD 20852. Internet: www.forestresources.org

* American Loggers Council. P.O. Box 966, Hemphill, TX 75948. Internet: www.americanloggers.org

* American Forest & Paper Association, 1111 19th St. NW, Suite 800, Washington, DC 20036. Internet: www.afandpa.org

Construction Trades
and Related Workers

Boilermakers

At a Glance

Boilermakers build, install, and repair boilers, vats, and other large tanks used for storing liquids and gases. Boilers supply steam for electric engines and for heating and power systems in buildings, factories, and ships. Tanks and vats are used to store and process everything from oil to beer. Because most boilers last for 35 years or more, repairing and maintaining them is a big part of a boilermaker's job. They inspect tubes, fittings, valves, and controls; clean the boilers; and repair or replace broken parts.

Data Bank

Education and Training: Long-term on-the-job training

Starting Salaries: $29,000

Average Earnings: $38,000–$60,000

Total Jobs Held: 19,000

Job Outlook: Little change

Annual Job Openings: 2,000

Related Jobs: Assemblers and fabricators; machinists; industrial machinery mechanics and maintenance workers; millwrights; pipelayers, plumbers, pipefitters, and steamfitters; sheet metal workers; tool and die makers; welding, soldering, and brazing workers

Personality Type: Realistic

Did You Know?

While the term *boilermaker* used to refer only to workers who actually made boilers (and graduates of Purdue University), today members of the boilermakers' union do a wide variety of jobs in construction, ship-building, and manufacturing. Some work at power plants and oil refineries. Others make heavy machinery, heaters, or even golf balls. Some produce cement, wallboard, and bricks, while others mine coal and other minerals.

Career in Focus: *Boilermaker Apprentice*

While there are many technical school programs available to teach the same skills, many boilermakers learn the trade through a formal apprenticeship. An apprenticeship usually consists of four or more years of on-the-job training, plus a hundred-plus hours of classroom instruction each year. Apprentices generally start at about half of what journey-level boilermakers earn. Apprenticeships are usually advertised by local unions when they are available.

Where and When

Boilermaker work is physically demanding, and workers often use potentially dangerous equipment such as torches and power grinders. Work may be done in cramped quarters or at high elevations. Extended periods of overtime are common, and boilermakers often may find themselves in between jobs.

For More Information

* International Brotherhood of Boilermakers, Iron Ship Builders, Blacksmiths, Forgers, and Helpers, 753 State Ave., Suite 570, Kansas City, KS 66101. Internet: www.boilermakers.org

Brickmasons, Blockmasons, and Stonemasons

At a Glance

These workers lay sidewalks and patios, build fireplaces, and install ornamental exteriors on buildings. Brickmasons work with (you guessed it) bricks. Blockmasons work with concrete blocks. Both brickmasons and blockmasons—who often are just called bricklayers—build and repair walls, floors, partitions, chimneys, and other structures. Stonemasons build stone walls and set stone exteriors and floors. They work with two types of stone: natural cut stone, such as marble, granite, and limestone, and artificial stone made from concrete, marble chips, or other materials. They often work on churches, office buildings, and hotels. Many masons are self-employed.

Career in Focus: *Refractory Mason*

A refractory mason is a brickmason who specializes in installing firebrick and refractory tile in high-temperature boilers, furnaces, ovens, and ladles for industrial companies. Most of these workers are employed in steel mills, where molten materials flow on refractory beds from furnaces to rolling machines. Work in such places can literally be hot and heavy.

Where and When

These individuals usually work outdoors in a variety of weather conditions. The work can be physically demanding. Masons stand, kneel, bend, and lift heavy materials. Injuries from tools and falls from scaffolds can be avoided with proper safety precautions and equipment.

For More Information

* Associated Builders and Contractors, Workforce Development Division, 4250 North Fairfax Dr., 9th Floor, Arlington, VA 22203. Internet: www.trytools.org

* International Union of Bricklayers and Allied Craftworkers, International Masonry Institute, The James Brice House, 42 East St., Annapolis, MD 21401. Internet: www.imiweb.org

* National Center for Construction Education and Research, P.O. Box 141104, Gainesville FL 32614-1104. Internet: www.nccer.org

* Associated General Contractors of America, Inc., 2300 Wilson Blvd., Suite 400, Arlington, VA 22201. Internet: www.agc.org

* National Concrete Masonry Association, 13750 Sunrise Valley Dr., Herndon, VA 20171-3499. Internet: www.ncma.org

Data Bank

Education and Training: Long-term on-the-job training

Starting Salaries: $24,000

Average Earnings: $31,000–$52,000

Total Jobs Held: 177,000

Job Outlook: Average increase

Annual Job Openings: 19,000

Related Jobs: Carpet, floor, and tile installers and finishers; cement masons, concrete finishers, segmental pavers, and terrazzo workers; plasterers and stucco masons

Personality Type: Realistic

Did You Know?

You may have heard of Boy Scout Camp and church camp, but have you heard of masonry camp? Each year, the International Masonry Institute sponsors a Masonry Camp on Swan's Island in Maine. For one week each summer, architects, engineers, and masonry apprentices spend a week working together to design and build a challenging new project. This way, workers from several fields learn how building plans go from paper to actual bricks and mortar.

Carpenters

At a Glance

Carpenters do all kinds of construction work, including woodworking, concrete work, drywall work, and many other jobs. They frame walls; build stairs; replace doors, windows, and locks; repair wooden furniture; and hang kitchen cabinets. They work with hand and power tools such as saws, drills, and levels, and they must be able to read blueprints. Most work in new construction or remodeling. Carpenters who remodel homes and other structures need a broad range of carpentry skills. These carpenters can switch from residential building to commercial construction or remodeling work, depending on which offers the best work opportunities.

Data Bank

Education and Training: Long-term on-the-job training

Starting Salaries: $22,000

Average Earnings: $27,000–$48,000

Total Jobs Held: 1,349,000

Job Outlook: Average increase

Annual Job Openings: 210,000

Related Jobs: Brickmasons, blockmasons, and stonemasons; cement masons, concrete finishers, segmental pavers, and terrazzo workers; electricians; pipelayers, plumbers, pipefitters, and steamfitters; plasterers and stucco masons

Personality Type: Realistic

Did You Know?

What do Han Solo, Jack Ryan, and Indiana Jones have in common? They were all former carpenters. Or at least they were played by one. Actor Harrison Ford was working as a carpenter when he got his role in the first *Star Wars* film. It's not surprising—carpenters make up the largest building trades occupation with more than a million workers. Of course we imagine Mr. Ford made a bit more cash as an actor (though the vast majority of actors would be better off financially as carpenters).

Career in Focus: *Brattice Builder*

Brattice builders are specialized carpenters who build tunnel bracing, or brattices, in underground passageways and mines. Brattices control the circulation of air through the passageways and to work sites. Brattice builders might also drill and blast obstructing boulders to reopen ventilation shafts. This is probably not a job for the claustrophobic.

Where and When

Carpentry work can be strenuous because of the prolonged standing, climbing, bending, and kneeling required. Work is done both indoors and out, and carpenters risk injury working with sharp tools and equipment or in situations where they might slip or fall. Many carpenters are self-employed and set their own schedules, although others work for contractors who set their hours for them.

For More Information

* Associated Builders and Contractors, 4250 North Fairfax Dr., 9th Floor, Arlington, VA 22203. Internet: www.trytools.org

* Associated General Contractors of America, Inc., 2300 Wilson Blvd., Suite 400, Arlington, VA 22201. Internet: www.agc.org

* National Center for Construction Education and Research, P.O. Box 141104, Gainesville, FL 32614-1104. Internet: www.nccer.org

* National Association of Home Builders, Home Builders Institute, 1201 15th St. NW, Washington, DC 20005. Internet: www.hbi.org

* United Brotherhood of Carpenters and Joiners of America, Carpenters Training Fund, 6801 Placid St., Las Vegas, NV 89119. Internet: www.carpenters.org

Carpet, Floor, and Tile Installers and Finishers

At a Glance

Carpet installers put carpet in new or old buildings and houses. Floor layers install flooring foundation materials such as rubber, laminate, vinyl, and linoleum. Tilesetters use grout to apply ceramic tiles to floors and walls, primarily in kitchens and bathrooms. Marble setters cut and set marble slabs in floors and walls of buildings. All of these workers use a wide variety of specialized tools. They do installations in homes, offices, hospitals, stores, restaurants, and many other types of buildings.

Career in Focus: *Floor Sander and Finisher*

After a carpenter installs a new hardwood floor or when a customer wants to refinish an old wood floor, floor sanders and finishers are called in. They smooth any imperfections in the wood using power sanders, wood chisels, and even sandpaper. Afterwards, they apply finish coats of varnish or polyurethane to both protect the floor and give it a glossy finish.

Where and When

Carpet, floor, and tile installers and finishers usually work indoors during regular daytime hours. Work done in stores and offices generally requires evening and weekend work. This work can be physically demanding. Workers spend much of their time bending, kneeling, pulling, and reaching, as well as lifting heavy rolls of carpet and moving heavy furniture.

For More Information

* Floor Covering Installation Contractors Association, 7439 Milwood Dr., West Bloomfield, MI 48322.

* Joint Apprenticeship and Training Fund, International Union of Painters and Allied Trades, 1750 New York Ave. NW, Washington, DC 20006. Internet: www.jatf.org

* International Union of Bricklayers and Allied Craftworkers, International Masonry Institute, The James Brice House, 42 East St., Annapolis, MD 21401. Internet: www.imiweb.org

* National Association of Home Builders, Home Builders Institute, 1201 15th St. NW, Washington, DC 20005. Internet: www.hbi.org

* National Tile Contractors Association, P.O. Box 13629, Jackson, MS 39236.

Data Bank

Education and Training: Moderate-term on-the-job training to long-term on-the-job training

Starting Salaries: $20,000

Average Earnings: $26,000–$47,000

Total Jobs Held: 184,000

Job Outlook: Average increase

Annual Job Openings: 26,000

Related Jobs: Brickmasons, blockmasons, and stonemasons; carpenters; cement masons, concrete finishers, segmental pavers, and terrazzo workers; drywall installers, ceiling tile installers, and tapers; painters and paperhangers; roofers; sheet metal workers

Personality Type: Realistic

Did You Know?

Do you know what a "knee kicker" is? It's actually not an angry four-year-old who is about to get into even more trouble. Instead, it is a tool used by carpet installers to stretch carpet into place. Contrary to the name, it is not actually kicked with the knee (which is a hard enough thing to do), but is pushed with the leg. Now can you guess what a "power stretcher" does? (Hint: It has nothing to do with aerobics.)

Cement Masons, Concrete Finishers, Segmental Pavers, and Terrazzo Workers

At a Glance

Cement masons and concrete finishers use a mixture of cement, gravel, sand, and water to build home patios, huge dams, and miles of roads. They pour the concrete and smooth the finished surface. Segmental pavers lay out flat pieces of masonry to form paths, patios, playgrounds, and driveways. These workers need a thorough knowledge of concrete's characteristics so that they can determine what is happening to the concrete and take measures to prevent defects. Many of these workers get their training through three-year or four-year apprenticeship programs.

Data Bank

Education and Training: Moderate-term on-the-job training to long-term on-the-job training

Starting Salaries: $20,000

Average Earnings: $25,000–$42,000

Total Jobs Held: 209,000

Job Outlook: Average increase

Annual Job Openings: 33,000

Related Jobs: Brickmasons, blockmasons, and stonemasons; carpet, floor, and tile installers and finishers; drywall installers, ceiling tile installers, and tapers; plasterers and stucco masons

Personality Type: Realistic

Did You Know?

The ancient Romans were serious road builders. Only Roman men of the highest rank were allowed to build and maintain roads. Those cement-block roads were so well constructed that they have lasted for more than 2,000 years. At the height of the Roman Empire, 29 different roads led from Rome to Northern Europe and the Middle East and even into parts of Africa. Hence the expression, "All roads lead to Rome."

Career in Focus: *Terrazzo Worker*

Terrazzo workers create attractive walkways, floors, patios, and panels by exposing marble chips on the surface of finished concrete. Much of the preliminary work of terrazzo workers is similar to that of cement masons. Terrazzo requires workers to add marble chips of various colors into concrete panels. Terrazzo workers then grind, clean, polish, and seal the dry surface for a lustrous and decorative finish.

Where and When

This work can be physically strenuous as most of it is done at floor level, requiring much bending and kneeling. Many jobs are outdoors and are generally stopped during bad weather. Workers wear kneepads and water-repellent boots when working with concrete. Most of these workers are employed by specialty trade contractors who set their hours. Overtime is sometimes needed to finish a job on schedule.

For More Information

* National Concrete Masonry Association, 13750 Sunrise Valley Dr., Herndon, VA 20171-3499. Internet: www.ncma.org

* Associated Builders and Contractors, Workforce Development Division, 4250 North Fairfax Dr., 9th Floor, Arlington, VA 22203. Internet: www.trytools.org

* Associated General Contractors of America, Inc., 2300 Wilson Blvd., Suite 400, Arlington, VA 22201. Internet: www.agc.org

* International Union of Bricklayers and Allied Craftworkers, International Masonry Institute, The James Brice House, 42 East St., Annapolis, MD 21401. Internet: www.imiweb.org

Construction and Building Inspectors

At a Glance

Construction and building inspectors make sure that the country's buildings, roads, sewers, dams, and bridges are safe. They may check electrical or plumbing systems, elevators, or the beams and girders on skyscrapers. In the United States, building construction is regulated by building codes. To monitor compliance with these codes, inspectors make an initial inspection during the first phase of construction and follow up with further inspections throughout the project. In areas where natural disasters—such as earthquakes or hurricanes—are more common, inspectors check for compliance with additional safety regulations. If necessary, inspectors notify the contractor, superintendent, or supervisor when they discover a violation. If the problem is not corrected, government inspectors have the authority to issue a "stop-work" order.

Career in Focus: *Home Inspector*

Home inspectors conduct inspections of newly built or previously owned homes, condominiums, town homes, and apartments. Typically, inspectors are hired by prospective home buyers to inspect and report on the condition of a home. In addition to examining structural quality, inspectors evaluate all home systems and features, including roofing as well as the exterior, garage or carport, foundation, interior, plumbing, electrical, and heating and cooling systems. Home inspection has become a standard practice in the home-buying process.

Where and When

Construction and building inspectors spend considerable time inspecting work sites, which pose their own dangers. They also spend a lot of time in a field office, reviewing blueprints, answering calls, and writing reports. Inspectors normally work regular hours, though if an accident occurs, they must respond immediately.

For More Information

* International Code Council, 5203 Leesburg Pike, Suite 600, Falls Church, VA 22041. Internet: www.iccsafe.org

* Association of Construction Inspectors, 1224 North Nokomis NE, Alexandria, MN 56308. Internet: www.iami.org/aci/home.cfm

* National Association of Home Inspectors, 4248 Park Glen Rd., Minneapolis, MN 55416. Internet: www.nahi.org

---

Data Bank

Education and Training: Work experience

Starting Salaries: $28,000

Average Earnings: $35,000–$56,000

Total Jobs Held: 94,000

Job Outlook: Above-average increase

Annual Job Openings: 6,000

Related Jobs: Carpenters; plumbers; electricians; architects, except landscape and naval; construction managers; engineers; cost estimators; drafters; engineering technicians; surveyors, cartographers, photogrammetrists, and surveying technicians

Personality Type: Conventional

Did You Know?

About 45 percent of all construction and building inspectors are employed by local governments. These local governments employ large staffs, including plan examiners or inspectors who specialize in steel, concrete, electrical, and elevator inspection. Getting a job working for state or local government almost always requires some type of certification, but the benefits are usually worth it.

Construction Equipment Operators

At a Glance

Construction equipment operators drive and operate the huge machinery used in building construction, road building and repair, and demolition. They might operate cranes, tractors, backhoes, pavers, cement mixers, tamping machines, or hoists, just to name a few. They work at construction sites, shipping docks, airports, mines, and on the nation's highways. They clear land, dig trenches, apply asphalt, and may even work on oil rigs. The pay for these jobs can be high, but the work may slow down in bad weather, reducing earnings.

Data Bank

Education and Training: Moderate-term on-the-job training

Starting Salaries: $22,000

Average Earnings: $27,000–$47,000

Total Jobs Held: 449,000

Job Outlook: Average increase

Annual Job Openings: 44,000

Related Jobs: Truck drivers and driver/sales workers, material moving occupations

Personality Type: Realistic

Did You Know?

A piledriver is more than a professional wrestling move. Piledrivers are large machines, mounted on skids, barges, or cranes, that hammer long, heavy beams of wood or steel (known as piles) into the ground. These beams are used to support retaining walls, bridges, piers, or building foundations. These machines are common in the oil industry. In fact, some piledriver operators work on offshore oil rigs.

Career in Focus: *Operating Engineer*

Operating engineers generally operate excavation and loading machines equipped with scoops, shovels, or buckets that dig sand, gravel, or earth, and load it into trucks or onto conveyors. Sometimes, they may drive and control industrial trucks or tractors equipped with forklifts or booms for lifting materials or with hitches for pulling trailers. They also may operate and maintain air compressors, pumps, and other power equipment at construction sites.

Where and When

Most construction equipment operators work outdoors in all kinds of conditions, though operations are usually stopped in the winter and during extremely wet weather. Operating heavy construction equipment can be dangerous, and it is usually dirty work. Operators may have irregular hours if work on the project continues around the clock, including late night and early morning shifts.

For More Information

* National Center for Construction Education and Research, P.O. Box 141104, Gainesville, FL 32614-1104. Internet: www.nccer.org

* Associated General Contractors of America, 2300 Wilson Blvd., Suite 400, Arlington, VA 22201. Internet: www.agc.org

* International Union of Operating Engineers, 1125 17th St. NW, Washington, DC 20036. Internet: www.iuoe.org

Construction Laborers

At a Glance

Construction laborers do a wide range of physically demanding jobs. They build skyscrapers and houses, roads and mine shafts. They remove waste materials and help tear down buildings. They load, unload, and distribute building materials; mix concrete; and use a variety of tools including jackhammers and torches. Construction laborers often help other craftworkers, including carpenters, plasterers, and masons. At other times, construction laborers may work alone, reading and following construction plans with little or no supervision. Many of the jobs they perform require physical strength and some specialized training and experience.

Career in Focus: *Road Construction Worker*

A good percentage of construction laborers are employed in highway, street, and bridge construction. These workers clear and prepare highway work zones, installing traffic barricades and markers. They also dig trenches; install sewer, water, and storm drain pipes; place concrete and asphalt on roads; and are responsible for the installation and maintenance of traffic control devices. This work can be dangerous because of the number of passing motorists.

Where and When

All of the lifting, carrying, stooping, kneeling, crouching, and crawling makes this a physically demanding job. Some laborers work at great heights or outdoors in all kinds of weather. Some jobs expose workers to harmful chemicals, loud noises, or dangerous equipment. To avoid injury, workers wear special gear and take safety precautions. Construction laborers generally work eight-hour shifts, though longer shifts are common and overnight work may be required, especially when working on highways. The work often stops due to bad weather.

For More Information

* Laborers-AGC Education and Training Fund, 37 Deerfield Road, P.O. Box 37, Pomfret Center, CT 06259. Internet: www.laborerslearn.org

* National Center for Construction Education and Research, P.O. Box 141104, Gainesville, FL 32614-1104. Internet: www.nccer.org

Data Bank

Education and Training: Moderate-term on-the-job training

Starting Salaries: $16,000

Average Earnings: $20,000–$35,000

Total Jobs Held: 1,009,000

Job Outlook: Little change

Annual Job Openings: 245,000

Related Jobs: Material moving occupations; forest, conservation, and logging workers; grounds maintenance workers

Personality Type: Realistic

Did You Know?

Who built the great pyramids of Egypt? Certainly, the pharaohs funded the projects, but it was the estimated 30,000 construction laborers who did the actual building. Using only the technology of ancient times, these workers cut huge stones from quarries, shaped them into building blocks, moved them from the quarries to the building sites, then raised them hundreds of feet, layer upon layer. It's a spectacular building feat, even by modern standards.

Drywall Installers, Ceiling Tile Installers, and Tapers

At a Glance

In most buildings, the walls and ceilings are made of drywall—a thin layer of gypsum sandwiched between two layers of heavy paper. Drywall and ceiling tile workers fasten drywall panels to a building's framework. Because drywall panels are produced in standard sizes, drywall installers must measure, cut, and fit some pieces around doors and windows and cut holes for electrical outlets, air-conditioning units, and plumbing. Installers glue, nail, or screw the wallboard panels to the wood or metal framework. Tapers then fill the joints between boards and prepare the wall for decorating. Some tapers apply textured surfaces to walls and ceilings with trowels, brushes, or spray guns.

Data Bank

Education and Training: Moderate-term on-the-job training

Starting Salaries: $21,000

Average Earnings: $28,000–$47,000

Total Jobs Held: 196,000

Job Outlook: Little change

Annual Job Openings: 22,000

Related Jobs: Carpenters; carpet, floor, and tile installers and finishers; insulation workers; plasterers and stucco masons

Personality Type: Realistic

Did You Know?

In part we have the military to thank for the drywall in our houses. During World War II, the government was looking for ways to build military barracks and bases faster and cheaper. Using lath and plaster took too long and was too expensive. Enter the United States Gypsum Company and its "Sheetrock" panels–later to become drywall. The subsequent housing boom after the war only increased drywall's popularity. Now it is the most common method for building interior walls.

Career in Focus: *Lathers*

Lathers fasten lath—strips of metal or other material—to walls, ceilings, and partitions of buildings. Lath forms the support for plaster, fireproofing, or other materials. Using hand tools and portable power tools, lathers nail, screw, staple, or wire-tie the lath directly to the framework. Due to the popularity of drywall, the lath and plaster method is not near as common as it used to be, and the number of lathers is dwindling.

Where and When

Almost all of this work is done indoors, though the work is sometimes strenuous. Drywall installers, ceiling tile installers, and tapers spend most of the day standing, bending, or kneeling. Some tapers even use stilts. Falls from ladders and scaffolds and injuries from power tools are the most common hazards. Many wear masks to help from breathing in too much dust. Most of them work for contractors, though nearly 20 percent of them are self-employed and set their own schedule.

For More Information

* Associated Builders and Contractors, 4250 North Fairfax Dr., 9th Floor, Arlington, VA 22203. Internet: www.trytools.org

* National Association of Home Builders, Home Builders Institute, 1201 15th St. NW, Washington, DC 20005. Internet: www.hbi.org

* Joint Apprenticeship and Training Fund, International Union of Painters and Allied Trades, 1750 New York Ave. NW, Washington, DC 20006. Internet: www.jatf.org

* United Brotherhood of Carpenters and Joiners of America, Carpenters Training Fund, 6801 Placid St., Las Vegas, NV 89119. Internet: www.carpenters.org

Electricians

At a Glance

Electricians work with the systems that provide electricity to homes and businesses. They may install, test, maintain, and repair wiring, heating, and air-conditioning systems. Electricians generally specialize in construction or maintenance work, though a growing number do both. Electricians in construction work primarily install wiring systems into new homes, businesses, and factories. Electricians specializing in maintenance work primarily upgrade existing electrical systems and repair electrical equipment. Electricians may install the wiring systems needed for telephones, intercoms, and fire alarm and security systems as well. Electricians also may install coaxial or fiber optic cable for computers and other telecommunications equipment. All electricians must follow government codes to ensure their own safety and the safety of the buildings they work on.

Career in Focus: *Maintenance Electrician*

Maintenance work for electricians varies greatly. Electricians who specialize in residential work may rewire a home and replace an old fuse box with a new circuit breaker box, or they may install new lighting and ceiling fans. Those who work in large factories may repair motors, transformers, generators, and electronic controllers on machine tools and industrial robots. Maintenance electricians in factories, hospitals, and other institutional settings may install new equipment.

Where and When

Electricians work at construction sites and in homes, businesses, and factories. The work can be physically demanding, involving standing, stooping, kneeling, and lifting heavy objects. Some electricians may commute long distances to job sites, and all electricians run some risk of injury from electrical shock, falls, and cuts. Most work a standard 40-hour week, and those in maintenance may work nights and weekends.

For More Information

* National Electrical Contractors Association (NECA), 3 Metro Center, Suite 1100, Bethesda, MD 20814. Internet: www.necanet.org

* International Brotherhood of Electrical Workers (IBEW), 1125 15th St. NW, Washington, DC 20005. Internet: www.ibew.org

* Independent Electrical Contractors, Inc., 4401 Ford Ave., Suite 1100, Alexandria, VA 22302. Internet: www.ieci.org

Data Bank

Education and Training: Long-term on-the-job training

Starting Salaries: $25,000

Average Earnings: $33,000–$56,000

Total Jobs Held: 656,000

Job Outlook: Average increase

Annual Job Openings: 68,000

Related Jobs: Heating, air-conditioning, and refrigeration mechanics and installers; line installers and repairers; electrical and electronics installers and repairers; electronic home entertainment equipment installers and repairers; elevator installers and repairers

Personality Type: Realistic

Did You Know?

Many of us learn in elementary school that Thomas Edison invented the lightbulb in 1879, but the truth is much more complicated. In fact, an English chemist named Humphry Davy invented the first electric light almost 70 years earlier. In addition, Edison's lightbulb was actually based on one developed by Henry Woodward in 1875. On top of that, a year before Edison's bulb, Sir Joseph Swan, an English physicist, invented a bulb that lasted for more than 13 hours. Just how many inventors does it take to make a lightbulb?

Elevator Installers and Repairers

At a Glance

Elevator installers and repairers assemble, install, repair, and replace elevators and escalators. They update older equipment and install new equipment. They also test the equipment to make sure it works properly. To install, repair, and maintain modern elevators, these workers must have a thorough knowledge of electronics, electricity, and hydraulics. Installers and repairers also install other moving devices such as dumbwaiters and material lifts, which are similar to elevators in design. They also build and maintain moving walkways, stair lifts, and wheelchair lifts.

Data Bank

Education and Training: Long-term on-the-job training

Starting Salaries: $36,000

Average Earnings: $47,000–$70,000

Total Jobs Held: 22,000

Job Outlook: Average increase

Annual Job Openings: 3,000

Related Jobs: Boilermakers, electricians, electrical and electronics installers and repairers, industrial machinery mechanics and maintenance workers, sheet metal workers, structural and reinforcing iron and metal workers

Personality Type: Realistic

Did You Know?

Many people have an intense fear of riding in elevators, so much so that they would rather take the stairs (which is generally a healthier option anyway). But did you know that escalators are actually more dangerous than elevators? According to some studies, escalator accidents are 15 times more likely than elevator accidents. The majority of escalator injuries come from falls, though there have been cases of individuals losing fingers and toes in the combs at the top and bottom of the escalator. Something to remember the next time you're at the mall.

Career in Focus: *Adjusters*

The most highly skilled elevator installers and repairers, called adjusters, specialize in fine-tuning all the equipment after installation. Adjusters make sure that an elevator works according to specifications and stops correctly at each floor within a specified time. Adjusters must be good troubleshooters, and often have a better understanding of electricity and electronics than other elevator installation workers.

Where and When

Most elevator installers and repairers work a standard 40-hour week, though some repairers are on call. Workers who specialize in maintenance are on their own most of the day and often service the same set of elevators according to a schedule. Elevator installers lift and carry heavy equipment and work in cramped spaces. Dangers include falls, electric shock, and muscle strain. Predictably, most of the work is done indoors.

For More Information

✳ International Union of Elevator Constructors, 7154 Columbia Gateway Dr., Columbia, MD 21046. Internet: www.iuec.org

✳ National Association of Elevator Contractors, 1298 Wellbrook Circle, Suite A, Conyers, GA 30012. Internet: www.naec.org

Glaziers

At a Glance

Glaziers select, cut, install, and remove all kinds of glass in doors, windows, showers, and baths. Residential glaziers replace glass in home windows; install glass mirrors, shower doors, and bathtub enclosures; and fit glass for tabletops and display cases. Commercial glaziers install decorative room dividers or security windows and replace storefront windows for supermarkets, auto dealerships, or banks. In large buildings, glaziers build the metal framework and install glass panels or curtain walls. Besides working with glass, glaziers also may work with plastics, granite, marble, and other glass substitutes. They may use cranes to lift large, heavy pieces into place. After the glass is mounted, glaziers secure it with bolts, cement, metal clips, or wood molding.

Career in Focus: *Window Repairer*

While they may not always be called glaziers, workers who install and repair windows in homes across the country do much of the same work. Window repairers fix and adjust metal and wooden casement windows, storm windows, and doors using hand tools and portable power tools. They may also repair or replace locks, hinges, and cranks; realign windows; and cut and install glass. Much of their work involves upgrading older windows to newer, more energy efficient ones.

Where and When

Glaziers often work outdoors, sometimes in bad weather. The work can result in injuries because they work with sharp tools and sometimes need to remove broken glass. Lifting and manipulating heavy glass panels while working on scaffolding or ladders can't be easy either. All of the kneeling, bending, and standing only adds to the physical demands of the job. Most glaziers work a standard 40-hour week. Almost two-thirds of them work for contractors in new construction and repair.

For More Information

* International Union of Painters and Allied Trades, 1750 New York Ave. NW, Washington, DC 20006. Internet: www.iupat.org

* National Glass Association, Education and Training Department, 8200 Greensboro Dr., Suite 302, McLean, VA 22102-3881. Internet: www.glass.org

* Associated Builders and Contractors, Workforce Development Department, 4250 North Fairfax Dr., 9th Floor, Arlington, VA 22203. Internet: www.trytools.org

---

Data Bank

Education and Training: Long-term on-the-job training

Starting Salaries: $20,000

Average Earnings: $26,000–$44,000

Total Jobs Held: 49,000

Job Outlook: Average increase

Annual Job Openings: 9,000

Related Jobs: Brickmasons, blockmasons, and stonemasons; carpenters; carpet, floor, and tile installers and finishers; cement masons, concrete finishers, segmental pavers, and terrazzo workers; painters and paperhangers; automotive body and related repairers

Personality Type: Realistic

Did You Know?

You've probably heard of or seen stained glass, but do you know how it's made? These days, only a small portion of glasswork in windows is actually "stained." Most stained glass today is actually clear glass that's been painted with silver oxide, or it's pot-metal glass that's been colored in its molten state. The earliest colored glass we know about today is from 306 B.C., when builders in the Far East used it for windows in homes and public buildings.

Hazardous Materials Removal Workers

At a Glance

These workers identify, remove, package, transport, and dispose of dangerous materials. They might deal with asbestos, lead, or radioactive materials. They also respond to emergencies where harmful substances are present. They use equipment ranging from brooms to personal protective suits, face shields, and respirators. Asbestos abatement workers and lead abatement workers remove asbestos, lead, and other materials from buildings scheduled to be renovated or demolished. Emergency and disaster response workers clean up hazardous materials after train derailments and trucking accidents. In facilities using radioactive materials, such as nuclear power plants, technicians and workers decontaminate areas and package radioactive materials for transportation or disposal.

Data Bank

Education and Training: Moderate-term on-the-job training

Starting Salaries: $22,000

Average Earnings: $26,000–$47,000

Total Jobs Held: 38,000

Job Outlook: Rapid increase

Annual Job Openings: 11,000

Related Jobs: Painters and paperhangers; insulation workers; sheet metal workers; power plant operators, distributors, and dispatchers; water and liquid waste treatment plant and system operators

Personality Type: No data available

Did You Know?

We've probably all heard about the Chernobyl meltdown or the oil spills in Alaska. But much of the hazardous material that threatens our health daily can be found in our own homes, schools, and offices. Lead was a common ingredient in house paint until the 1970s, when researchers began proving that it is toxic to humans, especially children. Likewise, asbestos, which was commonly used for insulation and fireproofing, can be harmful when breathed in, causing lung disease. Workers involved in testing for and removing these substances should have excellent job opportunities.

Career in Focus: *Treatment, Storage, and Disposal Worker*

These workers transport and prepare materials for treatment or disposal. At incinerator facilities, they transport materials from the customer to the incinerator, where they are destroyed by fire. At landfills, they follow a strict procedure for processing and storing hazardous materials. They organize and track the location of items in the landfill and may help change the material from a liquid to a solid state in preparation for storage. These workers typically operate heavy machinery, such as forklifts, bulldozers, and large trucks.

Where and When

As the name implies, this is probably not the safest job around, but every precaution is taken to ensure worker health when dealing with hazardous materials. Some workers may wear fully enclosed protective suits, and safety measures and guidelines are strictly followed. The work can be physically demanding, as it involves considerable standing, stooping, and kneeling. Most hazardous materials removal workers work a standard 40-hour week, though overtime and shift work are common. Those who remove materials from schools and businesses often work nights and weekends.

For More Information

* Laborers-AGC Education and Training Fund, 37 Deerfield Rd., P.O. Box 37, Pomfret, CT 06259. Internet: www.laborerslearn.org

* Heat and Frost Insulators and Asbestos Workers, 9602 M. L. King Jr. Hwy., Lanham, MD 20706. Internet: www.insulators.org

Insulation Workers

At a Glance

These workers put insulation in buildings to keep the heat in during the winter and the heat out during the summer. Insulation workers cement, staple, wire, tape, or spray insulation between the inner and outer walls or under the roof of a building. They often use a hose or blowing machine to spray a liquid insulation that dries into place. These workers must wear protective suits, masks, and respirators. Insulation workers use a variety of hand tools—trowels, brushes, knives, scissors, pliers—and some power tools, such as saws and compressors. Many are self-employed.

Career in Focus: *Pipe Coverer and Insulator*

Though most insulation workers are generalists, some specialize in providing insulation for pipes, vats, tanks, boilers, and refrigeration units in commercial and industrial buildings. This insulation not only prevents the wasteful loss of heat, but prevents moisture condensation and dampens sound as well. Though they no longer use asbestos, these workers may use cork, plastic, and magnesia as insulating materials.

Where and When

Insulation workers work indoors in residential and industrial settings. The work involves lots of standing, bending, or kneeling, and they may also work from ladders or in tight spaces. Work around pipes with varying temperatures can cause burns, and particles from insulation materials can be irritating to the eyes, skin, and lungs. Workers follow strict safety guidelines to prevent injury or irritation. Most work 40 hours per week, though overtime is common.

For More Information

* National Insulation Association, 99 Canal Center Plaza, Suite 222, Alexandria, VA 22314. Internet: www.insulation.org

* Insulation Contractors Association of America, 1321 Duke St., Suite 303, Alexandria, VA 22314. Internet: www.insulate.org

Data Bank

Education and Training: Moderate-term on-the-job training

Starting Salaries: $19,000

Average Earnings: $25,000–$45,000

Total Jobs Held: 61,000

Job Outlook: Little change

Annual Job Openings: 6,000

Related Jobs: Carpenters; carpet, floor, and tile installers and finishers; drywall installers, ceiling tile installers, and tapers; roofers; sheet metal workers

Personality Type: Realistic

Did You Know?

According to the U.S. Department of Energy, heating and air-conditioning account for 50 to 70 percent of the energy used in the average American home. And as any insulation installer will tell you, good insulation can cut that cost dramatically. With energy bills often tied to the price of natural gas, homeowners are always on the lookout for ways to keep their energy costs down. This is good news for insulation workers.

Painters and Paperhangers

At a Glance

Painters and paperhangers make walls and other surfaces attractive by applying paint, varnish, stain, or wallpaper to them. Painters first apply a primer or sealer to prepare the surface before adding the finish coat. Painters then brush, roll, and spray the paints onto surfaces. Painters paint outside walls with special paints that protect them from weather damage. Paperhangers apply wallpapers and add decorative borders. When redecorating, they may first remove the old covering by soaking, steaming, or applying solvents. When necessary, they patch holes and take care of other imperfections before hanging the new wall covering. Nearly half of all paper hangers and painters are self-employed.

Data Bank

Education and Training: Moderate-term on-the-job training

Starting Salaries: $20,000

Average Earnings: $25,000–$40,000

Total Jobs Held: 485,000

Job Outlook: Average increase

Annual Job Openings: 105,000

Related Jobs: Carpenters; carpet, floor, and tile installers and finishers; drywall installers, ceiling tile installers, and tapers; painting and coating workers, except construction and maintenance; plasterers and stucco masons

Personality Type: Realistic

Did You Know?

Painting isn't always a matter of "slapping it on there" using a brush or roller. Today, painters use a wide range of colors and techniques to jazz up walls. They might stencil, sponge, rag-roll, splatter, marbleize, or stipple paint onto a flat surface. They can also use appliqué or wallpaper borders. These days, many painters act as a kind of interior decorator, helping homeowners get the walls to look just right.

Career in Focus: *Maintenance Painter*

While the majority of painters are either self-employed or work for contractors involved in new construction or remodeling work, some are hired as part of a general maintenance staff. These maintenance painters usually work for organizations that own or manage large buildings or complexes, such as apartments, schools, hospitals, factories, and government agencies. Their work is similar to that of other painters, except that the employment is much more steady, and the work can be more routine.

Where and When

Most painters and paperhangers work 40 hours per week or less, and nearly a quarter work a variable schedule or only part-time. The job can require considerable standing, climbing, and bending, and some of the work is done on scaffolding and ladders. Painters often work outdoors, but generally only when the weather allows. Those who must remove lead-based paint work in a self-contained suit to prevent contact or inhalation of hazardous materials.

For More Information

* International Union of Painters and Allied Trades, 1750 New York Ave. NW, Washington, DC 20006. Internet: www.iupat.org

* Associated Builders and Contractors, Workforce Development Department, 4250 North Fairfax Dr., 9th Floor, Arlington, VA 22203. Internet: www.trytools.org

* Painting and Decorating Contractors of America, 11960 Westline Industrial Drive, Suite 201, St. Louis, MO 63146-3209. Internet: www.pdca.org

Pipelayers, Plumbers, Pipefitters, and Steamfitters

At a Glance

Pipelayers, plumbers, pipefitters, and steamfitters install, maintain, and repair many different types of pipe systems. Plumbers install and repair water, waste disposal, drainage, and gas pipe systems in homes and other buildings. They also install showers, sinks, toilets, and appliances. Pipelayers, pipefitters, and steamfitters install and repair the pipe systems used in manufacturing, creating electricity, and heating and cooling buildings. They also install the automatic controls that are used to regulate these systems. Steamfitters specialize in installing pipe systems that move liquids or gases under high pressure. Sprinklerfitters install automatic fire sprinkler systems in buildings.

Career in Focus: *Construction Plumber*

Construction plumbers are responsible for installing the new piping in a house or other building. They work from blueprints or drawings that show the planned location of pipes, plumbing fixtures, and appliances. To assemble a system, plumbers cut and bend lengths of pipe and connect them with fittings. After the piping is in place in the house, plumbers install the fixtures and appliances and connect the system to the outside water or sewer lines. Finally, using pressure gauges, they check the system to ensure that the plumbing works properly.

Where and When

Pipefitters and steamfitters generally work in industrial and power plants. Plumbers work in any commercial or residential setting where water and septic systems are required. Pipelayers work outdoors, sometime in remote areas. All of this work can be physically demanding, requiring extended periods of standing, lifting, crouching, and bending. Most work a standard 40-hour week, though those who provide maintenance services work evenings and weekends or are on call.

For More Information

* United Association of Journeymen and Apprentices of the Plumbing and Pipefitting Industry, 901 Massachusetts Ave. NW, Washington, DC 20001. Internet: www.ua.org

* Associated Builders and Contractors, Workforce Development Department, 4250 North Fairfax Dr., 9th Floor, Arlington, VA 22203. Internet: www.trytools.org

* Home Builders Institute, National Association of Home Builders, 1201 15th St. NW, Washington, DC 20005. Internet: www.hbi.org

Data Bank

Education and Training: Moderate-term on-the-job training to long-term on-the-job training

Starting Salaries: $24,000

Average Earnings: $31,000–$54,000

Total Jobs Held: 561,000

Job Outlook: Average increase

Annual Job Openings: 68,000

Related Jobs: Boilermakers; electricians; elevator installers and repairers; heating, air-conditioning, and refrigeration mechanics and installers; industrial machinery mechanics and maintenance workers; millwrights; sheet metal workers; stationary engineers and boiler operators

Personality Type: Realistic

Did You Know?

We may think of indoor plumbing as a modern convenience, or maybe we just take it for granted. But did you know that cultures as far back as 2600 B.C. had flush toilets attached to a sewage system? The Indus Valley Civilization had one in nearly every house, paving the way for Egyptian plumbing advances and the Roman aqueducts. Modern-day toilet paper, on the other hand, wasn't invented until 1857, by a man named Joseph Gayetty who had his name printed on every sheet.

Plasterers and Stucco Masons

At a Glance

Plasterers apply plaster to walls and ceilings to make them fire-resistant and more soundproof. They may also apply insulation to the outside of new or old buildings. They create smooth or textured finishes using trowels and combs. Skilled plasterers sometimes specialize in complicated decorative work. Stucco masons apply stucco—a mixture of cement, lime, and sand—over concrete, masonry, or lath. Stucco masons may also embed marble or gravel chips into the final coat to achieve a decorative finish. Plasterers and stucco masons should not be confused with drywall installers, who use drywall instead of plaster. Many plasterers and stucco masons are self-employed.

Data Bank

Education and Training: Long-term on-the-job training

Starting Salaries: $20,000

Average Earnings: $27,000–$43,000

Total Jobs Held: 59,000

Job Outlook: Little change

Annual Job Openings: 6,000

Related Jobs: Brickmasons, blockmasons, and stonemasons; cement masons, concrete finishers, segmental pavers, and terrazzo workers; drywall installers, ceiling tile installers, and tapers

Personality Type: Realistic

Did You Know?

Plastering is one of the oldest crafts in the building trades. Egyptians used a kind of gypsum plaster in building the Cheops Pyramid. In fact, the art of plastering goes back almost 9,000 years.

Career in Focus: *Restoration Plasterers*

While most plasterers work for independent contractors on new construction, some specialize in restorative projects. This skill is especially in demand in the Northeast, where older homes are being restored to preserve their historical look and value. Because of the degree of artistry required, these same workers may be hired to create special decorative effects, such as curved surfaces, on new construction as well.

Where and When

Most plastering work is indoors, though some work outside to apply wall insulation or exterior decorative finishes. The work is physically demanding, requiring considerable standing, lifting, and reaching. Most plasterers and stucco masons work on new construction sights, and many are employed in Florida, California, and the Southwest, where exterior stucco with decorative finishes is very popular.

For More Information

* Association of Wall and Ceiling Industries International, 803 West Broad St., Falls Church, VA 22046. Internet: www.awci.org

* Operative Plasterers' and Cement Masons' International Association of the United States and Canada, 14405 Laurel Place, Suite 300, Laurel, MD 20707. Internet: www.opcmia.org

* International Union of Bricklayers and Allied Craftworkers, International Masonry Institute, The James Brice House, 42 East St., Annapolis, MD 21401. Internet: www.imiweb.org

Roofers

At a Glance

Roofers install roofs made of tar or asphalt and gravel, rubber, metal, or shingles (themselves made of asphalt, slate, fiberglass, wood, or other material). They may install or repair the tiles on residential roofs, or repair old roofs on other buildings. Some may also waterproof concrete walls and floors. Roofers also install equipment that requires cutting through roofs, such as ventilation ducts and attic fans. Roofing has the highest accident rate of any of the construction trade occupations.

Career in Focus: *Estimator*

In most trade construction jobs there is room for advancement within a company. Roofers, for example, can advance to the role of supervisor or estimator for a roofing contractor. Estimators need a variety of skills in order to do their job, including the ability to read blueprints and even a little sales experience. They travel to the site, discuss the needs of the client, and put in a bid to do the work. If the price is right, the company gets the job. Most self-employed roofers naturally do their own estimating.

Where and When

Roofing work involves climbing, bending, kneeling, and heavy lifting. It also involves work outside, sometimes in rainy conditions. Workers risk slips or falls, not to mention that roofs can become quite hot during the summer. Almost all salaried roofers work for contractors who determine their working schedule, though one in four is self-employed.

For More Information

* National Roofing Contractors Association, 10255 W. Higgins Rd., Suite 600, Rosemont, IL 60018-5607. Internet: www.nrca.net

* United Union of Roofers, Waterproofers, and Allied Workers, 1660 L St. NW, Suite 800, Washington, DC 20036.

Data Bank

Education and Training: Moderate-term on-the-job training

Starting Salaries: $20,000

Average Earnings: $24,000–$41,000

Total Jobs Held: 162,000

Job Outlook: Average increase

Annual Job Openings: 38,000

Related Jobs: Carpenters; carpet, floor, and tile installers and finishers; cement masons, concrete finishers, segmental pavers, and terrazzo workers; drywall installers, ceiling tile installers, and tapers; plasterers and stucco masons; sheet metal workers

Personality Type: Realistic

Did You Know?

Not surprisingly, roofing is one of the top ten most dangerous occupations, according to the Bureau of Labor Statistics. While the majority of accidents and injuries are caused by falls, some are caused by burns due to the heat of bitumen—the hot, tar-like material used as a sealant. Doctors have researched various means of treating such burns, particularly searching for ways to remove tar or bitumen from burned skin without causing further damage. The results of their findings? Use good old-fashioned butter.

Sheet Metal Workers

At a Glance

Sheet metal workers use large sheets of metal to make ductwork for air-conditioning and heating systems. They also make roofs, rain gutters, skylights, outdoor signs, railroad cars, and other products. They may work with fiberglass and plastic materials. Sheet metal workers do both construction-related work and mass production of sheet metal products. Sheet metal workers first study plans and specifications to determine the materials they will need. They then measure, cut, shape, and fasten pieces of sheet metal to make ductwork, countertops, and other custom products. They take the parts to the construction site, where they further assemble the pieces as they install them. Sheet metal workers in manufacturing plants make parts for products such as aircraft or industrial equipment.

Data Bank

Education and Training: Moderate-term on-the-job training

Starting Salaries: $20,000

Average Earnings: $27,000–$51,000

Total Jobs Held: 198,000

Job Outlook: Average increase

Annual Job Openings: 50,000

Related Jobs: Assemblers and fabricators; machinists; tool and die makers; glaziers; heating, air-conditioning, and refrigeration mechanics and installers

Personality Type: Realistic

Did You Know?

You may already know that many insulation workers in the 1970s were exposed to asbestos—an insulation material that causes cancer in humans. But did you know that sheet metal workers had high exposures, too? In a survey taken in the late 1980s, more than 31 percent of sheet metal workers in construction, shipyard, and refinery work showed signs of asbestos-related diseases.

Career in Focus: *HVAC Technician*

In addition to installation, some sheet metal workers specialize in testing, adjusting, and servicing existing air-conditioning and ventilation systems to make sure they work efficiently. Properly installed duct systems are a key component to heating, ventilation, and air-conditioning (HVAC) systems, which is why duct installers are sometimes called HVAC technicians. These sheet metal workers are sometimes asked to perform a complete mechanical inspection of a building's HVAC, water, and lighting systems.

Where and When

Sheet metal workers usually work in shops where they create heavy pieces, or on site doing installation work. The job can involve considerable lifting, standing, climbing, and squatting. The work is done both indoors and out. Working with sharp metal, soldering and welding equipment, and scaffolds and ladders can be dangerous as well. Most sheet metal workers work a 40-hour week.

For More Information

* International Training Institute for the Sheet Metal and Air-Conditioning Industry, 601 N. Fairfax St., Suite 240, Alexandria, VA 22314. Internet: www.sheetmetal-iti.org

* Sheet Metal and Air-Conditioning Contractors' National Association, 4201 Lafayette Center Dr., Chantilly, VA 20151-1209. Internet: www.smacna.org

* Sheet Metal Workers International Association, 1750 New York Ave. NW, Washington, DC 20006. Internet: www.smwia.org

Structural and Reinforcing Iron and Metal Workers

At a Glance

These workers make the steel frames used to build bridges, high-rise buildings, and other structures. They also position and secure steel bars inside concrete in order to reinforce highways, buildings, bridges, and tunnels. In addition, they repair and renovate older buildings and structures. Even though the primary metal involved in this work is steel, these workers are still often known as ironworkers. These workers use a wide range of tools and heavy equipment to do their job.

Career in Focus: *Ornamental Ironworker*

Though most ironwork is not designed to be decorative (being sturdy and safe take priority), the work of ornamental ironworkers is different. They install stairs, handrails, curtain walls, and other miscellaneous metal items after the structure of the building has been completed. Ornamental ironworkers make sure that the pieces are properly fitted and aligned before bolting or welding them. They also dig postholes, mix concrete, and install ornamental fences.

Where and When

This work is usually done outside in all kinds of weather, though those working at great heights do not work during wet, icy, or extremely windy conditions. To prevent falls, ironworkers use safety harnesses, scaffolding, and nets for protection. Most structural and reinforcing iron and metal workers work in metropolitan areas, where most commercial and industrial construction takes place. Most work a standard week, though paid overtime is common.

For More Information

* International Association of Bridge, Structural, Ornamental, and Reinforcing Iron Workers, Apprenticeship Department, 1750 New York Ave. NW, Suite 400, Washington, DC 20006. Internet: www.ironworkers.org

* Associated Builders and Contractors, Workforce Development Department, 4250 North Fairfax Dr., 9th Floor, Arlington, VA 22203. Internet: www.trytools.org

* Associated General Contractors of America, Inc., 2300 Wilson Blvd., Suite 400, Arlington, VA 22201. Internet: www.agc.org

Data Bank

Education and Training: Long-term on-the-job training

Starting Salaries: $23,000

Average Earnings: $28,000–$55,000

Total Jobs Held: 107,000

Job Outlook: Average increase

Annual Job Openings: 19,000

Related Jobs: Assemblers and fabricators; boilermakers; engineers; cement masons, concrete finishers, segmental pavers, and terrazzo workers; welding, soldering, and brazing workers

Personality Type: Realistic

Did You Know?

The world's longest bridge, the Akashi Kaikyo Bridge, is located in Japan. It spans 1,991 meters (which makes it well over a mile long) and is supported by two 1,000-feet-high steel towers. It is more than 2,000 feet longer than the Golden Gate Bridge in San Francisco. How much steel does it take to make the world's longest bridge? A little more than 180,000 metric tons. That's about the same as the combined weight of 30,000 African elephants.

Installation, Maintenance, and Repair Occupations

Computer, Automated Teller, and Office Machine Repairers

At a Glance

Computer repairers install and fix computers, printers, and other computer equipment. Some repairers work on both computers and office equipment. Automated teller repairers install and fix ATMs—the machines that allow customers to carry out bank transactions automatically—at banks and credit unions. Most repairers travel to customers' workplaces to make repairs. These workers, known as field technicians, often have assigned businesses to which they provide regular maintenance. Bench technicians, on the other hand, work in repair shops located in stores, factories, or service centers. To repair or adjust equipment, workers use hand tools, such as pliers, screwdrivers, soldering irons, and wrenches. They work in many industries, and some are on call 24 hours a day to make emergency repairs.

Data Bank

Education and Training: Vocational/technical training

Starting Salaries: $21,000

Average Earnings: $28,000–$46,000

Total Jobs Held: 168,000

Job Outlook: Little change

Annual Job Openings: 31,000

Related Jobs: Broadcast and sound engineering technicians and radio operators, electronic home entertainment equipment installers and repairers, electrical and electronics installers and repairers, industrial machinery mechanics and maintenance workers, radio and telecommunications equipment installers and repairers

Personality Type: Realistic

Did You Know?

Statistics show that you can find a personal computer in more than 80 percent of American homes. That equates to millions upon millions of PCs out there waiting to break down. This is good news for computer repairers. Of course, like many electronics, it may soon become cheaper to *buy* a new computer than to get an old one fixed—especially since a computer gets "old" or outdated about the time you take it out of the box.

Career in Focus: *Office Machine and Cash Register Servicer*

Anyone who has ever worked in an office environment has probably seen one of these workers. Office machine and cash register servicers work on photocopiers, cash registers, mail-processing equipment, and fax machines. Office machine repairers usually work on machinery at the customer's workplace. Common malfunctions are caused by worn or dirty parts or problems with lamps, lenses, or mirrors. Servicers clean, replace, or repair the necessary parts.

Where and When

Most of this work takes place in clean, well-lighted surroundings. Field repairers must travel frequently. Because machines such as computers and ATMs are critical for organizations to operate, repairers and technicians often work around the clock. Shifts are usually decided on the basis of seniority. Though the job isn't strenuous, repairers may be required to lift heavy equipment.

For More Information

* ACES International, 5241 Princess Anne Rd., Suite 110, Virginia Beach, VA 23462. Internet: www.acesinternational.org

* Electronics Technicians Association International, 5 Depot St., Greencastle, IN 46135.

* International Society of Certified Electronics Technicians, 3608 Pershing Ave., Fort Worth, TX 76107-4527. Internet: www.iscet.org

Electrical and Electronics Installers and Repairers

At a Glance

These workers install and repair electrical and electronics equipment. Many of them work for the Department of Defense where they install radar, missile controls, and communication systems. Other electronic equipment repairers work for telephone companies, at hospitals, and in repair shops. They also may work in power plants and relay stations. Field technicians travel to factories or other locations to repair equipment. These workers often have assigned areas in which they perform preventive maintenance on a regular basis. Bench technicians work in repair shops located in factories and service centers, fixing components that cannot be repaired on the factory floor.

Career in Focus: *Motor Vehicle Electrical and Electronics Installer and Repairer*

These workers install, diagnose, and repair equipment in automobiles. Most installation work involves either new alarm or sound systems. Motor vehicle installers and repairers work with a growing range of electronic equipment, including DVD players, satellite navigation equipment, and passive and active car security systems.

Where and When

Some repairers work in comfortable repair shops while others may work on factory floors. Field technicians spend much of their time traveling to serve customers on site. Repairers may be required to carry heavy equipment and work in uncomfortable positions. Some risk of electric shock comes with the job, though precautions are taken against it.

For More Information

* ACES International, 5241 Princess Anne Rd., Suite 110, Virginia Beach, VA 23462. Internet: www.acesinternational.org

* Electronics Technicians Association International, 5 Depot St., Greencastle, IN 46135.

* International Society of Certified Electronics Technicians, 3608 Pershing Ave., Fort Worth, TX 76107-4527. Internet: www.iscet.org

Data Bank

Education and Training: Vocational/technical training

Starting Salaries: $26,000

Average Earnings: $33,000–$51,000

Total Jobs Held: 158,000

Job Outlook: Little change

Annual Job Openings: 16,000

Related Jobs: Broadcast and sound technicians and radio operators; computer, automated teller, and office machine repairers; electronic home entertainment equipment installers and repairers; radio and telecommunications equipment installers and repairers; industrial machinery mechanics and maintenance workers

Personality Type: Realistic

Did You Know?

Just what makes a smart bomb smart? It is, in fact, its precision-guided control system (installed by electronics specialists). These bombs and missiles are guided by radio, laser, and even satellite systems to more accurately hit the intended target and reduce the number of surrounding casualties. Of course, a smart bomb is still only as smart as the person using it.

Electronic Home Entertainment Equipment Installers and Repairers

At a Glance

These workers install and repair radios, TV sets, stereos, video games, and other home electronic equipment. They also may install and repair home security systems, intercom equipment, and satellite systems. They run tests to find problems and adjust and replace parts. Small equipment is usually brought into repair shops to be handled by bench technicians. Field technicians, on the other hand, travel to customers' homes to do installations and repairs. Improvements in technology have miniaturized and digitized many audio and video recording devices, which has only made repair work harder. Improved technologies have also lowered the price of electronic home entertainment equipment to the point where customers often replace broken equipment instead of repairing it.

Data Bank

Education and Training: Vocational/technical training

Starting Salaries: $17,000

Average Earnings: $23,000–$37,000

Total Jobs Held: 47,000

Job Outlook: Little change

Annual Job Openings: 6,000

Related Jobs: Broadcast and sound engineering technicians and radio operators; computer, automated teller, and office machine repairers; electrical and electronics installers and repairers; radio and telecommunications equipment installers and repairers

Personality Type: Realistic

Did You Know?

It can take decades for a new invention to catch on with the public. Push-button phones were first invented in 1896 and color television was first demonstrated in 1929, but neither product was in common use in America until the 1960s. Though it might take decades for a new invention to gain popularity, it sometimes doesn't take long for a new invention to be replaced or forgotten. Does anyone remember the laser disc?

Career in Focus: *Home Theater Installation Technician*

Big-screen televisions and surround-sound stereo systems have made it possible for people to create a theater-like experience in their own living room. This has created a need for home theater installation technicians, who specialize in installing home theater and satellite products. This job requires extensive travel to customers' homes, as well as complete knowledge of the equipment being installed and good people skills.

Where and When

Most repairers work in comfortable repair shops. Field technicians spend much of their time traveling to serve customers on site. Repairers may be required to carry heavy equipment and work in uncomfortable positions. They also must take precautions against electric shock. About one out of every three of these workers is self-employed.

For More Information

* ACES International, 5241 Princess Anne Rd., Suite 110, Virginia Beach, VA 23462. Internet: www.acesinternational.org

* Electronics Technicians Association International, 5 Depot St., Greencastle, IN 46135.

* International Society of Certified Electronics Technicians, 3608 Pershing Ave., Fort Worth, TX 76107-4527. Internet: www.iscet.org

Radio and Telecommunications Equipment Installers and Repairers

At a Glance

These workers install, repair, and maintain complex telephone and radio equipment. Most work either in a phone company's central office or in the field at customers' homes or offices. Others work on equipment for cable TV companies, railroads, or airlines. Radio mechanics install and maintain radio transmitting and receiving equipment. Telecommunications equipment installers work on equipment that transmits voice signals, data, graphics, and video, for example, installing or repairing telephone wiring and equipment. When problems with telecommunications equipment arise, repairers diagnose the source of the problem by testing each part of the equipment separately.

Career in Focus: *PBX Installers and Repairers*

These workers set up private branch exchange (PBX) switchboards, which relay incoming, outgoing, and interoffice calls within a single organization. They also install power systems, alarms, and telephone sets. The installer performs tests to verify that the newly installed equipment functions properly. Due to rapidly developing technologies, PBX installers must adapt and learn new technologies, including increasingly popular voice-over Internet protocol (VoIP) systems.

Where and When

These installers and repairers generally work in clean, comfortable surroundings such as an office or a service center. Telephone installers and repairers may work on rooftops, ladders, and telephone poles, however. While outdoors, these workers are subject to various weather conditions. Most installers and repairers work regular business hours, though some companies require shift work to meet round-the-clock servicing hours.

For More Information

* International Brotherhood of Electrical Workers, Telecommunications Department, 1125 15th St. NW, Room 807, Washington, DC 20005.

* Communications Workers of America, 501 3rd St. NW, Washington, DC 20001.

* Society of Cable Telecommunications Engineers, Certification Department, 140 Phillips Rd., Exton, PA 19341-1318. Internet: www.scte.org

Data Bank

Education and Training: Long-term on-the-job training to vocational/technical training

Starting Salaries: $30,000

Average Earnings: $41,000–$57,000

Total Jobs Held: 222,000

Job Outlook: Declining

Annual Job Openings: 22,000

Related Jobs: Broadcast and sound engineering technicians and radio operators; computer, automated teller, and office machine repairers; electronic home entertainment equipment installers and repairers; electrical and electronics installers and repairers; line installers and repairers; engineering technicians

Personality Type: Realistic

Did You Know?

We think of ourselves as living in the digital age, where everybody is "wired" into the information superhighway. But in fact only about 15 percent of the world's population has Internet access. Of course it is different in the United States, where nearly 70 percent of the population uses the Internet regularly. And that number is growing, which could mean steady work for telecommunications installers.

Aircraft and Avionics Equipment Mechanics and Service Technicians

At a Glance

Aircraft and avionics mechanics and service technicians inspect airplanes for problems. They make repairs and test equipment to make sure it is working properly and to complete the inspections required by the Federal Aviation Administration (FAA). Some work on several different types of planes, whereas others specialize in just one. Some mechanics even specialize in one part of an aircraft, such as the engine or electrical system of a DC-10. Much of an aircraft mechanic's work is preventive maintenance (thankfully). Mechanics inspect aircraft engines, landing gears, instruments, brakes, and other parts of the aircraft, repairing and replacing them as necessary. They also keep maintenance records of the work they perform.

Data Bank

Education and Training: Vocational/technical training

Starting Salaries: $29,000

Average Earnings: $38,000–$58,000

Total Jobs Held: 142,000

Job Outlook: Average increase

Annual Job Openings: 13,000

Related Jobs: Electricians, electrical and electronics installers and repairers, elevator installers and repairers

Personality Type: Realistic

Did You Know?

How safe is air travel? Statistics show that a good percent of Americans are afraid to fly, but those same people often don't think twice about driving on the interstate. Yet according to the U.S. National Safety Council, you are twenty times more likely to be killed in an auto accident than an airplane accident. Isn't that comforting?

Career in Focus: *Avionics Technician*

Avionics systems are an integral part of aircraft design. Avionics technicians repair and maintain the components used for aircraft navigation and radio communications, weather radar systems, and other instruments and computers that control flight. Technicians also may be required to analyze and develop solutions to complex electronic problems. These duties may require additional training and education. But you want the person repairing your airplane's radar system to be well educated, don't you?

Where and When

Mechanics typically work in hangers or other indoor areas. They often work under pressure to maintain flight schedules and still ensure the safety of passengers. They often lift objects weighing more than 70 pounds, and mechanics must stand, lie, or kneel in awkward positions. Ear protection is usually worn when working on and testing engines. Most aircraft mechanics work 40 hours per week in shifts around the clock, though overtime is frequent.

For More Information

* Professional Aviation Maintenance Association, 717 Princess St., Alexandria, VA 22314. Internet: www.pama.org

Automotive Body and Related Repairers

At a Glance

Automotive body repairers fix automobiles damaged in accidents. Although some work on large trucks, buses, or tractor-trailers, most work on cars and small trucks. They straighten bent bodies, hammer out dents, and replace parts that can't be fixed. Their supervisors usually decide which parts to fix and replace and how long the job should take. Body repair work has variety and challenges: Each damaged vehicle presents a different problem. Using their broad knowledge of automotive construction and repair techniques, repairers must develop appropriate methods for each job.

Career in Focus: *Automotive Glass Installer*

Some body repairers specialize in installing and repairing glass in automobiles and other vehicles. They remove broken, cracked, or pitted windshields and window glass. They then apply a moisture-proofing compound along the edges of new glass, place the glass in the vehicle, and install rubber strips around the sides of the windshield or window to make it secure and weatherproof. These specialists tend to make less money on average than general automotive body repairers.

Where and When

Most of these repairers work a standard 40-hour week, though some overtime is possible. They work indoors in noisy and dirty body shops, often working in awkward positions. Cuts, burns, and injuries from power tools are possible, though serious accidents are usually avoided when safety guidelines are followed.

For More Information

* Automotive Service Association, P.O. Box 929, Bedford, Texas 76095-0929. Internet: www.asashop.org
* National Automobile Dealers Association, 8400 Westpark Dr., McLean, VA 22102. Internet: www.nada.org
* Automotive Jobs Today, 8400 Westpark Dr., MS #2, McLean, VA 22102. Internet: www.autojobstoday.org
* National Glass Association. 8200 Greensboro Dr., Suite 302, McLean, VA 22102-3881. Internet: www.glass.org
* National Automotive Technician Education Foundation, 101 Blue Seal Dr. SE, Suite 101, Leesburg, VA 20175. Internet: www.natef.org

Data Bank

Education and Training: Long-term on-the-job training

Starting Salaries: $19,000

Average Earnings: $26,000–$45,000

Total Jobs Held: 223,000

Job Outlook: Average increase

Annual Job Openings: 20,000

Related Jobs: Automotive service technicians and mechanics; diesel service technicians and mechanics; painting and coating workers, except construction and maintenance

Personality Type: Realistic

Did You Know?

A "crumple zone" is a feature of automobiles designed to prevent injury in an accident by absorbing the energy from impact. They are typically found in the front of automobiles and work by lengthening the time it takes for the vehicle to come to a complete stop. This, in turn, reduces the amount of force applied to the body of the driver and passengers. While their benefits in high-speed accidents are unquestionable, they do have one obvious disadvantage: They crumple, often totaling the front of the car. This results in higher repair costs and more complicated work for automotive body repairers.

Automotive Service Technicians and Mechanics

At a Glance

Automotive mechanics and service technicians repair and service cars, trucks, and vans that have gas engines. During routine service work, mechanics inspect, adjust, and replace vehicle parts. Mechanics must be quick and accurate when they are diagnosing mechanical problems. This job is becoming more technically demanding as automobiles become more complex. As a result, these workers are now usually called "technicians" rather than "mechanics." The increasing complexity requires workers who can use computerized shop equipment and work with electronic components, while maintaining their skills with traditional hand tools.

Data Bank

Education and Training: Vocational/technical training

Starting Salaries: $18,000

Average Earnings: $24,000–$44,000

Total Jobs Held: 803,000

Job Outlook: Average increase

Annual Job Openings: 93,000

Related Jobs: Automotive body and related repairers, diesel service technicians and mechanics, small engine mechanics

Personality Type: Realistic

Did You Know?

Voluntary certification by the National Institute for Automotive Service Excellence (ASE) has become *the* credential to have for automotive service technicians. Certification is available in eight different areas, from electrical systems to engine repair to heating and air-conditioning. Technicians generally must have two years of experience in each field in order to pass the exam and earn their certification. In 2004, about 2,000 high school and postsecondary training programs had been certified by the ASE.

Career in Focus: *Tune-up Technician*

Most vehicles require regular tune-ups in order to run efficiently. Tune-up technicians adjust the ignition timing and valves, and adjust or replace spark plugs and other parts to ensure the best engine performance. They often use electronic testing equipment to isolate and adjust malfunctions in fuel, ignition, and emissions control systems. Like most other mechanics, they must be familiar with computers as well.

Where and When

More than half of all service technicians work more than 40 hours per week, including evenings and weekends. They generally work indoors. They may be required to do heavy lifting. Minor cuts, burns, and bruises are common.

For More Information

* National Automotive Technicians Education Foundation, 101 Blue Seal Dr. SE, Suite 101, Leesburg, VA 20175. Internet: www.natef.org

* Automotive Youth Educational Systems (AYES), 100 W. Big Beaver, Suite 300, Troy, MI 48084. Internet: www.ayes.org

* National Institute for Automotive Service Excellence (ASE), 101 Blue Seal Dr. SE, Suite 101, Leesburg, VA 20175. Internet: www.asecert.org

* National Automobile Dealers Association, 8400 Westpark Dr., McLean, VA 22102. Internet: www.nada.org

* Automotive Jobs Today, 8400 Westpark Dr., MS #2, McLean, VA 22102. Internet: www.autojobstoday.org

Diesel Service Technicians and Mechanics

At a Glance

Diesel mechanics and service technicians repair and maintain diesel engines in heavy trucks, buses, tractors, bulldozers, and cranes. They spend a lot of time doing preventive maintenance to make sure that the equipment operates safely and to reduce expensive breakdowns. It is common for technicians to handle all kinds of repairs, from working on a vehicle's electrical system one day to doing major engine repairs the next. This work is becoming increasingly complex, as more electronic components are used in diesel engines. Because of this new technology, technicians must regularly learn new skills.

Career in Focus: *School Bus Mechanic*

Each and every school day, buses transport millions of children to school through rain, sleet, and snow. Knowing the precious cargo they carry, school bus mechanics must be aware of the latest technologies in bus manufacturing. These mechanics often service every aspect of the vehicle, including the diesel engine. In small school districts, a single mechanic may be responsible for every aspect of the maintenance program. Because of the heavy responsibility they have, these mechanics are sometimes required to have a state certification in school bus inspection.

Where and When

Diesel technicians usually work indoors, though they sometimes make repairs to vehicles on the road. They are often required to do heavy lifting and stand or lie in awkward positions to make repairs. Like other automotive service technicians, they are prone to working more than 40 hours per week.

For More Information

❋ Association of Diesel Specialists, 10 Laboratory Dr., PO Box 13966, Research Triangle Park, NC 27709. Internet: www.diesel.org

❋ National Institute for Automotive Service Excellence (ASE), 101 Blue Seal Dr. SE, Suite 101, Leesburg, VA 20175. Internet: www.asecert.org

❋ Accrediting Commission of Career Schools and Colleges of Technology, 2101 Wilson Blvd., Suite 302, Arlington, VA 22201. Internet: www.accsct.org

❋ National Automotive Technicians Education Foundation, 101 Blue Seal Dr. SE, Suite 101, Leesburg, VA 20175. Internet: www.natef.org

Data Bank

Education and Training: Vocational/technical training

Starting Salaries: $23,000

Average Earnings: $29,000–$44,000

Total Jobs Held: 270,000

Job Outlook: Average increase

Annual Job Openings: 32,000

Related Jobs: Aircraft and avionics equipment mechanics and service technicians, automotive service technicians and mechanics, heavy vehicle and mobile equipment service technicians and mechanics, small engine mechanics

Personality Type: Realistic

Did You Know?

Diesel engines are heavier and last longer than gas engines. They're also more efficient because a diesel engine compresses its fuel—so it uses less to do more. Diesels get more power, better gas mileage, and are even better for the environment. Large trucks, buses, and trains have diesel engines, and nearly 40 percent of European cars run on diesel. So why isn't diesel more popular in the United States? In short, because it's harder to find, which makes it more expensive.

Heavy Vehicle and Mobile Equipment Service Technicians and Mechanics

At a Glance

These mechanics and technicians repair the machinery used in construction, logging, farming, and mining. They fix and maintain trenchers, backhoes, bulldozers, and cranes. They service and repair diesel engines and other machine parts. They may also repair the hydraulic lifts used to raise and lower scoops and shovels. Service technicians perform routine maintenance checks to ensure the equipment's performance and safety. In addition, service technicians adjust or replace defective parts and may also repair undercarriages and track assemblies. It is common for technicians in large shops to specialize in one or two types of repair. Technicians need training in electronics and the use of hand-held diagnostic computers to make engine adjustments and diagnose problems.

Data Bank

Education and Training: Long-term on-the-job training to vocational/technical training

Starting Salaries: $24,000

Average Earnings: $31,000–$45,000

Total Jobs Held: 178,000

Job Outlook: Little change

Annual Job Openings: 19,000

Related Jobs: Aircraft and avionics equipment mechanics and service technicians, automotive service technicians and mechanics, diesel service technicians and mechanics, industrial machinery mechanics and maintenance workers, small engine mechanics

Personality Type: Realistic

Did You Know?

Like many other industries, construction is highly sensitive to changes in the economy. When the economy experiences a downturn, investors are less likely to expand, new homes are less likely to be built, and bulldozers and cranes tend to sit idle. This in turn impacts those in the heavy vehicle and mobile equipment service trade. Still, most companies will try to retain experienced workers during slow periods, allowing for some job security.

Career in Focus: *Farm Equipment Mechanic*

What used to be a general repairer's job around the farm has evolved into a specialized technical career. These mechanics service, maintain, and repair farm equipment. They may also repair smaller lawn and garden tractors. Farmers have increasingly turned to farm equipment dealers to service and repair their equipment because the machinery is so complex. Farm equipment mechanics will generally work longer hours in the spring, summer, and fall, and much fewer hours in the winter.

Where and When

These service technicians usually work indoors, unless a repair is urgent or the machinery can't be moved from the worksite. Field service technicians work outdoors and spend most of their time away from the shop. Sometimes extensive travel is necessary. All technicians must be able to lift heavy parts and stand and lie in awkward positions while working. Minor cuts, burns, and bruises are part of the job. Most work a standard 40-hour week, though overtime is common.

For More Information

* The AED Foundation (Associated Equipment Dealers affiliate), 615 W. 22nd St., Oak Brook, IL 60523. Internet: www.aednet.org/aed_foundation

* National Automotive Technician Education Foundation (NATEF), 101 Blue Seal Dr., Suite 101, Leesburg, VA 20175. Internet: www.natef.org

* National Institute for Automotive Service Excellence (ASE), 101 Blue Seal Dr. SE, Suite 101, Leesburg, VA 20175. Internet: www.asecert.org

Small Engine Mechanics

At a Glance

The small engines that power motorcycles, motorboats, and outdoor power equipment share many characteristics with larger engines—including breakdowns. Small engine mechanics do routine engine checkups and repair everything from weed eaters to yachts. Motorcycle mechanics repair and overhaul motorcycles, motor scooters, mopeds, dirt bikes, and all-terrain vehicles. Other small engine mechanics service and repair lawnmowers, garden tractors, and chain saws. All engines require periodic service to minimize the chance of breakdowns and to keep them operating efficiently. Such routine maintenance is normally a major part of any mechanic's work. Many of these workers are self-employed.

Career in Focus: *Motorboat Mechanic*

Motorboat mechanics, or marine equipment mechanics, repair and adjust the equipment of boat engines. Most small boats have portable outboard engines that are removed and brought into the repair shop. Larger craft, such as cabin cruisers and commercial fishing boats, are powered by diesel or gasoline inboard or inboard-outboard engines, which are removed only for major overhauls. Most of these repairs are performed at the docks or marinas. Motorboat mechanics also may work on propellers, steering mechanisms, marine plumbing, and other boat equipment.

Where and When

Small engine mechanics usually work in well-lighted and ventilated repair shops, though motorboat mechanics commonly work outdoors at docks or marinas. Mechanics may work fewer than 40 hours a week during winter months, when motorcycles, motorboats, and lawnmowers are not in use (though we assume snow-blowers and snowmobiles need servicing, too).

For More Information

* Accrediting Commission of Career Schools and Colleges of Technology, 2101 Wilson Blvd., Suite 302, Arlington, VA 22201. Internet: www.accsct.org

Data Bank

Education and Training: Moderate-term to long-term on-the-job training

Starting Salaries: $17,000

Average Earnings: $23,000–$37,000

Total Jobs Held: 73,000

Job Outlook: Average increase

Annual Job Openings: 23,000

Related Jobs: Automotive service technicians and mechanics, diesel service technicians and mechanics, heavy vehicle and mobile equipment service technicians and mechanics

Personality Type: Realistic

Did You Know?

If you take a job in a restaurant, they usually supply you with the pots and pans. Likewise, janitors aren't expected to bring their own mop and bucket. But mechanics often must provide their own hand tools for their work. Most beginning mechanics start out with the basics, such as wrenches, pliers, screwdrivers, and power drills. As they gain experience, they collect more tools. Experienced mechanics might have thousands of dollars invested in tools.

Coin, Vending, and Amusement Machine Servicers and Repairers

At a Glance

These workers repair and maintain coin-operated machines that offer entertainment, soft drinks, snacks, and other items for sale. They retrieve money, stock the machines, and make sure they are clean and working properly. When installing machines, repairers must make the necessary water and electrical connections—following all plumbing and electrical codes—and check the machines for proper operation. Because many vending machines dispense food, these workers must also comply with state and local public health and sanitation standards. Preventive maintenance is a major job of repairers. Servicers and repairers also do some paperwork, such as filing reports, preparing repair cost estimates, ordering parts, and keeping daily records of merchandise distributed and money collected.

Data Bank

Education and Training: Moderate-term on-the-job training

Starting Salaries: $18,000

Average Earnings: $22,000–$35,000

Total Jobs Held: 46,000

Job Outlook: Little change

Annual Job Openings: 7,000

Related Jobs: Electrical and electronics installers and repairers; electronic home entertainment equipment installers and repairers; heating, air-conditioning, and refrigeration mechanics and installers; home appliance repairers

Personality Type: Realistic

Did You Know?

Though pinball machines had a brief stint of popularity during the Great Depression, it wasn't until the years right after World War II that they really caught on. Known as the Golden Age of Pinball, these postwar years saw new innovations in the pinball machine, including the addition of flippers in 1947, making it more a game of skill than simply one of luck. Today pinball machines have largely been replaced by interactive video games, though any repairer of coin-operated machines must still know how to fix a broken flipper.

Career in Focus: *Amusement Machine Repairer*

Amusement machine servicers and repairers work on jukeboxes, video games, pinball machines, and slot machines. They make sure that the various levers, joysticks, and mechanisms function properly. They update selections in jukeboxes, repair or replace malfunctioning parts, and rebuild existing equipment. Those who work in the gaming (gambling) industry must adhere to strict guidelines, because federal and state agencies regulate many gaming machines.

Where and When

Some of these repairers work in company repair shops, though many spend substantial time on the road, repairing machines on site. Most work a total of 40 hours per week. They may be on call to work nights, weekends, and holidays. This kind of repair work is relatively safe so long as repairers take care to avoid cuts and electrical shocks. Heavy lifting and moving is common.

For More Information

* National Automatic Merchandising Association, 20 N. Wacker Dr., Suite 3500, Chicago, IL 60606-3102. Internet: www.vending.org

* Vending Times, 1375 Broadway, New York, NY 10018.

* Automatic Merchandiser Vending Group, Cygnus Business Media, P.O. Box 803, 1233 Janesville Ave., Fort Atkinson, WI 53538-0803.

Heating, Air-Conditioning, and Refrigeration Mechanics and Installers

At a Glance

Heating and air-conditioning systems control the temperature, humidity, and air quality in most buildings. Refrigeration systems make it possible to store and transport food, medicine, and other perishable items. These mechanics install, maintain, and repair such systems. They may work for large companies or be self-employed. Technicians often specialize in either installation or maintenance and repair, although they are trained to do both. Because of the nature of the coolants used in air-conditioning and refrigeration, these workers must conform to strict guidelines to help protect the environment.

Career in Focus: *Refrigeration Mechanic*

Some mechanics may specialize only in refrigeration. Refrigeration mechanics install, service, and repair industrial and commercial refrigerating systems and a variety of refrigeration equipment. They follow blueprints to install motors, compressors, condensing units, evaporators, and other components. They connect this equipment to the ductwork, refrigerant lines, and electrical power source, and then charge the system with refrigerant and check it for proper operation.

Where and When

These mechanics and installers work in homes, stores, hospitals, office buildings, factories—just about anywhere. They may work outside in cold or hot weather or in buildings that are uncomfortable (the buildings usually don't have working heat or air-conditioning after all). Hazards include electrical shock, burns, and muscle strain. The majority of mechanics and installers work at least 40 hours per week, though during peak seasons (the summer and winter) overtime is common.

For More Information

* Air-Conditioning Contractors of America (ACCA), 2800 Shirlington Rd., Suite 300, Arlington, VA 22206. Internet: www.acca.org

* Refrigeration Service Engineers Society (RSES), 1666 Rand Rd., Des Plaines, IL 60016-3552. Internet: www.rses.org

* Plumbing-Heating-Cooling Contractors (PHCC), 180 S. Washington St., P.O. Box 6808, Falls Church, VA 22046. Internet: www.phccweb.org

* Air-Conditioning and Refrigeration Institute, 4100 North Fairfax Dr., Suite 200, Arlington, VA 22203. Internet: www.coolcareers.org or www.ari.org

Data Bank

Education and Training: Long-term on-the-job training

Starting Salaries: $23,000

Average Earnings: $29,000–$47,000

Total Jobs Held: 270,000

Job Outlook: Above-average increase

Annual Job Openings: 33,000

Related Jobs: Boilermakers; home appliance repairers; electricians; sheet metal workers; pipelayers, plumbers, pipefitters, and steamfitters

Personality Type: Realistic

Did You Know?

People working in this job can have a strong impact on the environment. CFCs and HFCs are coolants used in air-conditioning and refrigeration systems. These chemicals are dangerous if they escape into the atmosphere where they eat away at the ozone layer. Responsible technicians are careful to protect the environment from these chemicals. In fact, all technicians who work with them must be certified in their proper handling. Exams are administered by organizations approved by the U.S. Environmental Protection Agency.

Home Appliance Repairers

At a Glance

Anyone whose washing machine has ever exploded in a bubbly, watery mess knows the importance of a dependable appliance repair person. Home appliance repairers—sometimes called service technicians—repair ovens, washers, dryers, refrigerators, and other home appliances. Some repairers work specifically on small appliances such as microwaves and vacuum cleaners; others specialize in major appliances such as refrigerators and dishwashers. After identifying problems, home appliance repairers replace or repair defective belts, motors, heating elements, switches, gears, or other items. When repairing refrigerators and window air-conditioners, repairers must take care to recover and recycle refrigerants. All of these repairers must keep good records, prepare bills, and collect payments.

Did You Know?

The idea for the microwave oven started with a candy bar. Engineer Dr. Percy Spenser was working with radar equipment—more specifically a vacuum tube—when he noticed the candy bar in his pocket melting. Later experiments showed that the waves being emitted by the tube could pop popcorn and cause an egg to explode. Not too long afterward the first real microwave oven was built. It was nearly 6 feet tall and weighed more than 700 pounds. It probably would not have mounted easily under a kitchen cabinet.

Career in Focus: *Gas Appliance Repairer*

Many ovens use gas to produce heat rather than electricity. Repairers who specialize in gas appliances check the heating unit and replace tubing, thermocouples, thermostats, and valves. They may have to install pipes in a customer's home to connect the appliances to the gas line as well. They may have to saw holes in walls or floors and hang steel supports in order to hold gas pipes in place. They also answer emergency calls about gas leaks.

Where and When

Home appliance repairers either work in repair shops or make service calls to customers' homes. They may spend several hours a day driving to and from appointments. Repairers sometimes work in uncomfortable positions and tight spaces. Repairers must be conscious of the possibility of electrical shock and gas leaks. They usually work with little or no direct supervision. Most work a standard 40-hour week.

For More Information

* North American Retail Dealers Association, 10 E. 22nd St., Suite 310, Lombard, IL 60148.

* National Appliance Service Association, P.O. Box 2514, Kokomo, IN 46904.

* United Servicers Association, Inc., P.O. Box 31006, Albuquerque, NM 87190.

* International Society of Certified Electronics Technicians, 3608 Pershing Ave., Fort Worth, TX 76107. Internet: www.iscet.org

Industrial Machinery Mechanics and Maintenance Workers

At a Glance

A wide range of employees is required to keep sophisticated industrial machinery running smoothly—from highly skilled industrial machinery mechanics to lower skilled maintenance workers who perform routine tasks. Industrial machinery workers install and maintain the machines in factories or plants to keep the work on schedule. When repairs are needed, the repairer must work quickly so that production is not delayed. Primary responsibilities of industrial machinery mechanics also include preventive maintenance and installation of new machinery. By keeping complete and up-to-date records, mechanics try to anticipate trouble and service equipment before factory production is interrupted.

Career in Focus: *Machinery Maintenance Workers*

These employees are responsible for cleaning machinery, performing basic diagnostic tests, checking performance, and determining whether major repairs are necessary. They must adhere to strict maintenance schedules. Maintenance workers may perform minor repairs, but major repairs are generally left to machinery mechanics. As such, maintenance workers tend to earn less than mechanics, but they also don't need the same qualifications. Short-term on-the-job-training and a high school diploma are usually all one needs to be a machinery maintenance worker.

Where and When

Factories and other facilities can't afford to have machinery out of service, so mechanics are often on call to make emergency repairs. Overtime is common: About 30 percent work more than 40 hours per week. These workers are subject to cuts, bruises, and muscle strain, and they often must work on top of ladders or in cramped conditions. To protect themselves they wear hardhats, safety glasses, and hearing protection.

For More Information

* United Brotherhood of Carpenters and Joiners of America, 6801 Placid St., Las Vegas, NV 89119. Internet: www.carpenters.org

* National Tooling and Machining Association, 9300 Livingston Rd., Fort Washington, MD 20744. Internet: www.ntma.org

Data Bank

Education and Training: Short-term on-the-job training to long-term on-the-job training

Starting Salaries: $24,000

Average Earnings: $30,000–$47,000

Total Jobs Held: 306,000

Job Outlook: Little change

Annual Job Openings: 19,000

Related Jobs: Aircraft and avionics equipment mechanics and service technicians; automotive service technicians and mechanics; diesel service technicians and mechanics; elevator installers and repairers; heating, air-conditioning, and refrigeration mechanics and installers; heavy vehicle and mobile equipment service technicians and mechanics; machinists; maintenance and repair workers, general

Personality Type: Realistic

Did You Know?

About 25 percent of these workers are union members. Labor unions represent workers' rights to their employers and ensure fair pay and working conditions. Many workers in installation, maintenance, and repair occupations belong to unions. Those in industrial machinery repair may belong to one of several, including the United Steelworkers of America, the United Auto Workers, and the International Association of Machinists and Aerospace Workers.

Line Installers and Repairers

At a Glance

Line installers and repairers lay the wires and cables that bring electricity, phone service, and cable TV signals into our homes. They clear lines of tree limbs, check them for damage, and make emergency repairs when needed. They install new lines by constructing utility poles, towers, and underground trenches to carry the wires and cables. In addition to installation, these workers are responsible for the regular maintenance of electrical, telecommunications, and cable television lines. Bad weather or natural disasters can cause extensive damage to networks, so line installers and repairers must respond quickly to these emergencies to restore service.

Data Bank

Education and Training: Long-term on-the-job training

Starting Salaries: $25,000

Average Earnings: $34,000–$57,000

Total Jobs Held: 251,000

Job Outlook: Little change

Annual Job Openings: 34,000

Related Jobs: Broadcast and sound engineering technicians and radio operators, electricians, radio and telecommunications equipment installers and repairers

Personality Type: Realistic

Did You Know?

Fiber-optic cables are made of tiny strands of glass generally no wider than human hair. These tiny strands carry electricity, phone service, and cable TV signals to homes and businesses. One pair of optical fibers can carry more than 100,000 phone conversations at one time. The higher transmission capacity of fiber-optic cable has allowed services such as high-speed home Internet access. Splicing fiber-optic cable requires specialized equipment and training. Job prospects should be good for individuals with experience in working with such materials.

Career in Focus: *Electrical Powerline Installer*

While the work performed by telecommunications and electrical powerline installers is quite similar, they are two distinct occupations. Working with powerlines requires specialized knowledge of transformers, electrical power distribution systems, and substations. Workers on electrical powerlines install and replace transformers, circuit breakers, switches, fuses, and other equipment to control and direct the electrical current. Naturally, they take safety precautions to prevent electric shocks.

Where and When

This job can be dangerous because installers and splicers work underground or high above ground with various chemicals and electricity. They lift equipment and work in a variety of uncomfortable positions. They may have to travel long distances, and they often work in a variety of weather conditions. Many work a 40-hour week, though emergencies may require overtime. For example, when severe weather damages communication and electrical lines, installers and repairers may work long, irregular hours to restore them.

For More Information

* Communications Workers of America, 501 3rd St. NW, Washington, DC 20001. Internet: www.cwa-union.org

* International Brotherhood of Electrical Workers, Telecommunications Department, 1125 15th St. NW, Washington, DC 20005.

Maintenance and Repair Workers, General

At a Glance

General maintenance and repair workers have skills in many different crafts. They repair and maintain machines, mechanical equipment, and buildings. They also work on plumbing, electrical, and air-conditioning and heating systems. They build partitions; make plaster or drywall repairs; and fix or paint roofs, windows, doors, floors, and woodwork. They also maintain and repair specialized equipment and machinery found in cafeterias, hospitals, stores, offices, and factories. Typical duties include troubleshooting and fixing faulty electrical switches, repairing air-conditioning motors, and unclogging drains. General maintenance and repair workers inspect and diagnose problems and determine the best way to correct them, frequently checking blueprints, repair manuals, and parts catalogs. They also perform routine preventive maintenance and ensure that everything runs smoothly.

Career in Focus: *Maintenance Supervisor*

General maintenance workers often use their work experience to become craftworkers, such as electricians or plumbers, later in their careers. Those in large organizations who don't specialize can still advance to become the maintenance supervisor. In addition to many of the responsibilities of the general worker, maintenance supervisors plan work schedules and coordinate the work of other maintenance staff. They are responsible for inspecting and evaluating the work of maintenance employees as well as being the first to respond in the case of a maintenance emergency.

Where and When

These workers may have to stand for long periods, lift heavy objects, and work in uncomfortable environments or on ladders. Cuts, shocks, burns, falls, and bruises are potential hazards. Most work a regular 40-hour week, though some work evening, night, or weekend shifts or are on call for emergency repairs. The level of direct supervision varies.

For More Information

Information about job opportunities may be obtained from local employers and offices of the state employment service.

Data Bank

Education and Training: Moderate-term on-the-job training

Starting Salaries: $18,000

Average Earnings: $24,000–$41,000

Total Jobs Held: 1,332,000

Job Outlook: Average increase

Annual Job Openings: 154,000

Related Jobs: Carpenters; pipelayers, plumbers, pipefitters, and steamfitters; electricians; heating, air-conditioning, and refrigeration mechanics and installers; coin, vending, and amusement machine servicers and repairers; electrical and electronics installers and repairers; electronic home entertainment equipment installers and repairers; radio and telecommunications equipment installers and repairers

Personality Type: Realistic

Did You Know?

The general maintenance and repair worker is capable of fixing just about anything, so long as it doesn't require extensive knowledge or expertise. In that way he or she could be considered a "Jack of All Trades," a phrase meaning someone who is good at just about everything but does not excel at anything. The original figure of speech that this phrase comes from is "Jack of all trades, master of none, though ofttimes better than master of one."

Millwrights

At a Glance

Millwrights install, replace, and take apart the machinery and heavy equipment used in many industries. In addition to installing and dismantling machinery, many millwrights work with mechanics and maintenance workers to repair and maintain equipment. This includes preventive maintenance, such as lubrication and fixing or replacing worn parts. The development of new technology requires millwrights to keep their skills up-to-date—from blueprint reading and pouring concrete to diagnosing and solving mechanical problems. About half of all millwrights work in manufacturing.

Data Bank

Education and Training: Long-term on-the-job training

Starting Salaries: $27,000

Average Earnings: $35,000–$59,000

Total Jobs Held: 59,000

Job Outlook: Little change

Annual Job Openings: 5,000

Related Jobs: Industrial machinery installation, repair, and maintenance workers; tool and die makers; aircraft and avionics equipment mechanics and service technicians; structural and reinforcing iron and metal workers; assemblers and fabricators; heavy vehicle and mobile equipment service technicians and mechanics; welding, soldering, and brazing workers.

Personality Type: Realistic

Did You Know?

Millwright seems a strange name given that very few (if any) work in mills anymore. Though the name did originate from their work constructing flour mills, millwrights have historically been thought of more as engineers. They combined their knowledge of carpentry with that of blacksmithing and other mechanical arts to create everything from buildings to bridges. As the centuries progressed, millwrights became more and more focused on building and repairing machines, though their engineering and technical knowledge still shows through.

Career in Focus: *Turbine Installation and Repair*

Increasing automation in manufacturing means more complicated machines for millwrights to install and maintain. This requires them to specialize in certain machines or brand names. For example, some millwrights install and maintain turbines in power plants. These turbines can weigh hundreds of tons and contain thousands of parts. This machinery requires special care and knowledge, so millwrights receive additional training and are required to be certified by the manufacturer of the turbine in order to work on it.

Where and When

The working conditions of millwrights vary by industry. Those in manufacturing work in a shop setting, whereas those in construction may work outdoors in various weather conditions. They may also have to travel extensively from site to site. Advances in lifting and positioning equipment have made this job much safer. About 4 out of every 10 millwrights work more than 40 hours per week.

For More Information

* United Brotherhood of Carpenters and Joiners of America, 6801 Placid St., Las Vegas, NV 89119. Internet: www.carpenters.org

* Associated General Contractors of America, 333 John Carlyle St., Suite 200, Alexandria, VA 22314. Internet: www.agc.org

* Associated Builders and Contractors, Workforce Development Dept., 2300 Wilson Blvd., Suite 400, Arlington, VA 22201. Internet: www.trytools.org

* National Tooling and Machining Association, 9300 Livingston Rd., Fort Washington, MD 20744. Internet: www.ntma.org

Precision Instrument and Equipment Repairers

At a Glance

This job title covers a wide range of jobs. Precision instrument and equipment repairers may fix any number of smaller items from watches or cameras to defibrillators or violins. The most common jobs that fall into this trade include camera and photographic equipment repairers, watch and clock repairers, medical equipment repairers, and musical instrument repairers and tuners. They all use hand instruments and must possess a high level of skill, have good eye-hand coordination, and pay close attention to details. Many are self-employed and work in small workshops.

Career in Focus: *Piano Tuner*

Most piano tuners are also capable of making minor repairs. Tuning involves tightening and loosening different strings to achieve the proper tone or pitch. While the job used to be done with a tuning fork and a really good ear, nowadays handheld electronic tuners are used to match the pitch perfectly. Because pianos are difficult to transport, tuners normally make house calls. Some repairers specialize in restoring older pianos, which involves replacing one of the more than 12,000 parts found in some pianos.

Where and When

Most of these repairers work in comfortable workshops or repair shops, usually under minimal supervision. These workers often set their own schedules, and very few of them travel to do their work (piano tuners being one obvious exception). Those who repair medical equipment are often expected to be on call, but still tend to work normal daytime hours.

For More Information

* National Association of Photographic Equipment Technicians (NAPET), 3000 Picture Place, Jackson, MI 49201.
* National Association of Professional Band Instrument Repair Technicians (NAPBIRT), P.O. Box 51, Normal, IL 61761. Internet: www.napbirt.org
* Piano Technicians Guild, 4444 Forest Ave., Kansas City, MO 66106. Internet: www.ptg.org
* American Watchmakers-Clockmakers Institute (AWI), 701 Enterprise Dr., Harrison, OH 45030-1696. Internet: www.awi-net.org
* Association for the Advancement of Medical Instrumentation (AAMI), 1110 North Glebe Rd., Arlington, VA 22201-4795. Internet: www.aami.org

Data Bank

Education and Training: Moderate-term on-the-job training to associate degree

Starting Salaries: $22,000

Average Earnings: $30,000–$51,000

Total Jobs Held: 61,000

Job Outlook: Little change

Annual Job Openings: 7,000

Related Jobs: Computer, automated teller, and office machine repairers; coin, vending, and amusement machine servicers and repairers; dental laboratory technicians; ophthalmic laboratory technicians; industrial machinery installation, repair, and maintenance workers; jewelers and precious stone and metal workers; electronic home entertainment equipment installers and repairers

Personality Type: Realistic

Did You Know?

According to a Piano Technicians Guild membership survey, the majority of musical instrument repairers have some college work, and most have a bachelor's degree or higher. In addition, nearly all instrument repairers have a musical background, and many are musicians themselves. Very few colleges offer courses in instrument repair, so the majority of the trade is learned on the job as an assistant or apprentice. Still, it's one way for an aspiring musician to earn a living while waiting for his or her big break.

Production Occupations

Assemblers and Fabricators

At a Glance

Assemblers and fabricators put together complicated products such as computers, appliances, and electronic equipment. Their work is detailed and must be done accurately. They follow directions from engineers and use several tools and precise measuring instruments. Assemblers look for faulty parts and mistakes in the assembly process and then try to help fix problems before more defective products are produced. Some experienced assemblers work with designers and engineers to build prototypes or test products. Changes in technology have transformed the manufacturing and assembly process; automated manufacturing systems now use robots, computers, and programmable motion control devices. Assemblers must be comfortable using all of these new technologies.

Data Bank

Education and Training: Short-term on-the-job training to long-term on-the-job training

Starting Salaries: $16,000

Average Earnings: $20,000–$33,000

Total Jobs Held: 1,997,000

Job Outlook: Little change

Annual Job Openings: 393,000

Related Jobs: Welding, soldering, and brazing workers; machine setters, operators, and tenders—metal and plastic; inspectors, testers, sorters, samplers, and weighers

Personality Type: Realistic

Did You Know?

Manufacturing techniques are moving from traditional assembly line systems towards "lean" manufacturing systems. Lean manufacturing involves using teams of workers within "cells" to produce entire products. Team assemblers perform a group of tasks, rather than specializing in a single task as they would on an assembly line. The team also may decide how to assign the work and how to perform different tasks. This helps companies cover for absent workers, improve productivity, and increase their ability to respond to changes in demand.

Career in Focus: *Electrical and Electronic Equipment Assembler*

Electrical and electronic equipment assemblers build products such as electric motors, batteries, computers, and sensing equipment. Because dust might affect the operation of these products, electronic equipment assemblers tend to work in very clean, comfortable environments. There are about 200,000 workers directly employed in this field.

Where and When

Working conditions vary from plant to plant, but continue to improve. Most factories today are generally clean, well lit, and well ventilated. Some assemblers may come into contact with harmful chemicals or fumes, but safety precautions minimize any risk. Most full-time assemblers work 40 hours per week, though overtime and shift work is fairly common. The work can be repetitious and tedious.

For More Information

Information about employment opportunities for assemblers is available from offices of the state employment service.

Food Processing Occupations

At a Glance

These workers are responsible for producing many of the foods found in your pantry and refrigerator. Food processing workers work in grocery stores and production plants. They may work in a small market, in a large refrigerated room, or on an assembly line. Meat, poultry, and fish cutters and trimmers cut meat into pieces that are suitable for sale. Many work in animal slaughtering and processing plants, while butchers usually are employed in grocery stores. Bakers produce cakes, breads, and other baked goods. In manufacturing, bakers produce goods in large quantities, using high-volume mixing machines, ovens, and other equipment. Deli workers make salads and side dishes at grocery stores.

Career in Focus: *Food Batchmaker*

Food batchmakers set up and operate equipment that mixes, blends, or cooks ingredients to produce food products according to formulas or recipes. They generally work in assembly-line production facilities where much of the process is automated, and they are sometimes involved in quality control. They spend most of the work day on their feet. Kind of like those elves that make the cookies, except batchmakers make lots of different products, and they don't live in trees.

Where and When

Working conditions vary considerably. Butchers and meatcutters may work in slaughtering and processing plants or behind a meat counter. Those who work with meat and fish often work in cold, damp rooms to prevent the meat from spoiling. The cold, slippery conditions, sharp tools, and tiring, repetitive tasks make this one of the more dangerous jobs around. Bakers work in bakeries, hotels, restaurants, and supermarkets. They usually work in shifts, and morning, evening, weekend, and holiday work is common. Other food processing workers generally work in warm, noisy environments. Most work a regular 40-hour week, though that may include evenings and weekends.

For More Information

State employment service offices can provide information about job openings for food processing occupations.

Data Bank

Education and Training: Short-term on-the-job training to long-term on-the-job training

Starting Salaries: $15,000

Average Earnings: $18,000–$28,000

Total Jobs Held: 724,000

Job Outlook: Average increase

Annual Job Openings: 123,000

Related Jobs: Chefs, cooks, and food preparation workers

Personality Type: Realistic

Did You Know?

The slaughtering and meat packing industry is carefully regulated by the Food and Drug Administration (FDA), but it wasn't always. You may have read a book called *The Jungle* by Upton Sinclair. Though the political novel is about the immigration experience, it is often remembered for its stomach-churning descriptions of the meat packing industry at the turn of the 19th century. Its publication spurred the federal government to enforce stronger standards for both the safety of the workers and the general meat-eating public. In essence, the book helped create the FDA.

Computer Control Programmers and Operators

At a Glance

These workers use special computer numerically controlled (CNC) machines to cut and shape products such as car parts and compressors. These machines include lathes, milling machines, laser cutters, and water jet cutters. CNC programmers and operators follow blueprints from engineers to produce large quantities of a specific part. They use their knowledge of the working properties of metals and programming skills to design a set of instructions needed to make the product. These instructions are translated into a computer-aided manufacturing program containing a set of commands for the machine to follow. These commands describe where cuts should occur, what type of cut should be used, and the speed of the cut. In other words, these workers tell machines how to make stuff.

Did You Know?

While less-skilled CNC operators may need only a couple of weeks of on-the-job training, computer control programmers and skilled operators require more training and education. In fact, a growing number of them are receiving formal education from community or technical colleges. While these programs are still relatively new, they can provide the training needed to get a certification from the National Institute of Metalworking Skills, which in turn can expand career opportunities.

Career in Focus: *CNC Operator*

After the programming work is completed, CNC operators run the actual machines. They position the metal on the CNC machine and let the computer make the cuts. During a machining operation, the operator modifies the cutting program to account for any problems encountered. While many CNC operators are programmers as well, some manufacturers simply need CNC operators to be "button-pushers." They primarily start and stop machines, load cutting programs, and load and unload parts and tools. A single operator may monitor several machines simultaneously.

Where and When

Most computer control programmers and operators work a standard 40-hour week. They are increasingly working evening and weekend shifts, however, and overtime is common during peak production periods. Most machine shops are clean, well lit, and ventilated. Working around machine tools requires workers to wear protective equipment and exercise caution.

For More Information

* Precision Machine Products Association, 6700 West Snowville Rd., Brecksville, OH 44141-3292. Internet: www.pmpa.org

* National Tooling and Metalworking Association, 9300 Livingston Rd., Fort Washington, MD 20744. Internet: www.ntma.org

* Precision Metalforming Association Educational Foundation, 6363 Oak Tree Blvd., Independence, OH 44131-2500. Internet: www.pmaef.org

Machinists

At a Glance

Machinists make metal parts using lathes, drill presses, and milling machines. They often make specialized parts or one-of-a-kind items for companies that produce everything from cars to computers. Before they make a part, machinists must carefully plan and prepare the operation. After the layout work is completed, machinists position the workpiece on the machine tool, set the controls, and make the cuts. During the machining process, they must constantly monitor the rate and speed of the machine. Some machinists repair or make new parts for existing machinery. Because the technology in this field is changing rapidly, machinists must learn to operate a wide range of machines.

Career in Focus: *Production Machinist*

Production machinists produce large quantities of one part, especially parts requiring great precision. Frequently, machinists work with computer control programmers to determine how the automated equipment will cut a part. The programmer may determine the path of the cut, while the machinist determines the type of cutting tool, the speed of the cutting tool, and the feed rate.

Where and When

Most machine shops are relatively clean, well lit, and ventilated, and exposure to noise and debris is limited. Machinists still must wear protective equipment like safety glasses. Machinists stand most of the day and may need to lift heavy workpieces. Many machinists work a 40-hour week, though evening and weekend shifts are becoming more common.

For More Information

* Precision Machine Products Association, 6700 West Snowville Rd., Brecksville, OH 44141-3292. Internet: www.pmpa.org

* National Tooling and Machining Association, 9300 Livingston Rd., Fort Washington, MD 20744. Internet: www.ntma.org

* Precision Metalforming Association Educational Foundation, 6363 Oak Tree Blvd., Independence, OH 44131-2500. Internet: www.pmaef.org

Data Bank

Education and Training: Long-term on-the-job training

Starting Salaries: $21,000

Average Earnings: $27,000–$43,000

Total Jobs Held: 370,000

Job Outlook: Little change

Annual Job Openings: 33,000

Related Jobs: Tool and die makers; machine setters, operators, and tenders—metal and plastic; computer control programmers and operators; welding, soldering, and brazing workers

Personality Type: Realistic

Did You Know?

The vast majority of machinists work in manufacturing; however, a machinist's ability to create one-of-a-kind items makes the trade valuable in other fields as well. In fact, some machinists make copies of antique tools and machinery for museums and collectors. They use today's technologies to re-create yesterday's tools.

Machine Setters, Operators and Tenders–Metal and Plastic

At a Glance

Machine tool operators in the metalworking and plastics industries help produce most of the products we rely on daily. These workers fall into two groups: those who set up machines for operation and those who tend the machines while they work. They may work with drilling and boring machines, milling and planing machines, or lathe and turning machines. They work according to blueprints and other instructions to produce metal and plastic parts for everything from toasters to trucks.

Because the setup process requires an understanding of the entire production process, setters usually have more training and are more highly skilled than those who simply operate or tend machinery.

Data Bank

Education and Training: Moderate-term on-the-job training

Starting Salaries: $18,000

Average Earnings: $22,000–$36,000

Total Jobs Held: 1,129,000

Job Outlook: Declining

Annual Job Openings: 96,000

Related Jobs: Machinists; tool and die makers; assemblers and fabricators; computer control programmers and operators; welding, soldering, and brazing workers; inspectors, testers, sorters, samplers, and weighers

Personality Type: Realistic

Did You Know?

They call it "labor-saving machinery" in part because it cuts down on the amount of physical work required. But that, in turn, cuts down on the number of workers. The new advances in computer-controlled machine tools and robots have had a dramatic impact on this industry, causing an overall decline in the number of new workers needed in this field. The result is that those with the most experience and education and who are willing to adapt to the ever-changing technology will have the best job prospects.

Career in Focus: *Machine Setters, Operators, and Tenders–Plastic*

Plastic parts are steadily replacing metal ones in all kinds of manufacturing. These workers are required to set up and tend machines that transform plastic compounds into a wide variety of goods such as toys, tubing, and auto parts. These products are manufactured by various methods. They may use injection molding to make a spatula, an extruding machine to make a window frame, or blow molding to create a two-liter soft-drink bottle.

Where and When

These workers tend to be on their feet most of the day in clean, well-lit, and well-ventilated labs and workshops. The machines they use can be dangerous, so strict safety rules are observed, including the use of safety glasses and earplugs. Most machine setters, operators, and tenders work 40 hours per week. Because many shops operate more than one shift each day, some operators work nights and weekends.

For More Information

* National Tooling and Machining Association, 9300 Livingston Rd., Fort Washington, MD 20744. Internet: www.ntma.org

* Precision Metalforming Association Educational Foundation, 6363 Oak Tree Blvd., Independence, OH 44131. Internet: www.pmaef.org

* Precision Machine Products Association, 6700 West Snowville Rd., Brecksville, OH 44141-3292. Internet: www.pmpa.org

* Society of Plastics Industry, 1667 K St. NW, Suite 1000, Washington, DC 20006. Internet: www.plasticsindustry.org

Tool and Die Makers

At a Glance

Tool and die makers are among the most highly skilled workers in manufacturing. These workers produce tools, dies, and devices that enable machines to manufacture a variety of products—from clothing and furniture to heavy equipment and parts for aircraft. Tool makers create tools that cut, shape, and form metal and other materials. Die makers make the dies used to shape metal in stamping and forging machines. Some tool and die makers make prototypes of parts and then work with engineers to determine how best to manufacture the part. In addition to developing, designing, and producing new tools and dies, these workers also may repair worn or damaged tools, gauges, jigs, and fixtures. Tool and die makers must know about machining operations, mathematics, and blueprint reading.

Career in Focus: *Mold Maker*

A mold maker is not some scientist experimenting with bacteria and mildew in petri dishes. Rather, molds are used in a variety of manufacturing processes, most often to create plastic parts and goods. Mold makers specialize in creating the molds for the manufacturing industry. While some plastics companies may employ their own mold makers, the majority work out of specialty shops alongside other tool and die makers.

Where and When

Tool and die makers usually work in clean and cool toolrooms. Workers follow safety rules and wear safety glasses, earplugs, gloves, and masks. They spend much of their time on their feet and may do moderately heavy lifting. Most work 40 hours per week, traditionally during normal business hours.

For More Information

* Precision Machine Products Association, 6700 West Snowville Rd., Brecksville, OH 44141-3292. Internet: www.pmpa.org

* National Tooling and Machining Association, 9300 Livingston Rd., Ft. Washington, MD 20744. Internet: www.ntma.org

* Precision Metalforming Association Educational Foundation, 6363 Oak Tree Blvd., Independence, OH 44131-2500.

Data Bank

Education and Training: Long-term on-the-job training

Starting Salaries: $28,000

Average Earnings: $36,000–$55,000

Total Jobs Held: 103,000

Job Outlook: Declining

Annual Job Openings: 7,000

Related Jobs: Machinists; computer control programmers and operators; machine setters, operators, and tenders—metal and plastic; welding, soldering, and brazing workers

Personality Type: Realistic

Did You Know?

Many tool and die makers learn their skill through formal apprenticeship programs, which can take 4–5 years to complete. While requirements used to be limited to some on-the-job training and a certain number of courses, the National Institute of Metalworking Skills is developing new standards that would replace some of these requirements with competency tests. Don't say we didn't warn you.

Welding, Soldering, and Brazing Workers

At a Glance

These workers use the heat from a torch to melt and then permanently fuse metal parts together. Because of its strength, welding is used to build ships, cars, aircraft, and even space shuttles. Welding is also used to join beams when constructing buildings and bridges, and to join pipes in pipelines, power plants, and refineries. Welders may use a hand torch or a welding machine. There are about 100 different types of welding, though arc welding is the most common. Like welding, soldering and brazing use molten metal to join two pieces of metal. However, the metal added during the process has a melting point lower than that of the workpiece, so only the added metal is melted, not the workpiece itself. Highly skilled welders often are trained to work with a wide variety of materials in addition to steel, such as titanium, aluminum, or plastics.

Data Bank

Education and Training: Moderate-term on-the-job training to long-term on-the-job training

Starting Salaries: $20,000

Average Earnings: $25,000–$38,000

Total Jobs Held: 429,000

Job Outlook: Little change

Annual Job Openings: 59,000

Related Jobs: Machinists; machine setters, operators, and tenders–metal and plastic; computer control programmers and operators; tool and die makers; sheet metal workers; boilermakers; assemblers and fabricators

Personality Type: Realistic

Did You Know?

Say the word *welder*, and many people picture a man in a hard hat and goggles. But many of today's welders are women, and they can trace their history to the shipyards of World War II. During the war, the shipyards of San Francisco were so short of workers that they began hiring and training housewives and mothers to do the job. These women who came to work in America's factories during the war even had a popular song written and named for them: "Rosie the Riveter."

Career in Focus: *Cutter*

The work of cutters is closely related to that of welders. However, instead of *joining* metals, cutters use the heat from an electric arc, a stream of plasma, or burning gases to trim metal objects to specific dimensions. Cutters also dismantle large objects, such as ships, railroad cars, automobiles, buildings, or aircraft. Some operate and monitor cutting machines similar to those used by welding machine operators.

Where and When

These workers are exposed to a number of hazards, not the least of which are intense light, poisonous fumes, and very hot materials. They are like knights in armor, wearing safety shoes, goggles, hoods, and face shields. They may work both indoors and out, and may even work on scaffolding or platforms high off the ground. About half of these workers work a 40-hour week, though overtime is common, and some welders work up to 70 hours per week. In addition, some work in factories that operate around the clock, which requires evening and weekend shifts.

For More Information

＊ American Welding Society, 550 N.W. Lejeune Rd., Miami, FL 33126. Internet: www.aws.org

Bookbinders and Bindery Workers

At a Glance

Bookbinders and bindery workers use machines to bind the pages of books and magazines in a cover. These machines fold, cut, gather, glue, stitch, sew, trim, and wrap pages to form a book. Job duties depend on the kind of material being bound. In establishments that print new books, this work is done mechanically. In firms that do edition binding, workers bind books produced in large numbers or "runs." A small number of bookbinders work in hand binderies. These highly skilled workers design original or special bindings for limited editions, or restore and rebind rare books. Bookbinders and bindery workers in small shops may perform many binding tasks, while those in large shops usually are assigned only one or a few jobs.

Career in Focus: *Library Binder*

Library binders repair books and provide other specialized binding services to libraries. In libraries where repair work on rare books is needed, these bookbinders sew, stitch, or glue the printed sheets, shape the book bodies with presses and trimming machines, and reinforce them with glued fabric strips. Covers are created separately and then glued, pasted, or stitched onto the book bodies. If the book is especially old or rare, special precautions must be taken to preserve it.

Where and When

Binderies are noisy, and the job can be strenuous, requiring considerable lifting, standing, and carrying. Binders often work on an assembly line, and the task can be repetitive. Most work a 40-hour week.

For More Information

* Bindery Industries Association, International, 100 Daingerfield Rd., Alexandria, VA 22314.
* Graphic Arts Education and Research Foundation, 1899 Preston White Dr., Reston, VA 20191-5468. Internet: www.makeyourmark.org
* Printing Industries of America/Graphic Arts Technical Foundation, 200 Deer Run Rd., Sewickley, PA 15143.
* NPES The Association for Suppliers of Printing Publishing, and Converting Technologies, 1899 Preston White Dr., Reston, VA 20191-4367. Internet: www.npes.org/education/index.html

Data Bank

Education and Training: Short-term on-the-job training to moderate-term on-the-job training

Starting Salaries: $16,000

Average Earnings: $20,000–$33,000

Total Jobs Held: 81,000

Job Outlook: Declining

Annual Job Openings: 9,000

Related Jobs: Prepress technicians and workers; printing machine operators; machine setters, operators, and tenders–metal and plastic

Personality Type: Realistic

Did You Know?

Long before the printing press was invented, people were experimenting with book binding. The craft began in Rome during the first century with the invention of the codex. A codex was simply a series of sheets of vellum or parchment folded in half and sewed together across the fold. This was a vast improvement over the scrolls that were most popular at the time. Codices were easier to carry, easier to search through, and allowed for writing on both sides. They were the precursors to our modern books.

Prepress Technicians and Workers

At a Glance

Prepress technicians and workers prepare materials for printing presses. They do typesetting, design page layouts, take photographs, and make printing plates. With personal computers, customers can now show printing companies how they want their printed material to look. It is increasingly common for prepress technicians to receive files from the customer electronically. These files need to be formatted to fit on the paper the customer wants to use. The technician then creates proofs of the pages to give to the customer for a final check. Technicians use laser "imagesetters" to expose digital images of the pages directly onto thin aluminum printing plates which are then used to make the final product.

Data Bank

Education and Training: Long-term on-the-job training

Starting Salaries: $19,000

Average Earnings: $25,000–$42,000

Total Jobs Held: 141,000

Job Outlook: Declining

Annual Job Openings: 18,000

Related Jobs: Artists and related workers, graphic designers, desktop publishers, data entry and information processing workers, printing machine operators

Personality Type: Realistic

Did You Know?

Desktop publishing has changed the printing industry and the jobs of prepress workers. Today, they use high-tech computer programs to design and prepare materials for printing. These programs allow workers to separate color photos into the four basic colors that all printers use. The computer tells the printer precisely how much of each color of ink to apply so that the blend matches the original photos exactly. While this process is more efficient, it also means fewer jobs for prepress technicians.

Career in Focus: *Job Printer*

The printing process has three stages—prepress, press, and binding or postpress. Most of the time these three processes are handled by different workers who specialize in each stage. In small print shops, however, job printers are responsible for all three stages. They check proofs for errors and print clarity, correct mistakes, print the job, and attach each copy's pages together. They are the one-stop shopping of the printing world, though they are often not capable of handling large print runs.

Where and When

Prepress technicians and workers work in clean, comfortable environments with little noise. The extensive computer use can result in eyestrain and backaches. Platemakers who still work with chemicals run the risk of skin irritation. All of these workers are subject to the stress and pressure of tight deadlines. Most work an 8-hour day, though those employed by newspapers often work nights, weekends, and holidays.

For More Information

* Graphic Arts Education and Research Foundation, 1899 Preston White Dr., Reston, VA 20191-5468. Internet: www.makeyourmark.org

* Graphic Communications Conference of the International Brotherhood of Teamsters, 1900 L St. NW, Washington, DC 20036-5007. Internet: www.gciu.org

* Printing Industries of America/Graphic Arts Technical Foundation, 200 Deer Run Rd., Sewickley, PA 15143-2324.

Printing Machine Operators

At a Glance

Printing machine operators prepare, run, and maintain the printing presses in a pressroom. They check the paper and ink, make sure paper feeders are stocked, and monitor the presses as they are running. To prepare presses for printing, machine operators generally install the printing plate, ink the presses, load paper, adjust the press to the paper size and feed paper through the press cylinders. However, new technology skips these steps and sends the files directly to the press. Throughout the run, operators must regularly pull sheets to check for any printing imperfections, though much of this is now done by computers also. In most shops, press operators also perform preventive maintenance.

Career in Focus: *Screen Printing Machine Operator*

No doubt you have seen custom screen-printed t-shirts. Screen printing machines are capable of printing text and designs onto materials other than paper, including glass, plasticware, and cloth. Screen printing machine setters and operators determine all of the settings and adjustments necessary to create the design. They also monitor the printing process to ensure accuracy.

Where and When

This work can be physically and mentally demanding. Printing machine operators spend most of their time on their feet and are constantly under pressure to meet deadlines. Pressrooms are noisy, and working with the machinery can be hazardous, though new computerized controls make the job much safer. Many press operators work weekends, nights, and holidays, especially those who work for newspapers. Overtime is often needed to meet deadlines.

For More Information

* Graphic Communications Conference of the International Brotherhood of Teamsters, 1900 L St. NW, Washington, DC 20036-5007. Internet: www.gciu.org

* NPES The Association for Suppliers of Printing, Publishing, and Converting Technologies, 1899 Preston White Dr., Reston, VA 20191-4367. Internet: www.npes.org

* Printing Industry of America/Graphic Arts Technical Foundation, 200 Deer Run Rd., Sewickley, PA 15143.

* Graphic Arts Education and Research Foundation, 1899 Preston White Dr., Reston, VA 20191-5468. Internet: www.makeyourmark.org

Data Bank

Education and Training: Moderate-term on-the-job training

Starting Salaries: $18,000

Average Earnings: $23,000–$40,000

Total Jobs Held: 191,000

Job Outlook: Little change

Annual Job Openings: 26,000

Related Jobs: Machine setters, operators, and tenders–metal and plastic; bookbinders and bindery workers

Personality Type: Realistic

Did You Know?

Before the Middle Ages, few people in Europe could read. Manuscripts had to be copied by hand, a task often preformed by scribes who were employed by monasteries. Then in 1456 a man named Gutenberg made the first printing press using moveable type. His invention not only put a lot of scribes out of work, it also made books available to the common man for the first time in history. Gutenberg's printing press is considered to be one of the most important inventions in human history. In fact, in 1999, the Arts & Entertainment network named Gutenberg the most influential person of the last millennium.

Textile, Apparel, and Furnishings Occupations

At a Glance

Textile workers operate the machines that make goods such as fibers, cloth, and upholstery. These goods are then used in all kinds of products from sweaters to sofas. Jobs may involve computers, large industrial machinery, or substantial handwork. Textile machine setters, operators, and tenders run machines that make textile products out of fibers. Textiles are the basis of towels, bed linens, and nearly all clothing, but they also are a key ingredient in products ranging from roofing to tires.

Data Bank

Education and Training: Short-term on-the-job training to long-term on-the-job training

Starting Salaries: $14,000

Average Earnings: $17,000–$24,000

Total Jobs Held: 929,000

Job Outlook: Declining

Annual Job Openings: 116,000

Related Jobs: Assemblers and fabricators; medical, dental, and ophthalmic laboratory technicians; food-processing occupations; jewelers and precious stone and metal workers; woodworkers

Personality Type: Realistic

Did You Know?

Apparel workers are among the most rapidly declining work groups in the U.S. economy, in part because much of the work isn't being done in the U.S. anymore. Many U.S. companies are moving their production facilities abroad where labor is cheaper. Even tailors and dressmakers are feeling the sting, as it is now often cheaper to simply go out and buy new clothes rather than repair the old ones. Most of the patches you see on jeans today are there as a fashion statement, not to mend holes.

Apparel workers make cloth, leather, and fur into clothing and other products. They may also repair torn or damaged items, or tailor them to fit a customer. Upholsterers are skilled craft workers who make new furniture or repair old furniture. Laundry and dry cleaning workers clean garments, linens, draperies, blankets, and other articles.

Career in Focus: *Shoe and Leather Worker*

Shoe and leather workers work in manufacturing or personal services. In shoe manufacturing, they operate machines that do the cutting, joining, and finishing needed to create footwear. In personal services, they repair and customize leather goods for the public. They construct, decorate, or repair shoes, belts, purses, saddles, luggage, and other leather products. Shoe and leather workers and repairers who own their own shops also must keep records and supervise other workers.

Where and When

Working conditions vary considerably, though most people in these occupations work a standard 40-hour week. Evening and weekend work is common, especially for those employed in laundry and dry cleaning or in retail stores. Many textile mills use rotating shifts, which can make for unusual schedules. Work in these occupations can be physically demanding and repetitive. Upholsterers, for example, stand most of the day and do a lot of bending and heavy lifting.

For More Information

Information about job opportunities in textile, apparel, and furnishings occupations is available from local employers and offices of state employment services.

Woodworkers

At a Glance

Woodworkers use machines that cut, shape, assemble, and finish wood to make doors, cabinets, paneling, and furniture. In addition to these household goods, woodworkers also make sporting goods, such as baseball bats and oars, as well as musical instruments, toys, caskets, tool handles, and thousands of other wooden items. Precision woodworkers use hand tools to make rare or customized items. Production woodworkers use machines such as power saws, planers, sanders, and lathes. They may work in sawmills and plywood mills. Woodworkers have been greatly affected by the introduction of computer-controlled machinery, which has decreased the number of openings in this field.

Career in Focus: *Furniture Finisher*

Unlike those woodworkers who mass produce similar items, furniture finishers work on a job-by-job basis, often building one-of-a-kind pieces. These highly skilled precision woodworkers do all of the cutting, shaping, preparing, and assembling in order to make a finished product. For this reason, they normally need substantial training and an ability to work from detailed instructions and specifications.

Where and When

Working conditions vary by industry. Those in logging and sawmills have more physically demanding jobs and must adhere to rigid safety precautions. In furniture and cabinet manufacturing, employees still wear eye and ear protection and take precautions to guard against accidents. Prolonged standing, lifting, and fitting of heavy objects are common characteristics of the job.

For More Information

For information about woodworking occupations, contact local furniture manufacturers, sawmills, cabinetmaking or millwork firms, lumber dealers, or the nearest office of the state employment service.

Data Bank

Education and Training: Moderate-term on-the-job training to long-term on-the-job training

Starting Salaries: $16,000

Average Earnings: $20,000–$31,000

Total Jobs Held: 364,000

Job Outlook: Declining

Annual Job Openings: 44,000

Related Jobs: Carpenters, sheet metal workers, structural and reinforcing iron and metal workers, computer control programmers and operators, machinists, tool and die makers

Personality Type: Realistic

Did You Know?

Wood is one of the oldest materials to be shaped by man, whether it's making the shaft of a spear or carving out a canoe. Some of the stranger things to be created include a wooden car, wooden flowers, and wooden legs. However, through extensive testing, scientists have found that George Washington's false teeth were not, in fact, made of wood (as many of us are taught in elementary school). Rather his dentures were made of gold, ivory, lead, and human and animal teeth. So tongue splinters weren't a big problem, we guess.

Power Plant Operators, Distributors, and Dispatchers

At a Glance

Power plant operators control the turbines, generators, and boilers that generate electricity. Operators distribute power demands among generators, combine the current from several generators, and regulate the flow of electricity from the plant. When power requirements change, these workers start or stop generators and connect or disconnect them from circuits. Reactor operators are authorized to control the power output of the reactor in a nuclear power plant. The Nuclear Regulatory Commission (NRC) licenses operators of these plants.

Data Bank

Education and Training: Long-term on-the-job training

Starting Salaries: $37,000

Average Earnings: $46,000–$66,000

Total Jobs Held: 46,000

Job Outlook: Declining

Annual Job Openings: 7,000

Related Jobs: Stationary engineers and boiler operators, water and liquid waste treatment plant and system operators

Personality Type: Realistic

Did You Know?

Some parts of the world have grown accustomed to rolling blackouts–periods where they must go without electricity. But imagine being without power for more than two months. The longest peacetime blackout in history began on February 19, 1998, in Auckland, New Zealand. Four main power cables broke, causing electricity in the city center to be down for a total of 66 days.

Career in Focus: *Power Distributor and Dispatcher*

Also called load dispatchers or systems operators, these workers make sure that users receive enough electricity. They control the flow of electricity to industrial plants and substations, which supply everyone else's power needs. They monitor and operate current converters, voltage transformers, and circuit breakers. Dispatchers also record the status of connections. Dispatchers anticipate power needs, such as those caused by changes in the weather. They also handle emergencies, such as transformer or transmission line failures, by routing the electrical current around the affected areas.

Where and When

Because electricity is provided around the clock, this work is done in 8- or 12-hour shifts. Work on rotating shifts can be stressful and tiring because of disruptions in sleeping patterns. Those who work in control rooms generally sit or stand at a control station. The work requires constant attention. Those who work outside the control room may be exposed to danger from shocks, falls, and burns. Most workers at nuclear power plants are subject to random drug and alcohol tests.

For More Information

⁕ American Public Power Association, 2301 M St. NW, Washington, DC 20037-1484. Internet: www.appanet.org

⁕ International Brotherhood of Electrical Workers, 1125 15th St. NW, Washington, DC 20005. Internet: www.ibew.org

Stationary Engineers and Boiler Operators

At a Glance

Stationary engineers and boiler operators operate and maintain equipment that provides air-conditioning, heat, and ventilation to large buildings such as industrial plants. This equipment may include boilers, turbines, generators, pumps, and compressors, and may supply electricity, steam, or other types of power. These workers start up, regulate, repair, and shut down equipment. They ensure that the equipment operates safely and efficiently by monitoring meters and gauges. Stationary engineers typically use computers to operate the safety systems of new buildings and plants as well.

Career in Focus: *First-class Stationary Engineer*

There are several classes of stationary engineer licenses, each one specifying the type and size of equipment the engineer is allowed to use. A licensed first-class stationary engineer is qualified to run a large facility and operate equipment of all types and capacities. This person may be in charge of all mechanical systems in the building and may supervise the work of assistant stationary engineers, turbine operators, boiler tenders, and air-conditioning and refrigeration operators and mechanics. The license requires several years of on-the-job experience as well as passing a written examination.

Where and When

Stationary engineers and boiler operators generally work 40 hours per week all year round. Some facilities operate around the clock, creating the need for rotating shifts. These workers are often exposed to high temperatures, dust, dirt, and high noise levels. Workers spend much of their time on their feet. They may have to work in crouching and kneeling positions and crawl inside boilers to inspect, clean, or repair equipment.

For More Information

* International Union of Operating Engineers, 1125 17th St. NW, Washington, DC 20036. Internet: www.iuoe.org

* National Association of Power Engineers, Inc., 1 Springfield St., Chicopee, MA 01013.

* Building Owners and Managers Institute International, 1521 Ritchie Hwy., Arnold, MD 21012. Internet: www.bomi-edu.org

Data Bank

Education and Training: Long-term on-the-job training

Starting Salaries: $27,000

Average Earnings: $35,000–$56,000

Total Jobs Held: 50,000

Job Outlook: Little change

Annual Job Openings: 5,000

Related Jobs: Power plant operators, distributors, and dispatchers; water and liquid waste treatment plant and system operators; industrial machinery mechanics and maintenance workers; millwrights

Personality Type: Realistic

Did You Know?

Being a stationary engineer doesn't mean you can just sit in one place all day and monitor equipment (though the name may suggest otherwise). In fact, when they are not monitoring, cleaning, adjusting, inspecting, or repairing their usual equipment, they are given other maintenance responsibilities. Stationary engineers are often responsible for carpentry, plumbing, locksmithing, and electrical repairers. It would seem that stationary engineers are never in one place for very long.

Water and Liquid Waste Treatment Plant and System Operators

At a Glance

Water treatment plant operators make sure that the water we drink is safe. Water is pumped from wells, rivers, streams, and reservoirs to water treatment plants, where it is treated and distributed to customers. Wastewater travels through customers' sewer pipes to wastewater treatment plants. From there it is either treated and returned to streams, rivers, and oceans or reused for irrigation and landscaping. Operators in both types of plants control equipment that removes harmful materials, chemicals, and microorganisms from the water. They also control pumps, valves, and other equipment that moves the water or wastewater through the treatment process. They take water samples, perform analyses, and test and adjust chemicals in the water, such as chlorine. Occasionally, operators must work during emergencies, often caused by weather. Plant operators must also be familiar with the guidelines established by federal and state regulations.

Data Bank

Education and Training: Long-term on-the-job training

Starting Salaries: $22,000

Average Earnings: $27,000–$44,000

Total Jobs Held: 94,000

Job Outlook: Average increase

Annual Job Openings: 6,000

Related Jobs: Power plant operators, distributors, and dispatchers; stationary engineers and boiler operators

Personality Type: Realistic

Did You Know?

One of the hottest topics in water treatment today is desalination–the process of converting ocean and seawater into drinkable water by removing the salt and other minerals. It is an expensive process but a necessary one in places such as the Middle East, where fresh water is scarce. After all, with a planet covered in more water than land, it would be a shame to go thirsty.

Career in Focus: *Water Treatment Plant Attendant*

Every ladder has a first rung. Trainees in water treatment plants usually begin as attendants where they learn the majority of their skills on the job. They do routine tasks such as record meter readings, take samples of wastewater and sludge, and perform simple maintenance and repair work on pumps, motors, valves, and other plant equipment. This training is often combined with formal classroom experience.

Where and When

Water and wastewater treatment plant and system operators work both indoors and out. The work is physically demanding and is often performed in unsanitary locations. Because of this, operators pay close attention to safety procedures, especially around slippery walkways and dangerous gases. Because plants operate around the clock, operators work in rotating shifts, including weekends and holidays. They may be required to work overtime.

For More Information

* Association of Boards of Certification, 208 Fifth St., Ames, IA 50010-6259. Internet: www.abccert.org

* American Water Works Association, 6666 West Quincy Ave., Denver, CO 80235. Internet: www.awwa.org

* Water Environment Federation, 601 Wythe St., Alexandria, VA 22314-1994. Internet: www.wef.org

Inspectors, Testers, Sorters, Samplers, and Weighers

At a Glance

All products must meet certain quality standards before they can be sold to the public. These workers examine and sort products before releasing them to consumers. They may test by looking, listening, feeling, tasting, weighing, or smelling. Inspectors may reject a product, send it back to be fixed, or fix the problem themselves. Inspectors work in all kinds of industries producing all kinds of products, from food to clothing to glassware to cars. Some inspectors examine materials received from a supplier before sending them to the production line. Others inspect individual components or perform a final check on the finished product. Depending on their skill level, inspectors also may set up and test equipment, calibrate instruments, or simply record data.

Career in Focus: *Tester*

Testers repeatedly test existing products or prototypes under real-world conditions. For example, they may purposely abuse a machine by not changing its oil to see when it breaks down. They may devise automated machines to repeat a basic task thousands of times, such as opening and closing a car door. They subject products to extreme environments, such as scorching heat and freezing cold, to see how well they hold up. Through these tests, companies determine how long a product will last, what parts will break down first, and how to improve durability.

Where and When

Some inspectors may examine the same type of product for an entire shift, whereas others may inspect a variety. They are often on their feet all day and may be required to lift heavy objects. Plant conditions vary from noisy and dirty to clean and air-conditioned. Some inspectors do all of their analysis directly from electronic readouts on a computer. Evening, night, and weekend shifts are not uncommon, and overtime is sometimes required to meet production goals.

For More Information

✳ American Society for Quality, 600 North Plankinton Ave., Milwaukee, WI 53203. Internet: www.asq.org

---

Data Bank

Education and Training: Moderate-term on-the-job training

Starting Salaries: $17,000

Average Earnings: $22,000–$40,000

Total Jobs Held: 508,000

Job Outlook: Declining

Annual Job Openings: 85,000

Related Jobs: Construction and building inspectors, occupational health and safety specialists and technicians

Personality Type: Realistic

Did You Know?

You have probably seen video footage of crash test dummies, but did you know that automobile safety testing actually started with human cadavers? Long before the invention of crash dummies, researchers used dead bodies to simulate the effects of car accidents. Then in 1949, the first dummy was invented by Sierra Engineering Company. Named Sierra Sam, he was created for the United States Air Force in order to test aircraft ejection seats, finally answering the question, "What kind of dummy would do such a thing?"

Jewelers and Precious Stone and Metal Workers

At a Glance

These workers use precious metals and stones such as gold and diamonds to design and manufacture jewelry. Some specialize in one area, such as buying, designing, cutting, repairing, selling, or appraising jewels. This work requires a high degree of skill and attention to detail. Jewelers use chemicals, sawing and drilling tools, and torches in their work. They may work for large jewelry manufacturing firms, for small retail jewelry shops, or as owners of their own businesses. Those who own or manage stores or shops also hire and train employees, order and sell merchandise, and perform other managerial duties. Gemologists and laboratory graders analyze, describe, and certify the quality and characteristics of gem stones. They often work as quality control experts for retailers, importers, or manufacturers.

Data Bank

Education and Training: Vocational/technical training

Starting Salaries: $16,000

Average Earnings: $22,000–$40,000

Total Jobs Held: 42,000

Job Outlook: Little change

Annual Job Openings: 6,000

Related Jobs: Precision instrument and equipment repairers; welding, soldering, and brazing workers; woodworkers; artists and related workers; fashion designers; retail salespersons; sales representatives, wholesale and manufacturing

Personality Type: Realistic

Did You Know?

One of the most famous jewels in the world is the Hope Diamond. This 451-carat blue diamond was found in the early 1600s and has passed from kings to commoners. It has been stolen and recovered, sold and resold, cut and recut. But its fame is due to the bad luck it seems to bring its owners. Through the years, some of its owners have been beheaded, been killed by wild dogs, or committed suicide. More than 20 deaths have been blamed on the gem. You can see it at the Smithsonian Natural History Museum in Washington DC, though you probably shouldn't get too close.

Career in Focus: *Jewelry Appraiser*

Jewelry appraisers carefully examine jewelry to determine its value, after which they write appraisal documents. They determine the value of a piece by researching the jewelry market, using reference books, auction catalogs, price lists, and the Internet. They may work for jewelry stores, appraisal firms, auction houses, pawnbrokers, or insurance companies. Many gemologists also become appraisers.

Where and When

This work involves a great deal of concentration. The use of more comfortable jewelers' benches has eliminated most of the physical discomfort caused by spending long periods bent over in one position. Lasers, chemicals, sharp tools, and jewelers' torches all require proper safety precautions. In repair shops, jewelers usually work alone with little supervision. Those in retail stores may have extensive customer interaction. Because of the valuable nature of their products, jewelers must take involved safety precautions against theft.

For More Information

* Gemological Institute of America, 5345 Armada Dr., Carlsbad, CA 92008. Internet: www.gia.edu
* Manufacturing Jewelers and Suppliers of America, 45 Royal Little Dr., Providence, RI 02904.
* Jewelers of America, 52 Vanderbilt Ave., 19th Floor, New York, NY 10017. Internet: www.jewelers.org

Medical, Dental, and Ophthalmic Laboratory Technicians

At a Glance

These workers produce the devices that help patients see, speak, chew, or move better. Medical laboratory technicians construct artificial limbs, braces, and supports based on prescriptions from doctors. They are also referred to as orthotic and prosthetic technicians. Dental laboratory technicians make the products dentists use to replace decayed teeth. Using dentists' directions and molds of patients' mouths, they make dentures (false teeth), crowns, and bridges. In some laboratories, technicians perform all stages of the work, whereas in other labs, each technician does only a few specialized tasks.

Career in Focus: *Ophthalmic Laboratory Technician*

Ophthalmic laboratory technicians make prescription eyeglass or contact lenses. Some ophthalmic laboratory technicians manufacture lenses for other instruments, such as telescopes and binoculars. Ophthalmic laboratory technicians cut, grind, edge, and finish lenses according to specifications provided by opticians, optometrists, or ophthalmologists, and may insert lenses into frames to produce finished glasses. Although some lenses still are produced by hand, technicians are increasingly using automated equipment to make them.

Where and When

These technicians generally work in clean, comfortable laboratories where they have limited contact with the public. Most work a standard 40-hour week. At times they must wear goggles, gloves, and masks for safety. They may spend a great deal of time standing.

For More Information

* American Academy of Orthotists and Prosthetists, 526 King St., Suite 201, Alexandria, VA 22314. Internet: www.opcareers.org

* National Commission on Orthotic and Prosthetic Education, 330 John Carlyle St., Suite 200, Alexandria, VA 22314. Internet: www.ncope.org

* Commission on Dental Accreditation, American Dental Association, 211 E. Chicago Ave., Chicago, IL 60611. Internet: www.ada.org

* National Board for Certification in Dental Technology, 325 John Knox Rd., L103, Tallahassee, FL 32303. Internet: www.nbccert.org

* Commission on Opticianry Accreditation, 8665 Sudley Rd., #341, Manassas VA 20110.

Data Bank

Education and Training: Moderate-term on-the-job training to long-term on-the-job training

Starting Salaries: $18,000

Average Earnings: $22,000–$38,000

Total Jobs Held: 86,000

Job Outlook: Little change

Annual Job Openings: 6,000

Related Jobs: Dentists; opticians, dispensing; precision instrument and equipment repairers

Personality Type: Realistic

Did You Know?

What did people do before they had porcelain dentures? When Queen Elizabeth I lost all of her front teeth she put pieces of cloth under her lips to make her face appear fuller. Other members of the royal court had ornamental teeth made from silver or gold. Many early sets of dentures were made from bone or ivory, or from human teeth either donated by the dead (who didn't need them) or sold by the poor (who felt they needed the money more).

Painting and Coating Workers, Except Construction and Maintenance

At a Glance

Painting and coating machine operators cover everything from cars to candy with paints, plastics, varnishes, chocolates, or special solutions. Workers use various types of machines to coat a range of products, from giving paper its glossy finish to applying a mixture of silver, tin, and copper to glass to make mirrors. The most common methods of applying paints and coatings are spraying and dipping. Spray machine operators use spray guns to coat metal, wood, ceramic, fabric, paper, and food products with paint and other solutions. Other workers paint, coat, or decorate products such as furniture, glass, pottery, toys, cakes, and books. In response to concerns about air pollution and worker safety, manufacturers increasingly are using new types of paints and coatings on their products.

Data Bank

Education and Training: Short-term on-the-job training to moderate-term on-the-job training

Starting Salaries: $18,000

Average Earnings: $22,000–$37,000

Total Jobs Held: 185,000

Job Outlook: Little change

Annual Job Openings: 31,000

Related Jobs: Painters and paperhangers; woodworkers; machine setters, operators, and tenders—metal and plastic

Personality Type: Realistic

Did You Know?

Some lucky coating workers get to operate enrobing machines. These gizmos coat bakery goods, candy bars, and other treats with melted chocolate, sugar, or cheese. So some of the same skills that might help you paint a car can also help you make a Milky Way. Smaller candy makers may use a hand-dipping method to get a chocolate coating, but this process is much more time intensive, not to mention all the chocolate lost by workers licking their fingers.

Career in Focus: *Automotive Painter*

Although the majority of painting and coating workers are employed in manufacturing, perhaps the best known group of workers refinishes old and damaged cars, trucks, and buses. Automotive painters use a spray gun to apply successive coats of paint until the finish of the repaired sections of the vehicle matches that of the original. To speed drying between coats, they may place the freshly painted vehicle under heat lamps or in a special infrared oven. These painters also may do special detailing work.

Where and When

Painting and coating workers typically work indoors and may be exposed to dangerous fumes, though the painting is done in ventilated booths and operators typically wear masks or respirators. Operators have to stand for long periods when using a spray gun, as well as bend, stoop, or crouch in uncomfortable positions. Most operators work a normal 40-hour week, but self-employed automotive painters often work more.

For More Information

* National Institute for Automotive Service Excellence (ASE), 101 Blue Seal Dr. SE, Leesburg, VA 20175. Internet: www.asecert.org

Photographic Process Workers and Processing Machine Operators

At a Glance

Photographic process workers and processing machine operators develop film, make picture prints and slides, and enlarge and retouch photographs. These workers also restore damaged and faded photographs. Film process technicians operate machines that develop exposed photographic film in a series of chemical and water baths to produce images. Color printer operators use equipment to produce color prints from negatives. Photographic process workers perform more delicate tasks, such as retouching negatives, prints, and images to emphasize or correct specific features. Although computers and digital technology are replacing much manual work, some photographic process workers, especially those who work in portrait studios, still perform many specialized tasks by hand.

Career in Focus: *Airbrush Artists*

Airbrush artists restore damaged and faded photographs. They may also color or shade drawings to create a more photographic appearance. They first examine the drawing or photo to determine coloring, shading, and changes required. Then they use a template to spray ink or paint in order to fill in and blend missing parts of a photograph or give depth, perspective, and tone to a drawing.

Where and When

These workers spend most of their hours in clean, comfortable offices, laboratories, or one-hour minilabs. More and more photographic processing is being done on computers rather than in darkrooms. Workers take precautions to prevent exposure to chemicals and fumes. Many photo laboratory employees work a 40-hour week, including evenings and weekends. About one in four works part-time.

For More Information

✳ Photo Marketing Association International, 3000 Picture Place, Jackson, MI 49201. Internet: www.pmai.org

Data Bank

Education and Training: Short-term on-the-job training to moderate-term on-the-job training

Starting Salaries: $14,000

Average Earnings: $17,000–$26,000

Total Jobs Held: 86,000

Job Outlook: Declining

Annual Job Openings: 17,000

Related Jobs: Clinical laboratory technologists and technicians, computer operators, jewelers and precious stone and metal workers, prepress technicians and workers, printing machine operators, science technicians

Personality Type: Realistic; Artistic

Did You Know?

The first digital cameras came out in the 1980s, but only in the last decade have they exploded in popularity. Using digital cameras, both amateur and professional photographers can edit, touch up, and print their own photographs without ever taking the film to a processor. While this is incredibly convenient for the photographer, it isn't as convenient for photographic process workers who need something to do. As a result, job opportunities in this field are expected to steadily decline.

Semiconductor Processors

At a Glance

Semiconductors, also known as microchips, are the tiny brains inside today's computers and high tech equipment. Semiconductor processors are the workers who make these microchips. Semiconductors are produced in "cleanrooms"—production areas that must be kept free of any airborne matter, which can damage the chips. Processors must wear special coveralls called "bunny suits" to keep any dust away from the semiconductors. In creating these chips, operators use special equipment to imprint information on tiny silicon wafers. They spend a great deal of time at computer terminals, monitoring the operation of the equipment that makes the chips. They ensure that each of the tasks in the production of the chip is performed correctly.

Data Bank

Education and Training: Associate degree

Starting Salaries: $20,000

Average Earnings: $25,000–$38,000

Total Jobs Held: 45,000

Job Outlook: Declining

Annual Job Openings: 7,000

Related Jobs: Assemblers and fabricators, engineers, science technicians

Personality Type: Realistic

Did You Know?

Silicon Valley is the name given to the southern part of the San Francisco Bay area that became known for its creation of microchips. Over the past twenty years, the industry there has exploded. Now Silicon Valley has become synonymous with many high-tech products and inventions–and the people who got rich making them. In fact, the area has the highest number of millionaires per capita of anywhere in the United States.

Career in Focus: *Semiconductor Processing Technicians*

While technicians account for a smaller percentage of the workers in cleanrooms, they are crucial to the process. Technicians troubleshoot production problems and make equipment adjustments and repairs. They also take the lead in assuring quality control. To keep equipment repairs to a minimum, technicians perform diagnostic analyses to see whether an error is a flaw in one chip or in the process as a whole.

Where and When

Semiconductor processors work in rooms that must be kept free of dust and set at a comfortable 72 degrees. Workers wear suits that cover them entirely, minus the eyes which are protected by glasses. These workers may work with highly toxic chemicals, and they spend much of the day on their feet. The pace of the work is deliberately slow. Because these plants operate around the clock, night and weekend work is common.

For More Information

* Maricopa Advanced Technology Education Center (MATEC), 2323 West 14th St., Suite 540, Tempe, AZ 85281. Internet: www.matec.org

Transportation and Material Moving Occupations

Aircraft Pilots and Flight Engineers

At a Glance

Aircraft pilots fly airplanes and helicopters, test aircraft, and sometimes fight forest fires. Pilots may work for large airlines, charter services, the government, or private businesses. They must plan flights, check the aircraft and weather conditions, and keep records of each flight. Flight engineers act as a third pilot on large aircraft, monitoring and operating many of the instruments and systems. Most pilots are airline pilots and copilots who transport passengers and cargo, but one out of five pilots is a commercial pilot involved in tasks such as dusting crops, spreading seed for reforestation, testing aircraft, directing firefighting efforts, tracking criminals, monitoring traffic, and rescuing and evacuating injured persons.

Data Bank

Education and Training: Vocational/technical training to bachelor's degree

Starting Salaries: $41,000

Average Earnings: $54,000 (median annual earnings for commercial pilots); $129,000 (median annual earnings for airline pilots)

Total Jobs Held: 106,000

Job Outlook: Average increase

Annual Job Openings: 9,000

Related Jobs: Air traffic controllers

Personality Type: Realistic

Did You Know?

Not only are the earnings of airline pilots some of the highest in the nation, the job comes with its share of benefits as well. Airline pilots are usually eligible for life and health insurance, retirement benefits, and disability payments. They receive an expense allowance for every hour they are away from home and sometimes have an allowance for purchasing and cleaning their uniforms. In addition, pilots and their families usually are entitled to free flights. The drawback: The time away from home can be considerable.

Career in Focus: *Flight Instructor*

Some pilots are flight instructors. They teach their students in ground-school classes, in simulators, and in dual-controlled planes and helicopters. They teach student pilots about flight procedures and techniques, prepare lesson plans, and evaluate and monitor student performance. A few specially trained pilots are examiners. They periodically fly with other pilots or pilot's license applicants to test their proficiency.

Where and When

While the "where" should be obvious (if they aren't in the cockpit, they probably should be), the "when" varies considerably. FAA regulations state that pilots flying large aircraft cannot fly more than 100 hours a month or 1,000 hours a year. Most pilots fly about 75 hours a month and spend another 75 hours performing nonflying duties. Flight assignments are based on seniority, and most pilots work an irregular schedule and spend a lot of time away from home (at the expense of the airline). Commercial pilots also have irregular schedules and work at odd hours.

For More Information

* Air Line Pilots Association, International, 1625 Massachusetts Ave. NW, Washington, DC 20036.

* Air Transport Association of America, Inc., 1301 Pennsylvania Ave. NW, Suite 1100, Washington, DC 20004.

* Federal Aviation Administration, 800 Independence Ave. SW, Washington, DC 20591. Internet: www.faa.gov

* Helicopter Association International, 1635 Prince St., Alexandria, VA 22314. Internet: www.rotor.com

Air Traffic Controllers

At a Glance

Air traffic controllers are responsible for the safe movement of airport traffic both in the air and on the ground. With the help of radars, they direct landings, takeoffs, and ground movement of aircraft. They keep planes a safe distance apart during flights and inform pilots of current weather conditions. Their immediate concern is safety, but controllers also must direct planes efficiently to minimize delays. In emergencies they may search for missing aircraft. Airport tower controllers' main responsibility is to organize the flow of aircraft into and out of the airport. After each plane departs, airport tower controllers notify enroute controllers who take charge and ensure that the airplane safely arrives at its destination. There are 20 air route traffic control centers located around the country, each employing 300 to 700 controllers.

Career in Focus: *Flight Service Specialist*

In addition to airport towers and centers, air traffic controllers also work in flight service stations operated at more than 100 locations. These flight service specialists provide pilots with information on the station's particular area, including terrain, weather information, suggested routes, and other information important to the safety of a flight. Flight service specialists help pilots in emergency situations and coordinate searches for missing or overdue aircraft. However, they are not involved in managing air traffic.

Where and When

Controllers work about 40 hours per week. Because most control towers and centers operate around the clock, controllers rotate night and weekend shifts. The job requires intense concentration, as controllers are expected to keep track of several planes at once. The mental stress can be exhausting.

For More Information

* Federal Aviation Administration, 800 Independence Ave. SW, Washington, DC 20591. Internet: www.faa.gov

---

Data Bank

Education and Training: Long-term on-the-job training

Starting Salaries: $58,000

Average Earnings: $81,000–$131,000

Total Jobs Held: 24,000

Job Outlook: Average increase

Annual Job Openings: 2,000

Related Jobs: Aircraft pilots and flight engineers

Personality Type: Conventional

Did You Know?

The process to become an air-traffic controller is long and involved. A person must enroll in an FAA-approved education program and pass a pre-employment test. In addition, applicants must have three years of full-time work experience or have completed four years of college. After completing the FAA-approved program (and providing the applicant is under the age of 31), the applicant must pass a medical exam, undergo drug screening, and obtain a security clearance. Provided all of that goes well, he or she then attends a 12-week training session at the FAA Academy in Oklahoma. After graduating from there, the applicant begins on-the-job training as a "developmental controller," which can last between two and four years. After all of this, he or she is finally certified to be a full-fledged air traffic controller.

Bus Drivers

At a Glance

Buses provide transportation for millions of people every year, from commuters to school children to vacationers. Bus drivers transport people from place to place following a time schedule and a specific route, sometimes collecting fares and keeping a log of their activity. Some transit bus drivers transport people long distances within a state or throughout the country. School bus drivers drive students to and from school. Drivers must operate vehicles safely and have a valid commercial driver's license. Bus drivers operate a range of vehicles, from 15-passenger buses to 60-foot buses that can carry more than 100 passengers.

Data Bank

Education and Training: Short-term on-the-job training to moderate-term on-the-job training

Starting Salaries: $14,000

Average Earnings: $20,000–$33,000

Total Jobs Held: 653,000

Job Outlook: Average increase

Annual Job Openings: 110,000

Related Jobs: Taxi drivers and chauffeurs, truck drivers and driver/sales workers

Personality Type: Realistic

Did You Know?

More than 24 million students ride school buses every day in America. Some states now require that school buses be equipped with seat belts for all riders, and many other states are studying the idea. Proponents say seat belts will protect kids in a crash, but others say seat belts will slow down the time it takes to evacuate the bus in an emergency (not to mention give kids an additional means for torturing each other). It's a debate that has raged for decades.

Career in Focus: *Motor Coach Driver*

Some drivers operate motor coaches, which transport passengers on chartered trips and sightseeing tours. Drivers interact with customers and tour guides to make the trip as comfortable and informative as possible. They keep to strict schedules and follow the tour's itinerary. These drivers often act as customer service representative, tour guide, program director, and safety guide all in one. Trips frequently last more than a day.

Where and When

Most drivers work without any kind of direct supervision, but they also take full responsibility for their passengers. Intercity bus drivers may work nights, weekends, and holidays, and spend much of their time away from home. Senior drivers may have regular weekly work schedules, but schedules of other drivers vary. School bus drivers work only when school is in session, many for 20 hours per week or less. Those who work on tour and charter buses may work on any day and all hours, including weekends and holidays. The Department of Transportation regulates how many hours bus drivers can drive in a given week.

For More Information

* National School Transportation Association, 113 South West St., 4th Floor, Alexandria, VA 22314. Internet: www.yellowbuses.org

* National Association of State Directors of Pupil Transportation Services, 6298 Rock Hill Rd., The Plains, VA 20198-1916.

* United Motorcoach Association, 113 South West St., 4th Floor, Alexandria, VA 22314. Internet: www.uma.org

* American Bus Association, 700 13th St. NW, Suite 575, Washington, DC 20005. Internet: www.buses.com

Taxi Drivers and Chauffeurs

At a Glance

Taxi drivers and chauffeurs drive people in cars, limousines, and vans. Taxi drivers pick up passengers by "cruising" for fares, prearranging pickups, and picking up passengers from taxi stands. These professional drivers also help out-of-town business people and tourists get around in unfamiliar surroundings. Drivers should be familiar with streets in the areas they serve so that they can use the most efficient routes. They should know the locations of frequently requested destinations, such as airports, bus and railroad terminals, convention centers, hotels, and other points of interest. Chauffeur service differs from taxi service in that all trips are pre-arranged. Chauffeurs pamper their passengers by providing extras like newspapers, drinks, music, and television. All of these workers must lift heavy luggage and packages, drive in all kinds of weather and traffic, and sometimes put up with rude customers.

Career in Focus: *Paratransit Driver*

Many wheelchair-bound individuals may have difficulty getting into and out of a regular taxicab. Thankfully some taxi services have accommodations for such individuals. Some taxi drivers specialize in transporting individuals with special needs, such as those with disabilities and the elderly. These drivers, known as paratransit drivers, operate specially equipped vehicles. Some additional training on the equipment and passenger needs may be required.

Where and When

Driving for long periods can be tiring, stressful, and uncomfortable. Work hours of taxi drivers and chauffeurs vary greatly. Many work part-time, and schedules can change from day to day. Drivers may be on call, and evening and weekend work is expected. The job is attractive to individuals seeking a flexible work schedule, however. Improvements in cars have made the job safer and more comfortable, including satellite tracking systems and automated dispatch systems. Many chauffeurs wear formal attire such as a uniform or tuxedo.

For More Information

* National Limousine Association, 49 South Maple Ave., Marlton, NJ 08053. Internet: www.limo.org

---

Data Bank

Education and Training: Short-term on-the-job training

Starting Salaries: $13,000

Average Earnings: $16,000–$25,000

Total Jobs Held: 188,000

Job Outlook: Above-average increase

Annual Job Openings: 43,000

Related Jobs: Bus drivers, truck drivers and driver/sales workers

Personality Type: Realistic

Did You Know?

Some jobs you might anticipate being dangerous and sometimes even deadly. Roofers, fishers, and logging workers, for example, constantly face hazards as part of their daily work. But did you know that taxi drivers rank in the top ten most dangerous jobs in the United States? Granted, much of the danger comes from automobile accidents, but taxi drivers—who often work alone, carry large amounts of cash, and work at all hours in all areas of a city—may also find themselves victims of robbery and homicide.

Truck Drivers and Driver/Sales Workers

At a Glance

Truck drivers move and deliver goods among factories, warehouses, stores, and homes. Even if some goods travel most of the way by ship, train, or airplane, almost everything is carried by trucks at some point in its journey. Drivers maintain their trucks, check for fuel and oil, make sure their brakes and lights work, and make minor repairs. They also load and unload the goods they transport. The duration of runs vary according to the types of cargo and the destinations. Local drivers may provide daily service for a specific route or region, while other drivers make longer, intercity and interstate deliveries. Heavy truck and tractor-trailer drivers transport goods including cars, livestock, and other materials. Light or delivery services truck drivers operate vans and trucks weighing less than 26,000 pounds. They generally pick up or deliver merchandise and packages within a specific area.

Data Bank

Education and Training: Short-term on-the-job training to moderate-term on-the-job training

Starting Salaries: $18,000

Average Earnings: $23,000–$38,000

Total Jobs Held: 3,231,000

Job Outlook: Average increase

Annual Job Openings: 515,000

Related Jobs: Bus drivers, taxi drivers and chauffeurs

Personality Type: Enterprising; Realistic

Did You Know?

Long-distance trucking runs might last for several days or even weeks. Drivers stop only for gas, food, and loading and unloading. On such long runs, two drivers might work together. One driver sleeps in a berth built into the truck while the other drives. The berths often include refrigerators and televisions, though the quarters are still cramped.

Career in Focus: *Route Driver*

The primary responsibility of route drivers is to deliver and sell products over established routes. They sell goods, such as food products, or pick up and deliver items, such as laundry. They also respond to customer complaints and requests, take orders, and collect payments. Most have routes that deliver to businesses and stores, rather than to homes. After completing their route, route drivers place orders for their next deliveries based on product sales and customer requests.

Where and When

Driving for many hours at a time and loading and unloading cargo can be tiring. Some long-distance truck drivers may spend most of the year away from home, while local truck drivers usually return home in the evening. The U.S. Department of Transportation regulates the working conditions for truck drivers. Long-distance drivers may drive for 11 hours or work for 14 after 10 hours off-duty. Drivers on long runs face boredom, loneliness, and fatigue, and they often work nights, holidays, and weekends.

For More Information

* American Trucking Associations, Inc., 2200 Mill Rd., Alexandria, VA 22314. Internet: www.trucking.org

* Professional Truck Driver Institute, 2200 Mill Rd., Alexandria, VA 22314. Internet: www.ptdi.org

* The International Brotherhood of Teamsters, 25 Louisiana Ave. NW, Washington, DC 20001.

Rail Transportation Occupations

At a Glance

Railroads deliver billions of tons of freight and millions of travelers per year to destinations throughout the country, while subways and light-rail systems transport millions of passengers around metropolitan areas. This job includes railroad workers as well as subway and streetcar operators. Railroad engineers operate locomotives that transport passengers and cargo. Conductors are responsible for the cargo and passengers on trains. Those assigned to passenger trains also ensure passenger safety and comfort as they go about collecting tickets and fares, making announcements, and coordinating activities of the crew. Brakemen remove cars and throw switches to allow trains to change tracks. Yardmasters coordinate the activities of workers engaged in railroad traffic operations.

Career in Focus: *Subway and Streetcar Operator*

Subway and streetcar operators generally work for public transit authorities instead of railroads. Subway operators control trains that transport passengers through cities and their suburbs. The trains run in underground tunnels, on the surface, or on elevated tracks. Operators must start, slow, or stop their train; make announcements to riders; open and close the doors of the train; and ensure that passengers get on and off the subway safely. Streetcar operators drive electric-powered streetcars, trolleys, or light-rail vehicles that transport passengers around metropolitan areas. They don't *all* work in San Francisco.

Where and When

Many rail transportation workers work nights, weekends, and holidays, and may work more than a 40-hour week. The more desirable shifts are usually given based on seniority. Rail yard workers spend most of their time outdoors regardless of weather conditions. The work of conductors and engineers can be physically demanding as well. Those who work on trains operating between points hundreds of miles apart may spend a lot of time away from home.

For More Information

* Association of American Railroads, 50 F St. NW, Washington, DC 20001. Internet: www.aar.org
* American Public Transportation Association, 1666 K St. NW, Washington, DC 20006.
* Brotherhood of Locomotive Engineers and Trainmen, 1370 Ontario St. Mezzanine, Cleveland, OH 44113. Internet: www.ble.org

Data Bank

Education and Training: Moderate-term on-the-job training to vocational/technical training

Starting Salaries: $31,000

Average Earnings: $40,000–$68,000

Total Jobs Held: 112,000

Job Outlook: Declining

Annual Job Openings: 5,000

Related Jobs: Bus drivers, truck drivers and driver/sales workers, water transportation occupations

Personality Type: Realistic

Did You Know?

In the late 1800s, when the railroad was the fastest way to travel, wealthy people sometimes bought their own railroad cars. These cars were usually decorated with rich, expensive materials. Some even had luxury items such as sunken bathtubs, barber's chairs, and pipe organs. When they wanted to travel, these people simply had their cars hitched to a train. Most employed their own maids, chefs, and waiters to serve them on the trip as well. Some modern passenger trains still offer luxury travel accommodations, including fine linens and crystal stemware, impeccable service, and executive staterooms for sleeping. We doubt they have pipe organs, though.

Water Transportation Occupations

At a Glance

Workers in water transportation operate all kinds of boats on oceans, lakes, rivers, canals, and other waterways. Captains or masters are in charge of a vessel and the crew. Deck officers or mates help the captain. Sailors and deck hands do maintenance, steer, and load and unload cargo. Pilots guide ships through harbors and narrow waterways. On larger coastal ships, the crew may include a captain, a mate or pilot, an engineer, and seven or eight seamen. Unlicensed positions on a large ship may include a full-time cook, an electrician, and mechanics.

Data Bank

Education and Training: Short-term on-the-job training to vocational/technical training

Starting Salaries: $26,000

Average Earnings: $31,000–$55,000

Total Jobs Held: 72,000

Job Outlook: Little change

Annual Job Openings: 7,000

Related Jobs: Fishers and fishing vessel operators, job opportunities in the armed forces

Personality Type: Enterprising, Realistic

Did You Know?

Merchant mariners working on ships on the Great Lakes typically work for 60 days straight and then have 30 days off. Most sailors are hired for one voyage at a time, and during the winter months when the lakes are frozen, there is no work at all. Compared to many deep-sea mariners, however, those working on the Great Lakes are often not too far from home.

Career in Focus: *Ship Engineer*

Ship engineers operate, maintain, and repair propulsion engines, boilers, generators, pumps, and other machinery. Merchant marine vessels usually have four engineering officers: a chief engineer and a first, second, and third assistant engineer. Assistant engineers stand periodic watches, overseeing the safe operation of engines and machinery. These individuals combine their technical skills with their knowledge of seafaring, and many of them have a college degree.

Where and When

The "where" is usually a boat of some kind, hopefully in a body of water of some kind. The "when" various tremendously. Merchant mariners spend extended periods at sea, usually on voyages lasting several months. At sea, workers usually stand watch for 4 hours and then are off for 8 every day of the week. Workers on other ships may be on duty for 6 or 12 hours and then off for another 6 or 12. Extended periods of unemployment are common. People in water transportation work in all weather conditions and the jobs come with their share of hazards. The work is physically demanding and the stress of being away from home for long periods can take its toll.

For More Information

❋ Maritime Administration, U.S. Department of Transportation, 400 7th St. SW, Room 7302, Washington, DC 20590. Internet: www.marad.dot.gov/acareerafloat

❋ Paul Hall Center for Maritime Training and Education, P.O. Box 75, Piney Point, MD 20674-0075. Internet: www.seafarers.org/phc

❋ International Organization of Masters, Mates, and Pilots, 700 Maritime Blvd., Linthicum Heights, MD 21090-1941.

❋ U.S. Coast Guard National Maritime Center, 4200 Wilson Blvd., Suite 630, Arlington, VA 22203-1804. Internet: www.uscg.mil/stcw/index.htm

Material Moving Occupations

At a Glance

Material moving workers load and unload trucks and ships using cranes, bulldozers, shovels, and forklifts. They also move construction materials, logs, and coal around factories, warehouses, and construction sites. Material moving workers are categorized into two groups—operators and laborers. Operators use machinery to move construction materials such as earth, petroleum products, and other heavy materials. Some move materials onto or off of trucks and ships. They also may set up and inspect equipment, make adjustments, and perform minor repairs. Laborers manually handle freight, stock, or other materials; clean vehicles, machinery, and other equipment; and pack or package products and materials.

Career in Focus: *Hand Freight, Stock, and Material Mover*

These workers don't require cranes or bulldozers to do their work. Instead they manually move freight, stock, and other materials to and from storage and production areas, loading docks, delivery vehicles, ships, and containers. Their specific duties vary by industry. In factories, they may move materials or goods between loading docks, storage areas, and work areas. Specialized workers within this group include baggage and cargo handlers, who work in transportation industries, and truck loaders and unloaders.

Where and When

Material moving work is physically demanding and can be repetitive. Workers lift and carry heavy objects and stoop, kneel, crouch, or crawl in awkward positions. Some work at great heights, and many work outdoors in all kinds of weather. They often must wear gloves, hardhats, protective glasses, and other safety devices. Most material movers work eight-hour shifts, though overtime is common.

For More Information

* Industrial Truck Association, 1750 K St. NW, Suite 460, Washington, DC 20006. Internet: www.indtrk.org

* International Union of Industrial Engineers, 1125 17th St. NW, Washington, DC 20036. Internet: www.iuoe.org

* National Commission for the Certification of Crane Operators, 2750 Prosperity Ave., Suite 505, Fairfax, VA 22031. Internet: www.nccco.org

Data Bank

Education and Training: Short-term on-the-job training to related work experience

Starting Salaries: $15,000

Average Earnings: $18,000–$28,000

Total Jobs Held: 5,060,000

Job Outlook: Little change

Annual Job Openings: 1,190,000

Related Jobs: Bus drivers; construction equipment operators; machine setters, operators, and tenders–metal and plastic; rail transportation occupations; truck drivers and driver/sales workers; construction laborers

Personality Type: Enterprising; Realistic

Did You Know?

This job category covers a wide range of titles, from excavating machine operators who use scoops to load trucks with gravel to ship loaders who use hoists to load and unload sea vessels. But perhaps the unsung heroes of the category are the refuse and recyclable material collectors—more commonly known as garbage collectors. These workers gather the refuse from homes and businesses all across the nation for transport to dumps, landfills, and recycling centers. It's a heavy job for a country where every person produces an average of four pounds of trash per day.

Job Opportunities in the Armed Forces

Job Opportunities in the Armed Forces

At a Glance

The U.S. Armed Forces is the country's largest single employer with more than 2 million people serving, of which 1.4 million are on active duty. Maintaining a strong defense requires many activities, such as running hospitals, repairing helicopters, programming computers, and operating nuclear reactors. Military jobs range from clerical work to professional positions to construction work. People in the military must serve for a specified time and can be moved from one base to another. Enlisted personnel, who make up about 85 percent of the Armed Forces, carry out the fundamental operations of the military in areas such as combat, administration, construction, engineering, health care, and human services. Officers, who make up the remaining 15 percent of the Armed Forces, are the leaders of the military, supervising and managing all activities.

Data Bank

Education and Training: Moderate-term on-the-job training to related work experience

Starting Salaries: $13,700 (for new recruits)

Average Earnings: $28,500 (varies tremendously by pay grade; officers can make considerably more than enlisted personnel)

Total Jobs Held: 2,130,000

Job Outlook: Little change

Annual Job Openings: 170,000

Related Jobs: Almost all of them

Personality Type: No data available

Did You Know?

The military can provide you with the training to do almost any job once you've finished your commitment. The Armed Forces train doctors, nurses, journalists, cooks, lawyers, metalworkers, surveyors, meteorologists, computer specialists, pilots, sailors, electronics equipment repairers, mechanics, and craft workers, just to name a few. Many employers like hiring former military personnel because they know about discipline, honor, and getting the job done. In addition, the Montgomery GI Bill helps veterans pay for continued education at many colleges, universities, and training schools.

Career in Focus: *Combat Specialty Occupations*

When most people think of the military, they think of those enlisted men and women in combat specialty operations. They are the soldiers, such as infantry, artillery, and special forces, who are most directly involved in combat. They conduct military maneuvers, offensive raids, intelligence, demolitions, and search and rescue missions using aircraft, helicopters, ships, tanks, subs, and all other kinds of equipment. Enlisted personnel in this category only represent 15 percent of the total manpower for the military, however.

Where and When

To say that working conditions vary in the military is an understatement. A mechanic onboard an aircraft carrier has a vastly different work environment than a military counselor working with soldiers returning from combat duty or a bomb recovery specialist looking for landmines in city streets. The "where" could be a naval base in Hawaii, a recruitment center in Iowa, or a cave in Afghanistan. The "when" for an officer on a submarine is completely different than for a public affairs officer in Washington, DC. It also goes without saying that the work can sometimes be hazardous, even during peacetime—though much of the military's workforce is never directly involved in combat.

For More Information

✱ U.S. Department of Defense. *Military Career Guide Online.* Internet: www.todaysmilitary.com

Appendix A: Job Titles by Personality Type

Saying someone has a good personality after a first date usually means the person wasn't much of a looker. But personality counts for a great deal, especially in the world of work. It can even be valuable as a means of focusing your career research.

Many career counselors believe that people are more satisfied in a job or career if it suits their personality; people will stay at a job longer and be more productive if they like what they do and who they work with. The personality types used in the *EZ OOH* were developed in the 1950s by career guidance researcher John Holland, and his theory has since become the most widely used model for matching personality to career decisions. It is used in a wide variety of professional assessments and research materials including the *Self-Directed Search* and the Department of Labor's Occupational Information Network.

This appendix offers an index of job titles found in the *EZ OOH* arranged by personality type. You can use this index to quickly locate the jobs that might best match your interests. Simply review the descriptions of the six personality types, find the one or two that best describe you and your work preferences, and then scan the jobs listed under those categories to find ones you want to read about.

Descriptions of the Six Personality Types

Realistic

Realistic personalities like work activities that involve practical, hands-on problems and solutions. They enjoy dealing with plants; animals; and real-world materials such as wood, tools, and machinery. They also enjoy working outside, but often do not like paperwork or working closely with others.

Sample Work Activities: build kitchen cabinets, install flooring in houses, drive a taxicab, maintain the grounds of a park, refinish furniture, put out forest fires, work on a fishing boat, assemble electronic parts

Investigative

Investigative personalities like jobs that involve working with ideas and that require critical thinking and analysis. They like to search for facts and solve complex problems mentally rather than to persuade or lead people.

Sample Work Activities: study rocks and minerals, do laboratory tests to identify diseases, conduct chemical experiments, investigate crimes, invent new foods, diagnose and treat sick animals, study the history of past civilizations

Artistic

Artistic personalities like jobs that involve working with forms, designs, and patterns. They like self-expression and prefer to do their work without following a clear set of rules.

Sample Work Activities: conduct an orchestra, write poems or novels, play a musical instrument, act in a movie, paint sets for a play, announce a radio show, sing in a band, design artwork for magazines, create dance routines for a show

Social

Social personalities like work activities that assist others and promote learning and personal development. They like to teach, to give advice, to help, or to be of service to people in some way.

Sample Work Activities: perform nursing duties in a hospital, teach children how to read, give career guidance to people, do volunteer work at a nonprofit organization, help families care for ill relatives, work with juveniles on probation, teach a high school class

Enterprising

Enterprising personalities like work activities that involve starting up and carrying out projects. They like persuading and leading people, taking risks, and making important decisions. They prefer action rather than thought.

Sample Work Activities: buy and sell stocks and bonds, manage a retail store, buy and sell land, market a new line of clothing, negotiate contracts for professional athletes, represent a client in a lawsuit, run a toy store

Conventional

Conventional personalities like work activities that involve following set procedures and routines. They prefer working with data and details more than with ideas. They like working where there is a clear line of authority to follow.

Sample Work Activities: proofread records or forms, use a computer to generate customer bills, organize and schedule office meetings, keep shipping and receiving records, develop an office filing system, handle bank transactions

Index of Job Titles by Personality

Maintenance and Repair Workers, General, 257

Material Moving Occupations, 291

Medical, Dental, and Ophthalmic Laboratory Technicians, 279

Millwrights, 258

Painters and Paperhangers, 234

Painting and Coating Workers, Except Construction and Maintenance, 280

Pest Control Workers, 155

Photographic Process Workers and Processing Machine Operators, 281

Pipelayers, Plumbers, Pipefitters, and Steamfitters, 235

Plasterers and Stucco Masons, 236

Police and Detectives, 148

Power Plant Operators, Distributors, and Dispatchers, 274

Precision Instrument and Equipment Repairers, 259

Prepress Technicians and Workers, 270

Printing Machine Operators, 271

Probation Officers and Correctional Treatment Specialists, 69

Radio and Telecommunications Equipment Installers and Repairers, 245

Radiologic Technologists and Technicians, 133

Rail Transportation Occupations, 289

Roofers, 237

Science Technicians, 67

Semiconductor Processors, 282

Sheet Metal Workers, 238

Small Engine Mechanics, 251

Stationary Engineers and Boiler Operators, 275

Stock Clerks and Order Fillers, 205

Structural and Reinforcing Iron and Metal Workers, 239

Surgical Technologists, 134

Surveyors, Cartographers, Photogrammetrists, and Surveying Technicians, 49

Taxi Drivers and Chauffeurs, 287

Textile, Apparel, and Furnishings Occupations, 272

Tool and Die Makers, 267

Truck Drivers and Driver/Sales Workers, 288

Water and Liquid Waste Treatment Plant and System Operators, 276

Water Transportation Occupations, 290

Welding, Soldering, and Brazing Workers, 268

Woodworkers, 273

Investigative

Agricultural and Food Scientists, 53

Archivists, Curators, and Museum Technicians, 76

Atmospheric Scientists, 57

Biological Scientists, 54

Cardiovascular Technologists and Technicians, 122

Chemists and Materials Scientists, 58

Chiropractors, 105

Clinical Laboratory Technologists and Technicians, 123

Computer Programmers, 39

Computer Scientists and Database Administrators, 40

Computer Software Engineers, 41

Computer Support Specialists and Systems Administrators, 42

Computer Systems Analysts, 43

Conservation Scientists and Foresters, 56

Dentists, 106

Dietitians and Nutritionists, 107

Economists, 62

Engineering and Natural Sciences Managers, 13

Engineers, 50

Environmental Scientists and Hydrologists, 59

Financial Analysts and Personal Financial Advisors, 30

Fire Fighting Occupations, 147

Geoscientists, 60

Human Resources, Training, and Labor Relations
  Managers and Specialists, 18

Market and Survey Researchers, 63

Mathematicians, 44

Medical Scientists, 55

Nuclear Medicine Technologists, 129

Operations Research Analysts, 45

Optometrists, 109

Pharmacists, 110

Physician Assistants, 112

Physicians and Surgeons, 113

Physicists and Astronomers, 61

Psychologists, 64

Respiratory Therapists, 118

Science Technicians, 67

Social Scientists, Other, 66

Statisticians, 46

Surveyors, Cartographers, Photogrammetrists, and
  Surveying Technicians, 49

Teachers—Postsecondary, 82

Urban and Regional Planners, 65

Veterinarians, 120

Artistic

Actors, Producers, and Directors, 92

Advertising, Marketing, Promotions, Public Relations,
  and Sales Managers, 9

Announcers, 96

Architects, Except Landscape and Naval, 47

Archivists, Curators, and Museum Technicians, 76

Artists and Related Workers, 86

Barbers, Cosmetologists, and Other Personal
  Appearance Workers, 157

Commercial and Industrial Designers, 87

Dancers and Choreographers, 94

Demonstrators, Product Promoters, and Models, 169

Fashion Designers, 88

Floral Designers, 89

Graphic Designers, 90

Interior Designers, 91

Interpreters and Translators, 98

Landscape Architects, 48

Librarians, 78

Musicians, Singers, and Related Workers, 95

News Analysts, Reporters, and Correspondents, 99

Photographers, 100

Photographic Process Workers and Processing
  Machine Operators, 281

Teachers—Postsecondary, 82

Television, Video, and Motion Picture Camera
  Operators and Editors, 102

Writers and Editors, 103

Social

Animal Care and Service Workers, 156

Announcers, 96

Athletic Trainers, 121

Audiologists, 104

Child Care Workers, 158

Correctional Officers, 146

Counselors, 68

Dental Assistants, 138

Dental Hygienists, 124

Dispatchers, 200

Education Administrators, 12

Emergency Medical Technicians and Paramedics, 126

Financial Analysts and Personal Financial
  Advisors, 30

Fitness Workers, 159

Food and Beverage Serving and Related Workers, 152

Human Resources, Training, and Labor Relations Managers and Specialists, 18

Instructional Coordinators, 77

Interviewers, 193

Licensed Practical and Licensed Vocational Nurses, 127

Medical Assistants, 140

Nursing, Psychiatric, and Home Health Aides, 142

Occupational Health and Safety Specialists and Technicians, 130

Occupational Therapist Assistants and Aides, 143

Occupational Therapists, 108

Personal and Home Care Aides, 162

Physical Therapist Assistants and Aides, 145

Physical Therapists, 111

Podiatrists, 114

Police and Detectives, 148

Probation Officers and Correctional Treatment Specialists, 69

Psychologists, 64

Radiation Therapists, 115

Recreation Workers, 163

Recreational Therapists, 116

Registered Nurses, 117

Security Guards and Gaming Surveillance Officers, 150

Social and Human Service Assistants, 70

Social Workers, 71

Speech-Language Pathologists, 119

Teacher Assistants, 80

Teachers—Adult Literacy and Remedial Education, 81

Teachers—Postsecondary, 82

Teachers—Preschool, Kindergarten, Elementary, Middle, and Secondary, 83

Teachers—Self-Enrichment Education, 84

Teachers—Special Education, 85

Enterprising

Actors, Producers, and Directors, 92

Administrative Services Managers, 8

Advertising Sales Agents, 166

Advertising, Marketing, Promotions, Public Relations, and Sales Managers, 9

Appraisers and Assessors of Real Estate, 26

Athletes, Coaches, Umpires, and Related Workers, 93

Barbers, Cosmetologists, and Other Personal Appearance Workers, 157

Building Cleaning Workers, 153

Chefs, Cooks, and Food Preparation Workers, 151

Claims Adjusters, Appraisers, Examiners, and Investigators, 28

Computer and Information Systems Managers, 10

Construction Managers, 11

Demonstrators, Product Promoters, and Models, 169

Education Administrators, 12

Engineering and Natural Sciences Managers, 13

Engineers, 50

Farmers, Ranchers, and Agricultural Managers, 14

Financial Analysts and Personal Financial Advisors, 30

Financial Managers, 15

Flight Attendants, 160

Food and Beverage Serving and Related Workers, 152

Food Service Managers, 16

Funeral Directors, 17

Gaming Services Occupations, 161

Grounds Maintenance Workers, 154

Human Resources, Training, and Labor Relations Managers and Specialists, 18

Industrial Production Managers, 19

Insurance Sales Agents, 170

Judges, Magistrates, and Other Judicial Workers, 73

Lawyers, 74

Loan Officers, 32

Lodging Managers, 20

Management Analysts, 33

Material Moving Occupations, 291

Medical and Health Services Managers, 21

Meeting and Convention Planners, 34

Office and Administrative Support Worker
Supervisors and Managers, 211

Opticians, Dispensing, 131

Paralegals and Legal Assistants, 75

Police and Detectives, 148

Private Detectives and Investigators, 149

Property, Real Estate, and Community Association
Managers, 22

Public Relations Specialists, 101

Purchasing Managers, Buyers, and Purchasing
Agents, 23

Real Estate Brokers and Sales Agents, 171

Retail Salespersons, 172

Sales Engineers, 173

Sales Representatives, Wholesale and
Manufacturing, 174

Sales Worker Supervisors, 175

Securities, Commodities, and Financial Services Sales
Agents, 176

Top Executives, 24

Travel Agents, 177

Truck Drivers and Driver/Sales Workers, 288

Water Transportation Occupations, 290

Conventional

Accountants and Auditors, 25

Actuaries, 38

Air Traffic Controllers, 285

Appraisers and Assessors of Real Estate, 26

Bill and Account Collectors, 180

Billing and Posting Clerks and Machine
Operators, 181

Bookkeeping, Accounting, and Auditing Clerks, 182

Broadcast and Sound Engineering Technicians and
Radio Operators, 97

Brokerage Clerks, 187

Budget Analysts, 27

Cargo and Freight Agents, 198

Cashiers, 167

Claims Adjusters, Appraisers, Examiners, and
Investigators, 28

Communications Equipment Operators, 207

Computer Operators, 208

Construction and Building Inspectors, 225

Cost Estimators, 29

Counter and Rental Clerks, 168

Credit Authorizers, Checkers, and Clerks, 188

Customer Service Representatives, 189

Data Entry and Information Processing Workers, 209

Dispatchers, 200

File Clerks, 190

Fire Fighting Occupations, 147

Hotel, Motel, and Resort Desk Clerks, 191

Human Resources Assistants, Except Payroll and
Timekeeping, 192

Insurance Underwriters, 31

Interviewers, 193

Library Assistants, Clerical, 194

Library Technicians, 79

Medical Records and Health Information
Technicians, 128

Appendix B: Job Titles by Education and Training Requirements

According to the U.S. Department of Labor, a bachelor's or associate degree is the minimum requirement for 12 of the 20 fastest-growing occupations in the country, from physician assistants to computer software engineers. While it is no guarantee to getting a particular job, your education and training history is a primary qualification for even being *considered* for most jobs. The good news is there are millions of careers out there for all education levels (provided you have at least a high school diploma and are willing to learn on the job).

Because the number of jobs you have to choose from is dependent in part on your education or at least the education you are willing to get, we've broken the *EZ OOH* job titles down by their *minimum* education and training requirements. We recommend that you look for jobs that match your current level of education, but also ask yourself how far you are willing to go to get the job of your dreams. Consider the education and training level you would be willing to get, and look for jobs that match those criteria as well. Granted, postsecondary education isn't cheap, but there are resources out there that can help you fund your educational goals. In fact, you can find many of them referenced in the next appendix.

Jobs Requiring At Least Work Experience in a Related Job

Construction and Building Inspectors, 225

Cost Estimators, 29

Food Service Managers, 16

Gaming Services Occupations, 161

Industrial Production Managers, 19

Lodging Managers, 20

Office and Administrative Support Worker Supervisors and Managers, 211

Private Detectives and Investigators, 149

Purchasing Managers, Buyers, and Purchasing Agents, 23

Real Estate Brokers and Sales Agents, 171

Sales Worker Supervisors, 175

Teachers—Postsecondary, 82

Teachers—Self-Enrichment Education, 84

Jobs Requiring At Least Short-Term On-the-Job Training

Agricultural Workers, 216

Animal Care and Service Workers, 156

Assemblers and Fabricators, 262

Barbers, Cosmetologists, and Other Personal Appearance Workers, 157

Bill and Account Collectors, 180

Bookbinders and Bindery Workers, 269

Building Cleaning Workers, 153

Bus Drivers, 286

Cashiers, 167

Chefs, Cooks, and Food Preparation
Workers, 151

Child Care Workers, 158

Communications Equipment Operators, 207

Counter and Rental Clerks, 168

Couriers and Messengers, 199

Credit Authorizers, Checkers, and Clerks, 188

File Clerks, 190

Food and Beverage Serving and Related
Workers, 152

Food Processing Occupations, 263

Gaming Cage Workers, 183

Grounds Maintenance Workers, 154

Hotel, Motel, and Resort Desk Clerks, 191

Human Resources Assistants, Except Payroll and
Timekeeping, 192

Industrial Machinery Mechanics and
Maintenance Workers, 255

Interviewers, 193

Library Assistants, Clerical, 194

Library Technicians, 79

Material Moving Occupations, 291

Meter Readers, Utilities, 201

Nursing, Psychiatric, and Home Health
Aides, 142

Occupational Therapist Assistants and
Aides, 143

Office Clerks, General, 212

Order Clerks, 195

Painting and Coating Workers, Except
Construction and Maintenance, 280

Personal and Home Care Aides, 162

Pharmacy Aides, 144

Photographic Process Workers and Processing
Machine Operators, 281

Physical Therapist Assistants and Aides, 145

Postal Service Workers, 202

Procurement Clerks, 185

Production, Planning, and Expediting
Clerks, 203

Receptionists and Information Clerks, 196

Reservation and Transportation Ticket Agents and
Travel Clerks, 197

Retail Salespersons, 172

Security Guards and Gaming Surveillance
Officers, 150

Shipping, Receiving, and Traffic Clerks, 204

Stock Clerks and Order Fillers, 205

Taxi Drivers and Chauffeurs, 287

Teacher Assistants, 80

Tellers, 186

Textile, Apparel, and Furnishings
Occupations, 272

Truck Drivers and Driver/Sales Workers, 288

Water Transportation Occupations, 290

Weighers, Measurers, Checkers, and Samplers,
Recordkeeping, 206

Jobs Requiring At Least Moderate-Term On-the-Job Training

Advertising Sales Agents, 166

Announcers, 96

Billing and Posting Clerks and Machine
Operators, 181

Bookkeeping, Accounting, and Auditing
Clerks, 182

Broadcast and Sound Engineering Technicians and
Radio Operators, 97

Brokerage Clerks, 187

Cargo and Freight Agents, 198

Carpet, Floor, and Tile Installers and
Finishers, 223

Jobs Requiring At Least Long-Term On-the-Job Training

Jobs Requiring At Least Vocational/Technical Training

Jobs Requiring At Least an Associate Degree

Occupational Health and Safety Specialists and Technicians, 130

Paralegals and Legal Assistants, 75

Radiation Therapists, 115

Radiologic Technologists and Technicians, 133

Registered Nurses, 117

Science Technicians, 67

Semiconductor Processors, 282

Veterinary Technologists and Technicians, 135

Jobs Requiring At Least a Bachelor's Degree

Accountants and Auditors, 25

Actuaries, 38

Administrative Services Managers, 8

Advertising, Marketing, Promotions, Public Relations, and Sales Managers, 9

Agricultural and Food Scientists, 53

Architects, Except Landscape and Naval, 47

Archivists, Curators, and Museum Technicians, 76

Athletic Trainers, 121

Atmospheric Scientists, 57

Budget Analysts, 27

Chemists and Materials Scientists, 58

Commercial and Industrial Designers, 87

Computer and Information Systems Managers, 10

Computer Programmers, 39

Computer Software Engineers, 41

Computer Systems Analysts, 43

Conservation Scientists and Foresters, 56

Construction Managers, 11

Counselors, 68

Dietitians and Nutritionists, 107

Education Administrators, 12

Engineering and Natural Sciences Managers, 13

Engineers, 50

Fashion Designers, 88

Financial Analysts and Personal Financial Advisors, 30

Financial Managers, 15

Graphic Designers, 90

Human Resources, Training, and Labor Relations Managers and Specialists, 18

Insurance Sales Agents, 170

Insurance Underwriters, 31

Interior Designers, 91

Judges, Magistrates, and Other Judicial Workers, 73

Landscape Architects, 48

Loan Officers, 32

Management Analysts, 33

Medical and Health Services Managers, 21

Meeting and Convention Planners, 34

News Analysts, Reporters, and Correspondents, 99

Physician Assistants, 112

Probation Officers and Correctional Treatment Specialists, 69

Property, Real Estate, and Community Association Managers, 22

Public Relations Specialists, 101

Recreation Workers, 163

Recreational Therapists, 116

Sales Engineers, 173

Securities, Commodities, and Financial Services Sales Agents, 176

Social Workers, 71

Tax Examiners, Collectors, and Revenue Agents, 35

Teachers—Preschool, Kindergarten, Elementary, Middle, and Secondary, 83

Teachers—Special Education, 85

Top Executives, 24

Writers and Editors, 103

Jobs Requiring At Least a Master's Degree

Audiologists, 104

Economists, 62

Environmental Scientists and Hydrologists, 59

Geoscientists, 60

Instructional Coordinators, 77

Librarians, 78

Market and Survey Researchers, 63

Mathematicians, 44

Occupational Therapists, 108

Operations Research Analysts, 45

Physical Therapists, 111

Psychologists, 64

Social Scientists, Other, 66

Speech-Language Pathologists, 119

Statisticians, 46

Urban and Regional Planners, 65

Jobs Requiring At Least a Doctoral Degree

Biological Scientists, 54

Medical Scientists, 55

Physicists and Astronomers, 61

Jobs Requiring At Least a Professional Degree

Chiropractors, 105

Dentists, 106

Lawyers, 74

Optometrists, 109

Pharmacists, 110

Physicians and Surgeons, 113

Podiatrists, 114

Veterinarians, 120

Appendix C: Additional Sources of Career Information

Career Resources

While each entry in the *EZ OOH* recommends resources to further explore that particular job, there are many general resources that weren't listed. This appendix explains some of the more common career and education print resources and Web sites that you can use to further your research. Gathering as much information as possible will help you make a more informed decision and find a satisfying and rewarding career.

Personal contacts. Don't underestimate the power of the people you already know such as friends, colleagues, and family. Not only can they answer questions about a particular job, they can also put you in contact with people who can help you further. Such networking can help you make a decision about your career path and may also help you get a job once you've decided.

Local libraries. Libraries contain a tremendous amount of information on jobs and how to get them. They can also provide access to e-mail and the Internet for those individuals who don't have access at home. In addition to valuable reference books (like those listed later in this appendix), libraries may have information on job openings, colleges and financial aid, vocational training options, specific businesses, and trade magazines that can provide occupational information for specific industries. Librarians can help you find the information you need; after all, that's what they get paid for (see page 78 if you don't believe us).

Professional societies, trade groups, and labor unions. These groups are associated with workers in specific occupations. They are great resources for information on training requirements, earnings, and listings of local employers. Many offer apprenticeships for specific careers or can put you in contact with other organizations that can provide the training you need. Many of the sources listed at the end of each job description are professional societies, trade groups, and labor unions. In addition, the *Encyclopedia of Associations* (available at your local library) can give you the contact information you need for a particular organization.

Employers. Though contacting them requires some courage, employers are the main source of information on specific jobs. They can give you information on openings, application requirements, earnings and benefits, and advancement opportunities. Even if an employer has no job openings, they can still provide the information you need to decide whether the job is right for you to begin with.

Postsecondary institutions. Colleges, universities, and other postsecondary institutions frequently have career centers and libraries with information on different careers, job listings, and alumni contacts in various professions. They may have career counselors to help students and alumni as well.

Anyone enrolled in a postsecondary school or thinking about enrolling should be sure to take advantage of these resources.

Guidance and career counselors. Counselors can help you decide which careers might suit you best by determining your strengths and interests. They can help you evaluate your options and search for a job in your field or select a new field altogether. They can also help you further your education. Some counselors offer interview coaching, resume writing, and help with filling out applications. Counselors are most commonly found in high school guidance offices, college and vocational and technical school career planning and placement offices, community organizations, vocational rehabilitation agencies, and state employment service offices.

Internet resources. Many online career resources include job listings, resume posting services, and information on job fairs, training, and local wages. Most of the resources listed at the end of each job description have Internet addresses as well. In addition, individual companies may include job listings on their Web sites with information about required credentials, wages and benefits, and contact information. When using Internet resources, be sure that the organization is a credible, established source of information.

Online Sources from the Department of Labor and the Federal Government

✳ **Career OneStop.** Provides a wide range of workforce assistance and resources. Internet: www.careeronestop.org

✳ **O*NET Online.** This resource can provide even more information on specific occupations. Internet: www.onetcenter.org

✳ **Career Voyages.** Provided in collaboration with the U.S. Department of Education, Career Voyages has information on certain high-demand occupations. Internet: www.careervoyages.org

✳ **Bureau of Labor Statistics.** The Department of Labor's Bureau of Labor Statistics publishes a wide range of labor market information. Internet: www.bls.gov

✳ **Career Guide to Industries.** This publication discusses careers from an industry perspective. *The Career Guide* is also available at your local career center and library. Internet: www.bls.gov/oco/cg/home.htm

✳ **Wage Data.** For information on occupational wages. Internet: www.bls.gov/bls/blswage.htm

✳ **Education and Training Administration.** For information on training, workers' rights, and job listings. Internet: www.doleta.gov/jobseekers

✳ **USA Jobs.** Information on obtaining civilian positions within the federal government. Internet: www.usajobs.opm.gov

✳ **Today's Military.** For information on careers in the military, the Montgomery G.I. Bill, and military service. Internet: www.todaysmilitary.com

✳ **Equal Employment Opportunity Commission.** Information on how to file a charge of discrimination based on race, color, religion, sex, national origin, age, or handicap. Internet: www.eeoc.gov

Organizations for Specific Groups

Disabled workers:

✳ **State Vocational Rehabilitation Agency.** State counseling, training, and placement services for those with disabilities. Internet: www.ed.gov/Programs/EROD

✳ **National Organization on Disability.** Information on employment opportunities, transportation, and other considerations for people with all types of disabilities. Internet: www.nod.org

✳ **Job Accommodation Network (JAN).** Information on making accommodations in the work place for people with disabilities. Internet: www.jan.wvu.edu

✳ **Disability Information.** A comprehensive federal Web site of disability-related resources. Internet: www.disabilityinfo.gov

Blind workers:

✳ **National Federation of the Blind, Job Opportunities for the Blind (JOB).** Information on the free national reference and referral service for the blind. Internet: www.nfb.org

Older workers:

✳ **National Council on the Aging.** Internet: www.ncoa.org

✳ **National Caucus and Center on Black Aged, Inc.** Internet: www.ncba-aged.org

Veterans:

✳ **Credentialing Opportunities Online (COOL).** Explains how Army soldiers can meet civilian certification and license requirements related to their Military Occupational Specialty (MOS). Internet: www.cool.army.mil/index.htm

Women:

✳ **Department of Labor, Women's Bureau.** Resources for women in the workforce. Internet: www.dol.gov/wb

Education and Training Resources

Each entry in the *EZ OOH* provides the minimum education requirements for that job. This section explains the major sources of education and training required for most occupations in more detail. It also provides resources to help you get the education and training you need. Readers interested in researching jobs by the education and training level required should see Appendix B.

Four-year colleges and universities. Colleges and universities provide the knowledge and background necessary to be successful in many fields. They also can help place students in internships or co-ops to learn a job hands on. For more information on colleges and universities, go to your local library, consult a counselor, or contact individual colleges. Also check with your state's higher education agency.

A list of these agencies is available on the Internet: wdcrobcolp01.ed.gov/Programs/EROD/.

Junior and community colleges. Junior and community colleges offer programs that lead to associate degrees and training certificates. Community colleges tend to be less expensive than four-year colleges and universities, generally have more adult and part-time students, and are more tailored to the needs of local employers. Many offer weekend and night classes. For students who may not be able to enroll in a college or university because of their academic record, limited finances, or distance, junior or community colleges are a place to earn credits that can be applied toward a degree at a four-year college. For more information on junior and community colleges, go to your local library, consult a counselor, or contact individual schools. Also check with your state's higher education agency.

A list of these agencies is available on the Internet: wdcrobcolp01.ed.gov/Programs/EROD/.

Vocational and trade schools. These schools offer courses designed to provide hands-on experience. They tend to concentrate on trades, services, and other types of skilled work. Graduates of vocational and trade schools generally have an advantage over informally trained or self-trained job seekers. These schools also help students acquire any license or other credentials needed to enter the job market. For more information on vocational and trade schools, go to your local library, consult a counselor, or contact individual schools. Also check with your state's director of vocational-technical education.

A list of state directors of vocational-technical education is available on the Internet: wdcrobcolp01.ed.gov/Programs/EROD/.

Apprenticeships. An apprenticeship provides work experience as well as education and training for those entering certain occupations. Apprenticeships are offered by sponsors, who employ and train the apprentice. Apprenticeships generally last between one and four years. Some apprenticeships allow the apprentice to earn an associate degree. A state agency approved completion certificate is granted to those completing programs.

Information on apprenticeships is available from the Office of Apprenticeship on the Internet: www.doleta.gov/oa/.

Employers. Many employers provide on-the-job training. On-the-job training can range from spending a few minutes watching another employee demonstrate a task to participating in formal training programs that may last for several months. In some jobs, employees may continually undergo training to stay up to date with new developments and technologies or to add new skills.

Military. The United States Armed Forces trains and employs people in more than 4,100 different occupations. For more information, see "Job Opportunities in the Armed Forces" in this book.

Financial Aid Resources

Many people fund their education or training through financial aid or tuition assistance programs. Federal student aid is available as grants, work-study programs, and loans. All federal student aid applicants must first fill out a Free Application for Federal Student Aid (FAFSA), which provides a Student Aid Report (SAR) and eligibility rating. Forms must be submitted to the school, which then determines the amount of aid you will receive. The following resources can help you get the aid you need:

✳ For information on applying for federal financial aid, visit the FAFSA Internet site: www.fafsa.ed.gov.

✳ A U.S. Department of Education publication describing federal financial aid programs, called *The Student Guide*, is available at www.studentaid.ed.gov/students/publications/student_guide/index.html.

* Information on federal programs is available from www.studentaid.ed.gov and www.students.gov.

* Information on state programs is available from your state's higher education agency. A list of these agencies is available at wdcrobcolp01.ed.gov/Programs/EROD/.

Grants. A grant is money that is given to pay for education or training and any associated expenses. Grants are considered gifts and are not paid back. They are typically given on the basis of financial need. Federal grants are almost exclusively for undergraduate students.

Additional information on grants is available on the Internet: www.studentaid.ed.gov.

Federal Work-Study program. The Federal Work-Study program is offered at most institutions and consists of federal sponsorship of a student who works part-time at the institution he or she is attending. The money a student earns through this program goes directly toward the cost of attending the institution. There are no set minimum or maximum amounts for this type of aid, although, on average, a student can expect to earn about $2,000 per school year.

General information on the Federal Work-Study program is available at www.studentaid.ed.gov.

Scholarships. A scholarship is money donated to a student to help pay for his or her education or training. They are based on financial need, academic merit, athletic ability, or a wide variety of other criteria set by the organizations that provide the scholarships. Frequently, students must meet minimum academic requirements to be considered for a scholarship. Other qualifying requirements—such as intended major field of study, heritage, or group membership—may be added by the organization providing the scholarship. Information on scholarships is typically available from high school guidance counselors and local libraries.

The College Board has information on available scholarships at www.collegeboard.com/pay.

Student loans. Many institutions, both public and private, provide low-interest loans to students and their parents or guardians. The federal government also provides several types of student loans based on the applicant's financial need.

The College Board has information on available loans at www.collegeboard.com/pay.

Employer tuition support programs. Some employers offer tuition assistance programs as part of their employee benefits package. The terms of these programs depend on the firm. Consult your human resources department for information on tuition support programs offered by your employer.

Military tuition support programs. The United States Armed Forces offer various tuition assistance and loan repayment programs for military personnel. For more information go to www.todaysmilitary.com.

State and Local Resources

Most states have career information delivery systems (CIDS), which may be found in secondary and postsecondary institutions, as well as libraries, job training sites, vocational-technical schools, and employment offices. A wide range of information is provided, from employment opportunities to unemployment insurance claims.

Alabama

Director, Labor Market Information Division, Alabama Department of Industrial Relations, 649 Monroe St., Room 422, Montgomery, AL 36131.
Telephone: (334) 242-8859.
Internet: dir.alabama.gov

Alaska

Chief, Research and Analysis Section, Department of Labor and Workforce Development, P.O. Box 25501, Juneau, AK 99802-5501.
Telephone: (907) 465-4518.
Internet: almis.labor.state.ak.us

Arizona

Research Administrator, Arizona Department of Economic Security, P.O. Box 6123 SC 733A, Phoenix, AZ 85005-6123.
Telephone: (602) 542-5984.
Internet: www.workforce.az.gov

Arkansas

Division Chief, Labor Market Information, Department of Workforce Services, P.O. Box 2981, Little Rock, AR 72203-2981.
Telephone: (501) 682-3198.
Internet: www.arkansas.gov/esd

California

Chief, State of California Employment Development Department, Labor Market Information Division, P.O. Box 826880, Sacramento, CA 94280-0001.
Telephone: (916) 262-2160.
Internet: www.labormarketinfo.edd.ca.gov

Colorado

Director, Labor Market Information, Colorado Department of Labor and Employment, 633 17th St., Suite 600, Denver, CO 80202-3660.
Telephone: (303) 318-8850.
Internet: www.coworkforce.com/lmi/

Connecticut

Director, Office of Research, Connecticut Department of Labor, 200 Folly Brook Blvd., Wethersfield, CT 06109-1114.
Telephone: (860) 263-6275.
Internet: www.ctdol.state.ct.us/lmi

Delaware

Chief, Office of Occupational and Labor Market Information, Department of Labor, 4425 N. Market St., Fox Valley Annex, Wilmington, DE 19809-1307.
Telephone: (302) 761-8069.
Internet: www.delawareworks.com/oolmi

District of Columbia

Chief, Office of Labor Market Research and Information, 64 New York Ave. NE, Suite 3035, Washington, DC 20002.
Telephone: (202) 671-1633.
Internet: www.does.dc.gov

Florida

Director, Labor Market Statistics, Agency for Workforce Innovation, MSC G-020, 107 E. Madison St., Tallahassee, FL 32399-4111.
Telephone: (850) 245-7205.
Internet: www.labormarketinfo.com

Georgia

Director, Workforce Information and Analysis, Room 300, Department of Labor, 223 Courtland St., CWC Building, Atlanta, GA 30303.
Telephone: (404) 232-3875.
Internet: www.dol.state.ga.us/em

Hawaii

Chief, Research and Statistics Office, Department of Labor and Industrial Relations, 830 Punchbowl St., Room 304, Honolulu, HI 96813.
Telephone: (808) 586-8999.
Internet: www.hiwi.org

Idaho

Chief, Research and Analysis Bureau, Department of Commerce and Labor, 317 West Main St., Boise, ID 83735-0670.
Telephone: (208) 332-3570.
Internet: http://lmi.idaho.gov

Illinois

Deputy Director of Workforce and Career Information, Illinois Department of Employment Security, Economic Information and Analysis Division, 33 South State St., 9th Floor, Chicago, IL 60603.
Telephone: (312) 793-2316.
Internet: http://lmi.ides.state.il.us

Indiana

Director, Research and Analysis–Indiana Workforce
Development, SE 211, 10 North Senate Ave.,
Indianapolis, IN 46204-2277.
Telephone: (317) 232-7460.
Internet: www.in.gov/dwd

Iowa

Policy and Information Division, Iowa Workforce
Development, 1000 East Grand Ave., Des Moines,
IA 50319-0209.
Telephone: (515) 281-6642.
Internet: www.iowaworkforce.org/lmi

Kansas

Director, Kansas Department of Labor, Labor Market
Information Services, 401 SW Topeka Blvd., Topeka, KS
66603-3182.
Telephone: (785) 296-5058.
Internet: http://laborstats.dol.ks.gov

Kentucky

Research and Statistics Branch, Office of Employment
and Training, 275 East Main St., Mail Stop 2-WG,
Frankfort, KY 40621.
Telephone: (502) 564-7976.
Internet: http://oet.ky.gov

Louisiana

Director, Research and Statistics Division, Department
of Labor, 1001 North 23rd St., Baton Rouge, LA 70804-
9094.
Telephone: (225) 342-3141.
Internet: www.laworks.net

Maine

Director, Labor Market Information Services Division,
Maine Department of Labor, 19 Union St., Augusta, ME
04332.
Telephone: (207) 287-2271.
Internet: www.state.me.us/labor

Maryland

Maryland Department of Labor, Licensing and Regula-
tions, Office of Labor Market Analysis and Information,
Room 316, 1100 North Eutaw St., Baltimore, MD 21201.
Telephone: (410) 767-2250.
Internet: www.dllr.state.md.us/lmi

Massachusetts

Assistant Director of Economic Research, Massachusetts
Division of Unemployment Assistance, 19 Staniford St.,
Boston, MA 02421.
Telephone: (617) 626-6556.
Internet: www.detma.org/lmi

Michigan

Director, Bureau of Labor Market Information and
Strategic Initiatives, Department of Labor and Economic
Growth, 3032 West Grand Blvd., Suite 9-100, Detroit,
MI 48202.
Telephone: (313) 456-3100.
Internet: www.milmi.org

Minnesota

Research Director, Department of Employment and
Economic Development, Labor Market Information
Office, 1st National Bank Building, 332 Minnesota St.,
Suite E200, St. Paul, MN 55101-1351.
Telephone: (651) 296-6545.
Internet: www.deed.state.mn.us/lmi

Mississippi

Chief, Labor Market Information Division, Mississippi
Department of Employment Security, 1235 Echelon
Pkwy., Jackson, MS 39213.
Telephone: (601) 321-6262.
Internet: http://mdes.ms.gov

Missouri

LMI Research Manager, Missouri Economic Research
and Information Center, P.O. Box 3150, Jefferson City,
MO 65101-3150.
Telephone: (573) 751-3637.
Internet: www.missourieconomy.org

Montana

Research and Analysis Bureau, P.O. Box 1728, Helena,
MT 59624.
Telephone: (406) 444-2430.
Internet: www.ourfactsyourfuture.org

Nebraska

Administrator, Nebraska Workforce Development–Labor
Market Information, Nebraska Department of Labor, P.O.
Box 4600, Lincoln, NE 68509-4600.
Telephone: (402) 471-2600.
Internet: www.dol.state.ne.us

Nevada

Chief, Research and Analysis, Department of Employment, Training and Rehabilitation, 500 East Third St., Carson City, NV 89713-0020.
Telephone: (775) 684-0387.
Internet: www.detr.state.nv.us/lmi

New Hampshire

Director, Economic and Labor Market Information Bureau, New Hampshire Employment Security, 32 South Main St., Concord, NH 03301-4587.
Telephone: (603) 228-4123.
Internet: www.nhes.state.nh.us

New Jersey

Director, Division of Labor Market and Demographic Research, Department of Labor and Workforce Development, P.O. Box 388, Trenton, NJ 08625-0388.
Telephone: (609) 984-2593.
Internet: www.state.nj.us/labor

New Mexico

Research Chief, New Mexico Department of Labor, Economic Research and Analysis, 501 Mountain Rd. NE, Albuquerque, NM 87102.
Telephone: (505) 222-4684.
Internet: www.dol.state.nm.us

New York

Director, Research and Statistics, New York State Department of Labor, State Office Campus, Room 400, Albany, NY 12240.
Telephone: (518) 457-3805.
Internet: www.labor.state.ny.us

North Carolina

Director, Labor Market Information Division, Employment Security Commission, 700 Wade Ave., Raleigh, NC 27605.
Telephone: (919) 733-2936.
Internet: www.ncesc.com

North Dakota

Labor Market Information Manager, Job Service North Dakota, P.O. Box 5507, Bismarck, ND 58506-5507.
Telephone: (701) 328-3136.
Internet: www.jobsnd.com

Ohio

Director, Bureau of Labor Market Information, Office of Workforce Development, Ohio Department of Job and Family Services, 4300 Kimberly Pkwy., Columbus, OH 43232.
Telephone: (614) 752-9494.
Internet: www.ohioworkforceinformer.org

Oklahoma

Labor Market Information, Oklahoma Employment Security Commission, P.O. Box 52003, Oklahoma City, OK 73152.
Telephone: (405) 557-7221.
Internet: www.oesc.state.ok.us

Oregon

Oregon Employment Department, Attention: Research Division, Room 207, 875 Union St. NE, Salem, OR 97311.
Telephone: (503) 947-1200.
Internet: www.qualityinfo.org

Pennsylvania

Director, Center for Workforce Information and Analysis, Pennsylvania Department of Labor and Industry, 220 Labor and Industry Building, Seventh and Forster Sts., Harrisburg, PA 17121.
Telephone: (877) 493-3282.
Internet: www.paworkstats.state.pa.us

Puerto Rico

Economist, Labor Market Information Office, P.O. Box 195540, San Juan, Puerto Rico 00919-5540.
Telephone: (787) 754-5347.
Internet: www.net-empleopr.org

Rhode Island

Assistant Director, Labor Market Information, Rhode Island Department of Employment and Training, 1511 Pontiac Ave., Cranston, RI 02920.
Telephone: (401) 462-8767.
Internet: www.dlt.ri.gov

South Carolina

Director, Labor Market Information Department, South Carolina Employment Security Commission, 631 Hampton St., Columbia, SC 29202.
Telephone: (803) 737-2660.
Internet: www.sces.org

South Dakota

Director, Labor Market Information Center, Department of Labor, 420 S. Roosevelt St., Aberdeen, SD 57402-4730.
Telephone: (605) 626-2314.
Internet: www.state.sd.us/dol

Tennessee

Director, Research and Statistics Division, Department of Labor and Workforce Development, 500 James Robertson Pkwy., 11th Floor, Nashville, TN 37245-1000.
Telephone: (615) 741-2284.
Internet: www.state.tn.us/labor-wfd

Texas

Labor Market Information, Texas Workforce Commission, 9001 North IH-35, Suite 103A, Austin, TX 75753.
Telephone: (512) 491-4800.
Internet: www.tracer2.com

Utah

Director of Workforce Information, Utah Department of Workforce Services, 140 East 300 South, Salt Lake City, UT 84111.
Telephone: (801) 526-9401.
Internet: http://jobs.utah.gov

Vermont

Chief, Research and Analysis, Vermont Department of Labor, P.O. Box 488, Montpelier, VT 05601-0488.
Telephone: (802) 828-4202.
Internet: www.labor.vermont.gov

Virgin Islands

Chief, Bureau of Labor Statistics, Department of Labor, P.O. Box 303359, St. Thomas, VI 00803-3359.
Telephone: (340) 776-3700.
Internet: www.vidol.gov

Virginia

Director, Economic Information Services, Virginia Employment Commission, 703 East Main St., Room 327, Richmond, VA 23218.
Telephone: (804) 786-5496.
Internet: http://velma.virtuallmi.com

Washington

Director, Labor Market and Economic Analysis, Washington Employment Security Department, P.O. Box 9046, Olympia, WA 98507-9046.
Telephone: (360) 438-4804.
Internet: www.workforceexplorer.com

West Virginia

WORKFORCE West Virginia, Research, Information and Analysis Division, 112 California Ave., Charleston, WV 25303-0112.
Telephone: (304) 558-2660.
Internet: www.wvbep.org/bep

Wisconsin

Director, Bureau of Workforce Information, Department of Workforce Development, 201 E. Washington Ave., Madison, WI 53702.
Telephone: (608) 266-8212.
Internet: http://worknet.wisconsin.gov

Wyoming

Manager, Research and Planning, Wyoming Department of Employment, P.O. Box 2760, Casper, WY 82602-2760.
Telephone: (307) 473-3807.
Internet: http://doe.state.wy.us/lmi

Other Career Reference Materials

The *EZ OOH* is an ideal resource to get you started on your career search, but finding, getting, and keeping the right job requires more than just one book. The following resources, available from JIST, can help you further your career exploration and get the job you want.

Enhanced Occupational Outlook Handbook: Featuring more than 8,000 job descriptions, this reference book contains the full descriptions for each job in the *Occupational Outlook Handbook* plus related jobs from the U.S. government's Occupational Information Network (O*NET) database and *Dictionary of Occupational Titles.* Ideal for in-depth research.

New Guide for Occupational Exploration: This career reference allows individuals to explore all major jobs based on their interests. It organizes more than 900 jobs from the O*NET database into 16 interest areas based on the U.S. Department of Education career clusters. Helps job seekers get a real feel for the job through in-depth descriptions of job activities.

Exploring Careers: A Young Person's Guide to 1,000 Jobs: A career reference book designed for grades 7–12. Jobs are listed in 14 career clusters. Includes career "clues" to consider and profiles of real people working in related jobs. "Skill samples" help youths better understand whether they have the skills required for certain jobs.

College Majors Handbook: For anyone looking to find a college major that will help them get the job of their dreams. This handbook presents the actual jobs and earnings of college students in 60 majors. Use this guide to help you pick a course of study that matches your desired career path.

The *Best Jobs* Series: This series of books provides job descriptions of the best-paying and fastest-growing jobs based on any number of factors. Find the best jobs for your personality or your education level, the best jobs for baby boomers or college graduates, the best jobs to get through apprenticeships, or the best jobs for the 21st century.

The *Help in a Hurry* Series: Once you've used the *EZ OOH* and other career resources to discover the job of your dreams, let these quick and insightful books help you get it. Includes books to help you with career choices, resumes, interviews, and cover letters.

For more information about these and other career reference and exploration resources, please visit www.jist.com.

Editors' note: This section was adapted from the "Sources of Career Information" section of the *Occupational Outlook Handbook.* Specific non-government institutions, addresses, and Web sites are provided for your own research and do not constitute a specific endorsement by the Department of Labor or JIST Publishing.

Index of Job Titles

M

Machine Setters, Operators, and Tenders—Metal and Plastic, 266
Machinists, 265
Maintenance and Repair Workers, General, 257
Management Analysts, 33
Market and Survey Researchers, 63
Massage Therapists, 139
Material Moving Occupations, 291
Mathematicians, 44
Medical and Health Services Managers, 21
Medical Assistants, 140
Medical Records and Health Information Technicians, 128
Medical Scientists, 55
Medical Transcriptionists, 141
Medical, Dental, and Ophthalmic Laboratory Technicians, 279
Meeting and Convention Planners, 34
Meter Readers, Utilities, 201
Millwrights, 258
Musicians, Singers, and Related Workers, 95

N

News Analysts, Reporters, and Correspondents, 99
Nuclear Medicine Technologists, 129
Nursing, Psychiatric, and Home Health Aides, 142

O

Occupational Health and Safety Specialists and Technicians, 130
Occupational Therapist Assistants and Aides, 143
Occupational Therapists, 108
Office and Administrative Support Worker Supervisors and Managers, 211
Office Clerks, General, 212
Operations Research Analysts, 45
Opticians, Dispensing, 131
Optometrists, 109
Order Clerks, 195

P-Q

Painters and Paperhangers, 234
Painting and Coating Workers, Except Construction and Maintenance, 280
Paralegals and Legal Assistants, 75
Payroll and Timekeeping Clerks, 184
Personal and Home Care Aides, 162
Pest Control Workers, 155
Pharmacists, 110
Pharmacy Aides, 144
Pharmacy Technicians, 132
Photographers, 100

Photographic Process Workers and Processing Machine Operators, 281
Physical Therapist Assistants and Aides, 145
Physical Therapists, 111
Physician Assistants, 112
Physicians and Surgeons, 113
Physicists and Astronomers, 61
Pipelayers, Plumbers, Pipefitters, and Steamfitters, 235
Plasterers and Stucco Masons, 236
Podiatrists, 114
Police and Detectives, 148
Postal Service Workers, 202
Power Plant Operators, Distributors, and Dispatchers, 274
Precision Instrument and Equipment Repairers, 259
Prepress Technicians and Workers, 270
Printing Machine Operators, 271
Private Detectives and Investigators, 149
Probation Officers and Correctional Treatment Specialists, 69
Procurement Clerks, 185
Production, Planning, and Expediting Clerks, 203
Property, Real Estate, and Community Association Managers, 22
Psychologists, 64
Public Relations Specialists, 101
Purchasing Managers, Buyers, and Purchasing Agents, 23

R

Radiation Therapists, 115
Radio and Telecommunications Equipment Installers and Repairers, 245
Radiologic Technologists and Technicians, 133
Rail Transportation Occupations, 289
Real Estate Brokers and Sales Agents, 171
Receptionists and Information Clerks, 196
Recreation Workers, 163
Recreational Therapists, 116
Registered Nurses, 117
Reservation and Transportation Ticket Agents and Travel Clerks, 197
Respiratory Therapists, 118
Retail Salespersons, 172
Roofers, 237

S

Sales Engineers, 173
Sales Representatives, Wholesale and Manufacturing, 174
Sales Worker Supervisors, 175
Science Technicians, 67
Secretaries and Administrative Assistants, 213
Securities, Commodities, and Financial Services Sales Agents, 176
Security Guards and Gaming Surveillance Officers, 150
Semiconductor Processors, 282
Sheet Metal Workers, 238